CARPE DIEM

Carpe diem – 'eat, drink, and be merry, for tomorrow we die!' – is a prominent motif throughout ancient literature and beyond. This is the first book-length examination of its significance and demonstrates that close analysis can make a key contribution to a question that is central to literary studies in and beyond Classics: how can poetry give us the almost magical impression that something is happening here and now? In attempting an answer, Robert A. Rohland gives equal attention to Greek and Latin texts, as he offers new interpretations of well-known poems from Horace and tackles understudied epigrams. Pairing close readings of ancient texts with interpretations of other forms of cultural production such as gems, cups, calendars, monuments, and Roman wine labels, this interdisciplinary study transforms our understanding of the motif of *carpe diem*.

ROBERT A. ROHLAND is a Junior Research Fellow (under Title A) at Trinity College, Cambridge. His research focusses on two forms of ancient poetry: lyric and epigram, with equal attention to Greek and Latin material. He is also particularly interested in analysing poetry alongside other forms of ancient cultural production, such as artworks or calendars.

CAMBRIDGE CLASSICAL STUDIES

General editors
J. P. T. CLACKSON, W. M. BEARD, G. BETEGH,
R. L. HUNTER, M. J. MILLETT, S. P. OAKLEY,
R. G. OSBORNE, C. VOUT, T. J. G. WHITMARSH

CARPE DIEM

The Poetics of Presence in Greek and Latin Literature

ROBERT A. ROHLAND
Trinity College, Cambridge

CAMBRIDGE
UNIVERSITY PRESS

University Printing House, Cambridge CB2 8BS, United Kingdom

One Liberty Plaza, 20th Floor, New York, NY 10006, USA

477 Williamstown Road, Port Melbourne, VIC 3207, Australia

314–321, 3rd Floor, Plot 3, Splendor Forum, Jasola District Centre, New Delhi – 110025, India

103 Penang Road, #05–06/07, Visioncrest Commercial, Singapore 238467

Cambridge University Press is part of the University of Cambridge.

It furthers the University's mission by disseminating knowledge in the pursuit of education, learning, and research at the highest international levels of excellence.

www.cambridge.org
Information on this title: www.cambridge.org/9781316510827
DOI: 10.1017/9781009039789

© Faculty of Classics, University of Cambridge 2023

This work is in copyright. It is subject to statutory exceptions and to the provisions of relevant licensing agreements; with the exception of the Creative Commons version the link for which is provided below, no reproduction of any part of this work may take place without the written permission of Cambridge University Press.

An online version of this work is published at doi.org/10.1017/9781009039789 under a Creative Commons Open Access license CC-BY-NC-ND 4.0 which permits re-use, distribution and reproduction in any medium for non-commercial purposes providing appropriate credit to the original work is given. You may not distribute derivative works without permission. To view a copy of this license, visit https://creativecommons.org/licenses/by-nc-nd/4.0

All versions of this work may contain content reproduced under license from third parties.

Permission to reproduce this third-party content must be obtained from these third-parties directly.

When citing this work, please include a reference to the DOI 10.1017/9781009039789

First published 2023

A catalogue record for this publication is available from the British Library.

Library of Congress Cataloging-in-Publication Data
NAMES: Rohland, Robert A., author.
TITLE: Carpe diem : the poetics of presence in Greek and Latin literature / Robert A. Rohland.
OTHER TITLES: Poetics of presence in Greek and Latin literature | Cambridge classical studies.
DESCRIPTION: Cambridge, United Kingdom : Cambridge University Press, 2022. | Series: Cambridge classical studies | Includes bibliographical references and index.
IDENTIFIERS: LCCN 2022026168 | ISBN 9781316510827 (hardback) | ISBN 9781009018555 (paperback) | ISBN 9781009039789 (ebook)
SUBJECTS: LCSH: Horace – Criticism and interpretation. | Classical poetry – History and criticism. | Classical poetry – Themes, motives. | Pleasure in literature. | Time in literature. | BISAC: HISTORY / Ancient / General
CLASSIFICATION: LCC PA3021 .R64 2022 | DDC 874/.01–dc23/eng/20220627
LC record available at https://lccn.loc.gov/2022026168

ISBN 978-1-316-51082-7 Hardback
ISBN 978-1-009-01855-5 Paperback

Cambridge University Press has no responsibility for the persistence or accuracy of URLs for external or third-party internet websites referred to in this publication and does not guarantee that any content on such websites is, or will remain, accurate or appropriate.

Worzue dienet das studieren /
Als zue lauter vngemach?
Vnter dessen laufft die Bach
Vnsers lebens das wir führen /
Ehe wir es innen werden /
Auff jhr letztes ende hin;
Dann kömpt (ohne geist vnd sinn)
Dieses alles in die erden.

Hola / Junger / geh' vnd frage
Wo der beste trunck mag sein;
Nim den Krug / vnd fülle Wein.
Alles trawren leidt vnd klage /
Wie wir Menschen täglich haben
Eh' vns Clotho fortgerafft
Wil ich in den süssen safft
Den die traube giebt vergraben.

(Martin Opitz, *Ich empfinde fast ein grawen*, lines 9–24)

CONTENTS

List of Figures — page ix
Acknowledgements — xi
A Note on Ancient Texts and Translations — xiv
List of Abbreviations — xv

Introduction: In Search of Present Time — 1
  A Requiem for *Carpe Diem* — 1
  The Pleasure in Greek and Latin Texts — 8
  Performance, Text, and Evocation of Presence — 25
  The Structure of the Book — 35

1 The Archaeology of *Carpe Diem*: Sardanapallus, Monuments, Epigrams, and False Beginnings — 38
  1.1 The Invention of *Carpe Diem* — 41
  1.2 To Have and Have Not: Sardanapallus in Verse — 53
  1.3 The Art of Variation — 59
  1.4 The Professor of Desire, Sardanapallus in Rome — 68

2 A Moveable Feast: Wine Storage Places as Drinkable Calendars in Horace — 76
  2.1 Wine O'Clock: The Present Moment in Horace, *Epodes* 13 — 78
  2.2 Drinking Again and Thinking of When: Reperformance in *Odes* 3.8 — 82
  2.3 Horace's *Fasti*: Wine Storage Places at *C.* 3.8 (again), *C.* 2.3, *C.* 3.28 — 88
  2.4 Memories of Linguistic Wars: Tasting Language in *Odes* 3.14 — 101

3 Gathering Leaves: Horace, Choice of Words, Cyclical Time, and the Production of Presence — 108
  3.1 Words That Are Green Turn to Brown: Words and Leaves in the *Ars Poetica* — 109
  3.2 A Linguistic Turn Around and Around: Horace on Semantic Change — 117
  3.3 Bags Full of Leaves: Coinages in Horace's *Carpe Diem* Poems (*C.* 4.7, 1.11, 1.36) — 125

Contents

4 The Pleasure of Images: Epigrams and Objects
100 BC–AD 100   140
  4.1 Cups   143
  4.2 Gems   160
  4.3 Dining Halls and Tombs   176

5 As Is the Generation of Leaves, So Are
  the Generations of Cows, Mice, and Gigolos:
  Excerpe Diem! or Excerpts of *Carpe Diem*   183
  5.1 Plucking Grass: Cows, Flocks, Vergil, *Georgics* 3,
       and Seneca   187
  5.2 Plucking the Road, or Of Mice and Muses: Horace,
       Sermones 2.6   198
  5.3 Butchering Poetry: Trimalchio, Petronius' *Satyrica*, and
       Athenaeus   205
  5.4 Plucking Flowers: Naevolus in Juvenal 9   214

  Epilogue: Echoes of *Carpe Diem*   227

Bibliography   239
General Index   282
Index Locorum   290

FIGURES

0.1 Stele of the Seikilos epitaph. Photo © The National Museum of Denmark, Inv. 14897/photographer: John Lee. License type: CC-BY-SA. — page 2

0.2 Transcription of musical notation of the Seikilos epitaph. Transcribed into modern notation by D'Angour (2018) 69. — 3

1.1 Statue of 'Dionysus Sardanapallus'. Vatican Museum, Rome, Sala della Biga, Inv. 2363. Photo Copyright © Governorate of the Vatican City State – Directorate of the Vatican Museums. — 74

4.1(a, b, c) Silver cup with skeletons (Cup A). Cup A from the Boscoreale treasure, Paris, Louvre Bj 1923. Photo © RMN-Grand Palais (musée du Louvre)/photographer: Hervé Lewandowski. — 145

4.2(a, b, c) Silver cup with skeletons (Cup B). Cup B from the Boscoreale treasure, Paris, Louvre Bj 1924. Photo © RMN-Grand Palais (musée du Louvre)/photographer: Hervé Lewandowski. — 146

4.3 Berlin Gem with shepherd and skull. *AGD* ii Berlin 138, no. 349, table 64. Photo © Antikensammlung, Staatliche Museen zu Berlin – Preußischer Kulturbesitz, Inv. FG 417/photographer: Isolde Luckert. — 163

4.4 Munich Gem with shepherd and skull. *AGD* i.2 Munich 33, no. 729, table 84 (= Munich, Staatliche Münzsammlung, Inv. A 1700). Photograph taken from imprint. Photo © München, Staatliche Münzsammlung/photographer: Nicolai Kästner. — 164

List of Figures

4.5(a) Copenhagen Gem with shepherd and skull. 165
Photo © Thorvaldsens Museum, inv. no. I1204/ photographer: Jakob Faurvig. *Shepherd and Butterfly on a Skull*. Roman Republican ringstone, 100–30 BC. Carnelian, gold (modern gold ring). 1.2 x 0.9 cm.

4.5(b) Copenhagen Gem with shepherd and skull 166
(imprint). Photograph taken from imprint. Photo © Thorvaldsens Museum, inv. no. I1204/ photographer: Jakob Faurvig. *Shepherd and Butterfly on a Skull*. Roman Republican ringstone, 100–30 BC. Carnelian, gold (modern gold ring). 1.2 x 0.9 cm.

4.6 Lost gem with skull, table, and inscription. 169
Gori (1726–43) iii, appendix 21, no. 25 (Cambridge University Library classmark Mm.4.76–78); *CIG* 7298 = Kaibel 1129. Reproduced by kind permission of the Syndics of Cambridge University Library.

4.7 Lost gem with skeleton. Venuti and Boriani 170
(1736) table 80. Photo © The Fitzwilliam Museum, Cambridge.

4.8 Gem with image of lovers and inscription. 174
Photo © Rijksmuseum van Oudheden, Leiden. Inv. GS-01172/photographer: Robbert Jan Looman.

ACKNOWLEDGEMENTS

This is a book about pleasure. It is a particular pleasure to acknowledge the debts I have incurred when writing this book. My greatest debt is to the two supervisors of the Cambridge dissertation on which this book is based; I owe a great deal to my *Doktormutter* Emily Gowers for her generosity, learnedness, and inspiration. Every page benefited from her advice. I also owe a great deal to Richard Hunter, who provided erudition and advice throughout. For a book that makes a great deal of what it means to read *carpe diem*, I could not have wished for better readers.

I am extremely grateful to the examiners of my thesis, William Fitzgerald and Philip Hardie, for their numerous helpful suggestions and the exciting discussion during the viva. Their comments provided the stimulus for transforming the thesis into a book. Yet almost as often as I was returning to their written comments, I was returning to them, asking them for their opinions on draft chapters, on which they made numerous helpful comments. Stephen Oakley as editor of Cambridge Classical Studies read through a whole draft of the work. His comments not only saved me from many errors but also prompted me to rewrite one chapter and add an entirely new section at the beginning. I owe him my thanks for his detailed comments and helpful criticism. Thanks are also due to a number of people who read drafts of individual chapters and generously offered their comments: John MacGinnis, Emily Pillinger, William Race, and Caroline Vout. The book greatly benefited from their advice. David Sedley kindly offered some comments on a specific problem in writing. Giulia Maltagliati generously gave advice on a papyrus. On various occasions audiences listened to versions of several chapters. Their questions and comments have improved the work at a number of points.

After my doctorate I joined the University of Warwick for one year as a teaching fellow, where I was very fortunate to have

Acknowledgements

colleagues who generously offered advice on my project. David Fearn discussed the methodology and big picture with me already at a crucial stage of the dissertation and then again as I began the work on the transformation from thesis to book. Victoria Rimell offered probing questions that made me rethink the introduction of the book.

I wish to express my gratitude to the Cambridge School of Arts and Humanities, which funded my doctorate. It is thanks to their generosity that this project could be undertaken. I also owe thanks to the Faculty of Classics at Cambridge for a grant during the final stage of the doctorate. Yet my debt to the Faculty far exceeds material matters; Cambridge offered a congenial working environment for this project.

My election to a junior research fellowship at Trinity College, Cambridge gave me the time to turn the thesis into a book. I am extremely grateful to Trinity for providing me with the freedom and stimulating environment that allowed me to revise the book. Particular thanks are also due to the staff at the library of the Faculty of Classics at Cambridge, who helped me with many requests. Staff at the University Library got hold of numerous items via inter-library loans. For this I owe them my thanks. Parts of the book were written at the Combined Library of the Institute of Classical Studies and the Hellenic and Roman Societies. Research facilities that are second to none and outstanding staff make this a particularly stimulating place to work. The Roman Society generously funded a research stay at the Fondation Hardt, where I began to work on Chapter 4. At Cambridge University Press, Michael Sharp, Katie Idle, Nicola Maclean, and Dan Shutt guided the production of the book with great care.

I am deeply indebted to my Classics teachers at school, Stefan Gieseke and Wolfgang Krüger, whose inspiring classes at the Kaiser-Wilhelm- und Ratsgymnasium stand at the beginning of my educational journey in Classics. At St Andrews I was then fortunate to be taught by Alex Long, Jason König, and Emma Gee. At Oxford I learned much from Barnaby Taylor. During an exchange year at the University of North Carolina at Chapel Hill, I took fascinating classes by Sharon James and James O'Hara. It was also at Chapel Hill that I had the pleasure of

Acknowledgements

listening to William Race's wonderful classes on Horace. It is to the inspiration of these classes that this project goes back.

I do not believe that I can do justice here to debts of a more personal nature. My parents, Regine and Hans-Jürgen, have supported me with unfailing kindness. My sister Anna has been a constant source of advice in all matters of life. Most of all I wish to thank my wife, Janet. Without her love and support, this book could not have been written. As the thesis was nearing completion, our first son, Julius, was born, and as I was revising the book manuscript, our second son, Christian, was born. The book that follows has a thing or two to say about time and pleasure. But the most joyous time is the time spent with Janet, Julius, and Christian.

A NOTE ON ANCIENT TEXTS AND TRANSLATIONS

Texts and, where applicable, numeration of fragments are quoted according to the following editions unless otherwise noted. Alcaeus: Voigt (1971). Anacreon: Page's *PMG*. *Anacreontea*: West (1993). Horace: Klingner (1959). Juvenal: Clausen (1992). Martial: Shackleton Bailey (1990). Petronius: Müller (1995). Pliny the Elder: Rackham, Jones, and Eichholz (1938–63). Vergil: Mynors (1969). Comic fragments: Kassel and Austin (1983–2001). Elegy and iambus: West (1989–92). Wherever epigrams are included in Gow and Page's *HE*, *GP*, and *FGE*, their text is printed, and their numeration is given in addition to the source of the epigram (in most cases the *Greek Anthology*). The exception to this rule are the epigrams of Posidippus and Philodemus; here, Austin and Bastianini (2002) and Sider (1997) supersede *HE* and *GP*, respectively. Editions of less frequently quoted authors are noted in-text.

Textual apparatus are quoted selectively with the purpose of illuminating issues under discussion rather than giving a complete picture of textual problems of quoted passages. The apparatus and sigla are taken from the editions used. It should be noted, however, that for apparatus of Horace the sigla are taken from Shackleton Bailey (2001) rather than Klingner (1959) in the light of the findings of Brink (1971a) 1–43 concerning the transmission of Horace's text (cf. Tarrant (1983) and (2015b), and Shackleton Bailey (2001) i–viii). References to the *Theognidea* do not take a stance on the authenticity of individual fragments. They are thus generally cited as 'Thgn.' rather than '[Thgn.]'. All texts in languages other than English which appear in the body of the text are translated. Translations are my own.

ABBREVIATIONS

AGD	*Antike Gemmen in Deutschen Sammlungen*, 4 vols. (Munich 1968–9, Wiesbaden 1970–5).
Blänsdorf, *FPL*	J. Blänsdorf, ed. *Fragmenta poetarum Latinorum epicorum et lyricorum* (4th ed., Berlin and New York 2011).
BNJ	*Brill's New Jacoby*.
CA	J. U. Powell, ed. *Collectanea Alexandrina. Reliquiae minores poetarum Graecorum aetatis Ptolemaicae* (Oxford 1925).
CEG	P. A. Hansen, ed. *Carmina epigraphica Graeca*, 2 vols. (Berlin 1983–9).
CIG	*Corpus inscriptionum Graecarum*, 4 vols. (Berlin 1828–77).
CIL	*Corpus inscriptionum Latinarum* (Berlin 1863–).
CLE	*Carmina Latina epigraphica*. Final part of A. Riese, F. Bücheler, and E. Lommatzsch, eds. *Anthologia Latina* (Leipzig 1869–1926).
Courtney, *FLP*	E. Courtney, ed. *The fragmentary Latin poets* (Oxford 1993).
De ros. nasc.	*De rosis nascentibus*, a poem attributed to Ausonius. Green (1991) 669–71 provides a text and Green (1999) 263–4 provides a commentary.
DK	H. Diels and W. Kranz, eds. *Die Fragmente der Vorsokratiker* (6th ed., Berlin 1961).

List of Abbreviations

DNP	H. Cancik and H. Schneider, eds. *Der Neue Pauly. Enzyklopädie der Antike* (Stuttgart and Weimar 2000).
EO	S. Mariotti, ed. *Enciclopedia oraziana* (Rome 1996–8).
EV	F. Della Corte, ed. *Enciclopedia virgiliana* (Rome 1984–91).
FGE	D. L. Page, ed. *Further Greek epigrams* (Cambridge 1981).
FGrHist	F. Jacoby, ed. *Die Fragmente der griechischen Historiker* (Berlin 1923–30, Leiden 1940–58).
GL	H. Keil, ed. *Grammatici Latini*, 8 vols. (Leipzig 1855–80).
GP	A. S. F. Gow and D. L. Page, eds. *The Greek anthology. The Garland of Philip, and some contemporary epigrams*, 2 vols. (Cambridge 1968).
GV	W. Peek, ed. *Griechische Vers-Inschriften* (Berlin 1955).
HE	A. S. F. Gow and D. L. Page, eds. *The Greek anthology. Hellenistic epigrams*, 2 vols. (Cambridge 1965).
Hollis, *FRP*	A. S. Hollis, ed. *Fragments of Roman poetry* (Oxford 2007).
IG	*Inscriptiones Graecae* (Berlin 1873–).
Kaibel	G. Kaibel, ed. *Epigrammata Graeca* (Berlin 1878).
IK Kibyra I	T. Corsten, ed. *Die Inschriften von Kibyra, I. Die Inschriften der Stadt und ihrer näheren Umgebung. Inschriften griechischer Städte aus Kleinasien* 60 (Bonn 2002).
IK Kios	T. Corsten, ed. *Die Inschriften von Kios. Inschriften griechischer Städte aus Kleinasien* 29 (Bonn 1985).
L&S	C. T. Lewis and C. Short, eds. *A Latin dictionary* (Oxford 1879).

List of Abbreviations

LIMC	*Lexicon iconographicum mythologiae classicae*, 18 vols. (Zurich 1981–97).
LSJ	H. G. Liddell, R. Scott, H. Stuart-Jones, and R. McKenzie, eds. *A Greek-English lexicon* (9th ed. with supplement, Oxford 1968).
OCD	S. Hornblower, A. Spawforth, and E. Eidinow, eds. *The Oxford classical dictionary* (4th ed., Oxford 2012).
OLD	P. W. Glare, ed. *Oxford Latin dictionary* (Oxford 1968–82).
PMG	D. L. Page, ed. *Poetae melici Graeci* (Oxford 1962).
RE	A. von Pauly, G. Wissowa, W. Kroll, and K. Ziegler, eds. *Paulys Realencyclopädie der classischen Altertumswissenschaft* (Stuttgart 1893–1980).
SGO	R. Merkelbach and J. Stauber, eds. *Steinepigramme aus dem griechischen Osten*, 5 vols. (Stuttgart and Leipzig 1998–2004).
SH	H. Lloyd-Jones and P. Parsons, eds. *Supplementum Hellenisticum* (Berlin and New York 1983).
SSR	G. Giannantoni, ed. *Socratis et Socraticorum reliquiae*, 4 vols. (Naples 1990).
SVF	H. F. A. von Arnim, ed. *Stoicorum veterum fragmenta*, 4 vols. (Leipzig 1903–5).
TLL	*Thesaurus linguae Latinae* (Stuttgart, Munich, and Leipzig 1900–).
TrGF	B. Snell, R. Kannicht, and S. L. Radt, eds. *Tragicorum Graecorum fragmenta*, 5 vols. (Göttingen 1971–2004).
TrRF	W.-W. Ehlers, P. Kruschwitz, G. Manuwald, M. Schauer, and B. Seidensticker, eds. *Tragicorum Romanorum fragmenta*, 4 vols. (Göttingen and Bristol 2012–).

List of Abbreviations

Abbreviations of ancient authors and texts are taken from *LSJ* and *OLD*. In some cases these abbreviations have been extended. For instance, I use *Epist.* and *Epod.* for Horace's *Epistles* and *Epodes* rather than *Ep.* and *Epod.* as the *OLD* does. Abbreviations for journals follow the conventions of *L'Année philologique*.

INTRODUCTION

IN SEARCH OF PRESENT TIME

A Requiem for *Carpe Diem*

What does *carpe diem* sound like? Apparently, a bit like the Canadian rock star Neil Young – or at least this is how journalists described the experience of listening to the so-called Seikilos epitaph in a recording by the classicist David Creese.[1] The Seikilos epitaph is a remarkable inscription dating from the second century AD and found in Tralleis, near modern-day Aydın in Turkey. Extraordinarily, the epitaph features a song and some musical notation. Creese's recording of the song caused a media sensation, and news outlets dubbed the epitaph the 'world's oldest song'.[2] The central section of the epitaph, following an initial elegiac couplet, constitutes the song, over which musical notation is written. Its text proclaims that as long as one is alive, one should not be sad (*SGO* 02/02/07 Tralleis = *GV* 1955 = Pöhlmann and West (2001) 88–91, no. 23 = Copenhagen, National Museum of Denmark, Inv. 14897; see Figure 0.1 for a photograph of the stele and Figure 0.2 for the transcription of the musical notation).[3]

εἰκὼν ἡ λίθος | εἰμί· τίθησι μὲ | Σείκιλος ἔνθα
μνήμης ἀθανάτου | σῆμα πολυχρόνιον.

ὅσον ζῇς, φαίνου: |
μηδὲν ὅλως σὺ | λυποῦ·
πρὸς ὀλί|γον ἐστὶ τὸ ζῆν, |
τὸ τέλος ὁ χρό|νος ἀπαιτεῖ. |

Σείκιλος Εὐτέρ(που)· | ζῇ.

---

[1] The similarity to Neil Young was mentioned by news.com.au (www.news.com.au/ancient-seikilos-column-brings-worlds-oldest-song-back-to-life/news-story/f964606e93e78ce368a4e486ce1c7e47). The recording can be found on SoundCloud (https://soundcloud.com/info-1488/david-creese-sings-seikilos).
[2] This claim was also made by news.com.au.   [3] The text is taken from *SGO*.

I

Introduction: In Search of Present Time

I, the stone, am an image. Seikilos placed me here as long-lasting sign of immortal remembrance.

As long as you're alive, shine (?),[4] don't be sad at all; life is short, time asks for its due.

Seikilos, son of Euterpes; during his lifetime.

The message of the epitaph is clear enough: *carpe diem!* Eat, drink, and be merry, for tomorrow we die! The motif of *carpe diem*

Figure 0.1 Stele of the Seikilos epitaph
Copenhagen, National Museum of Denmark, Inv. 14897

---

[4] What Marx (1906) 146 said over 100 years ago still holds true: 'φαίνου imperatiuum nemo adhuc apte interpretatus est'. Marx understood Φαίνου as a vocative of a proper name, but no such name is attested. The translation 'trete auf (trete in Erscheinung)' at *SGO* is very odd for a *carpe diem* poem, but perhaps it is possible to understand the exhortation in the context of musical performance (i.e., 'trete [*sc.* als Musiker] auf'). The translation 'shine' of M. L. West (1992) 301, printed here with much hesitation, takes 'shine' as an exhortation to live. But one would wish for a closer parallel than 'Shine' by the pop group Take That, mentioned by D'Angour (2018) 66 n.51.

A Requiem for *Carpe Diem*

Song of Seikilos

Figure 0.2 Transcription of musical notation of the Seikilos epitaph
Transcribed into modern notation by D'Angour (2018) 69

prescribes the enjoyment of life as the result of insight into human mortality.[5] In the short Seikilos epitaph these two parts that constitute the motif are particularly apparent; 'shine, don't be sad at all' is the prescription to enjoyment. 'Life is short, time asks for its due' offers insight into human mortality. Other texts discussed in this book will sometimes express these two components in more complex or elusive ways, but all texts will fall under this definition of the *carpe diem* motif: a combination of insight into human mortality and an admonition to present enjoyment. Thus, some form of prescription has to be present in a text to qualify as *carpe diem*, though this can be implicit and does not have to be an admonition in the strict grammatical sense. Similarly, insight into human mortality can also be included implicitly, for example, by reference to worrisome old age or grievous cares.[6]

The motif of *carpe diem* is prominent throughout ancient literature and beyond; in early Greek poetry Alcaeus, Mimnermus and others proclaim it, and of course Horace makes the message central to his Latin lyric. It is written on numerous tombstones and carefully crafted on silver cups, while Roman satire even

---

[5] My definition of the *carpe diem* motif is deliberately simple. I follow the definitions of Davis (1991) 145–50 and Race (1993).
[6] See Davis (1991) 160–3 on 'forms of indirect prescription' in Horatian *carpe diem*, and 154 for how the simple mention of a 'long-lived crow' (*annosa cornix* at Hor. *C.* 3.17.13) implies a contrast with the brevity of human life (cf. Commager (1962) 261).

3

Introduction: In Search of Present Time

attributes the sentiment to a mouse. Today, the message appears on numerous T-shirts. This book attempts to understand the prominence and significance of the *carpe diem* motif: it does so by analysing how *carpe diem* poems are crucial places for negotiating textuality, performance and presence. These issues are naturally prominent in the Seikilos epitaph – an inscribed song. The song of Seikilos thus comes as the prelude to this study: in the present Introduction I offer a new interpretation of this important musical document, and I will show how this new interpretation of the Seikilos epitaph can serve as a model for reading *carpe diem*. Many motifs we can hear in the short song of Seikilos will reappear amplified in various permutations in the chapters of this book.

Because of its notation, the Seikilos epitaph has attracted much attention as one of the key sources for Greek music in general and musical notation in particular.[7] Its text, however – the *carpe diem* motif – is widely dismissed: one scholar, for instance, called the text 'embarrassingly banal' and another called it 'a ditty'.[8] To be sure, the text of the Seikilos epitaph is hardly original, and its expressions can easily be paralleled elsewhere.[9] Yet the text and the musical notes of the Seikilos epitaph need to be interpreted in conjunction. Thus, Armand D'Angour has recently shown how impressively the melody underlines the sense of the words.[10] I argue that the *carpe diem* text should be central to our understanding of the Seikilos epitaph: while the inclusion of a song on a tombstone is unparalleled and requires explanation, close attention to the text of the epitaph can help us appreciate more fully the function of song.[11]

---

[7] See Pöhlmann (1960) 80, (1970) 54–7 and the revised English version at Pöhlmann and West (2001) 88–91, no. 23 with further bibliography, Solomon (1986), M. L. West (1992) 280, 301–2, W. D. Anderson (1994) 222–7, Mathiesen (1999) 148–51, Landels (2009) 252–3, Hagel (2010) 286, Meier (2017), D'Angour (2018) 64–72 and (2019) 36–8, Lynch (2020) 286–90.

[8] W. D. Anderson (1994) 226, M. L. West (1992) 301. Also Marx (1906) 146: 'uerba ipsa produnt poetam misellum'. *Aliter* D'Angour (2018) 65: 'timeless maxim'.

[9] The closest verbal parallels in literary and epigraphic sources: Amphis *fr.* 8; *SGO* 02/09/32, 09/08/04 (= *GV* 1112), 18/01/20 (= *GV* 1219); Heberdey and Wilhelm (1896) 126, no. 211; Robert (1943) 182; *CIG* 7299; Cup B from the Boscoreale treasure, Louvre Bj 1924. The last two items are discussed in detail in Chapter 4.

[10] D'Angour (2018) 67–8, (2019) 38–40. He notes, for example, a falling melodic figure at λυποῦ. See Figure 0.2.

[11] My focus on the text distinguishes my explanation from the other two explanations for the unique occurrence of musical notation on the tombstone (though they are not mutually exclusive): according to Pöhlmann and West (2001) 91, the notation suggests

A Requiem for *Carpe Diem*

For any reader of the Seikilos epitaph, the notes mark the central section of the epitaph as a song, that is, as something that was properly performed rather than inscribed. Such a song would have been performed at a drinking party, the prime environment for the enjoyment of life.[12] This explains the function of song on Seikilos' tombstone: the song's placement and its overt and unique identification precisely as a song underline its content, the *carpe diem* message. As the words exhort the reader to enjoy life, so the notes point back to the enjoyment of music and evoke the banquet as the space of musical performance.[13] Yet these notes also mark a feeling of loss: once Seikilos is dead, he will never hear music again. Text and notation, then, work together in conveying the message of the epitaph that conjures up present enjoyment and its loss.

Notation is a sign system with a very clear function: one reads notes in order to make music. But did visitors to the graveyard look at the inscription and sing the song or play it on instruments? Perhaps they did so at the funeral itself, but it seems unlikely that the notation still served this function for the average visitor to the graveyard, who would glance at the inscription long after the funeral (note μνήμης ἀθανάτου σῆμα πολυχρόνιον; 'long-lasting sign of immortal remembrance'). Indeed, musical scores were primarily read and used by performers, and not destined for wide publication or readership.[14] In the case of the Seikilos epitaph, the

---

that Seikilos was a professional musician, as the name Seikilos, son of Euterpes, points to a family of professional musicians (following Marx (1906) 145. Cf. Φήμιος Τερπιάδης in the *Odyssey* and two inscriptions in Delphi that feature notation and were written by professional musicians at Pöhlmann and West (2001) 62–85, no. 20–1). Meier (2017) argues that the song, like some form of advertisement, makes the tombstone more notable.

[12] Cf. drinking songs featuring a *carpe diem* motif; particularly close are *PMG* 913 *apud* Amipsias *fr.* 21 and *P.Oxy.* 1795 (at *CA* 199–200 with commentary at Hopkinson (2020) 316–19), a drinking song preserved on a papyrus that predates the Seikilos epitaph by a century. Lucian *Merc. Cond.* 18, Plu. *Moralia* 622c, 711d and Gel. 19.9.4 attest to musical performances at banquets in the second century AD, the time of the Seikilos epitaph (cf. Hutchinson (2013) 68).

[13] My reading of the Seikilos epitaph does not necessarily prove earlier interpretations wrong; it is still possible to think with Pöhlmann and West (2001) 91 that Seikilos was a professional musician. My emphasis on the *carpe diem* motif would add something to this; Seikilos' life then consisted of spreading enjoyment.

[14] Barker (1995) 59–60, confirming the earlier assessment of Comotti (1988) 24 and (1989) 109.

Introduction: In Search of Present Time

notation thus constitutes a sign system bereft of its original function, which makes the system stand out all the more, for the notes clearly set the central section of the inscription apart from its paratext.[15] This paratext provides a strong contextualisation of a sepulchral inscription; preceding the song, there is the characteristically sepulchral elegiac metre as well as the sepulchral key terms σῆμα and μνήμη. Succeeding the song, Seikilos' own name in the nominative, along with his father's name in the genitive, and the epitaphic formula ζῇ ('during his lifetime') again manifest the sepulchral nature of the monument.[16] Yet, framed within this funerary paratext, the song, with its fast iambics and its notation, points back to life, where Seikilos was happily singing at the symposium. The Seikilos epitaph is thus both song and stone, both performance and text: the notes, permanently silent in the graveyard, create a *silent requiem* for *carpe diem*. The notation, just like the *carpe diem* text of the epitaph, both evokes the present moment and laments its loss. As a funerary inscription, the Seikilos epitaph is read, yet readers read not only an inscription but also a song and a moment of present time. They read *carpe diem*.

A feeling of loss not only applies to Seikilos' individual life but also to performance and music in literature more widely. For Seikilos, a life of song is succeeded by a written epitaph. I propose that the loss of present enjoyment in Seikilos' individual life and the way in which this loss is negotiated in his epitaph can offer a model for analysing the perceived loss of performance and music in a wider literary context.[17] In archaic Greece, songs at banquets expressed the sentiment of *carpe diem*; such songs

---

[15] The concept of the paratext is taken from Genette (1997) [1987]. For approaches to paratexts in ancient literature, see Jansen (2014).

[16] Admittedly, τίθησι [...] ἔνθα ('he placed here') has the appearance of a formula of dedicatory rather than sepulchral epigram. Yet, for such a formula in a sepulchral epigram, see the much earlier *CEG* 113. Besides other evidence, the formulaic ζῇ ('he is alive', i.e., he put up the monument in his lifetime) decisively points to epitaphs: the formula only makes sense in this context. For the formula, see Franz (1840) 341, Robert (1933) 123 and (1937) 225. For the form of the Seikilos stele as a funeral stele, see Meier (2017) 104–5.

[17] Cf. DuBois (1995) 29–30, Fearn (2020) 17–18 on lyric poetry and a sense of loss, and Peponi (2002) 21: 'the term *lyric* becomes the emblem of a non-entity, the mark of an absence'.

A Requiem for *Carpe Diem*

simultaneously praised and created present enjoyment. This book analyses what happens to the motif when it is not sung but appears in books, inscriptions, or on artworks. I argue that non-performative textual exhortations to *carpe diem* demonstrate nostalgia for an idealised notion of banquet songs: texts attempt to evoke music and presence.

To my knowledge, no monographic treatment of the ancient *carpe diem* motif exists yet; as we saw in the case of the Seikilos epitaph, the motif is usually dismissed as trite and unworthy of further analysis.[18] This book, by contrast, argues that close analysis of the *carpe diem* motif can make a key contribution to a question that is central to literary studies in and beyond Classics: how can poetry give us the almost magical impression that something is happening here and now? The book is also a study of lyric and its reception (throughout this book I use the term 'lyric' comprehensively to refer to elegy and iambus as well as melic);[19] I explore how lyric is inscribed into Greek and Latin epigrams (Chapters 1 and 4), how Horace transforms lyric in his Latin poetry books (Chapters 2 and 3), how lyric is cut up and bastardised in anthologies, satires, and other texts (Chapter 5), and, finally, how in all these contexts *carpe diem* exemplifies a lyric spirit which constantly oscillates between presence and textuality. The period of interest for this study reaches from Alexander the Great to the Latin satirist Juvenal, that is, from the dawn of the Hellenistic period to the Imperial period.

Though there exist some valuable contributions on individual aspects of the *carpe diem* motif,[20] a wider-ranging study is needed if we wish to understand the significance of the *carpe diem* motif

---

[18] For example, Giangrande (1968) 139 calls the motif 'banal' and 'platitudinous', resulting in 'dull' epigrams. For *carpe diem* in English Renaissance poetry, see now Hyman (2019). Krznaric (2017) is a book dedicated to *carpe diem*, but it belongs to the field of popular science rather than scholarship. It is a manifesto for regaining the lost art of seizing the day, described as a centuries-old wisdom recently hijacked by consumer culture and other ostensible modern evils. This is a nostalgic view. *Carpe diem* was already a call to indulge in luxury in the first centuries BC and AD, long before the consumer culture of the twentieth and twenty-first century (see Chapter 4).

[19] See Budelmann (2009b) 2–5 for the terminology.

[20] I have found particularly valuable Davis (1991) 145–88 on the rhetorical scope of Horatian *carpe diem*, Ameling (1985) on *carpe diem* in epigraphic sources, Dunbabin (1986) on the motif in material culture. Giangrande (1968) 102–5, 139–40, 165–71 gives a learned, albeit dismissive, account of the motif in Hellenistic epigram, which is

7

Introduction: In Search of Present Time

for the evocation of present time in poetry. This book will therefore take into account methods from a range of fields in order to do justice to the manifold appearances of *carpe diem* in ancient culture. I will pay equal attention to Greek and Latin material and I will employ methods from various fields, including philology, epigraphy, art history, music, ancient linguistics, and critical theory. It is only by taking these fields into account that we can understand either the motif of *carpe diem* or the significance of presence for poetry.

The Pleasure in Greek and Latin Texts

The *carpe diem* motif urges us to enjoy the pleasures of life. Arguably the most authoritative passage in ancient literature which tells of the pleasures of life is the beginning of *Odyssey* Book 9. There, Odysseus proclaims that the finest thing in life is to partake at a banquet, listen to the music of a bard, and enjoy wine and company.[21] When *carpe diem* poems extol the pleasures of life, these are pleasures of the banquet: eroticism and wine and lyric, an ancient counterpart of 'sex and drugs and rock 'n' roll'. Pleasure is almost synonymous with the banquet in its various forms, whether it is the Homeric feast, the Greek symposium, or the Roman *conuiuium*.[22] Thus, *carpe diem* poems tell their addressees to drink, eat, fool around (παίζω), not to deny sex, to enjoy dance and music, not to be greedy, to enjoy luxuries, and to enjoy one's youth.[23] Such exhortations regularly appear in pairs or

---

now complemented by Sens (2016). Race (1988) 118–41 analyses the *Nachleben* of the classical motif in later poetry.

[21] Hom. *Od.* 9.1–15, on which see Hunter (2018) 92–132.

[22] The bibliography on ancient banqueting is vast. For the symposium, see, above all: Rossi (1983), Lissarrague (1990) [1987], Murray (1990), Schmitt Pantel (1992), Murray and Tecuşan (1995), Slater (1992), Cameron (1995) 71–103, J. König (2012), Topper (2012), Hobden (2013), Węcowski (2014), Cazzato, Obbink, and Prodi (2016). The sympotic articles of Oswyn Murray are now collected in Murray (2018). For the *conuiuium* (and other meals), see, in particular: Dunbabin (2003), Donahue (2004), Vössing (2004) and (2008), Stein-Hölkeskamp (2005), Roller (2006), Schnurbusch (2011).

[23] *To drink*: for example, Alc. *fr.* 38a.1, Thgn. 976, Hor. C. 1.9.5–8, and Cazzato and Prodi (2016) 6–10, Gagné (2016) 226–7; *to eat*: for example, *SH* 335.4, *GV* 1368.1 *apud* Ath. 8.336d; *to fool around* (my attempt to render the difficult expression παίζω): for example, Thgn. 567, Amphis *fr.* 8.1, *SGO* 17/19/03 (sometimes *ludere* in Latin: *CLE* 85 (= *CIL* vi 16169), 1167 with Kajanto (1969) 362); *not to deny sex*: for example,

The Pleasure in Greek and Latin Texts

as a triad of merriment: eat, drink, and be merry....²⁴ Besides exhortations to specific actions, texts also tell their addressees simply to enjoy life – the most concise exhortation to *carpe diem* for which Greek and Latin use characteristic expressions.²⁵ One should not worry about the future, and indeed one should ignore anything other than sensuous pleasures.²⁶ Often we encounter the claim that the insight of *carpe diem* applies universally to all mankind.²⁷ We are also told to hurry and seek pleasures now while we may.²⁸ This sense of hurry suits the hunt for sensuous pleasures; conversely, we sense a mismatch when one poet proclaims that we must do righteous deeds as life is short (Bacchylides 3.78–84). An exhortation of this nature is an exception and should arguably be read as a reaction against the calls to sensuous pleasure-seeking elsewhere. There is also some obvious

E. *Alc.* 790–1, *AP* 5.85 = Asclepiades 2 *HE*, *AP* 5.79 = [Plato] 4 *FGE* (more simply, 'to fuck' (βινῶ): *CIG* 3846l); *to enjoy dance and music*: for example, Thgn. 975, Hor. *Epod.* 13.9–10; *not to be greedy*: for example, Thgn. 1007–12, Hor. *C.* 2.14.25–8, 4.7.19–20; *to enjoy luxurious living*: for example, *SGO* 16/34/37 (= *GV* 263), 16/32/05 (= *GV* 1016), *GV* 1978.17–22 with Robert (1965) 187–8, Kajanto (1969) 361; *to enjoy one's youth*: for example, Thgn. 877–8 (= 1070 ab), Hor. *C.* 1.9.15–18.

²⁴ For numerous examples, see Ameling (1985). Cf. Sens (2016) 235 n.14.
²⁵ In Greek 'to enjoy life' is usually expressed with τέρπω (e.g., Mimn. *fr.* 2.4, Thgn. 1047, *SH* 335.2), χαίρω (e.g., [Alexis] *fr.* 25.5 *apud* Ath. 8.336d–f), and εὐφραίνω (e.g., E. *Alc.* 788, *AP* 11.62.3 (Palladas), *SGO* 02/09/32, 10/05/04, 18/01/19, 18/01/20 (= *GV* 1219) with Ameling (1985) 40–1) and in Latin with pregnant sense *uiuo* (e.g., Cat. 5.1, Petron. 34.10, 72.2, Mart. 5.64.5, [Verg.] *Copa* 38; though the idiom is characteristic for Latin, the Greek equivalent ζήσαις is used at *CIG* 7299, discussed at pages 172–6; cf. Wilamowitz-Moellendorff (1924) ii.315). Latin *iucundus* can occasionally render τερπνός (Hor. *S.* 2.6.96, *Epist.* 1.6.65–6 translating Mimn. *fr.* 1.1). One common Greek idiom in *carpe diem* texts tells addressees to 'indulge their soul or heart', for example, *SH* 335.1 (σὸν θυμὸν ἄεξε), [Alexis] *fr.* 25.5 (τὴν ψυχὴν τρέφειν). This idiom sounds Greek when turned into Latin at Hor. *C.* 4.7.19–20 *amico quae dederis animo* and Pers. 5.151 *indulge genio* (see the learned note of Arnott (1996) 825 and pages 128–9 of this book in detail).
²⁶ For example, *P.Oxy.* 1795 (at *CA* 199–200), Anacreont. 8, Hor. *C.* 1.11.1–3, 2.11.1–5, 3.8.17, and see the rich note of Nisbet and Rudd (2004) 228.
²⁷ For example, Heracles at E. *Alc.* 782 says that his words on *carpe diem* are advice to all mortals (βροτοῖς ἅπασι). For this universalising aspect of the motif, see Chapter 5, page 197.
²⁸ Thus ἤδη, νῦν, *iam*, and *nunc* appear regularly (cf. Syndikus (1972–3) i.73–5). Horace uses the tag *dum licet* a number of times (*C.* 2.11.16, 4.12.26, *S.* 2.6.96, *Epist.* 1.11.20), which also appears at Prop. 1.19.25, Ov. *Ars* 3.61, Sen. *Phaed.* 774, Petron. 34.10, 114.9. Also note the variations *dum uirent genua* at Hor. *Epod.* 13.4, *dum loquimur* at Hor. *C.* 1.11.7, *dum loquor* at De ros. nasc. 37, and *dum fata sinunt* (and variations thereof) at Tib. 1.1.69, Prop 2.15.23, Sen. *Her. F.* 178. Cf. Citti at *EO* ii.646 s.v. 'tempo' (also Citti (2000) 60). Similar phrases in Greek can be found at, for example, [Alexis] *fr.* 25.5 (ἕως ἔνεστι τὴν ψυχὴν τρέφειν), *SGO* 02/02/07 = *GV* 1955 (ὅσον ζῇς).

9

Introduction: In Search of Present Time

humour at play when Ovid at *Ars Amatoria* 2.113–22 employs numerous *carpe diem* images only to say that the shortness of life demands that we study Greek and Latin! For Ovid's *praeceptor amoris*, knowledge of Greek and Latin literature is of course only the means for impressing women and having sex (and thus not after all very far removed from the regular *carpe diem* motif).[29] Others have been more serious than Ovid when they claim that one must study while one may. Still, when some philosophers and a poet proclaim that true pleasure is found in study, thought, and intellectual conversation, they plainly make these claims in an attempt to rewrite a well-known model that extols the sensuous pleasures of the banquet.[30] This is where all pleasure is located.[31] Admittedly, this statement needs some modification; we do not have to assume that every *carpe diem* poem addressing a lover is necessarily imagined as taking place at a banquet. Rather, what matters is that the erotic poetry is at home at the symposium, though erotic encounters surely also happened in other places. In addition, Roman *carpe diem* epitaphs repeatedly mention baths as one of the pleasures of life, something with a less close connection to the banquet (though Trimalchio takes his guests for a bath at the banquet).[32] Yet, despite these caveats, the general point still stands: the ancients would agree with Odysseus that the banquet is 'the finest thing'.

Although Odysseus' views on pleasure were formative for Greek culture, neither in this instance nor elsewhere do the Homeric epics urge their audience to *carpe diem*. Two possible exceptions need to be considered. When Priam visits Achilles in order to release the body of his son Hector, Achilles invites him to

---

[29] Yet there are, *mirabile dictu*, those who take Ovid seriously: Vredeveld (1993) i.xli–xlii and xli n.101 notes that that the passage was popular with Renaissance readers and in particular with Erasmus, who regularly says that one must devote life to study as time is short (cf. Chapter 5, pages 223–4).

[30] *SH* 355 Crates, *SH* 338 Chrysippus, and Call. *Aetia fr.* 43.12–17 Harder rewrite the hedonistic Sardanapallus epitaph, on which see in detail Chapter 1.

[31] Cf. Edwards (2007) 161–78, who analyses how *carpe diem* is a Roman attitude to death that permeates dining culture.

[32] Petron. 72.3 with Courtney (2001) 116. Cf. *AP* 5.12 = Rufinus 2 Page. On the motif: Kajanto (1969) 364–7, Ameling (1985) 37 n.11, Busch (1999) 517–34. Already at Hom. *Od.* 8.248–9, the Phaeacians list baths as one of the pleasures of life, along with dance, music, feasts, and luxurious clothes.

eat despite his suffering. Even Niobe, he says, ate after she had lost all her children (*Il.* 24.602–20). Similarly, after the death of Patroclus, Thetis tells her son Achilles not to refrain from sex, as his life would be short and he would die soon (*Il.* 24.128–32). Yet, in both these passages, characters are not so much told to enjoy life as to overcome grief: the sentiment is 'life goes on' rather than 'live it up'.[33]

While Homeric heroes have little interest in *carpe diem*, Homer's audience and readers are fascinated with the motif. The *carpe diem* motif is prominent in archaic Greek lyric, both melic and elegy, and it is elegy in particular that reworks Homeric words and images in order to tell its listeners to enjoy life while they may. When Glaucus compares the generations of men to the generations of leaves on the battlefield before Troy (*Il.* 6.145–9), *carpe diem* is far from his mind, but in an elegy of Mimnermus falling leaves become an image of human transience and a call to enjoy life.[34] Indeed, a number of Mimnermus' scarce fragments are preoccupied with *carpe diem* and the praise of youth.[35] Not only does he compare humans to leaves that fall in autumn, but he also speaks of the 'flower of youth' (ἄνθεα ἥβης/ἄνθος at *frr.* 1.4, 2.3, 5.2 if authentic), the 'fruit of youth' (καρπός ἥβης at *fr.* 2.7–8), and the 'season [*sc.* of youth]' (ὥρη at *frr.* 2.9, 3.1). Human life is compared to nature, then, withering away after a brief season of spring. This comparison between nature's withering and human transience would become a key trope of *carpe diem* poems, influencing poets from Horace to Herrick and beyond. Since words such as the flower or season of youth in Mimnermus are taken from the Homeric epics, it has been argued that elegy programmatically

---

[33] Compare and contrast Wankel (1983) 153, Race (1993). *AP* 10.47 (Palladas) makes Homer's Niobe an enjoinder for *carpe diem*, on which see Guichard (2017) 165–6, who also points to *TrGF Adespota* 331.

[34] Mimn. *fr.* 2 with Griffith (1975). For a detailed discussion of the image of leaves with further bibliography, see Chapter 3.

[35] *Carpe diem* poems: *frr.* 1 and 2. The *carpe diem* motif is also present in *fr.* 5 if West (1989–92) ii.86 is right to attribute all of Thgn. 1017–22 to Mimnermus (the first three lines of Mimnermus' fragment as quoted by Stobaeus 4.50.69 appear as the last three lines of the Theognidean passage; see Bowie (2012) 14–15). *Frr.* 3–6 concern joyful youth and/or grievous old age. It is tempting though speculative to assume a *carpe diem* motif for *fr.* 7 = *AP* 9.50 = Thgn. 795–6. See W. J. Henderson (1995) on Mimnermus and *carpe diem*.

11

Introduction: In Search of Present Time

appropriates Homeric words for new unheroic contexts: calls to merrymaking phrased in the words of martial epic.[36] Indeed, Archilochus in his elegies uses Homeric language even as he proclaims that the pleasures of the symposium and *carpe diem* are preferable to warfare.[37]

Boys and cups seem to be substitutes for Homer's kings and wars. One of the most influential theories for this apparent change was championed by Bruno Snell and Hermann Fränkel, who argued that a supposed lyric age of individuality witnessed a change of mentalities: lyric poets began to sing of their own life from a first-person perspective in the present tense.[38] Yet, this view has been challenged on methodological as well as chronological grounds; although the Homeric epics have been handed down to us as the oldest Greek poems, short lyric poetry probably existed already at the same time as, or before the composition of, the Homeric epics.[39] If so, it is conceivable that images such as the falling leaves were already part of short *carpe diem* pieces when the Homeric epics were composed.[40] Another example of Homeric engagement in elegy can be found in the Theognidean corpus, which includes numerous *carpe diem* poems;[41] one Theognidean poem seems to appropriate Odysseus' 'golden verses' on the pleasures of life to a sympotic piece that comes close to being a *carpe diem* poem (Thgn. 1063–8) – yet, it is also possible that the Theognidean poem gives us a glimpse into the sort of short lyric pieces that may have influenced Odysseus' words.[42] While it thus seems misguided to argue that lyric poets turned their thoughts to present enjoyment because of a change of mentality, it is arguably right that lyric appropriates epic language for a competing worldview – even

---

[36] Griffith (1975) 80–3, *passim*.
[37] Archil. *frr.* 2, 4, 11, 13 with Davis (2010b) 109–11. The *incipit* of *fr.* 19 is turned into a *carpe diem* poem at *Anacreont.* 8, though we cannot know whether Archilochus' original already included the motif.
[38] Snell (1953) [1946] 43–70, Fränkel (1975) [1962] 147–273.
[39] See, for example, A. P. Burnett (1983) 1–3, the first two chapters of R. L. Fowler (1987), Budelmann (2009b) 14–15.
[40] See Peliccia (2002) 220.
[41] *Carpe diem* poems: Thgn. 567–70, 719–28 (= Solon *fr.* 24), 877–8 (= 1070 ab), 973–8, 983–8, 1007–12, 1017–22 (= Mimn. 5.1–6), 1047–8, 1129–32, 1299–1304. Poems related to the motif: Thgn. 757–64, 879–84, 1063–8, 1069–70, 1119–22, 1191–4.
[42] Hunter (2018) 112–13, with further bibliography on 97.

The Pleasure in Greek and Latin Texts

though this worldview is grounded in genre rather than the mentality of the age.[43] Later these textual dynamics would become explicit in a fifth-century-BC elegy of Simonides, which quotes Homer's line on leaves and turns it into a *carpe diem* poem.[44]

In melic poetry, Alcaeus and Anacreon are most prominently associated with the *carpe diem* motif. Perhaps the most obvious feature of Alcaeus' sympotic poems is that they call for particularly heavy drinking. Thus, the fragment that most clearly brings out the message of *carpe diem* (*fr.* 38a) immediately begins with the imperative 'drink!' (πῶνε).[45] The same piece also includes two arguments that commonly support calls to enjoy life while one may: first, the argument that there is no return from death (lines 1–4); second, the *argumentum a fortiori*, according to which even greater men could not evade death (lines 5–10).[46] In a number of other Alcaean fragments the time of the year offers the justification for drinking; although the fragmentary status of these pieces does not allow us to say whether they would have included the *carpe diem* motif, this sort of argument certainly became prominent in Horace's poetry, in which insights from seasonal change offer the justification for *carpe diem*, as Gregson Davis has shown in detail.[47] It is then in the reception of Alcaeus' poetry more so than in his

---

[43] Thus Budelmann (2009b) 15.
[44] Simonides *frr.* 19 + 20 quoting Hom. *Il.* 6.146, discussed with bibliography in Chapter 3 at pages 111–15. Other Homeric passages receive a similar reception; when Odysseus at some point on the journey cheers up his companions and invites them to enjoy a good meal after they have weathered dangers, this may simply be good leadership (*Od.* 10.174–7; cf. 12.208–12 and 12.21–7 (Circe speaking)). In Horace's lyric it becomes a call to enjoy pleasures while one may (*C.* 1.7.25–32). Further, Hellenistic epigrams make the Homeric *hapax legomenon* ζωρός (*Il.* 9.203) a key term in *carpe diem* poems (discussed in Chapter 4).
[45] Alcaeus' other *carpe diem* poems say that it is best 'to get drunk' (μεθύσθην; *fr.* 335.4) or again begin with a call to drinks (πώνωμεν; *fr.* 346.1). See Trumpf (1973) for drinking in Alcaeus. Kantzios (2018) argues that *fr.* 42 is a *carpe diem* poem as well, but there is little in the fragment to support this reading.
[46] For the first argument on the finality of death, see, for example, Thgn. 973–8, Hor *C.* 1.4.17–20 (numerous more examples quoted by Nisbet and Hubbard (1970) *ad loc.*), 4.7.21–4; for the second argument, which proclaims that greater men have also died, see: Hor. *C.* 4.7.25–8, *SH* 335.3 Choerilus, *AP* 11.28.5–6 = Argentarius 30.5–6 *GP*, ultimately going back to Hom. *Il.* 21.107–8 with Wankel (1983) 135–7. Cf. Davis (1991) 163–7.
[47] There exist possible Alcaean models for Horace's treatment of the seasons: *spring* at Alc. *frr.* 286, 367 and Hor. *C.* 1.4/4.7; *summer* at Alc. *frr.* 347, 352 and Hor. *C.* 3.29.18–20; *winter* at Alc. *fr.* 338 and Hor. *C.* 1.9. Davis (1991) 145–50 analyses the 'rhetorical schema' of the Horatian *carpe diem* poem, in which a description of nature ('scene')

Introduction: In Search of Present Time

scarce surviving fragments wherein his importance for the *carpe diem* motif now lies. This is even more so the case with Anacreon; though Anacreon has the reputation of a *carpe diem* poet *par excellence*, this reputation is based on the later reception of his poetry, above all in the *Anacreontea*, a collection of poems passed under the name of Anacreon. While numerous Anacreontic poems include the *carpe diem* motif, we can find it in only one of Anacreon's own fragments.[48] Anacreon will almost certainly have composed more *carpe diem* poems, but it is the later tradition which tempts us to supply the *carpe diem* motif where a fragment itself does not include it.[49] To what extent melic poets other than Alcaeus and Anacreon engaged with the *carpe diem* motif is difficult to say. No one else has quite the reputation of a sympotic reveller that Alcaeus and Anacreon have, but some suggestive phrases that are scattered through lyric fragments of other authors suggest that they, too, occasionally exhorted their audience to make merry.[50]

Songs about *carpe diem* continued after the end of the archaic age. Yet, in some cases one can only speculate; in the classical age, Ion of Chios may have composed elegiac poems on that motif, but though some tantalising fragments extol merrymaking (*frr.* 26, 27), too little survives of his poetry to be certain.[51] We also

---

triggers a 'response' consisting of 'insight' (human life is transient) and 'prescription' (call to enjoyment).

[48] Anacr. *fr.* 395. Bernsdorff (2020) ii.616–18 and at *fr.* 395.5–6 convincingly argues that an exhortation to make merry is implied in the poem. The *carpe diem* motif would be clearer, though, if the poem were incomplete and such an exhortation had been explicitly included in omitted lines, which is possible. Iris Sticker at Bernsdorff (2020) ii.618 n.7 suggests that Anacreon, *fr.* 356a may belong to the same poem and offer this exhortation. Giangrande (1968) 109–11 sees the exhortation to enjoyment in a double entendre in *fr.* 395 (D. A. Campbell (1989) and Bernsdorff (2020) at *fr.* 395.11b–12 are rightly sceptical).

[49] Anacr. *fr.* 356 with Hor. *C.* 1.36.13–16, as analysed by Bernsdorff (2020) ii.426.

[50] Pindar's expression 'plucking youth' may have influenced the very expression 'carpe diem' at Hor. *C.* 1.11.8 (*P.* 6.48: ἥβαν δρέπων; cf. *fr.* 123.1–2 Maehler). Phillips (2014) traces an important element in a Horatian *carpe diem* poem back to Sappho: *permitte diuis cetera* (*C.* 1.9.9) alludes to τὰ δ' ἄλλα | πάντα δαιμόνεσσιν ἐπιτρόπωμεν (lines 9–10 of the 'Brothers poem' (at Obbink (2014), the provenance of which is problematic)). Gregson Davis analyses Sappho *fr.* 58 as a *carpe diem* poem (and suggests links between the motif and *fr.* 55) in an unpublished paper titled '"Time's arrow, time's cycle". Embodied temporality and the argument of Sappho's "Tithonos" poem (frg. 58)'. Bacchylides 3.78–84, too, engages with the motif (cf. *frr.* 11 + 12 Maehler).

[51] See LeVen (2014) 244–68 for presence and performance in late classical sympotic poetry.

know far too little about Hellenistic lyric, but if Asclepiades indeed wrote lyric poetry (as the metre that is named after him suggests) it would not be surprising if he had written *carpe diem* poems, since his surviving poetic output shows much interest in this motif as well as in Alcaeus.[52] It is generally assumed that such poems would have employed lyric metres not in the originally strophic form, but in stichic form: sequences of lines in the same metrical lengths, which were suitable for reading and recitation rather than song.[53] There is in fact an extant Hellenistic poem of this type that includes the *carpe diem* motif: Theocritus 29. Theocritus' poem uncovers a number of traits of archaic lyric in archaeological fashion:[54] the theme of pederastic love, the opening quotation from Alcaeus, and the Lesbian lyric metre (the Aeolic pentameter). Much like the later Seikilos epitaph, discussed at the beginning of this Introduction, Theocritus' poem also evokes music in a written medium; Lucia Prauscello has shown how the poem mimics distichic strophic form by creating end-stopped distichic sense units.[55] When Theocritus tells his addressee in the manner of Alcaeus to enjoy life while he may (Theoc. 29.25–34), we seem to hear momentary lyric song arising from the page of the book.

While hardly any Greek lyric on *carpe diem* survives from known authors after the archaic age, then, we possess a number of anonymous *carpe diem* poems, which are sometimes called 'popular' songs. Besides a few other examples, such *carpe diem* songs appear in particular in the *Anacreontea*.[56] Songs of this kind are an

---

[52] Cf. Hunter (1996b) 172–4, Sens (2011) xxxiii, 343–4. For *carpe diem* in Asclepiades' epigrams, see pages 16–17.

[53] Leo (1897) 65–70, Hunter (1996b) 4–5, 139–40, Fantuzzi and Hunter (2004) 27–8, Prauscello (2006) 186 n.2, Morgan (2010) 183–5. Compare and contrast Acosta-Hughes and Stephens (2012) 104–5.

[54] This is the argument and image of Hunter (1996b) 167–81. Cf. Pretagostini (1997).

[55] Prauscello (2006) 185–213, which is a revised version of Fassino and Prauscello (2001). Cf. the comparable technique of Meineke's Law in Horace's *Odes* discussed at page 29.

[56] *PMG* 913 *apud* Amipsias *fr.* 21, *PMG* 1009, *P.Oxy.* 1795 (at *CA* 199–200), *SGO* 02/02/07 = *GV* 1955 (the Seikilos epitaph discussed above in the Introduction), Anacreont. 7, 8, 32, 36, 38, 40, 45, 48, 50, 52A. For the *Anacreontea*, see, above all, Rosenmeyer (1992). M. L. West (1990) analyses the symposium in both the *Anacreontea* and *P.Oxy.* 1795. Fitzgerald (2021) chapter 4 interprets the *Anacreontea* as neoclassical poems which transform the literary past into a timeless present.

Introduction: In Search of Present Time

important reminder that *carpe diem* songs continued to be composed and performed after a so-called 'age of song'. Throughout this book they will be regularly adduced as a comparison to textual exhortations of *carpe diem*, though there is no space for a comprehensive interpretation of such songs. Still, it seems clear that any such interpretation in the future should not only take account of their performative nature, but should also consider to what extent books and writing influenced these songs. For instance, the *carpe diem* poem *Anacreontea* 8 begins with a motto taken from Archilochus *fr.* 19. Mottoes of this kind have received much attention in the context of Horace's book poetry, where they point to Horace's engagement with Alexandrian book editions, which catalogued early Greek lyric under such *incipit*s (I will return to Horatian mottoes in Chapters 2 and 5). The usage of the same technique in songs complicates this picture and opens up new avenues of research.

Epigrams offer the most sustained engagement with the *carpe diem* motif alongside lyric.[57] 'Epigram' describes verse inscriptions as well as the poetry genre that originated from these inscriptions, and the interplay between inscribed and literary epigrams is crucial for the genre in general and its treatment of the *carpe diem* motif in particular.[58] Epigram as a literary genre rose to prominence in the Hellenistic period, and we find *carpe diem* poems among the works of the first generation of Hellenistic epigrammatists such as Asclepiades of Samos (third century BC), as well as in late Hellenistic epigrams collected in the *Garland of Philip* (first century BC to first century AD), and also later still in Imperial and late antique epigrams (first century to sixth century AD).[59] In one epigram, the Hellenistic poet Leonidas

---

[57] Giangrande (1968) 102–5, 139–40, 165–71, Sens (2016).
[58] There is no clear dividing line between 'literary' and 'inscribed' epigrams, as Bing (1998) 29–40 shows. Despite this caveat the terms are still useful.
[59] Hellenistic *carpe diem* epigrams: see *AP* 5.85 = Asclepiades 2 *HE*, *AP* 7.217 = Asclepiades 41 *HE*, *AP* 7.452 = Leonidas 67 *HE*, *AP* 12.32 = Thymocles 1 *HE*, *AP* 12.50 = Asclepiades 16 *HE* with Hunter (2010) 284–8, Hedylus 5 *HE* with Sens (2016) 233–5 (Sens (2011) 202 also interprets *AP* 7.284 = Asclepiades 30 *HE* as a *carpe diem* poem). Late Hellenistic epigrams from the *Garland of Philip* are discussed in detail in Chapter 4, and see Rohland (2019) on *AP* 11.23 = Antipater of Thessalonica 38 *GP* (as well as on *AP* 5.39 (Nicarchus)). Imperial and late antique *carpe diem* epigrams: see *AP* 5.12 = Rufinus 2 Page, *AP* 5.72 (Palladas), *AP* 5.74 = Rufinus 28 Page, *AP* 7.32 (Julian), *AP* 7.33 (Julian), *AP* 10.47 (Palladas), *AP* 11.19 = Strato 99 Floridi, *AP* 11.62 (Palladas) with W. J. Henderson (2010) 252–7, *AP* 12.234 = Strato 74 Floridi. The precise dates of Rufinus Strato,

of Tarentum urges us to enjoyment, because even prudent Mr Temperance died (*AP* 7.452 = Leonidas 67 *HE*):[60]

μνήμην Εὐβούλοιο σαόφρονος ὦ παριόντες,
πίνωμεν· κοινὸς πᾶσι λιμὴν Ἀΐδης.

1 μνήμην Reiske : μνήμης codd. : μνήμονες Casaubon : μνῆμα τόδ᾿ Grotius

> You who pass by the grave[61] of sober Eubulus,
> let us drink! Hades is a common harbour for all of us.

The hexameter looks just like an epitaph and raises the expectation that this is precisely what we are reading. Yet as soon as we are imagining ourselves standing in front of the tombstone of Eubulus and reading the letters of its inscription, a call to drink screams at us at the beginning of the pentameter. The exhortation to drink seems to come straight out of the songs of a lyric poet and clashes with the epitaphic-writing of the previous line. We must revise our interpretation, then; what looked like a grave inscription turned out to be a piece of sympotic banter.[62] Yet it is of course precisely the play with epitaphic conventions that allows Leonidas to bring out the *carpe diem* message. Similarly, the epigrammatist Asclepiades of Samos plays with epitaphic formulae in a poem that tells a woman to sleep with him as life is short (*AP* 5.85 = Asclepiades 2 *HE*). Such an argument for seduction would of course become extremely common in later *carpe diem* poems.[63] While literary epigrams of this kind

---

Palladas, and Julian are a matter of debate. Pseudepigraphic and anonymous epigrams: see *AP* 5.79 = [Plato] 4 *FGE*, *AP* 11.3, *AP* 11.8 = *GV* 1906, *AP* 11.56.

[60] Giangrande (1968) 168–70 stresses the importance of σαόφρων ('prudent', 'chaste', here in particular 'sober'). The proper name Εὔβουλος, literally 'well-advised' or 'prudent', adds to this.

[61] μνήμη = μνῆμα ('tomb') is an unusual meaning, though Gow and Page (1965) cite some parallels. It still seems slightly preferable to the paradosis, a genitive of toast, ('let's drink to the memory (μνήμης) of Eubulus').

[62] I am here merely rehearsing the observations and interpretation of Giangrande (1968) 167–70.

[63] Especially in English Renaissance poetry, on which see Hyman (2019). Also see *AP* 7.217 = Asclepiades 41 *HE*, *AP* 5.79 = [Plato] 4 *FGE*, *AP* 5.80 = [Plato] 5 *FGE* = Philodemus 2 Sider, *AP* 5.74 = Rufinus 28 Page, Theoc. 23.29–32, 29.25–34, Cat. 5, Hor. *C.* 1.1.11, 3.28, Tib. 1.1.69–74, 1.4.27–38, *De rosis* at *Anthologia Latina* i.84 Riese = 72 Shackleton Bailey, Florus at *Anthologia Latina* i.87 Riese = 75 Shackleton Bailey, *De ros. nasc.*, and Ronsard's poetry with Race (1988) 118–41.

play with epitaphic conventions, the *carpe diem* motif was also common on actual epitaphs, which often address a wayfarer and exhort him with a triad of words of merriment to eat, drink, and be merry.[64] Epigrams thus share with lyric the figure of the addressee as a characteristic of the genre, which is relevant for the present study: a call to enjoyment has to be addressed to someone. Inscribed epitaphs that exhort to enjoyment may long precede Hellenistic literary epigrams; Christiane Sourvinou-Inwood argues that the word χαῖρε on fifth-century-BC epitaphs implies the meaning 'to rejoice' and is exclusively said by the deceased to the living.[65] If right, this is a concise early form of *carpe diem* in an epitaphic context. Epigram and lyric come from opposing sides to the *carpe diem* motif, then: while lyric is originally located at the banquet, the place of drinking and merrymaking, epigrams are located on tombs, the place of death.[66] Lyric and epigram also evoke different media: lyric is imagined as being sung, while epigrams are imagined as being written. Such extreme formalism needs to be modified, though. We have seen above how Leonidas juxtaposes an epitaphic line with a sympotic one. Indeed, 'sympotic' epigrams of this kind owe some debt to archaic elegy; deprived from their respective settings on stones or at symposia, Hellenistic epigrams and archaic elegy look rather alike.[67] Lyric and epigram thus share a relatively short form and a connection to the banquet. Verse inscriptions were of course not only a feature of epitaphs but also of dedications and objects other than tombs. Indeed, a number of *carpe diem* epigrams evoke inscriptions on objects such as cups and gems, which are part of the sympotic luxurious lifestyle.[68] Here, epigrams evoke a world of material objects that would have exhorted people to enjoy life while they may. In particular, the skeleton was an image for *carpe diem* that can be found on cups, gems, mosaics (on tables and elsewhere), and tombstones, as well as in the shape of little figurines.[69] One version of the

---

[64] Ameling (1985), and a fuller discussion with bibliography in Chapter 1.
[65] Sourvinou-Inwood (1995) 180–216.   [66] Sens (2016) 231–2.
[67] See Gutzwiller (1998) 115–22, Bing and Bruss (2007b) 11–12, Bowie (2007), Sens (2016) 231–2.
[68] See Chapter 4.   [69] Dunbabin (1986).

carpe diem argument that is particularly prominent in material culture is that death will make us all equal, so we may just as well enjoy ourselves while alive.[70] Latin literature follows Greek models in treating the *carpe diem* motif in particular in lyric. Thus, Catullus wrote a *carpe diem* poem that contrasts individual human life with the cycle of nature: 'The Sunne may set and rise, but we contrariwise sleepe after our short light one everlasting night.'[71] This contrast between nature's renewing cycle and the death of individual human life would become a key trope of *carpe diem* poems, in particular in Horace's poetry.[72] Indeed, while Catullus' *carpe diem* poem remains an isolated example in his corpus, in Horace the sentiment becomes a 'philosophical position advocated throughout the œuvre':[73] time and again Horace's odes tell their addressees to enjoy the present.[74] Horace famously writes himself into the canon of lyric poetry (*C.* 1.1.35–6). His poetry becomes a postscript to the Greek lyric tradition as numerous odes follow on from an initial quotation or motto from Greek lyric. Such poems collapse the time that separates Horace from archaic Greece, as Horace virtually joins the momentary celebrations of Alcaeus and the like: nunc *est bibendum!* ('*Now* we must drink!'). The generic self-consciousness of Horace guarantees that not only his own poetry but lyric as a genre becomes the poetry of *carpe diem*.[75]

Roman epitaphs, just like Greek ones, frequently include the *carpe diem* motif.[76] But Latin literature does not have an

---

[70] This relation between the theme *omnia mors aequat* and *carpe diem* is discussed by Dunbabin (1986) 212–15, and see pages 167–8 in Chapter 4. As Dunbabin points out, the theme is of course not restricted to art (see, e.g., Hor. *S.* 2.6.95, *C.* 1.4.13–14, 2.3.21–8, 2.14.9–12 with the discussion of Davis (1991) 163–7).
[71] Walter Raleigh's take on lines 4–6 of Cat. 5.
[72] See Hor. *C.* 1.4, 4.7. While the motif is not attested for *carpe diem* poems before Catullus, it is likely that such poems existed and are lost (thus Nisbet and Hubbard (1970) 60–1). Alcaeus' fragments in which he calls to drinks in different seasons are likely candidates (see page 13 n.47). For the motif in Horace, see, above all, Davis (1991) 155–60.
[73] Lowrie (1997) 57, and related comments on 50, 70. On page 1 Lowrie notes that according to common assumption *carpe diem* is the 'central didactic message of the *Odes*'.
[74] See Hor. *C.* 1.4, 1.7, 1.9, 1.11, 1.36, 2.3, 2.11, 2.14, 3.8, 3.14, 3.17, 3.28, 3.29, 4.7, 4.12. Besides the *Odes*, also note Hor. *S.* 2.6.93–7, 2.8.34, *Epod.* 13, *Epist.* 1.4, 1.5, 1.11.20–3, 2.1.144.
[75] See, for example, Culler (2015) 68–71 for the importance of Horace for the genre of lyric from a comparative perspective.
[76] See, for example, Ameling (1985) 42–3.

Introduction: In Search of Present Time

equivalent to the vast numbers of literary epigrams that the *Greek Anthology* preserves. Still, the epigrammatist Martial wrote a number of *carpe diem* poems.[77] Whether the pseudo-Vergilian elegiac poem *Copa* also belongs to the epigrammatic tradition is doubtful at best.[78] In this elegiac poem of thirty-eight lines a barmaid praises the features of her establishment and tells her addressee to live it up while he may. Wilamowitz argued that the poem is an embellished version of a tavern shop sign that would advertise its virtues; it would thus be an extended epigram.[79] Yet, there are no signs in the poem that hint at writing and shop signs; rather, the barmaid is said to dance and make music. It thus appears more likely to see connections between the piece and popular song and performance; we are invited to listen to the song of the barmaid and imagine her dancing.[80] The *Copa* is difficult to date, though may be a first-century-AD poem. In late antiquity we can find more Latin elegies on the *carpe diem* theme; these employ the elegiac metre for themes that owe much to Horace's lyric.[81]

While lyric and epigram are the two genres that show the most sustained engagement with *carpe diem*, there remain three categories that need to be addressed: the false, the lost, and the ugly. These will be discussed in turn. The false: the *carpe diem* motif is often characterised as Epicurean.[82] Yet, the *carpe diem* argument would not be possible without fear of death; it is this fear that compels us to hurried pleasure-seeking during our lifetime. Epicureans, such as Lucretius and Philodemus, thus explicitly disassociate *carpe diem* from true Epicureanism.[83] Indeed, as Lucretius is doing so, he tells of a banqueter who bewails the shortness of life and takes this as

---

[77] Mart. 1.15, 4.54, 5.20, 5.58, 5.64, 7.47, 8.44, 8.77, 10.23, 13.126, some of which are discussed in Chapter 4. A later example: Ausonius *Epigrams* 14 Green

[78] Text by Edward Kenney in Clausen et al. (1966), commentary at Goodyear (1977).

[79] Wilamowitz-Moellendorff (1924) ii.315. [80] Thus H. Morgan (2017).

[81] *De ros. nasc.*, a poem of Pentadius (*Anthologia Latina* i.235 Riese = 227 Shackleton Bailey, discussed in the Epilogue of this book. Very similar to *De. ros. nasc.* are also two short hexameter poems that are perhaps both late antique, although one is ascribed to the Hadrianic author Florus: *De rosis* at *Anthologia Latina* i.84 Riese = 72 Shackleton Bailey, Florus at *Anthologia Latina* i.87 Riese = 75 Shackleton Bailey with Courtney (1980b) 44–6 for date, authorship, and intertexts.

[82] For example, Hadot (1995) [1981] 224, Moles (2007) 168.

[83] Lucr. 3.912–30 with Kenney (2014) *ad loc.*, Martha (1867) 143–4, 169; Philodemus [*On Choices and Avoidances*] 17 with Indelli and Tsouna-McKirahan (1995) 35–6, 195–200,

an excuse for pleasure-seeking. Lucretius may take his aim here at the sort of poetry that is set at banquets, in which the *carpe diem* motif is common: lyric and epigram.[84] If so, this passage offers further support for the stance of this book, namely that the *carpe diem* motif belongs to banquet poetry, not philosophy. Although real Epicureans rejected the idea of *carpe diem*, many hedonists used Epicureanism as an intellectual pretence under which they sought pleasures. Seneca paints a vivid portrait of such people (*Dial.* 7.13), and popular or trivialised Epicureanism of this kind can also be seen on a silver cup that shows (among others) Epicurus in the form of a skeleton next to whom is written 'pleasure is the goal' (τὸ τέλος ἡδονή at Louvre, Bj 1923; see Figure 4.1c).[85] When Horace's *carpe diem* poems include Epicurean imagery and phrases, this, too, should be attributed to popular Epicureanism.[86]

While Epicureans would not subscribe to the idea of *carpe diem*, the question arises if other philosophical schools proclaimed this idea. It may seem intuitive to associate the idea of *carpe diem* with Aristippus and the Cyrenaics since their philosophy is associated with pleasure and seemed to exalt sensuous pleasures. Yet it is difficult to assess whether or not the Cyrenaics told their followers to make merry while they may. If Aristippus left behind any writings, they are lost to us, and we rely on later, sparse, often unreliable

---

Tsouna (2009) 260. Philodemus engages with the motif in his epigrams at *AP* 11.30 = 19 Sider and *AP* 5.80 = [Plato] 5 *FGE* = 2 Sider. *AP* 9.412 = 29 Sider seems to prompt us to enjoyment as we may die tomorrow (thus Sider (1997) 165, 168; the meaning of the poem is controversially discussed). Yet, Philodemus' argument in this epigram is somewhat different from the *carpe diem* argument; the poem suggests we should not discontinue our habitual pleasures because of a friend's death. Death is nothing to an Epicurean – neither something sad which interrupts pleasures, nor something to be feared that prompts to festivities as the *carpe diem* argument claims. See Sider (1997) 34 on similarities and rifts between Philodemus' personae as philosopher and poet.

[84] Kenney (2014) 208.
[85] See Dunbabin (1986) 224–30 on the cup, which is also discussed in Chapter 4. Erler and Schofield (1999) 642–3 analyse misconceptions of Epicurean ethics on the cup (cf. Rostovtzeff (1957) i.56 and his plate 7). On popular Epicureanism and *carpe diem*, see, in particular, Merlan (1949). On pages 170–1 I consider how popular Epicureanism may have influenced views on horoscopes in *carpe diem* contexts.
[86] Thus Merlan (1949). Cf. Traina (2009) [1991] 288–90. For verbal echoes of Epicurean philosophy in Horace, see *C.* 1.11.8 with Nisbet and Hubbard (1970) *ad loc.* and *C.* 3.29.41–3 with Nisbet and Rudd (2004) *ad loc.*, and note *Epist.* 1.4 for explicit mention of Epicurus in a *carpe diem* piece.

Introduction: In Search of Present Time

testimonies for his philosophy.[87] In one particularly suggestive fragment Aristippus says that pleasure can only be found in the present, though it is not clear whether this argument in a larger context would have amounted to *carpe diem*.[88] The question cannot be answered with certainty, then, and an additional difficulty concerns possible differences in the philosophical doctrines between Aristippus and later Cyrenaics; Hegesias, a later Cyrenaic philosopher, held the pessimistic view that happiness in life is so difficult to attain that death may be more pleasant, that is, the hedonistically preferable option.[89] This seems a far cry from *carpe diem*.

Seneca is arguably the philosopher who wrote most extensively on the shortness of life.[90] Yet, his teachings, too, differ from the idea of *carpe diem* in two important ways. First, the *carpe diem* argument poses that life is an absolute good and death is an absolute bad, for one can only find pleasure in the former and not in the latter. Seneca disagrees: life is not an absolute good and the wise man chooses to die rather than to live on in a miserable life. Seneca can thus criticise a certain Pacuvius, who seems to exemplify the *carpe diem* attitude as he celebrates each day his own funeral among wine, dinners, and male prostitutes who shout 'he has lived' (*Epist.* 12.9). Pacuvius' actions seem to reveal an overestimation of life as well as a fear of death.[91] For Seneca, this makes Pacuvius a fool. Second, the *carpe diem* argument urges to hurried pleasure-seeking in the present as the future is beyond our control. Seneca, however, claims that the wise man can bring past, present, and future all under his control.[92] Whoever finds pleasure only in the present is a fool (*Epist.* 99.5): *anguste fructus rerum determinat, qui tantum praesentibus laetus est* ('He who takes pleasure only in the present sets a narrow boundary to his enjoyment of things').[93] Despite the

---

[87] Lampe (2015) 16–25 gives an overview of the evidence of the Cyrenaics.
[88] *SSR* IV A 174, which is discussed in detail by Lampe (2015) 64–73. Cf. Sedley (2017) 91. Traina (2009) [1991] 288–90 argues on the basis of this fragment that Horatian *carpe diem* is closer to Aristippus than Epicurus.
[89] D.L. 2.93–6 with Sedley (2017) 97.
[90] Especially *De breuitate uitae*, but also note *De uita beata* and *Epistles* 12, 108.24–8.
[91] Thus Mann (2006). The behaviour of Petronius' Trimalchio is of course comparable (Petron. 78.5 with Schmeling (2011) *ad loc.*).
[92] G. D. Williams (2003) 22.
[93] See Vogt-Spira (2017) 204 on this passage, who contrasts it with the *carpe diem* argument at Hor. *C.* 3.8.27–8: *dona praesentis cape laetus horae:* | *linque seuera*.

difference in argument, readers of Seneca are frequently reminded of the *carpe diem* motif and Horace's treatment of it: numerous images, expressions, and quotations in Seneca are taken from poems that treat this motif.[94] It is, then, the poetic heritage of Seneca's language rather than the content of his philosophy for which *carpe diem* matters, and I will discuss one such example in Chapter 5.

It is time to turn to the lost. Lost lyric poems have already been mentioned. It is more difficult still to judge how lost works in other genres would have changed our understanding of the *carpe diem* motif. One poem from the classical period which may have offered us a different perspective on the *carpe diem* motif if it had survived is the *Hedypatheia* of Archestratus of Gela. In this didactic poem, Archestratus gives culinary insights in hexameters. For instance, he advises ignoring the cheap stuff and heading straight for lobster (*fr.* 25 Olson and Sens). Apart from timeless insights of this sort, the text also includes the *carpe diem* motif in one of the longest fragments (*fr.* 60 Olson and Sens): a free man should enjoy his drinks with dainties, and die if this is not possible. It is tempting – though ultimately speculative – to assume that this fragment would have been a programmatic passage; the whole justification of the work would then have been to enjoy good food because life is short.[95] If right, Archestratus' work may have shown us a side of *carpe diem* that differs in some respects from the texts discussed in this study. First, it would have put a strong emphasis on eating rather than drinking and merrymaking, as is the case in Alcaeus, Theognis, or Horace.[96] Second, the poem would have been comparatively long, unlike the short *carpe diem* poems in lyric and epigram, which are the focus of this study. Third, the fragment of Archestratus lets us see more clearly the formally instructive nature of *carpe diem* poems: didactic poetry and *carpe diem* poems share a first-person speaker, an addressee, frequent

---

[94] Sen. *Dial.* 10.8.5, 10.9 with G. D. Williams (2003) *ad loc.*, Stöckinger, Winter, and Zanker (2017b) 7–9, Vogt-Spira (2017).
[95] If this is the case, there was further incentive for Epicurus' distractors to claim that Archestratus' work was the origin for Epicurus' philosophy (see Chapter 1, page 67).
[96] Eating is of course a prominent theme in *carpe diem* epitaphs and close to the heart of Petronius' Trimalchio (Chapters 4 and 5).

Introduction: In Search of Present Time

imperatives, and the ostensible aim to instruct. The inclusion of the *carpe diem* theme in a didactic poem sheds light on these features.[97]

I have argued so far in this section that the *carpe diem* motif belongs to banquet poetry, that is, lyric and epigram. Yet the picture that is emerging may strike readers as rather too neat – after all, the *carpe diem* motif is scattered through a multitude of texts throughout different genres and ages. Thus, in tragedy a Persian king ends a speech with this sentiment (A. *Pers.* 840), and the drunk Heracles dedicates a little speech to the idea of merrymaking (E. *Alc.* 780–802).[98] In comedy, too, we see the motif in a number of fragments.[99] Pastoral poetry, Latin love elegy, epic, and didactic poetry all include the *carpe diem* motif.[100] Satirists attribute the sentiment to a mouse and a gigolo.[101] The *carpe diem* argument appears as a gnome or even cliché in these texts. Such messy, scattered pieces of *carpe diem*, which turn the motif into a cliché and can appear in contexts far removed from lyric settings, are what I have been calling 'the ugly'. Yet, while the motif appears in these texts, this does not make them all *carpe diem* texts; in other words, Aeschylus' *Persians* is not a tragedy on *carpe diem* just because a character voices this sentiment at one point. On the contrary, *carpe diem* sections that appear in longer texts regularly feel alien to their context: through their diction and imagery they

---

[97] Also see Alc. *fr.* 347 reworking Hesiod's didactic *Op.* 582–96 to a sympotic call to drinking, which may have included the *carpe diem* motif, and its adaption at Verg. *G.* 3.323–38 (Hunter (2014) 123–66 with bibliography, and see Chapter 5); Ov. *Ars* 3.59–80.

[98] Also see S. *Tereus TrGF* 593, E. *HF* 503–5, *Antiope TrGF* 196, *TrGF Adespota* 95. Dodds (1960) at E. *Ba.* 424–6 and 910–11 has rich notes with references to 'hedonism' in tragedy and beyond, though not all examples are *carpe diem* texts. Erler (2015) [2012] further discusses these 'hedonistic' passages. On the Latin side: Sen. *Her. F.* 175–83, *Phaed.* 443–54, 761–76; one would like to know more about the context of *TrRF Adespota* 21 apud Cic. *De orat.* 3.162 and *Ac.* 2.89: *uideo te, uideo: uiue, Ulixes, dum licet;* | *oculis postremum lumen radiatum rape!*

[99] Alex. *frr.* 222, 273, [Alex.] *fr.* 25, Amips. *fr.* 21, Amphis *frr.* 8, 21, Philetaer. *fr.* 7, Theophil. *fr.* 12.3–4 . On the Latin side, see the song at Pl. *Ps.* 1132–5.

[100] Pastoral: Theoc. 23.29–32, imitated at Verg. *Ecl.* 2.17–18. Elegy: Prop. 1.19.25–6, 2.15.23, 2.15.49–54, 4.5.59–62, Tib. 1.1.69–74, 1.4.27–38 with rich notes by K. F. Smith (1971) [1913] *ad loc.* Epic: Sil. 15.63–70. Didactic: Lucr. 3.912–30, Verg. *G.* 3.63–71, 3.323–38, Ov. *Ars* 3.59–80.

[101] Hor. *S.* 2.6.90–7, Juv. 9.124–9. Also see Pers. 5.151–3. In Petronius' *Satyrica carpe diem* is central for the *cena Trimalchionis*, and the sentiment also appears elsewhere in the work (discussed in Chapters 4 and 5).

evoke lyric poetry and look like quotations. Chapter 5 looks at some – though necessarily not all – instances of such *carpe diem* sections in longer texts.

The short survey of the *carpe diem* motif has pointed to lyric and epigram as the two genres in which the motif appears most frequently. I have so far only touched upon a key difference between these two genres: lyric hearkens back to performative song, while epigram looks back at written inscription. This difference in media is important for the *carpe diem* motif and will be addressed in the next section.

Performance, Text, and Evocation of Presence

Carpe diem poems proclaim the supreme importance of the present moment, the here-and-now. As such, these poems directly concern a topic that has been central in studies of lyric as well as literature more generally: the relation between lyric poems and their setting in the present. Literary scholars have tackled this theme of presence with divergent approaches – though they all agree on its importance.[102] In this section, I wish to show how my own approach relates to existing methodologies and how a close analysis of *carpe diem* poems can advance our understanding of this problem.

Carpe diem poems call their addressees to the momentary pleasures of the banquet. Early Greek lyric of that sort was also itself an element of the banquet, where it was sung. The ideal *carpe diem* poem would not only urge present enjoyment, but its performance at the symposium would make it a present event, and its music would create enjoyment. Yet, did such an ideal *carpe diem* poem ever exist? Research on early lyric, particularly from the 1980s onwards, has done much to highlight the significance of performance and the 'song culture' of Greece: numerous important studies have focused on the social function of the performance of lyric songs in their historical or ritual context.[103] Thus, the

---

[102] See Fearn (2020) 12–18 for a survey of different methodologies on presence in Greek lyric.
[103] The term 'song culture' is taken from Herington (1985). Also see Calame (1997) [1977], Gentili (1988 [1984]; 1990). Kurke (2000) gives a summary of the case for

function of Alcaeus' poetry, for instance, has been seen as forging bonds between men of the elite at the symposium.[104] When we encounter a *carpe diem* poem in early Greek lyric, in the Theognidean corpus, the likely performance context can add something to the poem (1047–8): νῦν μὲν πίνοντες τερπώμεθα, καλὰ λέγοντες· | ἄσσα δ' ἔπειτ' ἔσται, ταῦτα θεοῖσι μέλει ('now let's enjoy drink and good talk. But what will happen later is up to the gods'). As the speaker exhorts his fellow symposiasts to enjoyment in drink and good talk, they might indeed be drinking at the very moment of performance, and the poem itself creates the very enjoyment it asks for through its good talk and music. The words of the speaker are truly performative, according to J. L. Austin's definition of performative words:[105] the speaker does things with words as his utterance performs an action. When his words urge enjoyment through fine talk, they create enjoyment through fine talk (and music).[106] Through its performative power, the poem seems to assert an almost magical control over the present. Indeed, the hexameter seems to stress the poet's control over the present (νῦν μέν), while the pentameter notes that anything after this present moment is uncertain (δ' ἔπειτα).

The ideal *carpe diem* poem creates present enjoyment, then. And yet such a poem might be exactly this: nothing but an ideal.[107] For the stumbling block that stands in the way of this ideal is reperformance. Lyric was frequently reperformed. Lyric *carpe diem* songs thus did not in fact create a single wonderfully magical moment of present enjoyment that coincided with the performance

'song culture'. This approach has also been called 'pragmatic', 'historicist', or 'anthropological'. For the 'textualisation' of 'song culture', see Ford (2002).

[104] Rösler (1980).
[105] See the influential essay of Austin (1962). Cf. Nagy (1994–5) on Austin's performative utterances and archaic lyric, Culler (2015) 125–31 on such utterances and lyric more generally, Griffith (2009) 72 on the 'perlocutionary' force of Greek lyric, and Lowrie (2009a) 66–71 on performative utterances and Horace.
[106] I follow Bowie (1986) in assuming that sympotic elegy was musically performed. *Aliter* Budelmann and Power (2013), who argue that sympotic elegy sits between song and prose (and see their article for numerous references on this issue, including studies which argue for recitation of elegy). Even so, elegy would remain closely interwoven with performative song. See Sens (2016) 230–1 for a related interpretation of the *hic et nunc* in the *carpe diem* poem Thgn. 567–70.
[107] Halliwell (2008) 117: 'The ideal symposium is a dream, even a hallucination, of perfection'. See Goldhill (2017) 285, who discusses reperformance and states that performance is '"never only in the moment", however momentous an event may feel'.

of the song. Rather, from the beginning, this present moment was designed to be repeatable. The perfect unity of *carpe diem*, song, performance, and momentary present enjoyment is a nostalgic ideal. Indeed, a number of recent studies on Greek lyric have underlined the importance of reperformance and looked beyond a first performance or original audience of lyric.[108] This is not to deny the significance of the performative utterance in the Theognidean *carpe diem* piece. But reperformance cautions us against a too-pragmatic reading of performance. Already in the Theognidean corpus we can observe poems that evoke the present moment rather than simply being present: the moment (νῦν) will endlessly recur.

The turn to song culture in studies of archaic poetry has also had an impact on studies of later Greek and Latin poetry. This has taken two different forms. On the one hand, later poems came to be seen as songs embedded in rituals and social contexts, akin to Greek lyric. On the other hand, Latin as well as Hellenistic poetry has been described as detached book poetry, the polar opposite of early Greek song.[109] Thomas Habinek's book *The World of Roman Song* is the most notable contribution to the former approach.[110] Habinek's emphasis on song and its aspiration to enchant and do things with words is welcome. Yet, as Habinek takes statements of Roman poets about their *carmina* at face value and turns Roman poetry into indigenous, ritualised song, he risks ignoring both its literariness and Greek heritage.[111] The debate about Hellenistic literature in general and epigram in particular is comparable: Alan Cameron argued that sympotic epigrams were the product of a lively performance culture at symposia, whereas other scholars emphasised the importance of books and writing for such epigrams.[112] There thus seems to be a need to look at Greek and

---

[108] For reperformance, see, in particular, the articles in Hunter and Uhlig (2017) as well as Lowrie (1997) 31–2, Culler (2015) 294–5, Citroni (2017). Morrison (2007) 37–42 argues that literature is textualised through reperformance. Theognis seems to project reperformances of his poems at 237–54 with Hobden (2013) 23.

[109] Feeney (1993) 55–7 cautions us against this false dichotomy (the argument is now restated at Feeney (2021) 9–14).

[110] Habinek (2005).   [111] For such reservations, see Lowrie (2006), Citroni (2017).

[112] Cameron (1995) 71–103 reviving the position of Reitzenstein (1893) 87–192, who argued that sympotic epigrams were performed. Strong arguments in favour of the significance of books and writing in the context of epigram can be found in Gutzwiller

27

Introduction: In Search of Present Time

Roman material collectively. This is even more the case as scholars on early Greek poetry also started to look beyond performance and textuality in their research. A volume edited by Felix Budelmann and Tom Phillips analyses how early Greek lyric poems can be both text and event.[113] Thus Giambattisto D'Alessio's contribution in this volume argues that already Sappho's poems are not 'straightforward scripts of ritual performances' but rather '*evoke* such performances, or look at them sideways'.[114] I will show how Hellenistic and Roman poets take the cue from such archaic models when they evoke presence.[115]

The question of to what extent Latin poems should be understood as songs or written texts has been debated with particular intensity in the case of Horace.[116] The Latin lyrist Horace introduced the Romans to Greek-style lyric songs they had never heard before, and he found it pleasing that gentlemen read his poetry with their eyes and held it in their hands. These words are of course not my own but Horace's (*Epist.* 1.19.32–4), and they should give pause to anyone who maintains that Horace simply sung his lyric poetry.[117] Indeed, elsewhere Horace speaks of 'songs (*carmina*) that deserve preserving with cedar oil and keeping safe in smooth cypress', in an image borrowed from Callimachus.[118] Horace's songs are songs to be read and seen on the

---

(1998) 115–82, *passim*, Bing (2009), Höschele (2010) 27–37, *passim*. For Callimachus in this context, see Acosta-Hughes and Stephens (2012) 84–147, esp. 145–7.

[113] Budelmann and Phillips (2018), who note sources that look at lyric as literature at page 5 n.9. Compare and contrast Fearn (2020) 12–24, Foster, Kurke, and Weiss (2019b), Budelmann (2018) 2–7. Several recent studies on Pindar are noteworthy in this regard: Payne (2006), Phillips (2016), Fearn (2017), Spelman (2018).

[114] D'Alessio (2018) 61. Cf. Fearn (2020) 16–17.

[115] My study shares some concerns with two important recent books on Latin poetry: Curtis (2017) on the chorus and McCarthy (2019) on the first person. Yet, Curtis and McCarthy emphasise the gap between Roman written poetry and early Greek poetry embedded in ritual, while I wish to show how Hellenistic and Roman writers uncover effects of presence that were already part of archaic poetry (cf. Rimell (2020)).

[116] See Citroni (2017) for a nuanced survey of the debate that started with Heinze (1923) and includes notable contributions by Reitzenstein (1924), Lowrie (1997: 19–93; 2009a: 63–141), Edmunds (2001) 83–94 as well as Citroni's own contributions (1995; 2009 [1983]).

[117] This point about the passage is made by Lowrie (2009a) 254–5. *Aliter*, Wiseman (2015) 142.

[118] Hor. *Ars* 331–2 alluding to Call. *Aet. fr.* 7.12–14 Harder, on which see D. P. Fowler (1994) 251 n.46, Lowrie (1997) 60–1.

page of a book.[119] And yet songs they are, according to Horace. There thus arises the danger, if we avoid Charybdis and steer clear of the fiction of song, that we fall victim to Scylla and interpret Horace's poetry as detached literary book poetry in strongest contrast to allegedly organic pre-literary Greek lyric.[120] This is a difficult course to steer. A middle course needs to be taken – but, as Odysseus learned the hard way, it is advisable to stick somewhat closer to Scylla, which is in our case book poetry. In other words, Richard Heinze's well-known dictum, according to which Horace's song is nothing but fiction, helps us to see how striking the concept of lyric is on the pages of books.[121] It also makes us see more clearly how the page of the book mimics song: even Horace's stichic poems were apparently arranged in four-line stanzas (Meineke's Law).[122] Finally, it points to the influence of Hellenistic book editions of early lyric, which had already published lyric texts without accompanying musical notation.[123] The next question, though, is why this fiction of song still matters for Horace.

The preceding paragraph already hints at the influence of a number of scholars who have raised important questions concerning the textuality and performance of Horace's book poetry. Alessandro Barchiesi addressed such questions in an influential article, titled 'Rituals in Ink'.[124] Barchiesi notes that Horace writes himself into a tradition of Greek lyric poets (*C.* 1.1), but that two elements of Greek lyric are notably lost in his poetry: music and

---

[119] Regarding Horace, the argument against musical composition is made most convincingly by Rossi (2009) [1998], following earlier work by Seel and Pöhlmann (1959) and Pöhlmann (1965). Heinze (1918) laid the foundations. The exception is of course the *Carmen Saeculare*. In favour of musical composition and performance: Bonavia-Hunt (1969) 1–27, Wille (1977) 128, Albrecht (1993), Du Quesnay (1995), Lyons (2007; 2010, in particular pages 70–9), Wiseman (2015) 6–9, 139 and *passim*. Such theories are impressively refuted by Lowrie (2009a) 81–97. Cf. Parker (2009).
[120] I here rehearse the arguments of Feeney (1993) and Barchiesi (2000), which I will describe in more detail in the next paragraph. Also see the discussion of Budelmann and Phillips (2018) 15, from whom I take the imagery of Scylla and Charybdis in this context.
[121] Heinze (1923) 167.
[122] Barchiesi (2007) 147. See also page 15 for the comparable technique in Theoc. 29.
[123] The matter is contested; I repeat the stance of Wilamowitz-Moellendorff (1900) 41–2, augmented by Pöhlmann (1988). Hunter (1996b) 5 offers a short summary of the issue.
[124] Barchiesi (2000). Cf. W. R. Johnson (1982) 5, 126–7, Feeney (1993; 1998: 40–4), Barchiesi (2007; 2009), Clay (2010) 128–31. Mindt (2007) attempts to apply Barchiesi's thoughts to Horace's banquet poems.

Introduction: In Search of Present Time

performance. Yet, Barchiesi argues for Horace that 'what gets lost of a tradition continues to work *in absentia*':[125] Horace's poetry projects and recreates performance through textual means. That is to say, Horace is acutely aware of the performances, occasions, and moments in time of early Greek lyric, and he makes these features a major theme in his lyric.[126] Barchiesi also stresses how reperformance connects early Greek lyric with Horace's book poetry: though Greek lyric describes unique events in time, such as dinner parties or feasts for the gods, these should be reperformed. In Horace's lyric, 'every reading is a reperformance'.[127] Besides Barchiesi, Michèle Lowrie has extensively discussed the role of text and performance in Horace and Latin literature more widely in two monographs, *Horace's Narrative Odes* and *Writing, Performance, and Authority in Augustan Rome*.[128] Lowrie argues that Horace's poetry is centred on a tension between its professed status as momentary song and its reality as permanent text. A reader, Lowrie argues, is constantly invited to explore the tension between the media and to deconstruct Horace's 'poetics of presence'.[129] The subtitle of my book, 'The Poetics of Presence in Greek and Latin Literature', indicates my debt to Lowrie. Yet, while Lowrie sees in Horace' poetics of presence primarily a construction that invites its own deconstruction, I emphasise that poetic presence can also succeed in giving us the impression that something is happening here and now. The influential studies of Barchiesi and Lowrie have opened the door for others to look beyond a simple dichotomy between texts and performance. Thus, recent monographs that discuss Horace alongside other poets still wrestle with the problems that Barchiesi and Lowrie have set out: Lauren Curtis on choral performance, Kathleen McCarthy on the

---

[125] Barchiesi (2009) 334.
[126] Barchiesi (2000) 176: 'With profound insight, Horace first promotes the use of occasion as a marker of lyric to a generic convention, and then he shifts it from a convention to a theme. Being in time, the times of life, the passing of time, the unique nature of moments, and the caducity of moments will become, as the collection unfolds, the main preoccupations of the poet.'
[127] Barchiesi (2000) 176. Cf. Feeney (1993) 55–7.
[128] Lowrie (1997: 19–93, in particular 50; 2009a: 115 and *passim* (chapter 9 reworks Lowrie (2002)); see also Lowrie (2010).
[129] Lowrie (1997) 57, 70, and note her methodological considerations at Lowrie (2005), which point to her debt to Derrida (1980b) [1980a] (cf. Edmunds (1992) 116–23).

first-person form, and Adrian Gramps on occasion all argue that performance is a key issue with Horace and other poets.[130] These studies, as well as my own, tackle a problem which Lowrie neatly describes as the 'relationship between a text and its world or worlds'.[131] Where my own approach differs from previous ones is in that I attempt to include a world or worlds of things, such as monuments, inscriptions, gems, cups, and calendars, alongside my interpretation of texts.

It is not only in classical studies that debates around performance and presence have been prominent. In English and Comparative Studies, Jonathan Culler argues in his *Theory of the Lyric* that one distinctive feature of lyric is its ability to 'produce effects of presence'.[132] By this he means, for instance, the striking use of present tenses, addresses, and apostrophes in lyric poetry. The present tense is characteristic for lyric, and Culler argues that the tense creates a *now* that becomes repeatable; this, he says, is particularly the case of lyric written in English, which conventionally uses the simple present of habitual action, although the grammar would normally require a progressive tense ('I wander through each chartered street' rather than 'I am wandering').[133] According to Culler, address is another device that can produce effects of presence. When lyric poems address someone or something, they evoke the presence of this someone or something: 'if one puts into a poem *thou shepherd boy, ye blessed creatures, ye birds*, they are immediately associated with what might be called a timeless present but is better seen as a temporality of writing [...] – a special temporality which is the set of all moments at which writing can say "now"'.[134]

One of the most radical proponents of 'presence culture' (as he calls it) is Hans Ulrich Gumbrecht, a scholar of Romance and

---

[130] Curtis (2017) esp. 25–9, 132–5, McCarthy (2019) esp. 23–32, Gramps (2021) esp. ix–xviii, 76–84, 187–92. In addition to these three books, see, in particular, the article of Barber (2014).
[131] Lowrie (2005) 35. Cf. Feldherr (2010) 9, who says that in Ovid's *Metamorphoses* 'real objects bring the distant world of his stories into the present'.
[132] Culler (2015) 35–7. For theories on the nature of lyric by classical scholars, see W. R. Johnson (1982), Miller (1994). For an anthology of theories on lyric, see Jackson and Prins (2014).
[133] Culler (2015) 283–95.
[134] Culler (1981) 149, and see 135–54. Cf. Lowrie (1997) 20–6, Culler (2015) 186–243.

comparative literature.¹³⁵ According to Gumbrecht, the humanities in general and literary studies in particular have focused exclusively on hermeneutics and interpretation. Gumbrecht, conversely, argues that there is another dimension to texts beyond meaning and interpretation: presence, and the ecstatic moments art can create. What Gumbrecht advocates can perhaps be illustrated by a well-known anecdote from the life of the classical scholar A. E. Housman.[136] When lecturing, Housman came to Horace, *Odes* 4.7, a *carpe diem* poem that 'he dissected with the usual display of brilliance, wit, and sarcasm'. He then notably stepped aside from this usual habit of his and invited his class to look at the ode 'simply as poetry'. Housman proceeded to recite both the Latin poem and his own English translation. Afterwards he quickly confessed that he regarded the ode as 'the most beautiful poem in ancient literature', before he rushed out of the room. The anecdote shows us a development *in nuce*, in a single lecture, which Gumbrecht sees in the humanities at large: the attempt to tackle a text with traditional hermeneutic tools and to get to its meaning gives way to a turn to presence. It seems that Housman attempted to recapture a facet of the ode that goes beyond its meaning and which consists of its sound, its quality of being in the moment and making the moment present. Not by chance did Housman recite the poem and his translation in May, 'when the trees in Cambridge were covered with blossom': 'The snows are fled away, leaves on the shaws | And grasses in the mead renew their birth [...]'.

The occasion of Housman's recital matches the occasion of the poem, and young students are a fitting audience for *carpe diem* poems that tell their addressees to enjoy their bloom of youth.[137]

---

[135] Gumbrecht (2004). Gramps (2021) also brings Gumbrecht's concept of presence in dialogue with ancient literature and discusses in detail the potential interpretational benefits of Gumbrecht's approach over deconstructivism (esp. 76–84, 187–92). Interpretation and hermeneutics were also questioned as methods recently by Felski (2015) and long ago by Sontag (1966), who influenced the approach of Butler (2015) 59–87 in classical studies. Note that Lowrie (1997) 301 argues in her interpretation of Hor. *C.* 3.27 that the poem invites the reader to feel ecstasy and pleasure rather than to interpret the poem.

[136] The anecdote was originally included in a letter by T. W. Pym to *The Times* on 5 May 1936 and is quoted at A. Burnett (1997) 427.

[137] Housman could not have known that the poem would acquire further significance; a few months after the lecture the First World War broke out and killed at least one member of Housman's audience.

Performance, Text, and Evocation of Presence

In some ways, then, Housman's translation seems to grant us a poem that is grounded in occasion to an extent that some scholars of archaic Greek lyric only wish for. And yet the very word that means 'now' in the first line of Horace's poem is left untranslated: *redeunt iam gramina campis* ('And grasses in the mead renew their birth'). A closer translation would be '*now* the grass is returning to the fields'. Housman leaves out the word 'now', and rather than the momentary progressive present tense ('is renewing') uses the simple present tense of habitual action ('renew'). This suggests the iterability of the moment, and we can indeed find inscribed in the poem moments from Housman's past, when during his own undergraduate days he fell in love with his fellow student Moses Jackson. For Housman would later end a poem to Moses Jackson with words that are evocative of the last lines of Horace's ode and his translation.[138] The late spring moment that Horace experienced in Rome thus fuses with the very late spring moment at Housman's lecture in Cambridge, with such moments in his youth, and with countless other spring moments of their readers.[139]

Housman's treatment of the Horatian ode brings out qualities which Gumbrecht would call 'presence effects'.[140] These presence effects are, I argue, an inherent quality of *carpe diem* poems, which strive to evoke presence and momentary pleasure. Perhaps the most striking line in this regard can be found in the second stanza of Housman's translation: 'The swift hour and the brief prime of the year | Say to the soul, *Thou wast not born for aye*' (*inmortalia ne speres, monet annus et almum | quae rapit hora diem* at Hor. *C.* 4.7.7–8). Housman replaced Horace's indirect

---

[138] This is the observation of Wilkinson (1974) 44, who compares the last line of Housman's poem to Jackson (*et non aeterni uincla sodalicii*; 'and the bonds of comradeship that does not last for ever' at A. Burnett (1997) 289–91) with Hor. *C.* 4.7.27–8 (*nec Lethaea ualet Theseus abrumpere caro | uincula Pirithoo*) and Housman's translation ('And Theseus leaves Pirithoüs in the chain | The love of comrades cannot take away'). See, in more detail, Harrison (2002) 212–13.

[139] Indeed, prior to the well-known recitation in front of the class the poem had already been printed in 1897, and it would be printed again in 1922. Cf. Culler (2015) 294–5: 'Ever since Pindar and doubtless before, lyrics have been constructed for reperformance, with an iterable *now*: not timeless but a moment of time that is repeated every time a poem is read.'

[140] Note, however, that Gumbrecht understands 'presence' primarily in spatial rather than temporal terms. Yet such a distinction is difficult to maintain.

Introduction: In Search of Present Time

statement with direct speech. The direct speech, the address, the succession of six monosyllables, and the archaic diction suddenly change the atmosphere of the poem, as if death were kicking at the door. As we perceive this change of atmosphere, we feel the presence of a different voice in the poem that addresses us: the curt archaisms evoke the days of yesteryear.[141] But who is talking? It is of course 'the swift hour and brief time of the year'; in other words, it is time itself that is talking, addressing us. Readers for time to come are addressed with a stomping, capitalised 'Thou', as they are cast in the audience of Housman's lecture and as the listeners of Horace. For a moment we are in the presence of time, a presence that we feel rather than understand, and a time that is our own past as well as Housman's and Horace's. The task of this book is to listen to time talking.

The question of performance, presence, and textuality is, then, a major concern in literary studies in and beyond Classics. Yet, an extended treatment of the *carpe diem* motif has so far not been undertaken, although this motif is naturally paramount for any question concerning presence. This book will show that an analysis of the *carpe diem* motif is central for understanding how poetry writes *now*: as *carpe diem* poems aim to affect our senses as if they were music or wine, they become programmes of a poetry that produces presence. Another aim of this book is to show that Classics as a discipline is uniquely well-suited to explore how literature produces presence: as poems evoke a world of things, of inscriptions, monuments, music, books, wine labels, wine cellars, calendars, and cups, Classics, which is by its nature interdisciplinary, can explore this world of things.[142]

Culler ends his book on lyric by stressing lyric's heritage in song. He suggests that it might be profitable to experience lyric in the same spirit one may experience song: gaining a sensuous pleasure from sound and rhythm that transcends meaning.[143]

---

[141] Gumbrecht (2012) [2011] 6–7 argues that *Stimmung* ('atmosphere' or 'mood') is an important part of presence. Housman's translation also includes archaisms elsewhere, but they are uniquely concentrated in the present passage.

[142] Cf. Chapter 4, pages 140–1 for methodological considerations about presence and material studies, and the Epilogue for the potential of Classics in exploring presence.

[143] Culler (2015) 352–3. Cf. Gumbrecht (2004).

The Structure of the Book

This brings us back to the Seikilos epitaph. Here is a poem that invites its readers to do precisely this: to read it as song, to experience the pleasures of life and song, although it is permanently silent. The Seikilos epitaph invites us to read *carpe diem*.

The Structure of the Book

Chapter 1 starts by tracing the archaeology of *carpe diem*. Rather than speculating about the origin of a motif that is already attested in Akkadian and Egyptian sources, I look at the Greeks' own discourse of the past and how they constructed the origins of the motif. My focus is the hedonistic epitaph of the legendary last king of Assyria, Sardanapallus. Greeks were fascinated with this foreign *carpe diem* text, which seemed to precede their own history. In fact, however, it was by misunderstanding this foreign monument that they recreated its text: lurking behind Sardanapallus' Assyrian orgy are Greek banquets and the present tense of performative Greek lyric. As I discuss the reception of the Sardanapallus epitaph, I show how one of Epicurus' detractors forges a false link between Epicurus and *carpe diem*, when he changes one word of the epitaph.

Chapters 2 and 3 turn to Horace, who coined the expression *carpe diem* and wrote some of the most memorable *carpe diem* poems. Chapter 2 looks at wine in Horace. Rich Romans possessed thousands of wine amphorae, and consular dates marked the age of each amphora. I argue that this made wine storage places into huge drinkable calendars, in which the oldest wines were stored at the back and the younger wines at the front. Every time Horace mentions vintage wines, he accesses this calendar. Time is expressed through wine: opening an old wine creates a moment of present enjoyment which cannot be repeated. Yet, through vintage wines Horace also brings moments of the past to the present. Chapter 3 introduces a linguistic turn. In the *Ars Poetica*, Horace compares a language's lexical development to leaves falling from a tree: while some words disappear, old ones return. Both the image of leaves and the understanding of time as cyclical are also part of Horace's poetry of *carpe diem*. I show that the poems as well as the individual words of which they consist evoke present enjoyment.

35

Chapter 4 analyses epigrams and objects between 100 BC and AD 100, and discusses how objects and texts engage with one another in expressing the idea of *carpe diem*. Rarely studied Greek epigrams from the *Garland of Philip* and texts by the Latin authors Martial, Pliny the Elder, and Petronius point to exciting interplay between the textuality of epigrams and the presence of objects. Besides more conventional literary sources, my analysis also includes numerous artworks and inscriptions.

Chapter 5 looks at passages of *carpe diem* within longer texts. As *carpe diem* poems are read and re-read, they become independent textual objects: they can be inserted just about anywhere but never lose their lyric splendour. Thus, Vergil applies the *carpe diem* motif to a context as humble as cattle-breeding, while both Seneca and Samuel Johnson ignore the context and treat this section as vatic wisdom. I analyse how such excerpts relate to Latin satire, which bastardised other texts, to late antique anthologising, to medieval *florilegia*, and to early modern commonplace-books.

This book does not proceed chronologically; instead, its chapters are arranged thematically. A strictly chronological order is not realistic when so many inscriptions are difficult to date precisely, nor desirable when thematic arrangement allows us to compare, for example, reactions to the Sardanapallus epitaph from Aristotle, Crates, Chrysippus, and Cicero. The selection of material in the book will necessarily be selective, and not every occurrence of the *carpe diem* motif in the ancient world will be discussed. But it is hoped that the choices here will prove greater than the sum of its parts. Detailed analyses of the techniques with which texts evoke present enjoyment will arguably prove more useful than an extended list of *carpe diem* poems.

Last, it should be noted that the term *carpe diem* may be seen as problematic for several reasons. Taken from Horace, *Odes* 1.11, it is grossly anachronistic when used to refer to archaic Greek poetry. Moreover, as a quotation from Horace, the term may be strongly associated with Horace's own version of *carpe diem*: a cultured dinner party of elite Romans engaging with Greek-style poetry. The term's strong association with Horace may subsequently run the risk of making the analysis of *carpe diem*

The Structure of the Book

a search for the most 'Horatian' poetry, and thus lead to ignoring less 'Horatian' forms of *carpe diem* such as the radically hedonistic Sardanapallus epitaph. Nonetheless, I will resist the temptation to coin a new term to describe this motif. *Carpe diem* is a universally used and recognised term by scholars, and it is unlikely that others will adopt a new term. Indeed, the striking choice of words, the *callida iunctura*, is Horace's domain; whoever strives to rival him and soar to the heights of his ingenuity is likely to fall like Icarus, who, as we are told, gave his name only to the sea. Finally, the Horatian coinage also supports the retrospective approach of this study: as the study analyses acts of reading *carpe diem*, it is only natural to use a term that has struck a chord with many who read *carpe diem*.

I

THE ARCHAEOLOGY OF *CARPE DIEM*

Sardanapallus, Monuments, Epigrams, and False Beginnings

At the beginning of his work, Thucydides tells of the early history of Greece, making use of inference and adducing myth as well as material evidence (Th. 1–23). This section is commonly called the 'Archaeology', an appellation that was probably coined in the mid-nineteenth century.[1] Yet, a scholion that describes a passage within Thucydides' prooemium as ἀρχαιολογία might point to some awareness on the scholiast's part that this section goes beyond the scope of Thucydides' work: it deals with prehistory, myths, material remains, and heroic genealogies – in short, something that came to be known as ἀρχαιολογία or *antiquitates*.[2] In turn, the present chapter at the outset of this study will begin with an archaeology of the *carpe diem* motif: it will look at the prehistory of the motif, its myths, material remains, constructed genealogies, and false beginnings.

Thucydides' Archaeology of early Greek history turns eastward to Troy. A prehistory of *carpe diem* may take the same direction and discuss the interdependency of Sumerian, Akkadian, Egyptian, Hebrew, Greek, and Roman material. Such attempts have indeed been made.[3] But a genealogy of *carpe diem* which

---

[1] Rood (2015) 474–5.
[2] Scholion at Th. 1.12 (at Kleinlogel (2019) 294). The *locus classicus* for the Greek understanding of ἀρχαιολογία is Pl. *Hp. Ma.* 285d–e. See Momigliano (1950), Schnapp (1996) [1993] 45–65, Rood (2015) 474–5. Compare and contrast: Sergueenkova and Rojas (2017) 165–8, Anderson and Rojas (2017), especially the introduction and first contribution.
[3] The case for dependency is made by Gilbert (1946) (Egypt and Horace), M. L. West (1969) 128–31 (Egyptian and Hellenistic and Roman material), Fischer (1996) (Egyptian and Hebrew material), Schwienhorst-Schönberger (1996) 324–32 (Greek and Hebrew material), Tigay (1993) 252–3 (Babylonian and Hebrew material; with some valuable methodological considerations; bibliography at Suriano (2017)), *alii alia*; Dunbabin (1986) 208–12 and Wöhrle (1990) treat skeleton figures at dinner tables as an Egyptian

The Archaeology of *Carpe Diem*

makes the Egyptian Harper's Songs the source of Horace has to remain speculative – much like the genealogies of heroes and the foundations of cities, which constitute Greek ἀρχαιολογία. Indeed, the presence of the *carpe diem* motif in Chinese poetry should caution us that many parallels between 'Eastern' and Greco-Roman material may be accidental.[4] Nor are we likely to find the origins of *carpe diem* in a supposedly lyric age of individuality, in which an alleged shift of mentalities makes poets sing of present enjoyment rather than heroic deeds.[5] If we then cannot answer the question 'where does it come from?' in relation to *carpe diem*, it is perhaps the wrong question. Instead, we may rather ask the question why the origins of *carpe diem* matter or, better still, how the Greeks constructed the origins of *carpe diem*. Rather than establishing a historical sequence, I will look at the Greek discourse of the past – that is, their *Archaeology of carpe diem*.

This chapter's archaeology of *carpe diem* will thus be an archaeology in more than one sense; it considers the Greek discourse of ἀρχαιολογία, that is, an interest in material remains, prehistory, and genealogies – an early ancestor of modern archaeology. But the chapter also discusses an 'archaeology' of a motif – that is, a constructed origin of a literary mode. Finally, in describing a Greek discourse of the past rather than the Greek past itself, this approach owes something to Michel Foucault's *Archaeology of Knowledge*: 'in our time, history is that which transforms documents into monuments'.[6]

---

custom adopted by Greeks (Hdt. 2.78, Sil. 13.474–6, Plu. *Mor.* 148a, 357f, Lucian *Luct.* 21). A survey of 'Eastern' material and its possible influence on Greco-Roman literature can be found in Grottanelli (1995). Leaving aside the thorny issue of dependency, good starting points for *carpe diem* in Egyptian material are J. Assmann (1977; 1989), and for Sumerian material Alster (2005) 265–341.

[4] See, for example, Birrell (1993) chapter 4 on the *carpe diem* motif in popular songs of Han China.

[5] Thus Jaeger (1939–45) [1933–47] i.124–8. There is a certain affinity between Jaeger's claim here and Snell (1953) [1946] 43–70 and Fränkel (1975) [1962] 147–273, who champion the case for a cultural revolution of a lyric age, though Snell elsewhere is critical of Jaeger's work (cf. Lloyd-Jones (1967)). For criticism of Snell and Fränkel, pointing out methodological and chronological issues, see, for example, the first two chapters of R. L. Fowler (1987) and pages 12–13 in the Introduction to this book.

[6] For ἀρχαιολογία and links with modern archaeology, see Schnapp (1996) [1993] introduction and chapter 1, Boardman (2002). For an 'archaeology' of constructing poetic predecessors, see, above all, Hunter (1996b) for Hellenistic poetry, and cf. Sens (2007)

39

The Archaeology of *Carpe Diem*

The monument under investigation here is the Sardanapallus epitaph. Attributed to the legendary last king of Assyria, the epitaph became one of the most-often quoted and one of the most openly hedonistic *carpe diem* texts. Its alleged priority in both temporal terms and terms of hedonism make it a natural starting point for this discussion. The first section deals with the complex *Quellenkritik* of the epitaph and argues that the Greeks constructed it as an archaeological forerunner of the *carpe diem* motif in general and *carpe diem* in epigrams in particular. The Greeks *invent* the Sardanapallus epitaph in both senses of the Greek verb εὑρίσκω: they both *find* the epitaph and *devise* it (the ambiguity would also be true for Latin *inuenio*). The second section looks at elements of present time and performance in the epitaph. The third section looks at the art of variation in other epigrams dealing with the Sardanapallus epitaph and argues that these epigrams construct an Epicurean 'archaeology' of the *carpe diem* motif. The last section of this chapter analyses how one can read a theatrical performance of Sardanapallus' pleasures and how the epitaph is adapted in Rome. This chapter will analyse, then, how the Sardanapallus epitaph was constructed as the origin of a Greek tradition of *carpe diem*. Addressing this question, the chapter engages with the two main themes of this study: evocation of present time and reading *carpe diem*.

The figure of Sardanapallus has fascinated people for centuries. Indeed, Sardanapallus offers perhaps the only issue on which a classicist can vie with Isaac Newton, *qui genus humanum ingenio superauit*, as the Lucretian epigram on his statue in the chapel of Trinity College, Cambridge proclaims. For Newton, Sardanapallus was a real king, and Sardanapallus' alleged existence was one element in Newton's work on the chronology of the ancient

---

374 for epigram. Goldhill (1994) 197 speaks of 'a gesture of archaeological uncovering of a sedimented world of meaning' in Hellenistic poetry. Foucault (1972) [1969] discusses the 'Archaeology of knowledge': whereas documents used to be tools for historians with which they reconstructed the past, documents now become archaeological objects studied for their own sake. This thought can be found in a very similar form in Elsner (1994) 229: 'how monuments are turned into discourse, how objects become history'. Other important approaches to ruins and monuments: Price (2012), J. I. Porter (2011), and, in particular, Rosenmeyer (2018), who analyses Greek (and Latin) epigrammatic engagement with another foreign monument, the Egyptian Memnon colossus.

The Invention of Carpe Diem

world.⁷ Newton, as well as his contemporaries, took a legend for a fact, but the legend is worthy of investigation. This chapter will look at one of the best-known aspects of Sardanapallus' legend, his death, and how this is linked to *carpe diem*.

1.1 The Invention of *Carpe Diem*

ταῦτ' ἔχω ὅσσ' ἔφαγον καὶ ἐφύβρισα καὶ μετ' ἔρωτος
τέρπν' ἔπαθον· τὰ δὲ πολλὰ καὶ ὄλβια κεῖνα λέλειπται.⁸

I have what I ate and my kinks, and the pleasures I received in bed. But my many well-known riches are gone.

These words from Sardanapallus' epitaph were widely known, Strabo tells us (Str. 14.5.9: καὶ δὴ καὶ περιφέρεται τὰ ἔπη ταυτί). Indeed, when Strabo quotes the two lines in his *Geography*, written in the first centuries BC and AD, the lines had already been quoted, imitated, and parodied by Aristotle, Chrysippus, Cicero, and many more, sometimes with slightly varying words, sometimes in a longer version.⁹ And the fame of the epitaph does not stop there. Athenaeus would later talk of people who 'aspired to the lifestyle of Sardanapallus' (Ath. 8.335e–337a and 12.530c–531b): the poet Archestratus of Gela, a character from a play, and a man whose epitaph praises hedonism are all said to emulate Sardanapallus; even Homer's tale of the pleasure-loving Phaeacians is among the texts that are subsumed under the theme of Sardanapallus. Aristotle sees in Sardanapallus the prime representative of a life of pleasure when he discusses three different ways of life that are commonly thought to lead to the good (τὸ ἀγαθόν) or to happiness (ἡ εὐδαιμονία), namely the life of pleasure, the life of politics, and the life of contemplation (*EN* 1.3 1095b 22; cf. *EE* 1.5 1216a 16). Other writers link Epicurus' philosophy with Sardanapallus' lifestyle. For Athenaeus, Sardanapallus offers the archetype for anyone who aspired to

---

⁷ See the third chapter of Newton (1728). For the reception of Sardanapallus in Newton and elsewhere, see the stimulating article of Monerie (2015).
⁸ Text: *SH* 335 Choerilus Iasius (?).
⁹ See Lloyd-Jones and Parsons at *SH* 335 for a full account of readings and quotations. I return to this verse version on pages 53–9.

41

a lifestyle of *carpe diem*. How did Sardanapallus become this archetype? In order to answer this question, we will uncover layers of the legend of Sardanapallus as we follow a Greek expedition that tries to make sense of his alleged tomb.

Besides the hexameter version of Sardanapallus' epitaph, a prose version also circulated in Greek culture, which Strabo, for instance, quotes along with the verse version (Str. 14.5.9): Σαρδανάπαλλος ὁ Ἀνακυνδαράξεω παῖς Ἀγχιάλην καὶ Ταρσὸν ἔδειμεν ἡμέρῃ μιῇ· ἔσθιε, πῖνε, παῖζε· ὡς τἆλλα τούτου οὐκ ἄξια (τοῦ ἀποκροτήματος) ('Sardanapallus, the son of Anacyndaraxes, built Anchiale and Tarsus in a single day. Eat, drink, and fool around, because everything else is not worth this! ("This" refers to the snapping of the fingers)'). The epitaph, Strabo says, was written on a monument that featured a statue of a man snapping his fingers. The story of this epitaph is the story of Greeks who encounter a foreign ancient monument and interpret it as a monument of *carpe diem*. This story begins on the eve of the Battle of Issus in 333 BC, as the army of Alexander the Great comes to Anchiale near Tarsus in South Cilicia, where they see an ancient monument. Writers who accompanied Alexander on his campaign tell of the events in Anchiale. Thus, the Alexander historians Clitarchus and Callisthenes almost certainly will have told of the tomb, though their accounts are lost.[10] The account of another Alexander historian, Aristobulus, survives; Strabo and Athenaeus give us an almost identical text of the event, which they both attribute to Aristobulus.[11]

Aristobulus' text arguably also forms the basis of the most detailed description of the encounter in Anchiale, which

[10] We are only told that Clitarchus mentioned Sardanapallus' death, but F. Jacoby showed that the book number in which Clitarchus did so is where we would expect him to treat events in Anchiale (*FGrHist* 137 F 2 with Jacoby's commentary). Callisthenes is mentioned in the entry of Sardanapallus at Photius/Suda (*FGrHist* 124 F 34). While the entry seems to conflate numerous sources and it is not clear which part of it goes back to Callisthenes, it still offers evidence that Callisthenes may have mentioned Sardanapallus' epitaph in some form (cf. Burkert (2009) 507, 513–14). For Amyntas, see page 54 and 54 n.52.

[11] Aristobulus *FGrHist* 139 F 9a *apud* Ath. 12.530b–c and F 9b *apud* Str. 14.5.9. Possibly Clearchus *fr.* 51d Wehrli and Apollodorus *FGrHist* 244 F 303 also go back to Aristobulus, as Burkert (2009) 505–6 and 506 n.19 argues, but a conflation of sources or a different source cannot be excluded (Hermann Diels in F. Jacoby's commentary at *FGrHist* 244 F 303 thinks 'Apollodorus' may be a corruption of Aristobulus).

The Invention of *Carpe Diem*

the second-century-AD historian Arrian provides, though Arrian seems to rely on more than one source.[12] In Arrian's account, we enter 'archaeological' territory, as he makes inferences about the past based on material evidence: the foundations and circumference of Anchiale's walls attest to the power this town once had.[13] As the scene shows remains from a powerful past, Arrian describes the epitaph of Sardanapallus (*Anab.* 2.5.2–4):[14]

αὐτὸς δὲ ὕστερος ἄρας ἐκ Ταρσοῦ τῇ μὲν πρώτῃ ἐς Ἀγχίαλον πόλιν ἀφικνεῖται. ταύτην δὲ Σαρδανάπαλον κτίσαι τὸν Ἀσσύριον λόγος· καὶ τῷ περιβόλῳ δὲ καὶ τοῖς θεμελίοις τῶν τειχῶν δήλη ἐστὶ μεγάλη τε πόλις κτισθεῖσα καὶ ἐπὶ μέγα ἐλθοῦσα δυνάμεως. καὶ τὸ μνῆμα τοῦ Σαρδαναπάλου ἐγγὺς ἦν τῶν τειχῶν τῆς Ἀγχιάλου· καὶ αὐτὸς ἐφειστήκει ἐπ' αὐτῷ Σαρδανάπαλος συμβεβληκὼς τὰς χεῖρας ἀλλήλαις ὡς μάλιστα ἐς κρότον συμβάλλονται, καὶ ἐπίγραμμα ἐπεγέγραπτο αὐτῷ Ἀσσύρια γράμματα· οἱ μὲν Ἀσσύριοι καὶ μέτρον ἔφασκον ἐπεῖναι τῷ ἐπιγράμματι, ὁ δὲ νοῦς ἦν αὐτῷ ὃν ἔφραζε τὰ ἔπη, ὅτι Σαρδανάπαλος ὁ Ἀνακυνδαράξου παῖς Ἀγχίαλον καὶ Ταρσὸν ἐν ἡμέρᾳ μιᾷ ἐδείματο. σὺ δέ, ὦ ξένε, ἔσθιε καὶ πῖνε καὶ παῖζε, ὡς τἆλλα τὰ ἀνθρώπινα οὐκ ὄντα τούτου ἄξια· τὸν ψόφον αἰνισσόμενος, ὅνπερ αἱ χεῖρες ἐπὶ τῷ κρότῳ ποιοῦσι· καὶ τὸ παῖζε ῥᾳδιουργότερον ἐγγεγράφθαι ἔφασαν τῷ Ἀσσυρίῳ ὀνόματι.

Later he [i.e., Alexander] left Tarsus and arrived in Anchiale on the next day. It is said that Sardanapallus the Assyrian had founded this town. The circumference and the foundations of its walls clearly indicate that the town was great at its foundation and then became very powerful. Near the walls of Anchiale was the tomb of Sardanapallus. On top of it stood Sardanapallus himself, and his hands were brought together as if he was clapping; an epigram in Assyrian characters was inscribed upon the tomb. The Assyrians said that it was written in verse, and its sense was: '*Sardanapallus, the son of Anakyndaraxes, built Anchiale and Tarsus in a single day. But you, stranger, eat and drink and fool around, because all other human things are not worth this*' – the riddle was referring to the sound of the hand clap. Also, they said that the words 'fool around' were naughtier in Assyrian.

---

[12] Aristobulus *FGrHist* 139 F 9c *apud* Arrian *Anab.* 2.5.2–4. Arrian's version differs from Athenaeus and Strabo in particular in relation to the gesture, which Arrian describes as hand-clapping and the others as finger-snapping. Divergences from Athenaeus and Strabo are the result of either Arrian drawing on another source in addition to Aristobulus (F. Jacoby in his commentary; perhaps Clitarchus or Callisthenes?) or of Arrian following a different source (E. Meyer (1892–9) i.208 and Bosworth (1980–95) *ad loc.* both suggest Ptolemy) or of Arrian misunderstanding Aristobulus (Burkert (2009) 506, Brunt (2009) 481–2) or of Arrian conflating Aristobulus' account with his own observations of monuments in the region (Sergueenkova and Rojas (2017) 161).

[13] Sergueenkova and Rojas (2017) 164 n.80 also argue that the scene shows Aristobulus as a connoisseur of ancient material remains.

[14] Text: Roos (1967).

The Archaeology of *Carpe Diem*

The Greeks who look at the surroundings of a once-great city, marvel at a monument of a legendary king, and attempt to make sense of its inscription may remind us of Shelley's poem *Ozymandias* (= Ramesses II), in which a 'traveller from an antique land' marvels at a fragmented Egyptian statue and its inscription. The inscription extols Ozymandias' power and his empire, of which nothing remains in the desert. The 'archaeological' view of past empires is strikingly similar to the events in Anchiale, and perhaps not coincidentally both the Sardanapallus epigram and the Ozymandias epigram are among passages from Diodorus Siculus which are adopted in English Romantic literature.[15] Yet, more importantly, Shelley's traveller also engages in a similar 'act of reading' that pays attention to the inscription and its surroundings.[16] Indeed, the episode of the Sardanapallus epitaph gives us a glimpse into ways of reading epigrams and constructing a *carpe diem* of the past.

The whole story of the discovery of the Sardanapallus epitaph is rather shady (and not only because of a 'naughty' word in the 'Assyrian' inscription Arrian reports). As scholars have long recognised, there existed no Assyrian king who matches the characterisation of the 'Sardanapallus' in Greek sources: Sardanapallus was a figure of the Greek imagination, a legendary king, who was a symbol of wealth, luxury, *carpe diem*, and the decay of the Assyrian empire.[17] Whatever monument the Greeks saw in Anchiale was probably rather different in nature from the one they

---

[15] D.S. 2.23–7, 1.47. Lord Byron wrote a play titled *Sardanapalus* in 1821, which inspired Eugène Delacroix's famous painting (see Bernhardt (2009) 8–10). Also cf. the *Ozymandias* poem written by Shelley's friend Horace Smith.

[16] Bing (2002) 53–4 adduces Shelley's *Ozymandias* in an attempt to contrast the careful reading process of Shelley's traveller with the 'un-read Muse' of Greek inscriptions: 'The absence of any comparable scene in ancient literature is sobering.' On the contrary, the similarity to the scene of the Sardanapallus epitaph is striking. While this chapter owes much to Peter Bing and his concept of *Ergänzungsspiel*, the Sardanapallus epitaph is a case in point against an 'un-read Muse'.

[17] The name Sardanapallus may reflect the name of the Assyrian king Ashurbanipal, but this does not make Sardanapallus a historical person. Already Weißbach recognised this in his seminal article at *RE* i.A2 col.2457–66 s.v. 'Sardanapal': 'Als geschichtliche Persönlichkeit ist S. einfach nicht fassbar'. Also F. Jacoby at *RE* xi.2 col.2052 s.v. 'Ktesias' on Sardanapallus: 'mehr eine griechische, als eine orientalische Sagenfigur'. Thus also, more recently, Rollinger (2017) 576. MacGinnis (1988) considers parts of Assyrian history that may have inspired the Sardanapallus legend (cf. Waters (2017) 40, 84–5). Haubold (2013) 108–11 shows that even Berossus, who had access to the

tell of. A reasonable theory is that the monument was a victory monument of the Assyrian king Sennacherib, whose name the Greeks misunderstood as Sardanapallus.[18] Already Eduard Meyer had argued that the Alexander historians engage in an *interpretatio Graeca* of a foreign monument.[19] The Greeks are then not so much reading an inscription as misreading or constructing it so that meaning is created by the reader rather than the writer. In a manner Stanley Fish could have only wished for, the Greek interpretive community approach a text, read it through their interpretive framework, and create meaning as readers. All we have of the 'text' is their reading.[20]

Before we turn in detail to the Greek interpretation of the monument, a short excursus is necessary in order to explore a deeper stratum of the Sardanapallus legend. Alexander's expedition came to the East with the preformed opinion of Sardanapallus as one of the most famous Assyrians in history and as a character who stood for *carpe diem*. This cultural formation determined how the Greeks misread the Assyrian monument. It cannot be said with certainty at what point in time the figure of Sardanapallus emerged in Greek culture, but he is mentioned in Greek sources of the fifth century BC: Herodotus mentions his wealth, the antiquarian Hellanicus distinguished between two kings called Sardanapallus – a virtuous one and a less virtuous one – and the name was so well-known that 'a Sardanapallus' appears as a stereotype for a flashy inspector in a comedy of Aristophanes.[21] For a long time scholars had thought that the prose epitaph of Sardanapallus also goes back to this time,

---

Mesopotamian sources, felt compelled to mention Sardanapallus in order to suit the expectations of his Greek readership.

[18] Thus Weißbach at *RE* i.A2 col.2466–7 s.v. 'Sardanapal' and Rollinger (2017) 578. Cf. Dalley (1999).
[19] E. Meyer (1892–9) i.203–9, ii.541–4. More recently, Bernhardt (2009) and Rollinger (2017) 576–9 have followed Meyer. For the dynamics of *interpretatio Graeca*, see Rosenmeyer (2018) 15 n.41 with further references. Conversely, Burkert (2009), Fink (2014), and Sergueenkova and Rojas (2017) consider genuine 'Eastern' source texts. Frahm (2003) 44 knows of a reference to 'eating, drinking, and merrymaking' in one of Ashurbanipal's inscriptions.
[20] For the theory of interpretive communities and reading, see Fish (1976).
[21] See Hdt. 2.150, Hellanic. *FGrHist* 4 F 6, 687a F 2, Ar. *Av.* 1021. This is laid out succinctly by Lenfant (2001) 46–7. The attribution of the story of Sardanapallus' death to lost/fragmentary *logoi* of Herodotus as suggested by Drews (1970) did not convince me.

as ionicisms in the epitaph seemed to point to a fifth-century-BC Ionian historiographer.²² Yet, Walter Burkert showed in an important article that the ionicisms do not go back to an earlier source but were added by the Alexander historians in an attempt to render the original 'Assyrian' language through dialect.²³

The earliest source that tells us of Sardanapallus' death and associates him with the idea of *carpe diem* is, then, Ctesias, a Greek historian who was physician to the Persian king (late fifth to early fourth century). Ctesias describes in his *Persica* how Sardanapallus burns himself along with his precious possessions and his concubines on a pyre when he realises that the enemy forces of the Medes will defeat him.²⁴ In Athenaeus' rendering of Ctesias, Sardanapallus essentially constructed a massive banqueting hall on his pyre, including 150 gold couches with as many tables to accommodate Sardanapallus, his wife, and an improbably high number of concubines. The essence of the *carpe diem* motif was thus already present in Ctesias: death and dining.²⁵ This was not just any death, but the death of the first world empire; nor was it just any feast, but one of enormous proportions, which was directly linked to the end of this empire. Ctesias combines a Greek idea of death and dining with some 'Eastern' flavouring; the absence of male aristocrats seems 'Eastern', and so does the magnitude of a banquet that includes – if each couch accommodated a single diner – a staggering 150 people, consisting of Sardanapallus and his wife and concubines (in Diodorus, also his eunuchs). Yet, despite some 'Eastern' flavouring, most ingredients of Sardanapallus' banquet are decidedly Greek. In

---

²² Niese (1880) ix–xi first noted the ionicisms Ἀνακυνδαράξεω, ἔδειμεν, and ἡμέρῃ μιῇ at Aristobulus *FGrHist* 139 F 9, Clearchus *fr.* 51d Wehrli, and Photius/Suda s.v. Σαρδαναπάλους, which only Apollodorus *FGrHist* 244 F 303 and Arrian *Anab.* 2.5.4 fully atticise to Ἀνακυνδαράξου, ἐδείματο, and ἡμέρᾳ μιᾷ. Scholars suggested various Ionian historians as the source for the epitaph: Hellanicus (Niese (1880) ix–xi, Boncquet (1987) 144 and 144 n.674 with further support), Dionysius of Miletus (E. Meyer (1892–9) i.203), Hecataeus (Maas (1895) 216 n.15), Ctesias (Prentice (1923) 78–80).
²³ Burkert (2009) 506–7, adducing as a parallel Timotheus *PMG* 791.149, where Persians speak in Ionic (cf. A. *Pers.* 13, 61, 556, 761 with Hall (1991) 79).
²⁴ Ctes. *fr.* 1b 27 Lenfant *apud* D.S. 2.27; *fr.* 1q Lenfant *apud* Ath. 12.529b–d.
²⁵ These features are less clear in Diodorus' rendering of Ctesias, but I follow Lenfant (2004) 247, who says that Athenaeus gives us a more complete account of Ctesias here. Athenaeus tells us that most historians said Sardanapallus was stabbed to death (Ath. 12.529a singling out Duris *FGrHist* 76 F 42). Ctesias, who speaks of self-burning, is the odd one out, and the detailed account of the self-burning in Athenaeus must go back to him.

The Invention of *Carpe Diem*

fact, an unbelievably high number of fifty prostitutes had already characterised an extravagant Greek symposium; or, in other words, the staggering number of prostitutes at Sardanapallus' banquet is part of a Greek sympotic discourse to mark extravagance.[26] Furthermore, the emphasis on communal reclining during the banquet is more Greek than Assyrian.[27] Spectacular and 'oriental' as Sardanapallus' death may seem, lurking behind it is the *carpe diem* of the Greek symposium.[28]

Ctesias' account almost certainly did not include an epitaph, but his story of a party that ended the Assyrian empire was distilled into an epitaph at a later point.[29] It is probable, though not certain, that the two famous hexameters quoted at the beginning of this chapter emerged in Greek culture in the fourth century and were already known to the Greeks when they encountered the monument in Anchiale in 333 BC.[30] Whether or not the Sardanapallus epitaph already circulated in Greek culture before 333, the Greeks were certainly eager to add material evidence to a well-known tale and figure – perhaps comparable to their 'discoveries' of armour of Homeric heroes.[31]

---

[26] A skolion Pindar composed for a symposium of Xenophon of Corinth speaks of courtesans 'with 100 limbs', which I take to mean 50 prostitutes (*fr.* 122.19 Maehler). Others take this to refer to 100 or 25 or very many courtesans (see Groningen (1960) 41–3, Kurke (1996) 58 n.22, and see pages 50–1 for the sympotic setting of the skolion; cf. Liberman (2016) 54–7).

[27] Murray (2016) 23–4 notes that Assyrian rulers were depicted as single reclining banqueters, while others around them were seated. Murray contrasts the Greek style of communal reclining. A difficult topic; see also: Fehr (1971), Dentzer (1982) 68–9, Burkert (1991), Grottanelli (1995) 71–2, Reade (1995), Topper (2012) 13–52, Węcowski (2014) 141–9.

[28] For the concept of Orientalism, see Said (1978); for Orientalism and the Greeks, see Hall (1991) 99–100, *passim*. Aeschylus had already attributed a *carpe diem* sentiment to an Eastern ruler, the Persian king Darius (A. *Pers.* 840 with Maas (1895) 214 n.13, Dornseiff (1929), Wankel (1983) 153).

[29] Ctesias is generally treated as the source for Diodorus' account of Sardanapallus' death (*fr.* 1 b 23–7 Lenfant *apud* D.S. 2.23–7), but the section that mentions the epitaph in Diodorus is not attributed to Ctesias in *FGrHist*, nor is it by F. W. König (1972) or Lenfant (2004). In this section, Sardanapallus is said to have told his 'successors on the throne' (D.S. 2.23.3: τοῖς διαδόχοις τῆς ἀρχῆς) to inscribe the epitaph on his tomb. This is not compatible with Ctesias' emphasis on Sardanapallus as the last king of Assyria, as already C. Jacoby (1875) 609–10 had shown: no successors to the throne here. I thus find it unconvincing that Boncquet (1987) 148–51, Stronk (2010) in his commentary on page 158, and Lanfranchi (2011) 216–17 and 217 n.142 attribute this section of Diodorus to Ctesias.

[30] For this tradition, see most succinctly Lloyd-Jones and Parsons at *SH* 335. I return to this question on pages 53–5 and 54 n.54.

[31] See Paus. 3.3 with Schnapp (1996) [1993] 46–8. Cf. Hartmann (2013), who discusses the fascination of ancient readers with old inscriptions, and Busine

The Archaeology of *Carpe Diem*

The popular Sardanapallus legend influenced the Greeks' interpretation of the monument in Anchiale – and so did their reading practice of epigrams. The role of the reader has been the focus of several studies of Hellenistic epigram.[32] Crucially, in the case of Sardanapallus' epitaph, we can observe the act of reading in action. For as Alexander and his fellow travellers from an antique land encounter a difficult inscription, they apply their usual toolkit of reading methods. Let us, for a moment, imagine that a different epigram had been written about the events in Anchiale. In this alternative epigram, the writer might have said: 'What is the meaning of this monument in an old town in Cilicia? I can discern some foreign letters, and above them is the image of someone in precious Eastern clothes. Is he perhaps a king? And what does the movement of his hands signify? I think I have found a solution: the king is Sardanapallus and he playfully snaps his fingers, because everything in life is not worth more than this snap of the finger!' There are of course Hellenistic epigrams which describe exactly such an act of reading: the act of making sense of riddling monuments and inscriptions, the attempt to create a literary epigram through *reading* riddling images, and the act of understanding language as a primarily visual, not an oral, medium.[33] The difference is that in such Hellenistic epigrams the act of reading is self-conscious and problematised, whereas it is not in the case of the Sardanapallus epitaph;[34] but I maintain that the act of reading as described in Hellenistic epigrams is based on actual practice in life, which preceded Hellenistic literature.[35] The Sardanapallus episode thus

---

(2012), who discusses the discovery of forged 'old' inscriptions in pagan and Christian antiquity.

[32] See, for example, D. Meyer (1993; 2005; 2007) with further sources on reader-response theory (*Rezeptionsästhetik*) in the tradition of Jauß (1967). Cf. Bing (1995), Petrovic (2005) 34–7, Day (2019). For the act of reading epigrams in the archaic period, see Day (2010).

[33] See *AP* 7.428 = Mel. 122 *HE*, *AP* 7.427 = Antip. Sid. 32 *HE*, and *AP* 7.422 = Leon. 22 *HE* with Goldhill (1994), also *AP* 7.429 = Alcaeus of Messene 16 *HE*, and the late antique example of Ausonius *Epigrams* 37 Green. Cf. Gutzwiller (1998) 265–76, Fantuzzi and Hunter (2004) 328–38 with further examples and references, Squire (2009) 160–5.

[34] Goldhill (1994) 205 speaks of the 'self-conscious and self-reflexive dramatization of viewing – seeing oneself as seeing'. Cf. Zanker (2004).

[35] This argues against Bing (2002), who claims that this act of reading could only arise in book poetry. Bing's notion is opposed by, for example, Day (2007; 2010), Bruss (2010), Cairns (2016) 3–4 and 3n.10. For reading in the Greek world, see Svenbro (1993) [1988], Johnson and Parker (2009).

The Invention of *Carpe Diem*

shows the complex ways in which Greeks were reading epigrams before the advent of either the Hellenistic period or book epigrams. The reading of the Sardanapallus epitaph is an extremely elaborate reverse *Ergänzungsspiel*. While Peter Bing described how *Ergänzungsspiel* in numerous Hellenistic literary epigrams invites the reader to supply the surroundings of the epigram now that the epigram appears isolated from its surroundings on the scroll,[36] the opposite happens in the case of the Sardanapallus epitaph: monument and surroundings were present to the Greeks in Anchiale, but almost the entire inscription was added (*ergänzt*) by the readers. The only part of the epitaph that may have belonged to the actual inscription in Anchiale are the place names Anchiale and Tarsus, which could have been part of a victory monument of Sennacherib.[37]

The Greeks supplied the epigram as they tried to make sense of the puzzling Assyrian monument. The monument arguably would have featured a statue or relief of an Assyrian ruler making a gesture with an extended thumb and a pointed index finger, which indicates the presence of a god (*ubāna tarāṣu* in Akkadian), as Eduard Meyer argued in a seminal article.[38] The Greeks were puzzled at the odd gesture of the statue and assumed that the inscription must have supplied an explanation. Consequently, they supplied the deictic τούτου in the inscription as a reference to the hand gesture (Aristobulus' account at Str. 14.5.9): τἆλλα τούτου οὐκ ἄξια ('everything else is not worth *this!*'). There arguably was no such deictic marker in the 'Assyrian' inscription. Rather, we can see how the Greeks read the material surroundings of the epitaph and construct a text that reflects their interpretation. As a result, we find a deictic

---

[36] Bing (1995). For supplementation (*Ergänzung*) in Hellenistic visual art, see Zanker (2004) 72–102.
[37] Thus Weißbach at *RE* i.A2 col.2466–7 s.v. 'Sardanapal', Bosworth (1980–95) i.193–4. Sergueenkova and Rojas (2017) 162 stress that this part of the epitaph was probably owed to local interpreters. Sennacherib may have celebrated the subjugation and rebuilding of the two towns in 696 BC. The Greeks would have misunderstood Sennacherib's name for Sardanapallus and added the *carpe diem* text.
[38] E. Meyer (1892–9) i.203–9. See also Weißbach at *RE* i.A2 col.2466–71 s.v. 'Sardanapal', Furlani (1927), Forsberg (1995) 64, 67–9, Lanfranchi (2003) 83, Rollinger (2017) 578. Sergueenkova and Rojas (2017) 161 suggest a different gesture of a Hittite or Luwian monument. Riemschneider (1955) thinks the gesture on the monument might have been one of greeting, but her interpretation is based on the Greek 'inscription', which is a questionable methodology, as Ameling (1985) 38 n.16 noted. Papadopoulou (2005) is also too ready to accept the 'inscription' as genuine.

pronoun in the epitaph, which can also be found in numerous Greek epigrams as a particularly strong marker of interplay between text and monument.[39]

It is not only the Greeks at Anchiale who were puzzled at a monument. Puzzlement is a reaction that many Hellenistic epigrams describe when viewers look at art.[40] Already an epitaph roughly contemporary to the events in Anchiale asks the viewer not to be surprised when seeing the accompanying relief that depicts a man mortally wounded by a lion.[41] In the case of Sardanapallus' gesture, viewers were also surprised and expected that here, too, the inscription would provide clarity. What is remarkable is that once meaning is constructed, the Alexander historians reverse the dynamics between clues and solutions in their accounts; they quote an inscription including the demonstrative τούτου, which is unintelligible on its own and requires an explanation that relates the pronoun to the statue (Aristobulus' account at Str. 14.5.9): 'everything else is not worth *this* (τούτου)! ("This" refers to the snapping of the fingers)'.[42] They thus present the image as a supplement to text in the conventional way, though in fact the text was originally a supplement to the image.[43] Beside the deictic pronoun, there are several other features of the epigram which were arguably formed by the assumptions that Greek readers had about the style of epitaphs. This includes the verse form, the deceased as a first-person speaker, the second-person verbs that address a wayfarer, the paraenetic tone, and the father's name of the deceased.[44]

---

[39] See Ecker (1990) 122–3, Bing (1995) 118, 121, Petrovic (2005) 31, Tsagalis (2008) 217–19 for inscribed epigram. Such pronouns were already common in the sixth century, for example, *CEG* 37 (= *GV* 58).

[40] Gutzwiller (2002) 95–6.

[41] *CEG* 596 (second half of the fourth century BC) with Bruss (2010) 401–3.

[42] While sources generally speak of snapping of the fingers and Pl. *Mor.* 336c adds dancing to the finger snapping, Arrian at *Anab.* 2.5.4 speaks of a handclap. See page 43 n.12 for attempts to explain the different gesture in Arrian.

[43] Cf. Bing (1995) 117, Petrovic (2007) 56, S. West (1985) on Herodotus' technique of presenting supplementing information for his epigrams.

[44] The deceased as speaker of an epigram is first attested around 500 BC (*CEG* 159 = *GV* 1228) and becomes common in the classical period (Sourvinou-Inwood (1995) 280–1, Tueller (2008) 14–15, 17–22); the passer-by as addressee is first attested for the mid-sixth century BC (*CEG* 28 (= *GV* 1225) with Tueller (2008) 14–15; cf. the sequence *GV* 1209–1383, Sourvinou-Inwood (1995) 280, Tueller (2010)); for paraenetic epitaphs, see, for example, the sequence *GV* 1359–69; the patronymic is already attested for the eighth century BC (Ecker (1990) 45).

The Invention of *Carpe Diem*

As the Greeks believe that they have successfully deciphered the monument, they present their solutions with a rhetoric of expertise. Several features of the narratives of the Alexander historians stress their thorough research methods. This is particularly clear in Arrian's account. There it is noted that the Greeks inspected the site of Anchiale. The former greatness of this town, inferable from the circumference of its walls, lends credence to the presence of a monument there, which is associated with the Assyrian king best known to the Greeks. The Greeks also stress the foreignness of the inscription, which they deciphered. They mention its Assyrian letters, they note the explanations of locals, and they render the foreign language in Ionic dialect. The different dialect marks the epigram as 'Asian' and attempts to give readers a closer impression of the original. And yet, here, just as in the content of the inscription, what is meant to look foreign turns out to be Greek. Other remarks also aim to show expertise; thus, it is mentioned that the epigram was originally written in verse. This was hardly a feature of the Assyrian inscription; rather, the tradition of the well-known verse version of Sardanapallus' epitaph (or indeed the general Greek tradition of verse epitaphs) influenced the Greek reading here. The boasting about the knowledge of connotations of an Assyrian word for having sex in Arrian can be explained in two ways. If this section goes back to Aristobulus, then Aristobulus already attempted to boast about his scholarly credentials. Alternatively, it is possible that Arrian compares accounts of different Alexander historians and notes the discrepancy between παῖζε and ὄχευε in these sources.[45] But one thing is clear: as Greek authors argue whether Sardanapallus exhorted readers to 'fool around' or to 'fuck', they believe they are discussing a reliable source, which they scrutinise with scholarly methods.[46]

---

[45] Sergueenkova and Rojas (2017) 163–4 overstate the importance of local interpreters, who, according to them, claimed knowledge of the script, identified the diction, and recognised words as obscene. It is much more likely that these comments come from the Greeks and their experiences in reading epigrams. Why would locals attribute an obscenity to someone they venerated as a hero, as Sergueenkova and Rojas think? Apollodorus *FGrHist* 244 F 303 and the Photius/Suda entry of Sardanapallus read ὄχευε, Plutarch *Mor.* 336c ἀφροδισίαζε, all other sources παῖζε.

[46] An instructive parallel is Piglet's interpretation of the inscription 'Trespassers W' in *Winnie-the-Pooh*. Piglet says that the sign reads 'Trespassers William', supposedly the

The Archaeology of *Carpe Diem*

Although the Greeks are fascinated with Sardanapallus' exhortations to present enjoyment, and although they ostensibly stress how one of these exhortations has rather peculiar connotations in Assyrian, in the end all these exhortations look very Greek.[47] Such exhortations to merriment were at home in sympotic poetry. Thus, we can read the following words in an elegiac fragment of Ion of Chios (*fr*. 27.7): πίνωμεν, παίζωμεν ('let's drink, let's fool around!'). This is not to say that we can draw a direct line from Ion to the Sardanapallus epitaph, where Arrian and others read ἔσθιε καὶ πῖνε καὶ παῖζε. The alternative ὄχευε in place of παῖζε in some sources lessens the verbal similarity to a degree. Nor should we assume that Ion's words were of such proverbial nature that the Alexander historians had them in mind. Rather, it seems likely that the fragment of Ion allows us a glance at the type of exhortations that would have been common in many sympotic poems. Thus, we encounter commands that pair πῖνε and παῖζε also in a different elegiac fragment of Ion and – in a *carpe diem* context – in a fragment from comedy.[48] Sympotic poets also used pairs of other commands, told their addressees to drink and eat (Thgn. 33: πῖνε καὶ ἔσθιε), to be joyful (or greeted?) and drink (Alc. *fr*. 401a: χαῖρε καὶ πῶ τάνδε), and very often simply to drink.[49] The Sardanapallus epitaph urges to drink and merriment, and its text evokes lyric exhortations to present enjoyment. As the Greeks ostensibly uncover the words of an Assyrian king, they actually engage in an archaeology of their own literary past: Sardanapallus speaks in the familiar language of a Greek sympotic tradition that reaches at least as far back as Alcaeus and Theognis.[50] Sardanapallus speaks to the

---

name of one of his ancestors, who erected this sign in front of his house. The scene is expertly illuminated by Elsner (1994) 224–6.

[47] Bernhardt (2009) 16–24, Rollinger (2017) 577.

[48] Ion *fr*. 26.15–16: δίδου δ' αἰῶνα [...] | πίνειν καὶ παίζειν καὶ τὰ δίκαια φρονεῖν ('grant us time [*sc*. Dionysus] to drink and to fool around and to have just thoughts'; Amphis *fr*. 8.1: πῖνε, παῖζε ('drink, fool around!'). Thgn. 567 has παίζω in a *carpe diem* context.

[49] The *carpe diem* poem Alc. *fr*. 38a begins with the imperative πῶνε. The exhortatory πώνωμεν/πίνωμεν can be found at Alc. 346, 352, Thgn. 763, 1042. Cf. *PMG* 902.1: σύν μοι πῖνε συνήβα συνέρα συστεφανηφόρει ('together with me drink, enjoy your youth, love, wear a garland!'). See Cazzato and Prodi (2016) 6–9, Gagné (2016) 226–7 on the sympotic invitation to drink. Already in the *Odyssey* verbs of eating and drinking are frequently coupled (e.g., *Od*. 2.305: ἐσθιέμεν καὶ πινέμεν). Such expressions may not yet have had the same ring in Homer that they would acquire in Alcaeus or Theognis.

[50] My interpretation here is influenced by Sens (2016) 234–5, who argued that traditional sympotic commands in Hellenistic epigram point to a self-conscious engagement with

To Have and Have Not: Sardanapallus in Verse

Greeks as if he were a symposiast whose banquet they join. The Sardanapallus epitaph, then, unearths traditional commands from Greek sympotic poetry and makes them present; the imperatives that call to merriment construct the fiction of Sardanapallus speaking to his readers in their presence. For a moment we seem to party with Sardanapallus.

Reading the Sardanapallus epitaph and writing it comes down to one and the same thing. The interpretive process of reading signs can create a new text, in a way that is probably best explained by Stanley Fish. The Sardanapallus story tells us much more about the Greek readers than about any Assyrian king. The way in which the Greeks read the Sardanapallus epitaph is notable in particular for two concerns. First, the account of the events in Anchiale points to a sophisticated way of viewing and reading that is commonly associated with the Hellenistic period. Yet, as the events in Anchiale show, this way of reading precedes the Hellenistic period, and it thus offers us valuable information concerning the prehistory of Hellenistic epigram. Second, the way the Greeks read the Sardanapallus epitaph points to an archaeological method with which they attempt to make sense of the distant past. As they apply these methods to the Sardanapallus epitaph they invent its *carpe diem* message. It seemed to fascinate Greeks that in Anchiale they found themselves in the material presence of Sardanapallus; though long dead, the king seemed to momentarily snap his fingers and tell his readers to live it up. The story of Sardanapallus gained traction after the spectacular discovery in Anchiale, so that Plutarch could say some centuries later that there was no difference between Sardanapallus' life and his tombstone (Plu. *Mor.* 336d). Pleasure had become text.

1.2 To Have and Have Not: Sardanapallus in Verse

The game of supplementing the Sardanapallus inscription goes further. The sight of Sardanapallus' supposed tomb gave rise not only to the prose epitaphs with which the previous section was

---

the literary past. For the engagement with the literary past as a form of archaeology, see Hunter (1996b).

occupied but also new impetus to the verse epitaph. Thus, one account of Alexander's campaign, written by Amyntas, tells us that a certain Choerilus made a verse translation of the inscription in 'Chaldean letters'.[51] Amyntas gives us a prose paraphrase of Choerilus' verses, which he apparently took and shortened from an earlier source. Amyntas' testimony is then secondary, which may account for some confusions within it — not least of which is that the tomb of Sardanapallus is moved from Anchiale to Nineveh in order to suit his supposed place of death.[52] Despite these caveats, Amyntas' testimony offers support for placing the verse version of the Sardanapallus epitaph into the environment of Alexander's campaign; Choerilus of Iasus, a poet who accompanied Alexander on his campaign, responded to the sight of the foreign inscription with his 'translation'.[53] In fact, Choerilus was not so much translating an Assyrian inscription into Greek as transferring Greek material to an Assyrian monument. As I briefly mentioned above, two hexameters of Sardanapallus' epitaph were particularly popular and probably already circulating before Alexander (lines 4–5).[54] Choerilus, then, added lines 1–3 to the well-known lines 4–5, creating an epitaph of five lines. Later,

---

[51] Amyntas *FGrHist* 122 F 2 *apud* Ath. 12.529e–530a.

[52] The epitaph in Amyntas' prose paraphrase begins with the particle δέ: ἐγὼ δὲ ἐβασίλευσα καὶ ἄχρι ἑώρων τοῦ ἡλίου <τὸ> φῶς, ἔπιον, ἔφαγον, ἠφροδισίασα [...] ('I was a king, and for as long as I saw the light of the sun, I drank, ate, and had sex [...]'). Unless Athenaeus shortened here or there is a lacuna in the manuscripts, Amyntas cut from his source the opening of Choerilus' epitaph. This offers further support to Burkert (2009) 506–7, who argues that Amyntas is a later author assembling material, and not a surveyor (bematist) of Alexander (thus also F. Jacoby in his commentary at Amyntas *FGrHist* 122 F 2 against Schwartz at *RE* ii col.2008 s.v. 'Amyntas' no. 22; cf. Cinzia Bearzot at *BNJ* Amyntas 122, 'Biographical Essay').

[53] The authorship is not uncontested. Strabo 14.5.9 notes that Choerilus wrote a verse epitaph. As only one canonical verse epitaph is known, this must be the one in question, which Choerilus wrote. The question is then 'which Choerilus?' — the fifth-century-BC epic poet Choerilus of Samos, or Choerilus of Iasus, who accompanied Alexander? Amyntas' testimony decisively favours the Iasian, who was first championed as the author by Naeke (1817) 206–7. For the tradition of the verse epitaph, see, above all, Lloyd-Jones and Parsons at *SH* 335.

[54] The chronology is not certain. Aristotle, who first quotes the two famous hexameters (*Protrept. fr.* 16 Ross = 90 Rose, but date and attribution to work uncertain), could still have written about them after the events in Anchiale, and the same is true for Crates (Aristotle may have read about the events in Anchiale in the work of his nephew Callisthenes, as Burkert (2009) 513–14 suggests). Yet, the two hexameters seemed to have been proverbial already in Aristotle's times, which suggests that they had already emerged earlier in the fourth century.

To Have and Have Not: Sardanapallus in Verse

two more lines were added. I print the text of Lloyd-Jones and Parsons (*SH* 335 Choerilus of Iasus (?)):

εὖ εἰδὼς ὅτι θνητὸς ἔφυς σὸν θυμὸν ἄεξε (1)
τερπόμενος θαλίῃσι· θανόντι τοι οὔτις ὄνησις.
καὶ γὰρ ἐγὼ σποδός εἰμι, Νίνου μεγάλης βασιλεύσας.
ταῦτ᾽ ἔχω ὅσσ᾽ ἔφαγον καὶ ἐφύβρισα καὶ μετ᾽ ἔρωτος
τέρπν᾽ ἔπαθον· τὰ δὲ πολλὰ καὶ ὄλβια κεῖνα λέλειπται. (5)
[ἥδε σοφὴ βιότοιο παραίνεσις, οὐδέ ποτ᾽ αὐτῆς
λήσομαι· ἐκτήσθω δ᾽ ὁ θέλων τὸν ἀπείρονα χρυσόν.]

Make yourself happy and enjoy feasts in the knowledge that you are mortal. Nothing is of any use for a dead man. For even I am dust, though I was king of great Nineveh. I have what I ate and my kinks, and the pleasures I received in bed. But my many well-known riches are gone. [These are wise words to live by, and I will never forget them. But let anyone who wants that amass endless gold.]

Choerilus virtually inscribes a proverbial epitaph upon a monument, and as he does so he expands it. His additions in lines 1–3 reflect the physical encounter with the monument during Alexander's campaign; the admonition to the reader conforms to the prose versions of the epitaph that arose in Anchiale. The cultural dynamics of Choerilus' verse epitaph are then comparable to those of the prose epitaph: Choerilus' reading of a foreign monument turns out to be a creative adaption of an already well-known Greek text.

The verses of Sardanapallus' epitaph are endlessly quoted,[55] but it is rarely noted how striking they are. The exceptions are perhaps Aristotle and Cicero, who refer to the oldest part of the epitaph, lines 4–5. In *De finibus*, Cicero discusses Sardanapallus' epitaph and the possibility of enjoying bodily pleasures when they are past. According to him, Aristotle asked, 'how could a sensation last with a dead man which even in his lifetime he could only feel while he was actually enjoying it?' (Aristotle *Protrept. fr.* 16 Ross = 90 Rose *apud* Cic. *Fin.* 2.106 and *apud* Cic. *Tusc.* 5.101). To be sure, Cicero here makes a philosophic argument about the nature of pleasure, which relates to more general discussions in Epicurean and Stoic philosophy about what is and is not attainable in life and how self-mastery

---

[55] For a full account of quotations, see Lloyd-Jones and Parsons at *SH* 335. Cf. Preger (1891) 183–7, no. 232.

55

can be achieved (and the implications of pairing Sardanapallus with Epicurus and past pleasures will be discussed below);[56] but the comment cuts to the nature of the epitaph and indeed of this book: how does enjoyment work in the past tense?

The paradoxical nature of Sardanapallus' statement, which Aristotle discerns, is further underlined in its choice of words. The most striking word in the epitaph is arguably its usage of ἔχω. The verb ἔχω is very common in epitaphs. Crucially, though, it almost always takes the deceased as the object, while the subject is the tomb, the monument, or something similar.[57] The word is formulaic to the extent that Asclepiades would later play with its meaning in an epigram, which begins with the words: 'I hold (ἔχω) Archeanessa the hetaera of Colophon' (*AP* 7.217 = Asclepiades 41 *HE*). Who is holding the hetaera? A lover or a tomb? The impossibility of determining this is precisely the point of the poem, which plays with generic boundaries, as Richard Thomas has shown. And it is the formulaic nature of ἔχω that makes such a play possible.[58] Being dead is a question of to have and have not. No dead man can be the agent of ἔχω; there is nothing to *have* in the underworld; only the tomb *has* the corpse. This is of course reversed in the Sardanapallus epitaph: Sardanapallus *has* all the things eaten, his kinks and the pleasures he received in bed. Indeed, the surprising usage of ἔχω is highlighted by the more conventional usage of λείπω: all other things are left behind. The verb λείπω is another formulaic expression on epitaphs. This verb almost always takes the deceased as the subject (in the passive construction of the Sardanapallus epitaph the deceased is of course the logical subject).[59] Dead people conventionally leave things behind and do not have or own anything anymore. While Sardanapallus does leave almost everything behind, he still has pleasure. Aristotle is rightly struck by this assertion.

---

[56] Already the Cyrenaics discussed self-mastery; Aristippus supposedly said about the famous prostitute Lais (*SSR* IV A 96): 'I have (ἔχω!) Lais, but I am not had by her (οὐκ ἔχομαι).'
[57] Tueller (2008) 50–2. Cf. Bruss (2005) 19.
[58] Thomas (1998) 208–13 and Sens (2011) *ad loc.* with further examples and references.
[59] On λείπω in epitaphs, see Tueller (2008) 48–9, Tsagalis (2008) 110–13.

To Have and Have Not: Sardanapallus in Verse

A later poem by the Hellenistic poet Machon might be an instructive comparison. In this poem, perhaps influenced by Sardanapallus, Machon tells of an absurd form of convivial death:[60] having eaten a giant octopus, the dithyrambic poet Philoxenus is told by his doctor that he will die (Machon 9 Gow *apud* Ath. 8.341a–d). Philoxenus then asks to be served the head of the octopus that had still been left, intending to run off to the underworld *having all the things that are his* (ἵν' ἔχων ἀποτρέχω πάντα τἀμαυτοῦ κάτω). In this anecdote, Philoxenus succeeds in keeping the things he ate even after death; he has his octopus and eats it. Yet, Philoxenus has of course to go to absurd lengths in order to achieve this, and the ingenuity displayed by Philoxenus illustrates the difficulty in extending possessions and pleasure after death.

The case of Sardanapallus presents an even more extreme version of extending pleasures. The Greeks read that Sardanapallus still *has* the things he ate, and so forth – in the present tense! This present-tense ἔχω points to present enjoyment, although it is long gone. It constitutes an attempt to bring back present time, which simultaneously points to its loss. And yet, the gap in time is enormous in this case: when Choerilus rewrote the epitaph in Alexander's times, Sardanapallus had been dead for centuries. Indeed, Choerilus' addition of three lines emphasises the gap; he inserts a reference to Sardanapallus' rule over ancient Nineveh right before Sardanapallus tells us in the present tense of his enjoyment (*SH* 335.3–4): Νίνου μεγάλης βασιλεύσας | ταῦτ' ἔχω ὅσσ' ἔφαγον καὶ ἐφύβρισα [...] ('though I was king of great Nineveh. I have what I ate and my kinks [...]'). Greeks would have assumed an even longer gap. While modern historians date the fall of Nineveh to 612 BC, Greek sources from Ctesias in the fifth century BC to Eusebius in the fourth century AD locate Sardanapallus' reign somewhere in the ninth century BC. The

---

[60] See Scodel (2010) 262–3, who notes the similarity of Machon's anecdote to the description of Ninus (a king modelled on Sardanapallus) by the poet Phoenix of Colophon *CA* 231–2, fr. 1. Cf. LeVen (2013; 2014: 137–44). In another absurd form of convivial death, Babrius 60 tells a fable of a mouse who fell into a soup; the mouse's last words are strongly reminiscent of the Sardanapallus epitaph: 'βέβρωκα' φησί [sc. ὁ μῦς] 'καὶ πέπωκα καὶ πάσης τρυφῆς πέπλησμαι· καιρός ἐστί μοι θνῄσκειν.' Cf. pages 198–205 in Chapter 5 for mice and *carpe diem*.

The Archaeology of *Carpe Diem*

mere fact that the Greeks were wrong is of little interest for the present study. Nor does the addition of approximately two centuries matter in itself. Rather, I wish to stress the probable reasoning behind the Greek chronology and how this affects the reading of the Sardanapallus epitaph. For Ctesias and for Alexander's expedition, Assyrian history preceded Greek history; that is, they locate the end of the Assyrian empire in a time in which there were no known Greek historical events, just a transition period between myth and history proper. Many centuries later, around AD 300, this chronology would become more pronounced when Eusebius compiled chronological tables that synchronised events of world history, for he dates the fall of Nineveh before the first Olympic Games, that is, neatly on the other side of the demarcation line of history.[61] Naturally, the Greeks who encountered the Sardanapallus epitaph in the fourth century BC did not have anything comparable to the sophisticated synchronisation tables of Eusebius. Yet, as Denis Feeney has argued, Eusebius' tables go back to a Greek historiographical tradition, which in the fifth century BC already noted that 'Eastern' history preceded Greece's own.[62] In other words, Sardanapallus is quite literally *pre*-history, and his story is best investigated with *archaeological* methods. The monument from pre-history comfortably stands at the beginning of a Greek tradition of *carpe diem*. Though in actual fact the fall of Nineveh is roughly contemporary with the poetry of Mimnermus, such a thought would arguably never have crossed Greek minds.[63] Sardanapallus precedes their tradition.

---

[61] The expressions 'dividing up the past' and 'demarcation lines of history' are taken from Feeney (2007) 77–92, and see 28–32 for Eusebius.

[62] Feeney (2007) 29; at 59–67 Feeney argues that the incorporation of Asian dates into universal history was as a particularly Roman concern of the first century BC; earlier, Greeks were aware of the greater antiquity of Eastern empires but often chose to ignore that. Despite this caveat, the greater antiquity of the Assyrian empire must have mattered for readers of the Sardanapallus epitaph; the encounter of Anchiale took place on the eve of the Battle of Issus, when Alexander would have been able to write himself into a succession of empires that began with the Assyrians (cf. Momigliano (1982) 545 on the *translatio imperii*). Further, Burkert (2009) 504 notes Ctesias' wrong chronology for the end of the Assyrian empire as well as his influence on Eusebius. Dionysius of Halicarnassus says that the Assyrian empire reaches back to the time of myth (*Antiquitates Romanae* 1.2.2), as Feeney (2007) 78 notes. See Mosshammer (1979) 182–3 on the synchronism of Sardanapallus with Greek history.

[63] Eusebius, naturally, dates lyric poets according to the Olympic games; that is, he locates them on this side of the demarcation line of history.

The Art of Variation

As Greeks encounter the monument in 333 BC and read the words 'I have what I ate [...]', they must assume that they encounter a daring present tense that bridges centuries and links pre-history with the present moment. Indeed, Greek epitaphs conventionally assume that they will be read for time to come, so that the words they use and the time frame they construct must be true for an indefinite future.[64] In the case of the Sardanapallus epitaph, this means not only that this striking present tense has been there for immeasurable time, but also that it will persist in being there. In eternity, Sardanapallus always has his pleasures. While Ctesias described a last monumental banquet Sardanapallus enjoyed, the banquet had become a monument in Anchiale. Expressions from banqueting, the 'eat, drink, and be merry' of sympotic lyric, are still present, but they are *monumentalised*: enjoyment lasts in an eternal present, as people read *carpe diem*.

1.3 The Art of Variation

An epigram is never alone. It belongs to the core of the genre that inscriptions are surrounded by other inscriptions, vie for the attention of a wanderer, and share a set of formulae. Once collected in books, epigrams create meaning through juxtaposition with neighbouring epigrams, and series of allusive epigrams are common.[65] The following section turns to the 'art of variation' in epigrams similar to the Sardanapallus epitaph.[66]

Following their extensive 'archaeology', it is only natural that Greeks treat Sardanapallus as the archetype for similar inscriptions.[67] Thus, Athenaeus says that 'a certain Bacchidas, who enjoyed the same lifestyle as Sardanapallus, after his death

---

[64] See Tueller (2008) 36–42 on present time in epitaphs.
[65] See Tarán (1979), Gutzwiller (1998) 227–322, Kirstein (2002), Fantuzzi (2010).
[66] On epitaphs and *carpe diem*, see Lier (1904) 56–63, Tolman (1910) 95–6, Galletier (1922) 79–82, L. Friedländer (1923) iii.302–5, Brelich (1937) 49–53, Robert (1943): 182–3, 186–7; 1965: 184–92), Lattimore (1942) 260–3, Kajanto (1969), Ameling (1985), and the category 'Geniesse das Leben' in the index at *SGO* v.339.
[67] Some modern scholars also treat the Sardanapallus epitaph as the model for all epitaphs of this kind (Kajanto (1969) 361, Nollé (1985) 125). Yet, not all Greek epitaphs that include exhortations to merriment consciously attempt to follow the Sardanapallus epitaph, which at any rate was not the first of its kind (Ameling (1985) 38).

also has inscribed on his tomb' the following epigram (*GV* 1368 *apud* Ath. 8.336d):

πιέν, φαγὲν καὶ πάντα τᾷ ψυχᾷ δόμεν·
κἠγὼ γὰρ ἔστακ' ἀντὶ Βακχίδα λίθος.

Drink, eat, and make yourself happy! For I stand here in Bacchidas' place: a stone.

Naturally, no one knows whether Bacchidas' life really resembled that of Sardanapallus', as Athenaeus claims. Most likely this conclusion is drawn from the content of the epitaph, which belongs to an otherwise unknown person ('a certain Bacchidas'; Βακχίδας δέ τις; the name may have reinforced Athenaeus' interpretation). Yet, there is something to learn from Athenaeus' reception of the epitaph. At least for a reader who was as learned in literature and sympotic affairs as Athenaeus, the conclusion is clear: through his epitaph and (by extension) through his life, Bacchidas aims to emulate Sardanapallus. Though the Sardanapallus epitaph is not the archetype of the *carpe diem* theme on epitaphs, it was treated as an archetype in the reception of such epitaphs. Thus, Athenaeus collects material of people who 'aspire to the lifestyle of Sardanapallus' and are 'similar to Sardanapallus'.[68]

The content of Bacchidas' epitaph is less interesting than its framing by Athenaeus. Walter Ameling collected dozens of parallels.[69] One aspect in the second line is noteworthy, though: κἠγὼ γὰρ ἔστακ' ἀντὶ Βακχίδα λίθος ('For I stand here in Bacchidas' place: a stone'). This line is strongly evocative of the third line of Choerilus' epigram: καὶ γὰρ ἐγὼ σποδός εἰμι, Νίνου μεγάλης βασιλεύσας ('For even I am dust, though I was king of great Nineveh'). In both cases the deceased is substituted by inanimate substance – in one case dust and in the other stone.[70]

---

[68] Within the sequence Ath. 8.335e–337a and 12.530c–31b, Athenaeus treats Sardanapallus figures. Aspiring to Sardanapallus' lifestyle is Archestratus of Gela (Ath. 8.335f: ὁ καλὸς οὗτος ἐποποιὸς καὶ μόνος ζηλώσας τὸν Σαρδαναπάλλου τοῦ Ἀνακυνδαράξεω βίον). A character from a lost play is described as similar to the Assyrian king (Ath. 8.336b: καὶ ἄλλος δέ τις [. . .] τῷ Σαρδαναπάλλῳ παραπλήσιος).
[69] Ameling (1985).
[70] Note also the very similar *CEG* 153 (fifth century BC), ἀντὶ γυναικὸς ἐγὼ Παρίο λίθο ἐνθάδε κεῖμαι | μνημόσυνον Βίττης, μητρὶ δακρυτὸν ἄχος, as well as *AP* 7.271.3–4 = Callimachus 45.3–4 *HE*, ἀντὶ δ' ἐκείνου | οὔνομα καὶ κενεὸν σᾶμα.

But whatever Bacchidas' qualities in life were, he certainly was not the ruler of a world empire. The *argumentum a fortiori*, 'even I who used to rule great Nineveh am dust and bones', does not work in his case. Instead, his epigram plays with the role of the speaker. At least, anyone with knowledge of the Sardanapallus epitaph would most naturally assume that the speaker is the deceased. Only the last three words of the epigram reveal the identity of the speaker: not Bacchidas, but a stone (λίθος). This is the point of the epigram; the sympotic exhortations for the living are contrasted with the voicelessness and non-existence of the deceased. There are no pleasures for Bacchidas anymore, who is replaced by a stone. Bacchidas' voicelessness is in strong contrast to Sardanapallus' present-tense voice, which bridges centuries.

An epitaph similar to Sardanapallus', which predates the events in Anchiale, was found on the tomb of a Lycian dynast. Michael Wörrle dated it to the early fourth century and discussed it in detail (*SGO* 17/19/03, from where I take the text).[71]

> τῇδε θανὼν κεῖμαι Ἀπολλώνιος Ἑλλαφίλου παῖς.
> ἠργασάμην δικαίως, ἡδὺν βίον εἶχον ἀεὶ ζῶν,
> ἐσθίων καὶ πίνων καὶ παίζων. ἀλλ' ἴθι χαίρων.
>
> I lie here dead, Apollonius, the son of Hellaphilus. I acted justly; I always had a pleasant life, while I was alive, eating and drinking and fooling around. But go and farewell.

Apollonius' epitaph confirms the striking nature of the present-tense ἔχω in the Sardanapallus epitaph, discussed in Section 1.2. For in Apollonius' epitaph we encounter the imperfect εἶχον; he used to have all sorts of pleasures while alive. This is, of course, a much more natural understanding of death, and there are numerous parallels on like epitaphs, in which ἔχω describes the absence of pleasures in the underworld. One deceased, for instance, can speak with the authority of autopsy that 'down here you *have* none

[71] Wörrle (1998), and in more detail Wörrle (1996–7). For the architecture of the monument, see Borchhardt (1996–7) 8–14, tables 11–16. Richard Hunter has pointed out to me that sense demands taking ἀεί with εἶχον, although word order seems to suggest that ἀεί goes with ζῶν. The odd word order then points to the writer's lack of ease with Greek. As I gratefully accept Hunter's argument, my translation differs in this point from the German translations of Wörrle and Burkert.

of these [sc. pleasures]'.⁷² Against the comparison of the Apollonius epitaph and its parallels, the usage of ἔχω in the Sardanapallus epitaph is a remarkable invention. The cultural dynamics are perhaps the most striking aspect of Apollonius' epitaph. Wörrle discussed them in some detail, and he showed that Apollonius, a Lycian dynast, here presents himself as adopting a Greek lifestyle. As the son of Hella-philus, a name not attested elsewhere, as Wörrle notes, he might have been prone to philhellenism. If the design of his tomb goes back to Apollonius himself, then he chose to present himself as an aristocratic Greek symposiast in image and text: a *Totenmahl*-relief depicts Apollonius raising a cup, and the epitaph below picks up Greek sympotic vocabulary. Burkert notes that the writer struggles at points with the Greek metre, and that the expression ἠργασάμην δικαίως might be a syntactic code-switch from a Semitic language, where 'making justice' sounds more idiomatic than in Greek.⁷³ According to Burkert, the linguistic shortcomings suggest that Apollonius' family only recently came under the influence of Greek culture and might have spoken more commonly Luwian-Lycian. The question is what part of Greek culture influenced Apollonius or the writer of the epitaph. Wörrle thinks that the mention of justice could have been influenced by fourth-century Greek philosophical thought, and the *carpe diem* theme by sympotic culture. While the latter seems entirely convincing, the single word δικαίως does not seem a strong enough marker to philosophical influence. In fact, as Wörrle himself sees, Greek lyric already combined drinking, merrymaking, and justice in ways comparable to Apollonius' epitaph (Ion of Chios *fr.* 26.16): πίνειν, καὶ παίζειν, καὶ τὰ δίκαια φρονεῖν ('to drink and to fool around and to have just thoughts').⁷⁴ The Greek symposium, then, seems to be the cultural

---

⁷² *CIG* 3846l: Ἄνθος τοῖς παροδείταις χαίρειν. λοῦσαι, πίε, φάγε, βείνησον· τούτων γὰρ ὧδε κάτω οὐδὲν ἔχις. Note the deictic. For the verb βινῶ ('to fuck'), see Bain (1991) 54–62. Further examples are *AP* 11.56.6 (Anon.): σὺ δ' οὐδὲν ἔχεις, *SGO* 09/08/04.10 (= *GV* 1112.10). The opposite, a usage of ἔχω in the sense of the Sardanapallus epitaph, can be found at *IK* Kibyra I 300–2, no. 362. Latin versions of the Sardanapallus epitaph with present-tense *habeo* are discussed on pages 71–3.
⁷³ Burkert (2009) 510.
⁷⁴ Wörrle (1996–7) 36, Bernhardt (2009) 16–17, and see Wörrle (1998) 80–3 for arguments in favour of philosophical heritage in the epitaph. Reitzenstein (1893) 50

institution that the epitaph attempts to emulate throughout. Strikingly, Apollonius' epitaph displays the opposite dynamics of cultural transfer from the Sardanapallus epitaph; before Greeks in Anchiale believed that they uncovered an 'Eastern' sentiment, Apollonius' epitaph already presents this very sentiment as something Greek for people in the 'East'.[75]

One parallel epigram to the Sardanapallus epitaph was written by the Cynic philosopher Crates of Thebes (*AP* 7.326 = Crates 8 Diels = *SH* 355):[76]

ταῦτ' ἔχω ὅσσ' ἔμαθον καὶ ἐφρόντισα, καὶ μετὰ Μουσῶν
σέμν' ἐδάην· τὰ δὲ πολλὰ καὶ ὄλβια τῦφος ἔμαρψεν.

I have what I studied and thought and the venerable things I learnt with the Muses. But delusion seized my many riches.

Crates' parody follows the Sardanapallus epitaph in the *Greek Anthology*, and Plutarch also quotes the two epigrams as a pair (Plu. *Mor.* 546a). 'Companion pieces', that is, epigrams which can only be understood as a response to different epigrams, are a common feature of the genre.[77] Crates' epigram is such a companion piece, as there is little point in the epigram without the reference to Sardanapallus. Kathryn Gutzwiller thinks that the two epigrams might have circulated orally as a pair before book editions grouped parallel epigrams.[78] At any rate, Crates' epigram is certainly an early example of a non-inscriptional parallel epigram.[79]

Crates engages with Sardanapallus' text as epigram, that is, he recognises epitaphic conventions and makes use of them himself: τὰ δὲ πολλὰ καὶ ὄλβια τῦφος ἔμαρψεν ('but delusion seized my many riches'). The verb μάρπτω ('seize') is not part of the tradition of the Sardanapallus epigram, but is Crates' invention. Invention is perhaps the wrong word, though, since the verb can be found on numerous epitaphs. On these epitaphs, it is usually

---

underlines the sympotic setting of Ion's poem. Bacchylides 3.78–84, perhaps comparably, admonishes his audience to 'righteous' or 'pious' deeds (ὅσια) as life is short.
[75] Thus Wörrle (1996–7). [76] Text: *SH*. [77] See Tarán (1979), Kirstein (2002).
[78] Gutzwiller (2010) 243. On the relation between the epigrams of Sardanapallus and Crates, also see Heusch (1951).
[79] For inscribed predecessors, see Fantuzzi (2010).

Hades, a Moira, or another agent of death who is the subject of the seizing.[80] The scribes of the *Palatine* and *Planudean Anthologies* also recognised the epi-*taphic* language, but did not recognise the Cynic philosophy. And thus their readings τάφος (P) and τύμβος (Pl) in place of τῦφος (Diogenes Laertius) are telling: in their mind, death takes away everything, and this should be the point of an epigram in Book 7 among other sepulchral epigrams. In fact, Crates replaces the agent of death with the Cynic concept of τῦφος; whether this is best translated as 'mist', 'fog', or 'delusion', at any rate it describes a Cynic concept of an incorrect perception of the world. Crates' sentence is similar to a famous saying that is usually attributed to Crates' follower and fellow Cynic Monimus (*SSR* V G 2): τῦφος τὰ πάντα ('everything is delusion'). In contrast to the way the scribes of the *Anthology* understood it, Crates' epigram does not necessarily refer to death.[81] A real Cynic already has no possessions in life, so that being dead makes no difference to this; and this is precisely the point of three epigrams on the Cynic Diogenes which play with this meaning of ἔχω.[82] Crates' epigram is thus not primarily sepulchral in its purpose, but it plays with sepulchral language. Indeed, his usage of μάρπτω is rather daring: a 'fog' or a 'mist' cannot easily 'seize' anything. Parallels from epitaphs, in which even Charon's boat seizes someone, might ease the boldness of the *iunctura*. The act of seizing and grasping is an important action in both epitaphs and *carpe diem* poems: while Hades seizes young people on epitaphs, *carpe diem* poems reverse these dynamics and here humans can take control of time and seize it (I will revisit this issue in Chapter 2 and in Chapter 3). Sardanapallus, too, is *holding onto* his pleasures. Admittedly, ἔχω is an extremely weak haptic word. But since Crates says that he 'holds' the things that have not been 'seized' (μάρπτω), and Cicero says that Sardanapallus was able to 'carry off' his pleasures (*aufero*), the Sardanapallus epitaph was at least

---

[80] *LSJ* s.v. μάρπτω. Cf. *GV* 818, 973, 1155, and 1903 with Vérilhac (1978–82) ii.180.
[81] The more so as Cynics did not believe in an afterlife (cf. Fantuzzi and Hunter (2004) 324–5). Lucian *DMort.* 2.1, 20.6 also shows the opposition of Cynics to Sardanapallus.
[82] *AP* 7.66 (Honestus), *AP* 7.67 = Leonidas 59 *HE*, *AP* 7.68 (Archias), adduced in this context by Lier (1904) 60 n.11. Cf. Clayman (2007) 497–9.

read as a struggle over seizing pleasure.[83] All this does not make a Callimachus out of Crates. But the epitaph is notable for its play with epitaphic formulae in a non-epitaphic context, something characteristic of many later Hellenistic literary epigrams. The epigram is also notable as an early companion piece. Indeed, if Gutzwiller is right and these companion pieces circulated orally for a while, then Crates' epigram in many ways looks forward to the development of the Hellenistic book epigram. The Sardanapallus epitaph thus becomes part of a development of reading *carpe diem*, in which readers add their own versions of the epitaph by adopting epigrammatic conventions. One reason for Crates to attack Sardanapallus is that he is an easy straw man.[84] A Cynic life in poverty might not appeal to many, but neither does the extreme 'Eastern' luxury of Sardanapallus. By contrasting his lifestyle with Sardanapallus', Crates creates a false dichotomy: you don't agree with Sardanapallus' luxury? Then you should join us Cynics in the barrel!

Sardanapallus did not serve as a foil for Crates alone. In the *Aetia*, Callimachus notably says about symposia that only the fruits of intellectual enquiry proved lasting, whereas the pleasures of wreaths and food quickly faded (*fr.* 43.12–17 Harder). Like Crates, Callimachus reverses the stance of the Sardanapallus epitaph.[85] Indeed, Callimachus seems to flag up that he joins in a conversation of people who disagree with Sardanapallus, as he introduces his statement with the words καὶ γὰρ ἐγώ ('for in my case, *too*', polemically taken from the Sardanapallus epitaph at *SH* 335.3 Choerilus). On the face of it, Callimachus here arguably expresses his agreement with a preceding statement of his interlocutor, now lost. But Callimachus' assertive answer can also be extended to Crates, with whom he virtually joins in a dialogue. At any rate, soon Crates and Callimachus would be joined in their criticism of the Sardanapallus epitaph. For the Stoic philosopher

---

[83] Reid (1925) at Cic. *Fin.* 2.106 points to parallels for *aufero* in literature and on tomb inscriptions. A strong haptic word for plucking is ἀπεκαρπισάμην ('I reaped the fruits' or 'I enjoyed'; cf. *carpe diem* at Hor. *C.* 1.11.8!) at Kaibel 546.16 with Peek (1979) 258–9.
[84] Cf. Wankel (1983) 150–1.
[85] Noted by, for example, Barigazzi (1975) 9–11, Richard Hunter at Sider (2017) 201.

The Archaeology of *Carpe Diem*

Chrysippus also adapted Sardanapallus' epitaph, in this case all five lines of Choerilus (*SH* 338 = *SVF* iii.200 fr. 11 apud Ath. 8.337a):[86]

εὖ εἰδὼς ὅτι θνητὸς ἔφυς σὸν θυμὸν ἄεξε,
τερπόμενος θαλίῃσι· φαγόντι σοι οὔτις ὄνησις.
καὶ γὰρ ἐγὼ ῥάκος εἰμί, φαγὼν ὡς πλεῖστα καὶ ἡσθείς.
ταῦτ' ἔχω ὅσσ' ἔμαθον καὶ ἐφρόντισα καὶ μετὰ τούτων
ἐσθλ' ἔπαθον· τὰ δὲ λοιπὰ καὶ ἡδέα πάντα λέλειπται.

Make yourself happy and enjoy conversations in the knowledge that you are mortal. Nothing is of any use to you once you have eaten it. For I, too, am tattered, although I ate as much as possible and enjoyed myself. I have what I studied and thought, and the good things I experienced along with this. But all the rest is gone, though it was pleasant.

Chrysippus takes over the entire first line of Choerilus without change, and even the initial word of the second is the same, until he substitutes θαλίῃσι for μύθοισι. In the whole piece, only very few words are altered; in line 2 Chrysippus reads φαγόντι instead of θανόντι; in line 3 he reads ῥάκος instead of σποδός (arguably in order to make the epigram sound less sepulchral), and omits the reference to ruling Nineveh. The final two lines are for the most part taken from Crates. A notable change is Chrysippus' ἡδέα instead of ὄλβια in Choerilus and Crates.[87] While Chrysippus' alterations, for the most part, reverse the sense of the epigram, there is no such great difference between ἡδέα and ὄλβια; either way, good things are left behind. And yet, Chrysippus made a point of changing this word, though his epigram elsewhere shows the aim to stick as closely to Choerilus and Crates as possible. But in writing ἡδέα, his epigram alludes to Epicurus' philosophy, which proclaims that ἡδονή is the highest good. Chrysippus' method is perhaps slightly more subtle than accusing Epicurus of frequenting a prostitute called Ἡδεία, as others did,[88] but the motif is the same in either case: a smear-campaign against Epicurus, the philosopher

---

[86] Text: *SH*. The same straw-man argument was still welcome for the teachings of a certain preacher from Nazareth; see Luke 12:18–20 and 1 Corinthians 15:32 with Ameling (1985).
[87] Phoenix of Colophon *CA* 231–2, fr. 1 also speaks of ὄλβια.
[88] For this charge, see D.L. 10.6–8 with Gordon (2012) 100–103. For such strategies in general, Sedley (1976) is fundamental.

of shady pleasures. By putting Epicurus' words into Sardanapallus' mouth, Chrysippus creates a straw man of a truly hedonistic philosophy. Epicurus is then just a follower of Sardanapallus. Elsewhere Chrysippus claims that the origin of Epicurus' philosophy is the *Hedypatheia* of the didactic poet Archestratus of Gela.[89] The strategy is the same in each case; Epicurus is not a serious philosopher, but simply added the label of philosophy to the teachings of a weak Eastern despot and a debauched gourmand (for good measure the prostitute/erotic writer Philaenis is thrown into the mix). The Sardanapallus epitaph, of course, presents a case of *carpe diem*, and so does one of the fragments of Archestratus which was perhaps programmatic in Archestratus' poem and which Athenaeus explicitly associates with Epicurus (Archestratus *fr.* 60 Olson and Sens *apud* Ath. 3.101f). Epicurus, however, would arguably not have made this argument.[90] If death is nothing to us, then it can hardly provide the urgency for hurried pleasure-seeking. Indeed, Lucretius, whose Epicurean credentials are beyond doubt, explicitly condemns this attitude (Lucr. 3.912–30). But for critics of Epicurus, such as Chrysippus, Epicurus can be placed in a line of decadence that begins with Sardanapallus and includes Archestratus and Philaenis. This argument develops the *archaeology of carpe diem* further, as it constructs a genealogy in which Sardanapallus becomes the origin of Epicurean philosophy. Naturally, the king of Nineveh and the Athenian philosopher sound rather similar once Epicurus' words are inserted into Sardanapallus' mouth. The damage was lasting.[91] Cicero, in discussing Epicureanism, in *De finibus*, still adduces the Sardanapallus epitaph (2.106): in proper Epicurean fashion, Sardanapallus seems to enjoy past pleasures (*bona praeterita*).

---

[89] Chrysippus *SVF* iii.178 *fr*.709 *apud* Ath. 3.104b and 7.278e–f (= Archestratus *test.* 6 Olson and Sens). See Olson and Sens (2000) xliv–xlv for Archestratus' association with Epicurus.
[90] See Epicurus *Letter to Menoecus* 130–2 with Sedley (1976) 129–30 for Epicurus' rejection of drinking, parties, luxurious seafood (Archestratus!), and dinners. Though Epicurus would not have made the *carpe diem* argument, it can be found in *popular* Epicureanism, on which see in detail pages 20–1 in the Introduction.
[91] See Sedley (1976) for the success of the anti-Epicurean smear campaign in general. The article on Ennius in the *OCD* still draws a connection between Archestratus and Epicureanism. No doubt Chrysippus would be pleased to see that.

The Archaeology of *Carpe Diem*

1.4 The Professor of Desire, Sardanapallus in Rome

A fragment from comedy directly precedes Chrysippus' 'emended' version of the Sardanapallus epitaph in Athenaeus. This fragment is allegedly a passage from a lost play of Alexis, a playwright of Middle Comedy. Athenaeus gives its title as Ἀσωτοδιδάσκαλος ('The instructor in profligacy'). Athenaeus' editing choice shows that he noticed the similarity between this passage and the Sardanapallus epitaph. Indeed, the speaker of the passage seems to be virtually responding to Crates and Chrysippus, as he launches into an attack against philosophers.[92] In his introduction to the passage, Athenaeus says that it tells how a slave called Xanthias exhorts his fellow slaves to live it up ([Alexis] *fr.* 25 *apud* Ath. 8.336d–f):

τί ταῦτα ληρεῖς, φληναφῶν ἄνω κάτω
Λύκειον, Ἀκαδήμειαν, Ὠιδείου πύλας,
λήρους σοφιστῶν; οὐδὲ ἓν τούτων καλόν.
πίνωμεν, ἐμπίνωμεν, ὦ Σίκων, <Σίκων>,
χαίρωμεν, ἕως ἔνεστι τὴν ψυχὴν τρέφειν.   (5)
τύρβαζε, Μάνη· γαστρὸς οὐδὲν ἥδιον.
αὕτη πατήρ σοι καὶ πάλιν μήτηρ μόνη,
ἀρεταὶ δὲ πρεσβεῖαί τε καὶ στρατηγίαι
κόμποι κενοὶ ψοφοῦσιν ἀντ' ὀνειράτων.
ψύξει σε δαίμων τῷ πεπρωμένῳ χρόνῳ·   (10)
ἕξεις δ' ὅσ' ἂν φάγῃς τε καὶ πίῃς μόνα,
σποδὸς δὲ τἆλλα, Περικλέης, Κόδρος, Κίμων.

> Why are you talking this nonsense and are making a mess of the Lyceum, the Academy, and the gates of the Odeon, the gibberish of the sophists? None of this is any good. Let's drink! Let's drink up, Sicon, Sicon! Let's enjoy ourselves as long as we can make ourselves happy! Live it up, Manes! Nothing gives more pleasure than the belly. Only the belly is both your father and your mother. But the prestige from ambassadorships and generalships is pompous vanity and rings as hollow as dreams. At the destined time some god will finish you off. All you'll have is what you eat and drink; all the rest is dust: Pericles, Codrus, Cimon.

The textual history of this fragment is difficult. Athenaeus tells us that he has found no play called Ἀσωτοδιδάσκαλος in over 800 Middle Comedies (though the number might be conventional),

---

[92] Thus Wankel (1983) 152 on the first two lines.

and he says that it was neither catalogued by Callimachus, nor by Aristophanes, nor in Pergamum. Athenaeus encountered the excerpt in the work of the philosopher Sotion of Alexandria. As the fragment further includes some linguistic oddities and a probable anachronism, it is likely that it was not authentic, as has been argued in detail by Geoffrey Arnott.[93]

Arnott originally assumed that the play was forged for reasons of financial gain, but revised this assumption later, and in his commentary argued that the passage is a 'bogus quotation designed to illustrate the enemy viewpoint in an anti-Epicurean pamphlet composed in the third or second century'.[94] This is a very plausible suggestion. Indeed, the association of Epicurus with Sardanapallus is arguably more pronounced than Arnott assumes. For he argues that Ettore Bignone, who earlier linked the passage to Epicureanism, 'fails to prove any positive relationship between Epicurus and epitaph beyond their common hedonism'.[95] Yet, the case of Chrysippus, who makes Sardanapallus sound like Epicurus, points to this relationship. The fact that Cicero adduces the Sardanapallus epitaph in a discussion of Epicurean pleasures further strengthens the case (*Fin.* 2.106). Just like Chrysippus, Pseudo-Alexis merges the Sardanapallus epitaph with Epicurean sentiments. This includes notably the rejection of public offices in lines 8–9,[96] and I wonder if the equation of public prestige with hollow sound is not a faint ring of the assertion of the Sardanapallus epitaph, according to which any human achievements do not even equal the sound of snapping of the fingers. The mention of the belly also looks suspiciously like an attack on Epicurus.[97] Arnott disagrees and thinks that the passage on the belly lacks a direct verbal tie to Epicurus. But need there be one? Is it not more significant that the belly appears as a stock motif in *anti*-Epicurean writing rather than in Epicurus? And here the charge is clear: Epicurus is a philosopher of the belly. Indeed, the closest parallel for the belly in

---

[93] Arnott (1955; 1996: 819–30), who notes that the Odeon was not yet a haunt of philosophers during Alexis' lifetime. Notable proponents of the authenticity of the fragment include Kassel and Austin (1983–2001), Nesselrath (1990) 69–70. Cf. Tammaro (2014).
[94] Arnott (1996) 821.
[95] Arnott (1996) 820, 830 pointing to Bignone (1936) i.335, ii.228–36.
[96] Noted by Arnott (1996) *ad loc.* with further references.
[97] Thus Bignone (1936) i.335, ii.228–236, Gordon (2012) 33–5.

The Archaeology of *Carpe Diem*

Pseudo-Alexis is a fragment from New Comedy, in which Hegesippus attributes the saying to Epicurus that men always seek pleasure and that 'nothing is better than chewing' (τοῦ γὰρ μασᾶσθαι κρεῖττον οὐκ ἔσθ' οὐδὲ ἕν | ἀγαθόν, Hegesippus *Philetairoi fr.* 2.5–6).[98] As a mock-quotation of the Sardanapallus epitaph in a philosophic context, the Ἀσωτοδιδάσκαλος is comparable to Crates' and Chrysippus' versions of the Sardanapallus epitaph. Moreover, there is perhaps another such text, if Adelmo Barigazzi is right to assume that a Hellenistic iamb, which also adopts the Sardanapallus epitaph, would have included in lost lines some criticism on this epitaph.[99]

The slave Xanthias in Pseudo-Alexis asserts that it is only possible to hold onto pleasures, whereas everything else is void. While Pseudo-Alexis expresses the same sentiment as the Sardanapallus epitaph and also copies its phrasing, the words do not refer to Sardanapallus anymore; we are still told that worldly prestige is dust and ashes, but the prestige is now associated with the Athenians Pericles, Codrus, and Cimon rather than with the Assyrian king. The sentiment is translated and made present to suit a conversation in Athens; the fiction of the Eastern king is given up. And so is the fiction of the epitaph; Choerilus' σποδός ('dust') makes it into the text of Pseudo-Alexis and may remind us of its epitaphic heritage, but the text of Pseudo-Alexis constitutes a piece of a conversation, not an inscription. As the fragment abandons the illusion of the epitaph, Xanthias in Pseudo-Alexis exhorts with first-person-plural verbs in the present tense: πίνωμεν, ἐμπίνωμεν, ὦ Σίκων, <Σίκων>, | χαίρωμεν, ἕως ἔνεστι τὴν ψυχὴν τρέφειν ('Let's drink! Let's really drink, Sicon, Sicon! Let's enjoy ourselves as long as we can stay happy!'). These are exhortations among the living, where everyone – speaker as well as addressees – can join in the drinking.[100] As we have seen, such exhortations are

---

[98] This and other anti-Epicurean criticisms of the belly are collected by Sedley (1976) 129–31, who also mentions the Pseudo-Alexis fragment at 130 n.42. Many of these texts appear in the sequence Ath. 7.278e–9d, in which Epicurus' adherence to Archestratus is mentioned and several comic passages support the charge.

[99] Barigazzi (1981) on Phoenix of Colophon *CA* 231–2, *fr.* 1 *apud* Ath. 12.530e–531a. A recent commentary of the fragment is provided by Claudio de Stefani at Sider (2017) 518–24. Barigazzi (1981) 33–4 suggests that Phoenix of Colophon *CA* 234, *fr.* 3 *apud* Ath. 10.421d, which shares the theme, may be a fragment of the same work. Cf. Perri (2011).

[100] Cf. pages 16–17 in the Introduction for a discussion of *AP* 7.452 = Leonidas 67 *HE*, where the adhortative πίνωμεν interrupts the epitaphic mode.

The Professor of Desire, Sardanapallus in Rome

evocative of sympotic poetry which urges symposiasts to enjoyment (Ion of Chios *fr.* 27): πίνωμεν, παίζωμεν· ἴτω διὰ νυκτὸς ἀοιδή, ὀρχείσθω τις ('let's drink, let's fool around; let singing continue through the night, let someone dance'). The theatrical performance seems to approximate the performative quality of lyric *carpe diem*: leaving behind the heritage of stones and inscriptions, the comedic fragment seems to enact present enjoyment.[101] And yet, also this passage in the tradition of Sardanapallus is at least as much about reading *carpe diem* as it is about performing *carpe diem*. The forgery imagines a scene never to be performed, but always to be read by anti-Epicureans with scorn; they neither hear the call πίνωμεν at the symposium, where they can enact it, nor do they watch it on stage, where others perform it, but they read *carpe diem* and reject it.

It is not only Pseudo-Alexis who inserts the Sardanapallus epitaph into character speech.[102] Sardanapallus' epitaph continued to fascinate readers, and still in Latin epic we find a version of it inserted. Rabirius was an epic poet who probably lived under Augustus and wrote a work that included a description of Mark Antony's death.[103] Seneca provides a quotation from this scene along with some context (Sen. *Ben.* 6.31 quoting Rab. *poet. fr.* 2 Courtney, *FLP* = 2 Blänsdorf, *FPL* = 231 Hollis, *FRP*):

egregie mihi uidetur M. Antonius apud Rabirium poetam, cum fortunam suam transeuntem alio uideat et sibi nihil relictum praeter ius mortis, id quoque, si cito occupauerit, exclamare:
hoc habeo, quodcumque dedi.

I think that in the poet Rabirius Mark Antony put it very well, when he witnessed that his fortune went to someone else and that nothing was left to him except the right to determine his own death, and that too only if he seized it quickly; then he exclaimed: 'I have whatever I have given away.'

Only half a hexameter survives of Rabirius' scene of Mark Antony's death. The commentators have long noticed that this fragment adapts and reverses Cicero's translation of the

---
[101] See Lowrie (2009a) 70 on links between performative discourse and performance media.
[102] For Callimachus, see page 65.
[103] See *OCD* s.v. 'Rabirius' no. 2, Hollis, *FRP* 384–5.

Sardanapallus epitaph by addition of one letter (*Tusc.* 5.101):[104] *haec habeo, quae edi, quaeque exsaturata libido | hausit; at illa iacent multa et praeclara relicta* ('*I have what I ate* and all the kinks I enjoyed fully. But my many well-known possessions are gone'). The main point of Rabirius' fragment is apparently to contrast Mark Antony's well-known generosity with Sardanapallus' self-centred hedonism; it is his generosity that gives Mark Antony lasting benefits.[105] Whether it would have mattered for Rabirius' poem that both Sardanapallus and Mark Antony committed suicide as the control of a world empire was slipping away from them cannot be said with certainty on the basis of the short fragment. But what we can say is that Rabirius lets Mark Antony virtually speak a 'self-epitaph';[106] that is, the résumé that Mark Antony draws at the end of his life consciously evokes the form of a tomb inscription. For we can find the words of the Sardanapallus epitaph also as a motif on Roman tomb inscriptions (Courtney (1995) 160, no. 169 = *CLE* 244 = *CIL* vi 18131): *quod edi bibi, mecum habeo, quod reliqui perdidi* ('I have what I ate and drank. I have lost what I left behind'). Another Roman proclaims on his epitaph in Sardanapallus' fashion that 'he has everything' (*omnia se habet*), before he lists sensuous pleasures.[107] The Sardanapallus epitaph was, then, both part of discussions in Roman philosophy about the good life, as Cicero attests, and a very real material presence, as the epitaphs show which extol the lasting benefits of the hedonistic life (not all of them may have thought of Sardanapallus, but for a leaned reader the link is clear).

Scholars have noticed how epitaphic gestures in Vergil and other poets are important techniques through which poets engage with epigrammatic qualities, such as the medium of written text, its public nature, the materiality of everlasting

---

[104] For example, Courtney, *FLP ad loc.*, and in particular Dahlmann (1983–7) ii.17–19 in more detail.
[105] Thus Courtney, *FLP ad loc.* pointing to Plu. *Ant.* 4.7, 43.5, 67.8.
[106] Hollis, *FRP* in his commentary on page 386.
[107] *CIL* vi 15258 with Busch (1999) 523–5, who notes that *habet* in this epitaph picks up the phrasing of the Sardanapallus epitaph. Courtney (1995) 369 notes that the sentiment is also paralleled at *CLE* 187 = *CIL* ix 2114 (*quod comedi et ebibi, tantum meu est*), *CLE* 2207 = *CIL* iii 14524 (*quot comidi, mecum aue[o]*). Cf. Kajanto (1969) 363.

The Professor of Desire, Sardanapallus in Rome

stone, or the role of the reader.[108] Rabirius, in turn, joins an epigrammatic tradition of rewriting the Sardanapallus epitaph; Crates, Chrysippus, and others have rewritten the Sardanapallus epitaph in order to flaunt their philosophies, which stand in opposition to Sardanapallus' lifestyle. As Rabirius lets Mark Antony look at his past life at one of the most momentous points of Roman history, we are invited to compare him with Sardanapallus, whose epitaph espouses momentary pleasures and *carpe diem*. The gesture towards epitaphs, texts which by their very nature keep people in memory and memorialise them, here becomes also part of an intertextual memory that looks back at the various versions and rewritings of the Sardanapallus epitaph.[109] Rabirius' adaption of the Sardanapallus epitaph brings us to Augustan Rome. In the next chapter we will turn to *carpe diem* poetry under (and about) Augustus.

This chapter has traced the archaeology of *carpe diem*, as Greeks try to make sense of a monument in Cilicia. Their reading of the monument proved extremely influential. Sardanapallus is made to stand at the beginning of a tradition of *carpe diem*, and anyone else – whether it is the philosopher Epicurus or someone who chose similar sentiments on his tombstone – becomes part of a constructed genealogy of *carpe diem* which begins with the legendary Assyrian king. At least since the Greeks saw a monument in Anchiale in 333 BC, Sardanapallus' *carpe diem* has been associated with reading and writing. In reading his inscription, Greeks wrote it, and the subsequent history of the Sardanapallus epitaph has been one of rewriting it by adopting epigrammatic conventions. And yet, some of these texts also evoke presence and performance: Choerilus' Sardanapallus epitaph speaks in the present tense.[110] Though it is centuries old, Sardanapallus' enjoyment is always present.

---

[108] See, in particular, Dinter (2005) on Vergil's *Aeneid* and its models, with bibliography. Cf. Breed (2006) on Vergil's *Eclogues*, especially chapter 3, and Bettenworth (2016) on Latin elegy, especially the methodological considerations in chapter 3.

[109] For what it is worth, a statue of James I greets visitors to the Bodleian Library with Rabirius' epigram as James is giving books to statues that represent fame and the university: *haec habeo quae dedi* (and *haec habeo quae scripsi*; see Reid (1925) 212–13).

[110] Cf. Culler (2015) 283–95 on the present tense in lyric.

The Archaeology of *Carpe Diem*

A Roman statue provides a postscript to Sardanapallus' story. Sardanapallus continued to fascinate and one Roman, who may have regarded Sardanapallus as a model of hedonism, wrote the name ΣΑΡΔΑΝΑΠΑΛΛΟΣ upon a Dionysus statue, thus effectively transforming the god of wine into the Assyrian king (Figure 1.1).[111]

Figure 1.1 Statue of 'Dionysus Sardanapallus'
Rome, Vatican Museum, Sala della Biga, Inv. 2363

[111] The statue, now in the Vatican Museum (Sala della Biga, Inv. 2363), dates back to Claudian times, and was found in the so-called villa of Cato Uticensis at Frascati. The name of

The Professor of Desire, Sardanapallus in Rome

Another misinterpretation of a statue (in this case perhaps a conscious one), another inscription added to a statue finally allows a Roman to be in the material presence of Sardanpallus.

Sardanapallus was not added by the sculptor, but later (though still in antiquity). The statue is a copy of a type that is dubbed Dionysus-Sardanapallus and goes back to an original from classical Athens. See, above all, Megow at *LIMC* suppl. viii.1075–6 s.v. 'Sardanapallos'. Cf. Weißbach at *RE* i.A2 col.2473–4 s.v. 'Sardanapal', Bernhardt (2009) 21 and his figure 4, Rollinger (2017) 578.

2

A MOVEABLE FEAST

Wine Storage Places as Drinkable Calendars in Horace

It is a truth universally acknowledged that Horace wrote his poems in order to provide posterity with quotations for any circumstance. A particularly well-known example of quoting Horace is the story of Patrick Leigh Fermor and the German general who bonded over Horace during the Second World War.[1] In 1944, Fermor abducted the German commander of Crete, General Karl Heinrich Kreipe. As they climb up Mount Ida, General Kreipe looks at the mountain and quotes the beginning of Horace, *Odes* 1.9: *Vides ut alta stet niue candidum Soracte* ('do you see how Mount Soracte stands there glistening with deep snow?'). Fermor overhears the quotation and responds by quoting the rest of the poem. According to Fermor, he and his prisoner looked at each other 'as though, for a long moment, the war had ceased to exist'.[2] As Kreipe and Fermor quote Horace's *carpe diem* poem and form a strange bond between enemies in the middle of the Second World War, they resemble Diomedes and Glaucus, who meet on the battlefield before Troy and discuss how *leaves that are green turn to brown*.

If we wish to understand the appeal of the *carpe diem* motif, which created an Iliadic encounter in the Second World War, the two most common interpretations of the motif will not do: neither if we regard this motif as a banal call to drinks nor if we regard it as Epicurean will we understand *carpe diem*. In Chapter 1 as well as in the Introduction I showed in detail why the *carpe diem* motif is not Epicurean, and it is unnecessary to repeat the arguments here.[3] Rather, it seems profitable to focus on the ways through which

---

[1] In turn much quoted in Horatian scholarship: Ziolkowski (2005) 183–4, Holzberg (2009) 11–12, Edmunds (2010) 343–4, Mayer (2012) 113.
[2] Fermor (2002) [1977] 73–4.
[3] See pages 20–1 and 63–71. Nonetheless, Epicurean interpretations of Horace's *carpe diem* abound; see, for example, Conte (1994) [1987] 307–8, Lefèvre (1993a) 207–9, Moles (2007) 168.

A Moveable Feast

Horace's *carpe diem* creates effects of presence. Fermor claims that, after the quotation of the poem, 'for a long moment, the war had ceased to exist'. *Carpe diem* thematises precisely such present moments in time. In the Soracte ode, Horace thus tells his addressee to focus on the banquet in the present and to leave everything else to the gods, who will at some point calm the storm that rages outside (*C.* 1.9.9–12). So, too, for Fermor and the German general the intense present moment that the poem evokes makes them forget the storm of war that rages through the world. If, then, the poem is about a moment in time, it is equally important that such a moment is repeatable: Mount Ida can stand in for Mount Soracte. Memory makes moments repeatable. Thus, Fermor notes that he and the general 'had both drunk at the same fountains long before'.[4] For Horace, however, it is a different drink that triggers the recollection of the past: not water from clear fountains, but wine.

Time and *carpe diem* have been recognised as crucial themes of Horace's poetry.[5] In this and the next chapter I will analyse the concept of time we find in Horace's *carpe diem* poems. I will argue that we can find the essence of his *carpe diem* in wine and words. This in itself may be hardly surprising, but I hope to show how Horace's treatment of wine and words allows him to write *carpe diem* poems which could have never been created in early Greece. I argue that it is precisely through his choice of wine and words that Horace thematises presence, present time, enjoyment, performance, and reperformance in his *carpe diem* poems. Thus, in the Soracte ode, Horace addresses a certain Thaliarchus and asks him to 'serve the four-year-old wine more generously than usual from its Sabine jar' (*C.* 1.9.6–8):

---

[4] Compare and contrast the different reaction of Byron's Childe Harold with Edmunds (1992) 71–4; when the Childe reaches Mount Soracte, he regrets that his classical education had only prepared him 'to understand, not love' Horace's lyric.

[5] I note here only studies solely dedicated to these themes. Time: Gagliardi (1975–6), Deschamps (1983), Ancona (1994), Schwindt (2004b; also 2005b: 15–18), Broccia (2007), Evans (2016), Vogt-Spira (2017), Citti at *EO* ii.645–53 s.v. 'tempo' (also Citti (2000) 54–64). *Carpe diem*: Bardon (1944), D'Anna (1979), Pöschl (1992). Bardon diagnoses Horace with a melancholic soul; D'Anna describes the motif as Epicurean; Pöschl analyses Horace's 'Lebenskunst' biographically. Neither of these approaches convinced me. For a short but learned account on death, time, and *carpe diem* in Horace, Traina (1975–98) [1985] v.134–43 repays reading. Davis (1991) 145–88 offers a rich analysis of the rhetorical scope of Horatian *carpe diem*.

77

benignius | deprome quadrimum Sabina, | o Thaliarche, merum diota. This is the exhortation to *carpe diem* in the poem. Horace evokes the present moment through his usage of wine and words; a wine from four years back points to the ever-changing nature of the year, and its presence at the symposium spreads enjoyment. The Greek word Horace uses to describe the jar, *diota*, is an informal word, which underlines the intimate setting and Horace's concern for the immediate present.[6]

This chapter analyses wine in Horace – hardly, of course, an overlooked topic.[7] Yet the connection between wine and time has received less attention, though Ernst Schmidt and Courtney Evans made valuable contributions to this aspect of wine.[8] In this chapter, I will analyse wine as a key element in Horace's *carpe diem* poems. The chapter falls into four sections. In the first section, I will show how Horace's old wines can paradoxically create effects of presence and contribute to enjoyable moments in the present time. In the second section, I turn to reperformance and show how old wines repeat occasions of the past. The third section argues that wine storage places function as a drinkable consular calendar in Horace. The fourth section shows how wine can preserve the taste of old words. I will pay close attention to Roman wine labels, painted inscriptions on amphorae, so that this chapter does not fully leave the epigraphic territory of the preceding one.

2.1 Wine O'Clock: The Present Moment in Horace, *Epodes* 13

Before Horace made *carpe diem* poems one of the leitmotifs of the *Odes*, he already wrote a poem of this kind in the *Epodes* (for *carpe diem* in the *Sermones*, see Section 2 of Chapter 5).[9] In *Epodes* 13, a raging storm prompts the poet to reflections on

---

[6] The argument of Gitner (2012) 112–15. As I serve the four-year-old Sabine wine of *Odes* 1.9 here only as an aperitif in the introduction, I will not point to the enormous bibliography on this poem.

[7] See Pierson (1860), Kießling (1867) 5–8, Gemoll (1892) 97–104, Apperson (1905), McKinlay (1946; 1947), Commager (1957), A. Richter (1970), Frieman (1972), Griffin (1985) 65–87, Murray (1985), Davis (1991: 145–88; 2007), La Penna (1995), Broccia (2006), Mundt (2018) 99–115, Fedeli at *EO* ii.262–9 s.v. 'vino'. For wine as a poetological image in Greek poetry, see Nünlist (1998) 199–205.

[8] Schmidt (2002) [1980] 248–65, Evans (2016) 127–245.   [9] See Davis (1991) 146–50.

The Present Moment in Horace, *Epodes* 13

mortality and to drinking while it is still possible (I quote the first eight lines).

> Horrida tempestas caelum contraxit et imbres
> niuesque deducunt Iouem; nunc mare, nunc siluae
> Threicio Aquilone sonant. rapiamus, amici,[10]
> occasionem de die, dumque uirent genua
> et decet, obducta soluatur fronte senectus.   (5)
> tu uina Torquato moue consule pressa meo.
> cetera mitte loqui: deus haec fortasse benigna
> reducet in sedem uice.

A chilling storm has given the sky a gloomy appearance, and the god of the sky is overcast by rain and snow. Now the sea, now the forests resound with the Thracian North Wind. Friends, let's snatch the opportunity from the day! And while our legs are vigorous and it's proper, let the old wrinkles relax on the overcast face. You, get wine that was pressed in my birthyear when Torquatus was consul. Don't talk of anything else; perhaps a god will bring a welcome change and let this turbulence settle.

August Meineke said that the whole poem exhales the spirit of a Greek model. The wine with the consular date, however, reeks of pure Romanness:[11] the dating of vintages according to consular dates is a decidedly Roman custom, which this chapter will discuss in some detail. In Rome, the names of consuls were visible on amphorae as part of some sort of wine label. These are often referred to as *tituli picti* in scholarship, while ancient sources call them *pittacia* (Petron. 5.34), *notae* (Hor. *C.* 2.3.8), or *tituli* (Juv. 5.34). There is ample evidence for wine labels and the practice of naming vintage wines after consuls in both literary and epigraphic sources.[12] But while the careful blending of Greek symposia with Roman *conuiuia* is characteristic for Horace's

---

[10] Shackleton Bailey (2001) prints the conjecture *Amici* (vocative singular of the proper name Amicius) of Housman (1972) [1923] iii.1087, which attempts to resolve the supposedly undesirable switch from plural to singular addressees. This conjecture is also recommended by Brink (1982b) 41–2. Other conjectures have been suggested. Yet, commands to one person (even after plural verbs) make good sense in the context of the banquet: Cavarzere (1992) 202 points to Alc. *fr.* 346.

[11] L. C. Watson (2003) 423 notes that the wine defies the statement of Meineke (1854) xxii: *totum carmen Graecum exemplar spirat*. Still, for some notably Greek features of the poem, in particular allusions to Alc. *fr.* 338, see Cavarzere (1992) 200 with further sources.

[12] See Pl. *Poen.* 834–8, Cat. 68.28, Cic. *Brut.* 287–8, Hor. *C.* 3.8.12, 3.21.1, 3.28.8, *Epod.* 13.6, *S.* 1.10.24, *Epist.* 1.5.4, Tib. 2.1.27, Vell. 2.7.5, Luc. 4.379, Petron. 34.6, Plin. *Nat.*

A Moveable Feast

Greek-style Latin lyric,[13] the question arises as to why Horace mentions this particular wine, or, in other words: what is the significance of a wine that is as old as he is? Scholars have rightly argued that the age of the wine matters, but while some of their interpretations advance our understanding of the wine, other interpretations are rather elaborate.[14] In contrast, my interpretation is extremely simple: the wine is chosen because it is delicious, that is to say, it is the right moment to drink a wine of this age. This seems the most natural reason for choosing a particular vintage. Thus, we can infer from Cicero that a Falernian wine from the preceding year might be too young, and one from the consulship of Opimius or Anicius might be so old that it has lost its sweetness or is not even drinkable anymore (*Brut.* 287). When Horace specifies the vintage, he asks for a vintage between these extremes of first youth or excessive maturation, a wine that is at its prime for drinking.[15]

If we accept that the wine is chosen because it is at the right age for being drunk, this neatly underlines the *carpe diem* motif of the

---

14.55, Mart. 1.26.7, 1.105, 2.40.5, 3.26.3, 3.82.24, 9.87.1, 10.49.2, 13.113.1, Juv. 5.30–1, and Galen *Ant.* 2.15 = xiv.25–6 Kühn. For epigraphic evidence, Rigato and Mongardi (2016) offer a catalogue of Roman wine labels. Also see the labels at *CIL* iv 2551–880 (and in particular 2551–61 for consular dates), xv 4529–8998, Warmington (1935–40) iv.208–11, Crawford (2012). Cf. Dressel (1878) 167, Marquardt and Mau (1964) [1886] 462–3, Gemoll (1892) 101–2, Blümner (1911) 152, Callender (1965) 5–6, Courtney (1980a) at Juv. 5.28 (and already the scholiasts on that passage: Grazzini (2011–18) 246), Tchernia (1986) 30–1, appendix 2, 321–41, Weeber (1993) 25–6, Nisbet and Rudd (2004) 247–8, Desbat (2004), Stein-Hölkeskamp (2005) 203–11, Thurmond (2017) 206.

[13] See, for example, *C.* 1.20 with Commager (1962) 325–6, and *C.* 1.9, briefly mentioned in the introduction of this chapter. For Horace's transformation of the Greek symposium, see Murray (1985).

[14] Kilpatrick (1970) is particularly laboured; according to him, the poem describes how Horace offers a wine from his own birth year to Cassius at the latter's birthday on the eve of Philippi. None of this has any basis in the poem, as L. C. Watson (2003) 418 notes. Other suggestions are that Horace serves a precious wine for a precious friend who is to be identified with Maecenas, and the wine from the year of his birth also links him with Achilles, who is called an *alumnus* (Lyne (2005) 5, 10, 18–19); the poem may be set on Horace's own birthday (Mankin (1995) *ad loc.*). I profited especially from the following readings: the wine evokes mortality (Lowrie (1992) 416); the wine marks Horace as ordinarily Roman, in contrast to Achilles (Mankin (1995) *ad loc.*); the age of the wine lets Horace reflect on his life (Schmidt (2002) [1980] 249–50). Recently, Evans (2016) 192–4 argued that Chiron's advice to Achilles in the second half of the poem takes place on the day Achilles was born and is thus connected to the wine from Horace's year of birth.

[15] For ideal drinking ages of various grapes, see Ath. 1.26c–27d. For luxurious wine as old as the person drinking it, see Sen. *Dial.* 10.17.2.

The Present Moment in Horace, *Epodes* 13

poem in several ways. First, the wine is strongly identified with Horace; it is pressed in the year he was born, the year of *his* consul Torquatus: *uina Torquato* [...] *consule pressa meo*. Horace's year of birth and the wine are interwoven in the chiastic line. Wine and Horace are identified.[16] In the preceding lines, Horace stresses that now is the right time for him and his companions to enjoy themselves, before the advent of gloomy old age. Given the close temporal identification of Horace with his wine, the wine might be on the verge of becoming too old to be still drinkable, and the link between Horace and wine invites readers to transfer the feared prospect of grievous old age to the wine. Indeed, the description of old wine as a metaphorical old man is conventional and arguably would have made the connection between Horace's age and the age of the wine easier.[17] Horace is the wine. The same moment calls them to enjoyment in *Epodes* 13.

There is one more side to the wine. Before Horace mentions the wine, he exhorts his companions to 'snatch the opportunity from the day' (3): *rapiamus, amici,* | *occasionem de die*. Horace here translates the Greek concept of καιρός, the opportune time or right moment. The expression exudes the Greek spirit that August Meineke discerned in the poem. The καιρός must be seized before it passes by. The divine allegory of Καιρός illustrates the point well: the young god Καιρός has a lock of hair in his front, which can be snatched, but he is bald on his back.[18] In Latin, *occasio* is the proper translation for καιρός, and the act of snatching also looks back to Greek models where expressions such as καιρὸν λαμβάνειν are common, as Alfonso Traina has observed.[19]

---

[16] It is generally noted that Horace mentions a wine from the same vintage at *C*. 3.21.1: *O nata mecum consule Manlio*. Schmidt (2002) [1980] 249–50 stresses the identification of the wine with Horace. He, however, argues that Horace asks for a wine from his birth year as he reviews his life, before he is prepared to die in battle (so already Commager (1962) 282). Lowrie (1992) 417–18 says that the poem 'grounds its own writer in existence' by mentioning the vintage.

[17] See, for example, Archestr. *fr.* 59.2–3 Olson and Sens with numerous parallels in their commentary, and Arnott (1970). For the idea of drinking wine before it is too late in Horace, see *C.* 2.14.25–8.

[18] The *locus classicus* for this depiction of Καιρός is an epigram of Posidippus, which describes a statue by Lysippus (*APl* 275 = Posidippus 142 Austin and Bastianini). For καιρός, see Trédé-Boulmer (2015).

[19] Traina (1973) 7–8, quoting A. *Sept.* 65 (cf. Babcock (1978) 110). Traina notes that καιρὸν ἁρπάζειν is not used in Greek before Plu. *Phil.* 15. For *occasio* as a translation of

81

Horace's exhortation to snatch the right moment is followed by the exhortation to get hold of the particular wine. This suggests that the wine, too, is opportune, and that it is the right moment to drink it. As we have seen, the wine is as much a date, a unit of time, as it is something to drink. As Horace talks about time in *Epodes* 13, he blends a Greek concept of time with a Roman dating system.

The wine in *Epodes* 13 is opportune and should be drunk in this moment. This present quality of the wine needs stressing. It is perhaps natural to focus on the past when it comes to old wines, and this chapter will indeed also consider how vintage wines allow Horace to include the past in his banquets. But equally important is the present nature of wine: it can be drunk once and then it is gone. As we have seen in *Epodes* 13, a vintage wine can present an opportune moment in the present time, a wine that must be drunk now (cf. Hor. *C.* 1.37.1–6). In Horace's exhortation to *carpe diem* in *Epodes* 13, the wine evokes the present time.

2.2 Drinking Again and Thinking of When: Reperformance in *Odes* 3.8

In this section, I wish to look in some more detail at vintage wines as a calendrical mechanism in Horace. *Odes* 3.8 already features a date in its *incipit* and might thus be well suited for an analysis of wine as a dating mechanism:

> Martiis caelebs quid agam kalendis,
> quid uelint flores et acerra turis
> plena miraris positusque carbo in
> caespite uiuo,
>
> docte sermones utriusque linguae: (5)
> uoueram dulcis epulas et album
> Libero caprum prope funeratus
> arboris ictu.

καιρός, see *Distichs of Cato* 2.26, Phaedr. 5.8, Ausonius *Epigrams* 12 Green. In Latin, the allegory undergoes a gender change from masculine καιρός to feminine *occasio*. The peculiar hairstyle of the Opportunity is arguably as strange for female allegories as it is for male ones (*RE* x.2 col.1516 s.v. 'Kairos': 'recht unästhetisch'). Also cf. Plin. *Nat.* 14.142, who tells us that in his time drunkards commonly claimed 'to snatch life' (*rapere se ita uitam praedicant*).

Reperformance in *Odes* 3.8

hic dies anno redeunte festus
corticem adstrictum pice dimouebit (10)
amphorae fumum bibere institutae
   consule Tullo.

sume, Maecenas, cyathos amici
sospitis centum et uigiles lucernas
perfer in lucem: procul omnis esto (15)
   clamor et ira.

mitte ciuilis super urbe curas:
occidit Daci Cotisonis agmen,
Medus infestus sibi luctuosis
   dissidet armis, (20)

seruit Hispanae uetus hostis orae
Cantaber sera domitus catena,
iam Scythae laxo meditantur arcu
   cedere campis.

neglegens, ne qua populus laboret, (25)
parce priuatus nimium cauere et
dona praesentis cape laetus horae:
   linque seuera.

Although you are well-versed in both Greek and Latin discourses, you are puzzled what a single like me is doing on the first of March? And what the point of the flowers is? And why the boxes are full of incense? And why there are charcoals on the altar of fresh turf? The reason is, I had vowed to Liber a delicious meal and a white goat when a tree almost struck me and sent me six feet under. As the year comes round, this holiday will remove the cork that had been sealed with pitch from an amphora which was taught to drink smoke under the consulship of Tullus.

    Raise a hundred toasts, Maecenas, to the rescue of your friend and keep the lights burning till daylight. Here's no place for shouting and anger. Don't worry about the domestic affairs of the city. The army of Cotiso the Dacian has fallen. The hostile Medes tear one another apart with weapons that bring themselves grief. The Cantabrian, our old enemy on the Spanish coast, is finally conquered and in chains. The Scythians have now unstrung their bows and are preparing to withdraw from their plains.

    Stop caring if the Roman people is in trouble; don't be too concerned: you're not a politician. Be happy and take the gifts of the present hour. Let go of serious matters.

A Moveable Feast

'This ode begins with a parody of an aetiology', Nisbet and Rudd state.[20] As they point out, this manner of aetiology is closely linked to the Roman calendar, and Ovid's *Fasti* provides the best example for this type of literature. Indeed, the *Fasti* also includes an aetiology for the Calends of March (1 March), that is, the *Matronalia*, a holiday for Juno Lucina. Ovid asks Mars why mothers celebrate the first day of March (Ov. *F.* 3.170: *dic mihi matronae cur tua festa colant*). Questions about a celebration also prompt the aetiology in Horace, and his sequence of two indirect questions might point to the (mock-) didactic nature of the passage. Pointedly, the questions in the ode arise because Horace celebrates the first day of March as a bachelor, and is thus quite the opposite of Ovid's celebrants.[21] The riddle – impossible to solve for Maecenas despite his Greek and Latin learning – is resolved when Horace reveals that he celebrates his delivery from a fallen tree with an annual holiday (*C.* 3.8.6–12. Cf. *C.* 2.13, 2.17).[22] Horace's new aetiology leads to a re-attribution of the holiday; suddenly, Juno Lucina is not the honoured goddess anymore, but Bacchus (6–7): *uoueram dulcis epulas et album | Libero caprum* ('I had vowed to Liber a delicious meal and a white goat').[23] Bacchus takes over this holiday and, as the following stanza reveals, Bacchus also provides a system for measuring time in this ode.

This day is a yearly recurring feast (9–11): *hic dies anno redeunte festus | corticem adstrictum pice dimouebit | amphorae* ('as the year comes round, this holiday will remove the cork that had been sealed with pitch from an amphora').[24] Such recurring

[20] Nisbet and Rudd (2004) 123.
[21] Nisbet and Rudd (2004) *ad loc.* note the witty enclosure of *caelebs* within *Martiis kalendis*, and point out that Juv. 9.53 speaks of 1 March as *femineis* [...] *Kalendis*. Fulkerson (2017) 77–8 cites numerous references for the *Matronalia*.
[22] Oftentimes there exist both Greek and Latin aetiologies for Roman festivals, as Ov. *F.* 2.359, for instance, testifies for the Lupercalia. Though Greek and Latin learning is essential for identifying calendrical traditions, it is of little use for solving the riddle of Horace's celebration (cf. Fraenkel (1957) 222).
[23] New holidays commemorating events of the recent past became common under Caesar, as Kießling and Heinze (1966) note at *C.* 3.8.9. See Rüpke (2011) [1995b] 124–34 on new holidays instated by or associated with Augustus, and recently again Rüpke (2017) 59–63. Beard (1987) 10–11 argues that one of the fundamental qualities of the Roman calendar is its openness to reinterpretations of festivals. Cf. Feeney (1998) 127–31.
[24] Nisbet and Hubbard (1970) 244 clarified that *anno redeunte* 'in no way implies a first anniversary', which is 'a view that depends on a mistranslation'. For feasts in Horace, see Lieberg (1965).

Reperformance in *Odes* 3.8

feasts often offer a ritualistic reperformance of an original event on which they are supposedly based. Thus, Ovid's *Fasti* explains in some detail that Romans run naked through the town and slap women on the Lupercalia (Ides of February = 15 February) because Romulus and Remus were naked when they once pursued cattle thieves (Ov. *F.* 2.267–380). Similarly, Horace also reperforms his delivery from the falling tree. In the second stanza, Horace mentions that Liber saved him from a tree falling on his head, and Nisbet and Rudd are right to point out that the literal meaning of Lyaeus, 'the loosener', suits the god very well in this context.[25] The following stanza deals with reperformance. This time, not a tree (*arbor*) but one of its constituents, namely rind (*cortex*), is the object that must be removed.[26] *Cortex*, the metonymic, ritualistic signifier, makes way for Bacchus, just as the tree made way for him. When Horace put an amphora into storage and destined it to be drunk on the anniversary of the tree incident, this marked the preparations for the ritualistic reperformance. In other words, 'teaching' the amphora to drink smoke in the storage place, Horace was already 'inaugurating' his celebrations, and this is exactly the double-meaning that is entailed in Horace's use of *institutus*, as Nisbet and Rudd observe (11–12):[27] *amphorae fumum bibere institutae | consule Tullo* ('an amphora which was taught [or inaugurated] to drink smoke under the consulship of Tullus').

Odes 3.8 shows the significance of reperformance for Horace's poetics of the present. The party Horace describes in the poem is a unique moment in present time. At the end of the poem, Horace makes this explicit, as he exhorts Maecenas to 'gladly *take* the gifts of the present hour' (27: *dona praesentis* cape *laetus horae*). This is the exhortation to *carpe diem*.[28] As we have already seen in *Epodes* 13, here, too, an exhortation to seize time is semantically

---

[25] Nisbet and Rudd (2004) *ad loc.*
[26] A comparison between the parallel sentences in Hor. *C.* 3.8.9–11 and *C.* 3.14.13–14 shows that *corticem* is in the place of *atras curas*; the happy holiday removes cork and sorrows to make time for wine. For similarities between the two poems, see Santirocco (1986) 128–31. For wine removing sorrows, see Broccia (2006). For forgetting (and remembering) at banquets, see Hutchinson (2016) 253–4, 267–8.
[27] Nisbet and Rudd (2004) *ad loc.*
[28] As Commager (1962) 244 n.9 notes, the insight into human mortality, a requirement for a *carpe diem* poem, is implied in the cause for the party: Horace's escape from death.

linked with an exhortation to enjoy wine; Horace tells Maecenas earlier in the poem to '*take* a hundred cups' (13–14) (*sume, Maecenas, cyathos amici | sospitis centum*).[29] Yet, the wine is not just the 'gift of the present hour'. It also recreates the enjoyment of the present hour every single year, and in doing so looks back at the fall of the tree, an event from several years ago. Horace is *drinking again and thinking of when* the tree almost killed him. Removing the cork from the bottle creates a reperformance, a ritual, and Horace's own religious calendar.[30] As Horace expresses time through wine, *carpe diem* materialises: enjoying time and enjoying wine becomes the same thing, though this notably entails a strange blend of past and present time.

Every time Horace uses the phrase *dies festus* in the *Odes* and the *Epistles*, he also mentions an old wine (*C.* 2.3.6–7, 3.8.9, 3.14.13, 3.28.1; *Epist.* 1.5.9–10). In Horace, a holiday or festival is more than a time of intense celebration of the present. In the perfectly cyclical Roman calendar in which any *dies festus* is identical to last year's *dies festus* or that of any previous year, celebration of the present is naturally evocative of the past.[31] Vintage wine brings the time of the past to the symposium, and a clear distinction between past and present becomes impossible, as Horace's book poetry conflates occasions of past and present.[32]

The inauguration of Horace's yearly ritual happened under the consulship of Tullus. At this point we encounter a second form of the Roman calendar. As Denis Feeney has reminded us, there existed two types of *fasti*: the calendrical *fasti*, an annual calendar of celebrations (which has concerned us so far in *Odes* 3.8), and

---

[29] The parallel between the present poem and *Epod.* 13 would be even stronger if the *uaria lectio* of *rape* in place of *cape* was accepted at *C.* 3.8.27. Traina (1973) 8–9, following Bentley (1713) *ad loc.*, gives a detailed account on the semantic qualities of the words and why *cape* should be preferred. Cf. Citti (2000) 58–9 and Graziosi (2009) 151–2. Putnam (1996b) brings out the urgency of the exhortations. Lieberg (1965) 414 and Delignon (2017) 85 wish to see an Epicurean sentiment in the exhortation.
[30] Cf. Griffin (1997), Schwindt (2004b) 83–4. Hor. *C.* 3.22 similarly creates a personal religious calendar, as has been analysed by Cairns (1982), J. Henderson (1995), Feeney (1998) 134–5. For the importance of reperformance in Horace, see Barchiesi (2000) 175–6.
[31] See Feeney (2007) 158–63 on the identity of dates in different years of Caesar's calendar.
[32] See, in particular, Schmidt (2002) [1980] 264–5 on occasion, wine, and celebrations. Cf. Lieberg (1965), A. Richter (1970) 5–6, Griffin (1997), O'Gorman (2002) 90–3, Evans (2016) 245.

Reperformance in *Odes* 3.8

the consular *fasti*, a list of Roman magistrates that denotes years.³³ The date 'under the consulship of Tullus' can refer to the year 66 BC as well as to the year 33 BC. While older commentaries generally favour the earlier date, with the somewhat artificial reasoning that Horace often mentions older wines, Nisbet and Hubbard as well as Ernst Schmidt have made the compelling point that *consule Tullo* gives us a date for the tree incident, so that 33 BC is almost certainly the right date.³⁴ Indeed, since the storage of the wine marks the inauguration of Horace's annual festival, this seems sensible: the *cortex* that Horace removes from the amphora dates back to the tree incident. Wood from that year is again removed, and wine from that year signifies freedom.³⁵

As Schmidt says, dating events by wine is typical for Horace.³⁶ Yet, this is a peculiar system of dating and deserves further scrutiny. For it is one thing to say that '1945 is the year that marked the end of the Second World War', but it is an altogether different thing to say this: 'Château Mouton Rothschild of 1945 is a stellar example [*sc.* of a truly great vintage] and to celebrate the Allied victory and mark the return of Baron Philippe to his estates, he [i.e., Baron Philippe de Rothschild] commissioned the artist Philippe Jullian to illustrate the wine's label with the 'V' for Victory.'³⁷ In the latter case the Allied victory is contextualised through an outstanding wine vintage, and more specifically through a peculiar wine label: a unique moment in history becomes recallable through a wine, which some people still buy and drink today. In Rome, most wines were probably drunk after a minimal time of maturation.³⁸ Yet, vintage wines also existed and they took their names from the consuls of the year of the vintage, or of the year when the wine was transferred from the *dolium* to the

---

[33] Feeney (2007) 166–9. Cf. Wolkenhauer (2011) 190–1.
[34] Schmidt (2002) [1980] 258–60. The later date was first suggested by Ensor (1902) 210. Nisbet and Hubbard (1970) 244 first suggested a connection between the date of the wine and the tree incident. The earlier date is favoured by Kießling and Heinze (1966) *ad loc.*, Syndikus (1972–3) ii.106.
[35] Did the rind come from the very tree that almost killed Horace?
[36] Schmidt (2002) [1980] 248–65, Evans (2016) 127–245.
[37] www.idealwine.info/2015/05/08/1945-the-victory-year/. In the following years, well-known artists, among them Picasso, Chagall, and Warhol, would design the wine label for each new vintage of Mouton Rothschild – perhaps the most artistic take on wine labels since Horace.
[38] Tchernia (1986) 29–30, Thurmond (2017) 189.

amphora, or both. This is natural enough; after all, the names of consuls *were* the year, as Feeney says,[39] and a date *ab urbe condita* for wine would have been absurd.[40] In the case of *Odes* 3.8, the year 33 BC would have been known to Romans as 'Imp. Caesar Diui f. and L. Volcatius Tullus'. Wines sometimes took the name of only one of the two consuls.[41] For 33 BC, the year in question, Tullus was the only sensible choice out of the two, as Augustus accumulated a total of thirteen consulships (eleven of them by the publication of the tribiblos), so that it seems impossible to put his name elegantly into poetry.[42] These practical considerations do not mean that Augustus is altogether absent: the date 'under the consulship of Tullus' refers to a year in which Augustus was consul, a year that was named after him. Thus, Augustus is present, however elusively. Horace's worries and the danger to his life are gone, and when he marks this day Augustus is somewhere there.[43] But probably Horace would warn us not to ask where exactly Augustus is, just as he in fact warns Maecenas not to ask about the political state of the empire (*C.* 3.8.15–28): everything is taken care of and must not be mentioned at the banquet.

2.3 Horace's *Fasti*: Wine Storage Places at *C.* 3.8 (again), *C.* 2.3, *C.* 3.28

Consular wines are a synonym for vintage wines. This is exactly the punchline in the following epigram of Martial (13.111):

> De Sinuessanis uenerunt Massica prelis:
> condita quo quaeris consule? nullus erat.

---

[39] Feeney (2007) 171.
[40] Though, for contextualisation, Pliny *Nat.* 14.55 gives an additional *ab urbe condita* date for the famous Opimian wine.
[41] Nisbet and Rudd (2004) at *C.* 3.21.1, citing Plin. *Nat.* 14.94. For epigraphic evidence, see, for example, *CIL* iv 9313 (= Rigato and Mongardi (2016) 113, no. 51).
[42] Horace manages to describe the wine label 'second consulship of Taurus' at *Epist.* 1.5.4: *uina bibes* iterum Tauro *diffusa*. Mentioning the number of a consulship is common on actual wine labels, for example, *CIL* iv 2554–9.
[43] Cf. Hor. *Epod.* 9.37–8, *C.* 3.14 (discussed below). In *C.* 4.5, Horace explicitly mentions that Augustus drives out any cares. Syndikus (1972–3) ii.108 says that in *C.* 3.8 the carefree life points to Augustus, though he is not named (cf. Griffin (1997) 58). Yet the wine label does and does not include Schrödinger's Caesar. See page 89 for an actual wine label from 33 BC, which does not include Augustus.

Wine Storage Places at *C.* 3.8, *C.* 2.3, *C.* 3.28

Massic wine has come from Sinuessan presses. You are asking under which consul it was put to storage? There wasn't any.

The hyperbole is telling. A wine that predates the existence of consuls is an absurd impossibility in more than one sense; it is not only unrealistic but also subverts the whole system. A wine that predates the Republic also predates Roman time and, in particular, Roman oenological time.[44]

As we have seen, wine labels, which were painted on amphorae, are commonly mentioned in literary sources, and just over 160 such labels are known to have survived.[45] Among the existing wine labels, we also have a label for the wine Horace mentions in *Odes* 3.8, the vintage dating back to 33 BC (*CIL* xv 4566):[46]

FVN. P.
L. TULL. L. AUT
COS

The abbreviations stand for *Fun(danum). P(asianum)* | *L. Tull(o). L. Aut(ronio)* | *co(n)s(ulibus)*, so that the label refers to a wine from Fundi from the year when L. Volcacius Tullus and L. Autronius Paetus were consuls, the latter a suffect consul.[47] As wine labels were most commonly written in ink, they faded over time. At *Odes* 3.8.11–12, Horace says that his wine bottle was taught to drink smoke: *amphorae fumum bibere institutae* | *consule Tullo* ('an amphora which was taught to drink smoke under the consulship of Tullus'). 'Drinking smoke' refers to a Roman way of storing wine; Nisbet and Rudd note that Romans sometimes stored wine in an *apotheca* under the roof, where smoke supposedly improved

---

[44] This is also the point in 13.117, where Martial says that he has an amphora from the time of Nestor, which 'can bear any name you please'. Cf. Mart. 1.105, where an amphora is so old that it has lost its label.
[45] Helpfully collected by Rigato and Mongardi (2016). See page 79 n.12 for wine labels in literary and epigraphical sources as well as in scholarship.
[46] Rigato and Mongardi (2016) 111, no. 29. The second inscription of the amphora reads: *Fund(ani)* uel *fundi). Pasiani. A[e]mil(–).* | *(amphora) III* | *Tull(o). et A[ut]ron(io). co(n)s(ulibus).* Another wine label from this year is *CIL* viii 22640, 3 (= Rigato and Mongardi (2016) 121, no. 115). Some fragmentary labels which mention Augustus could date to 33 BC as well as any other year in which he held the consulate (Rigato and Mongardi (2016) 125, no. 159–61).
[47] Autronius Paetus became suffect consul when Augustus stepped down as consul on 1 January. For consuls and suffects of this year, see Bodel (1995) 287–9. For wines from Fundi, see Plin. *Nat.* 14.65, Mart. 13.113.

89

its taste.[48] Whether or not this was the case, at any rate the smoking process changed both the taste of the wine and the appearance of the amphora. The older an amphora is, the darker its label, so that the past becomes gradually more illegible.[49] The taste of the wine becomes smokier as well as stronger, while the liquid diminishes.[50] When Horace serves a wine which has 'drunk smoke' in *Odes* 3.8 he and Maecenas will be able to taste the past gone by.

Some wealthy Romans owned thousands of amphorae (Varro *De uita populi Romani fr.* 125a Riposati *apud* Plin. *Nat.* 14.96 and *fr.* 125b *apud* Nonius 544 Mercier, Hor. *S.* 2.3.115–17, Galen *Ant.* 2.15 = xiv.25–6 Kühn).[51] Seneca therefore speaks of 'storehouses filled with the vintages of many ages' (*Epist.* 114.26): *aspice ueteraria nostra et plena multorum saeculorum uindemiis horrea: unum putas uideri uentrem cui tot consulum regionumque uina cluduntur?* ('Look at our grand crus and the storehouses that are filled with the vintages of many ages. Do you think that the wines of so many consular years and so many regions were put into storage for the enjoyment of a single belly?'). Elsewhere he notes that old wines were stored according to taste and age (*Nat.* 4B.13.3: *ueteraria per sapores aetatesque disponere*; 'to store vintage wines by type and age'). The sight of such storage places, then, resembled a huge, drinkable consular calendar, possibly no less spectacular than Augustus' famous *Fasti Capitolini*. Consular calendars were essentially lists of past consuls: an orderly sequence of yearly dates denoted by the names of the consuls for each year. We can also discern in other contexts the underlying grid of the consular calendar; the best-known example is arguably

---

[48] Nisbet and Rudd (2004) *ad loc.*, Tchernia and Brun (1999) 136–8 with numerous further references.
[49] Cf. Mart. 1.105, Juv. 5.33–5: *cras bibet Albanis aliquid de montibus aut de | Setinis, cuius patriam titulumque senectus | deleuit multa ueteris fuligine testae.*
[50] The most famous old wine is the so-called Opimian from 121 BC. Plin. *Nat.* 14.55–6 says that by his time this wine had diminished to strong dregs, which were highly valued and used to spice other wines.
[51] For these and the following references, see Tchernia (1986) 33–4, who also notes that Cicero could attack Piso for not having a wine cellar but buying his wines from the tavern (*Pis.* 67). Cf. Tchernia (1995) 300, Tchernia and Brun (1999) 34, 133–4. Also see now Van Oyen (2020) 50–3, who makes important points on the transformative quality of wine storage.

Wine Storage Places at C. 3.8, C. 2.3, C. 3.28

Roman annalistic historiography, which charted the past on a calendrical grid.[52] Wine storage places are another such calendrical structure, as the wines were arranged according to consular years. The sequence of consular names that a wine storage place displays is the sequence of such names in the *fasti*. Entering the storage space, one could slowly make (or drink) one's way further into the past, while reading the names of consuls in ink on the amphorae, which gradually recalled an ever more distant past. Wine storage places thus offered a spatial visualisation of time.[53] Indeed, the physician Galen made his way through the emperor's wine storage place, reading the consular years, and drinking his way from old bitter wines at the back of the storage place to younger wines that lack this bitterness at the front (Galen *Ant*. 2.15 = xiv.25–6 Kühn):[54]

κομιζομένων γὰρ τοῖς βασιλεῦσι τῶν ἀρίστων ἀπανταχόθεν, ἐξ αὐτῶν πάλιν τούτων τὸ κάλλιστον αἱρήσεται, ἔγωγέ τοι τῶν οἴνων τῶν Φαλερίνων ἑκάστου τὴν ἡλικίαν ἀναγινώσκων ἐπιγεγραμμένην τοῖς κεραμίοις, εἰχόμην τῆς γεύσεως, ὅσοι πλειόνων ἐτῶν ἦσαν εἴκοσι, προερχόμενος ἀπ' αὐτῶν ἄχρι τῶν οὐδὲν ὑπόπικρον ἐχόντων.

For the best things are brought to the emperors from everywhere, and from these again the best will be chosen. Thus, I read the age written on the jars of each of the Falernian wines, and had a taste of all those which were more than twenty years old and from these I went further until the wines had no bitterness in their taste.

Horace is the poet who mentions wine storage most frequently. Thus, Horace mentions at one point a Sabine wine that he had 'stored away' at a special occasion (*C*. 1.20: *conditum*), and at another point a 'stored away Caecuban wine' (*C*. 3.28.2–3: *reconditum* [...] *Caecubum*). The verb Horace uses, *condo*, appropriately describes the process of storing away wine for future use. Yet, Horace's usage of this verb goes further. At one point Horace

---

[52] Feeney (2007) 190 calls annalistic historiography 'the narratological correlative to the monumental *fasti* with their paired consuls'. Cichorius at *RE* i.2 col.2250 s.v. 'Annales' argued that such historiography derived from consular *fasti*. Conversely, Rüpke (1995a) argued that consular *fasti* took their information from historiography.
[53] For spatial prepositions and their application to time in Latin, see Bettini (1991) [1988] 113–93. Evans (2016) 5–29 applies Bettini's findings to verbs of movement in Horace.
[54] Text: Kühn (1821–33).

speaks of 'times that are stored in the public records of the *fasti*' (*C.* 4.13.13–16):[55]

> nec Coae referunt iam tibi purpurae
> nec cari lapides tempora, quae semel
>   *notis condita fastis*
>   inclusit uolucris dies.
>
> Neither purple dresses from Cos nor precious gems can any longer bring back the years once winged time has stored them away and locked them up in the public *fasti*.

To be sure, the comparison in this passage is made with tongue in cheek; the aging Lyce is made aware of the flight of time, and the evocation of the public consular *fasti*, which record time, strongly contrasts in register with her licentious love life.[56] And yet, the mention of the Roman calendar system of the *fasti* in Greek-style lyric is striking. Denis Feeney thus says about this passage that 'no Greek lyric poet could have thought or written in such manner'.[57] Jörg Rüpke notes that the *fasti* appear in Horace as an 'authorised form of collective memory'.[58] Significantly, Horace strongly links calendars with wine storage places; thus, time is 'stored away' in the *fasti* as if they were a wine cellar.[59] This is an apt choice of words, since wine cellars in turn also act as *fasti*, which preserve the names of consuls. Another significant usage of *condo* is noted by Michael Putnam; Horace uses the word also for writing poetry, and at one point says that he composes and stores up what he might soon again remove from storage, in words that are wholly evocative of wine storage (*Epist.* 1.1.12): *condo et conpono quae mox depromere possim* ('I'm storing and putting away what I may soon bring forth again').[60] What I wish to stress is that storing wine,

---

[55] For this poem as 'anti-*carpe diem*', see Davis (1991) 223–4.
[56] Thus Feeney (1993) 58, and already Orelli and Baiter (1850) *ad loc.* Cf. T. S. Johnson (2004) 177–8. Conversely, Fedeli and Ciccarelli (2008) *ad loc.* argue that the *fasti* in the ode refer to the aediles' registers of prostitutes.
[57] Feeney (1993) 58, and see 58–60.
[58] Rüpke (1997) 76 and 76 n.61 quoting besides the present passage also Hor. *S.* 1.3.112, *C.* 3.17.2–4, 4.14.1–6, *Epist.* 2.1.48. Cf. Mugellesi at *EO* ii.134–5 s.v. 'calendario', Lowrie (1997) 54 on the calendar in *C.* 1.4, Barchiesi (2007) 153–5, Evans (2016) 47–8.
[59] See *OLD* s.v. 'condo' 2c, where *C.* 4.13.15 is listed as a transferred meaning of storing something (thus also Bo (1965–6) s.v.).
[60] Putnam (1969) 153–4. Mayer (1994) *ad loc.* is on point: 'metaphors for poetic composition [...] elegantly revert to more basic senses'. For the storage imagery, see also

Wine Storage Places at *C.* 3.8, *C.* 2.3, *C.* 3.28

storing dates, and storing poetry are semantically interwoven realms in Horace's book poetry: all this can be stored and accessed later. As Horace says farewell to lyric and begins to write literary letters, he proclaims to 'put away' his lyric, but we might wonder if he does not merely put it into storage (*Epist.* 1.1.10): *nunc itaque et uersus et cetera ludicra pono* ('so now I put away poetry and other trifles').[61] At any rate, ten years after the publication of the tribiblos Horace returns to lyric again in *Odes* 4 and he accesses his self-storage facility: at the beginning of *Odes* 4.11, he mentions that he has kept a jar of Alban wine for over nine years.[62]

Horace's wine storage place is closely linked to Augustan forms of memorialising. Thus, Augustus' deeds in war and peace are perhaps virtually preserved in wine bottles for future ages (*Epist.* 1.3.8): *bella quis et paces longum diffundit in aeuum?* ('who disseminates his [i.e., Augustus'] deeds in war and peace for long time to come?'). Nisbet has suggested that *diffundo* may be a wine metaphor here: 'the poet bottles up the great deeds of the present for the delectation of future generations'.[63] Just as wine storage places preserve the *tituli* ('wine labels') of numerous vintages, so library catalogues or indeed Horace's poetry preserve the *tituli* ('titles') of numerous poems.[64] Appropriately, Horace

---

D. West (1967) 24, 27. The passage is appropriately listed under the lemma of storing, preserving, and bottling at *OLD* s.v. 'condo' 2b (thus also Bo (1965–6) s.v.), not under the lemma for composing literature (14a). For *conpono*, meaning 'to put away/store', see Bo (1965–6) s.v. See Nisbet and Rudd (2004) at *C.* 2.3.2–3 on *promo*. Sullivan (2014) interprets Horace's lyric monument (*C.* 3.30) as a basket of papyrus scrolls, commonly arranged in pyramid form. If right, Horace's scrolls will outlast anything, and readers will always access them.

[61] Cf. Hor. *S.* 2.3.115–16: *positis intus Chii ueterisque Falerni mille cadis*.
[62] Thus Murray (1985) 50, Bernays (1996) 41–2, T. S. Johnson (2004) 152, Thomas (2011) *ad loc.*, Evans (2016) 237–8. Fedeli and Ciccarelli (2008) *ad loc.* rightly stress the similarity to *Ars* 388, where Horace recommends a nine-year wait between the draft and publication of a poem. Did Horace mark the tribiblos with a stamp of its publication year, akin to a wine label? His address to Sestius in *C.* 1.4 might indicate the publication year of 23 BC, in which Sestius was suffect consul. Sestius' name also appears as a stamp on numerous amphorae, since he was a rich amphora producer (for this and the relevance of the addressee for the ode, see Will (1982)). Hutchinson (2008) 131–61, however, argues against publication of the three books together (see 138–9 on Sestius).
[63] Nisbet (1966) 327, pointing to Hor. *Epist.* 1.5.4: *uina* [...] *iterum Tauro diffusa*. One could add Ov *F.* 5.517–18: *quaeque puer quondam primis diffuderat annis | promit fumoso condita uina cado*.
[64] For these two meanings of *titulus*, see *OLD* s.v. 1 and 3 (and 2 for the oddity of an attached label at Petron. 34.6). The dictionary entry points to Ov. *Tr.* 1.1.7 (among other

envisages in *Odes* 4.14 that Augustus may be kept in eternal memory through *tituli* (here: 'commemorative inscriptions') and *fasti* ('public records', but also 'calendars');[65] but it is of course also his own poetry that inscribes Augustus and numerous other people and events upon *tituli* and *fasti*.

While the act of storing wines and dates in calendrical order is important in Horace's poetry, the act of accessing this calendar is equally important. This is the message of *carpe diem*: if the wine is not taken from storage for enjoyment, only an heir will profit after death (*C.* 2.14.25–8). Time and time again, Horace asks for wines to be brought forth from storage places. One such instance can be found in *Odes* 2.3, a *carpe diem* poem. Horace begins the poem by telling Dellius to keep an even-minded disposition in all circumstances (*C.* 2.3.1–8):

> Aequam memento rebus in arduis
> seruare mentem, non secus in bonis
>   ab insolenti temperatam
>   laetitia, moriture Delli,
>
> seu maestus omni tempore uixeris, (5)
> seu te in remoto gramine per dies
>   festos reclinatum bearis
>   interiore nota Falerni.

> Keep this in mind: be level-headed when things are arduous; likewise in good times tone done your excessive joy, Dellius. For you are sure to die, whether you spend every moment of your life in misery or at each holiday you lie down in a secluded meadow and enjoy yourself with a Falernian vintage wine from the back of your cellar [literally: 'treat yourself to an interior label of Falernian wine'].

These lines show some awareness of the spatial dimension of wine storage places. Horace speaks of the 'interior label of a Falernian wine' (*interiore nota Falerni*). As Porphyrio informs us, this expression refers to the custom that the youngest wines were stored at the front of the storage place and the oldest at the back,

---

passages) for the meaning 'title', so that *L&S* s.v. seem wrong in stating that 'title of a book' is a post-Augustan meaning of *titulus*.

[65] Hor. *C.* 4.14.1–4, where Feeney (2007) 185 and A. Russell (2019) 178 n.69 are arguably right to insist that the meaning 'calendar' for *fasti* need not be excluded here, though Ps-Acro and all the modern commentators think so.

Wine Storage Places at *C.* 3.8, *C.* 2.3, *C.* 3.28

that is, its most 'interior' place.[66] We can observe the same spatial structure that we saw when Galen drank his way through the emperor's wine cellar: the past is a place far away at the back of the cellar. Yet, Horace strongly links the past with the present: he says that Dellius may drink old wines 'at each holiday' (*per dies festos*).[67] The old wine with 'the interior label' becomes part of the present feast. This is indeed what we have seen in *Odes* 3.8, in which Horace serves a vintage wine for a peculiar holiday. *Odes* 2.3 thus explicitly comments on Horace's method of blending old wine with present festivities. But the ode also puts this theory into practice, when Horace asks for some wine (*C.* 2.3.9–16):

> quo pinus ingens albaque populus
> umbram hospitalem consociare amant (10)
> ramis? quid obliquo laborat
> lympha fugax trepidare riuo?
>
> huc uina et unguenta et nimium breuis
> flores amoenae ferre iube rosae,
> dum res et aetas et sororum (15)
> fila trium patiuntur atra.

> Why do the huge pine and the white poplar love to join their branches and create inviting shade? Why does the quick-flowing water bother to rush along the river's twisted course? Tell them to bring wine here and perfumes and the all-too-short-lasting blossoms of the lovely rose, while matters and your age and the black threads of the three sisters of fate allow it.

The transition between these two stanzas and the two preceding ones is difficult. In the first two stanzas Horace made a general statement on the good life: keep your nonchalance, Dellius, whether times are difficult or you are enjoying a banquet with old wine on a remote meadow. But there is no suggestion yet that the poem's setting is this very banquet on the meadow.[68] Horace characteristically embellishes one part of the doublet and gives us

---

[66] Porphyrio *ad loc.*: *hoc est: uetustiore, quoniam interiores lagynae solent esse, quae prius stipatae sunt*. Also note that there is a semantic overlap between a wine label (*nota*) and a mark in the calendar for an auspicious day (*nota* at *C.* 1.36.10).
[67] Not 'throughout the holidays'. For the distributive usage of *per*, see Kießling and Heinze (1966) *ad loc.*
[68] For banquets *en plein air* in literature, see Cazzato (2016).

an attractive vignette of the banquet, while the description of the sad life remains colourless.[69] Nonetheless, his words are gnomic and do not seem to refer to a particular situation in the present:[70] the tenses in the second stanza are future-perfects, and they describe the balance of a life when it is over, not the present situation. In the third stanza, however, Horace seems to move from a general statement to a particular place. Attempts have been made to ease the boldness of the transition by adopting different readings in the third stanza.[71] This will not do. For the beginning of the fourth stanza is even bolder. Rather than adopting different readings, we should appreciate with Nisbet and Hubbard the 'immediacy' and 'urgency' of Horace's lyric here.[72] The strongest sign of this immediacy is the first word of the fourth stanza: *huc*. This opening of the stanza is striking, and meant to be so. For the deictic *huc*, 'here', points to the *hic et nunc* of the banquet.[73] With this word we have left behind the generalising statements of the poem's beginning. The timeless banquet from the beginning is transformed into a banquet of the present moment. This inner movement of the poem mirrors the movement of wine: as Horace asks for wines to be brought to the banquet and be made present (*huc*), so the poem becomes present.[74]

---

[69] Thus Woodman (1970) 169–70, Harrison (2017) *ad loc*. For this technique, see Davis (1991) 163–4, who notes that often one member of the doublet is 'marked', the other one 'unmarked' (the terms of Palmer (1981) 95–6).

[70] Nisbet and Hubbard (1978) 52–3: 'In the third stanza the poem moves from generalizations to the description of a particular parkland [...] In the fourth stanza, with another abrupt development Horace uses the poet's prerogative to issue directions for a symposium.' The issue is that lyric poems show movement, and 'setting' is anything but a stable category, as Hutchinson (2018) discusses in detail.

[71] Brink (1971b) 19–21 strongly argues in favour of *qua* instead of *quo* in line 9 (Lambinus saw this in manuscripts) and Haupt's *ramisque et* instead of *ramis quid* in line 11. Shackleton Bailey (2001) prints *qua*, as well as Fea's *et* in place of *quid* in line 11.

[72] Nisbet and Hubbard (1978) at *C.* 2.3.9.

[73] Cf. Heinze (1923) 155 on the demonstrative *harum* [...] *arborum*, which perhaps introduces a sympotic setting at the *carpe diem* poem Hor. *C.* 2.14.22. Barchiesi (2005) 155–7 adduces *C.* 2.11.13–14 additionally to these two passages, in a short discussion of lyric deixis of trees in Horace's sympotic poems. Rösler (1983) discusses *demonstratio ad oculos* and 'deixis am Phantasma' in relation to Greek lyric, and treats Horace's deictics in this tradition on pages 23–5. Mindt (2007) applies Rösler's concepts to several Horatian banquet poems. Lefèvre (1993b) 149–50 takes the deictics as evidence that *C.* 2.3 and *C.* 2.11 were actually performed in a park.

[74] Pöschl (1994) 126 argues that the poem moves between dark and light notes as well as between generalising and personal aspects.

Wine Storage Places at *C.* 3.8, *C.* 2.3, *C.* 3.28

Wines have to be 'moved' to the symposium (*Epod.* 13.6: *tu uina Torquato moue consule pressa meo*; 'you, *get* wine that was pressed in my birthyear when Torquatus was consul'), or 'brought forth', as they had been 'put away' (*C.* 3.2.2–3: prome reconditum, | *Lyde, strenua Caecubum*; 'Lyde, quickly *bring forth* the Caecuban wine, *which has been stored away*');[75] or in a mock-hymn the wine jar has to 'descend' from its storage place (*C.* 3.21.7: *descende*).[76] Vintage wines in Horace leave the *apotheca*, something of a storehouse of memory, and enter the intense presence of the symposium. The incarnate date, an amphora with a consular year, thus enters the present time of the symposium. This concept of dates and past time, which can be carried around, is possibly comparable to the concept of language among Jonathan Swift's Lilliputians. In *Gulliver's Travels* the Lilliputians do not use spoken language but carry objects around with which they communicate. In Horace, we can observe a moveable feast: in the form of wine bottles, past feasts and occasions are literally moved to the present moment. The manifest date is brought from its place in the calendar to the banquet. This also allows Horace to move his celebrations to unusual dates: as Horace gets the appropriate wine, he moves the feast for Bacchus to the first day of March in *Odes* 3.8.

Using consular dates is a dating system that comes with some peculiarities. When Pliny mentions the age of the well-known Opimian wine from 121 BC, the date 'Opimius' immediately evokes political events that are associated with the consul (Plin. *Nat.* 14.55): *anno* [*sc. claritas*] *fuit omnium generum bonitate L. Opimio cos., cum C. Gracchus tribunus plebem seditionibus agitans interemptus est* ('one year was distinguished as it was excellent for all types of wine; this was the year when Lucius Opimius was consul and when Gaius Gracchus, the tribune of the people, was first causing civil discord and was then killed'). Pliny's passive verb *interemptus est* ('he was killed') may be

---

[75] Nisbet and Rudd (2004) *ad loc.* note that *prome* is 'a natural word for bringing out wine', also appearing in Hor. *C.* 1.36.11, 3.21.8. Cf. *Epod.* 9.1: *Quando repostum Caecubum ad festas dapes* [*sc. bibam?*]. At Ov. *F.* 5.517–18 an old man serves a wine he had stored as a child (quoted on page 93 n.63).
[76] On hymnic features of Hor. *C.* 3.21, see Norden (1956) [1913] 143–63.

A Moveable Feast

slightly obscuring: it was Opimius who promised to give anyone bringing him Gracchus' head the equivalent weight of gold. Pliny's way of recalling history through a wine vintage in this passage is very similar to the case of the Allied victory and the Mouton Rothschild quoted above.[77] In Horace we have already seen a possible allusion to politics in his mention of Tullus in *Odes* 3.8: the co-consul Augustus is latently lurking behind that date. In other odes the mention of consular dates seems to serve different purposes.[78] In *Odes* 3.28, Horace tells a certain Lyde to celebrate the feast day of Neptune together with him and bring some wine from the consulship of Bibulus (*C.* 3.28.5–8):

> inclinare meridiem (5)
>   sentis et, ueluti stet uolucris dies,
> parcis deripere horreo
>   cessantem Bibuli consulis amphoram?

> You can feel that the midday sun is about to enter its downward course, and yet – as if the winged day were standing still – are you hesitating to snatch from storage the sluggish amphora from the year that Bibulus was consul?

The consulship of Bibulus marks the year 59 BC, when Julius Caesar and M. Calpurnius Bibulus were consuls. Suetonius, however, asserts that Romans jokingly referred to the year as 'Julius and Caesar' instead of 'Caesar and Bibulus', as Bibulus was notoriously inactive (Suet. *Jul.* 20.2).[79] Bibulus attempted to prevent his co-consul Caesar's legislation by procrastinating. Some people even used this date jokingly in testamentary documents,

---

[77] See page 87. The reverse is also possible: at Velleius 2.7.5 the account of Gracchus' story triggers the mention of the Opimian wine.

[78] Note that in Hor. *C.* 1.20 Maecenas becomes part of a quasi-consular date for wine, as Cairns (1992) 92 recognises: an acclamation for Maecenas provides the date for the wine in place of the usual consular date.

[79] Evans (2016) 223–34 also points to this section of Suetonius as well as to the one I quote in the following paragraph, and he stresses that Bibulus' political (in)activity mirrors the hesitating amphora. This interpretation goes back to D. West (1973) 43–4. Evans notes that Cic. *Att.* 2.19.2 describes Bibulus in the famous words that Ennius coined for Fabius Cunctator: *unus homo nobis cunctando restituit rem* (Enn. *fr.* 363 Skutsch). Cassius Dio 38.6 reports that people broke the *fasces* of Bibulus in 59, which takes his consular power away from him. For consuls that were so bad that they should have been deleted from the *fasti*, see Cic. *Sest.* 33 and *Pis.* 30 with A. Russell (2019) 174. Russell further notes on page 171 that Mark Antony's name was first deleted then reinscribed upon the *fasti*. Tiberius rejected the suggestion to delete the names of bad consuls in the *fasti* (Tac. *Ann.* 3.17–18).

Wine Storage Places at *C.* 3.8, *C.* 2.3, *C.* 3.28

according to Suetonius. Moreover, the following verses were supposedly common knowledge at that time (Suet. *Jul.* 20.2):

> non Bibulo quiddam nuper sed Caesare factum est:
> nam Bibulo fieri consule nil memini.
>
> An event recently happened not in the year of Bibulus but in the year of Caesar. For I do not remember anything to have happened in the year of Bibulus.

Horace's choice of dating the wine seems strange at first sight: while Romans have wittily asserted that such a thing as a consulship of Bibulus does not exist, Horace nonetheless asks for a wine from that time. In *Odes* 3.8 above we have already seen how Horace's mention of one consul, Tullus, provokes his readers to think of the absence of the other consul, Augustus. In the case of Bibulus and *Odes* 3.28, incompleteness and absence is very much the essence of the date. This serves different purposes; for once, the hesitant amphora is evocative of the consul Bibulus, who famously procrastinated Caesar's legislation, as David West notes.[80] Indeed, Horace's interlocking word order keeps the 'consul Bibulus' neatly embedded between (or inscribed on?) the 'hesitating amphora'.

The date on the wine label in *Odes* 3.28 also serves another purpose. Victor Pöschl stresses, in a wonderful interpretation of the poem, that Lyde is only characterised through her hesitation, and he notes that her hesitation finds a parallel in the hesitating amphora.[81] Horace attempts to overcome Lyde's hesitation, and Pöschl is arguably right to see a lover's pleas in Horace's urging.[82] This is a common situation in *carpe diem* poems; thus, Horace urges Leuconoe to seize the day in *Odes* 1.11, and several Greek epigrams urge women to submit to their lovers' pleas before time runs out. Indeed, the word *parco* ('to spare, be sparing'), which expresses Lyde's hesitation, may point to Greek models where φείδομαι ('to spare, be sparing') is used in exactly

---

[80] D. West (1973) 43–4, T. S. Johnson (2004) 152 n.46, Evans (2016) 223–34. Bibulus also hesitated to leave his house as a governor of a province while there was still a single enemy outside (and he still wanted a triumph), as Cicero jokes at *Att.* 6.8.5.
[81] Pöschl (1970) 186, Schmidt (2002) [1980] 255–6, Evans (2016) 231.
[82] Pöschl (1970) 188–91.

A Moveable Feast

this context.[83] As Horace mentions the midday sun, he introduces a sense of urgency; this is the reminder of time passing by, possibly pointing to the approaching evening of life in the typical fashion of a *carpe diem* poem.[84]

When Horace urges Lyde to submit to his pleas, he tells her not to hesitate to 'snatch' (*deripere*) an amphora from the year of Bibulus. The word for getting hold of the amphora, *deripio*, is a comparatively violent term. Elsewhere Horace uses more neutral (*moueo, fero, peto*) or technical vocabulary (*promo, depromo*). The exhortation to snatch the wine rapidly and violently is an attempt to overcome Lyde's hesitation.[85] But this also points again to the peculiar calendar Horace uses. We have seen how Horace exhorts his companions in *Epodes* 13 to 'snatch' (*rapio*) the occasion and to 'move' (*moueo*) some wine to the banquet. As Horace addresses Lyde, he conflates time and wine: Lyde is asked to snatch an amphora as well as an elusive moment in time. Just as Bibulus' consulate is a fleeting date, so the amphora is hesitant to be brought from storage. The moment in past time, 59 BC, which is difficult to locate but promises 'bibulous' enjoyment,[86] finds some parallel in the moment in present time: here, Horace's date with Lyde promises enjoyment if only he can convince her to seize the day (and the wine).

Feeney has stressed that the consular *fasti* served a symbolical purpose, while 'the utilitarian dimension [...] is less clear'.[87] At first sight wine labels may offer such a utilitarian dimension; identifying the right wine is, after all, quite useful. Closer inspection, however, has revealed that Feeney's statement also holds true for amphorae: it is the symbolic value of consuls on wine labels that Horace exploits with his drinkable calendar.

---

[83] See *AP* 5.85.1 = Asclepiades 2.1 *HE, AP* 9.439.6 = Crinagoras 47.6 *GP, AP* 11.25.3 = Apollonides 27.3 *GP, P.Oxy.* 1795.3 (at *CA* 199–200, if restored correctly) and already *PMG* 913.2 at Amipsias *fr.* 21.5. Asclepiades' epigram is close in spirit. I discuss the other epigrams in detail in Chapter 4.
[84] Thus Pöschl (1970) 182–6. This is the reference to death of the *carpe diem* poem. Cf. Evans (2016) 231–2.
[85] Thus Pöschl (1970) 186.
[86] For the pun on Bibulus and *bibulus*, see Kießling and Heinze (1966) *ad loc.*, who point to Hor. *Epist.* 1.14.34 [*sc. scis*] *quem bibulum liquidi media de luce Falerni.*
[87] Feeney (2007) 170 referring to Wallace-Hadrill (1987) 223–4, Rüpke (1995a).

2.4 Memories of Linguistic Wars: Tasting Language in *Odes* 3.14

The oldest wine Horace mentions in his poetry appears in *Odes* 3.14. In this poem, Horace celebrates Augustus' happy return from Spain (*C.* 3.14.13–28):

> hic dies uere mihi festus atras
> exiget curas: ego nec tumultum
> nec mori per uim metuam tenente   (15)
> Caesare terras.
>
> i pete unguentum, puer, et coronas
> et cadum Marsi memorem duelli,
> Spartacum siqua potuit uagantem
> fallere testa.   (20)
>
> dic et argutae properet Neaerae
> murreum nodo cohibere crinem:
> si per inuisum mora ianitorem
> fiet – abito.
>
> lenit albescens animos capillus   (25)
> litium et rixae cupidos proteruae:
> non ego hoc ferrem calidus iuuenta
> consule Planco.

19 uagantem *codd.* : uagacem *Charis. GL i.66*

> This is a real holiday for me as it will banish my dark worries: I will not fear civil strife or violent death, because Caesar controls the world. Slave, come and get perfume and garlands and a cask that remembers the Marsian feud, if anywhere a jar was able to elude marauding Spartacus.
>
> And tell Neaera with her clear voice to hurry and to tie her myrrh-scented hair with a band. If the detested doorman makes you wait, just give up and come back. My hair is turning white and that's softening my temper; I used to welcome altercations and violent quarrels. I would not have put up with this in my youth when I was hot-blooded and when Plancus was consul.

Augustus returns victorious from Spain, and Horace celebrates. The ode thus seems a good example for a celebration of the present moment in typical lyric fashion. On closer inspection, however, much of the ode deals with the past as a foil for present celebrations; as Horace praises Augustan peace, he recalls the civil wars of the past (14–15: *tumultus* and *uis*). Parts of this recollection of political unrest in Rome are also the Social War (18), Spartacus' revolt (19–20), and Plancus' consulship that marks the year of Philippi (27–8).

When Horace asks a slave to bring a wine jar to the symposium, the wine also provides a historical date (17–20): *i pete unguentum, puer, et coronas | et cadum Marsi memorem duelli, | Spartacum siqua potuit uagantem | fallere testa* ('slave, come and get perfume and garlands and a cask that remembers the Marsian feud, if anywhere a jar was able to elude marauding Spartacus'). The wine dates back to the Social War of 91–87 BC (or even precedes it), a revolt of Rome's Italian allies.[88] This date makes it of course an old and therefore choice wine, thus befitting the occasion.[89] Yet, apart from these concerns for the symposiasts' enjoyment, the vintage also makes the wine a historical fact.[90] Horace's instructions to his slave are generic for a symposium, and they are common in early Greek lyric. The wine jar, however, which is firmly placed in Roman history, is distinct from the usual commands at a Greek symposium. As we have seen in *Odes* 2.3, again an old wine enters the present moment of the banquet and marks a holiday. This time the wine had to escape from the dangers of wars of the past in order to make it to the banquet. Wines were indeed easy victims in war; Polybius tells us that Hannibal washed his horses in old wine in order to cure them of scabies as he marauded through Italy.[91] Horace's wine escaped the notice of Spartacus' marauding hordes. The wine thus evokes Roman history; in fact, it is even said to remember it (18): *cadum Marsi memorem duelli* ('a cask that remembers the Marsian feud').[92]

---

[88] Putnam (1996a) 453 understands the line as referring to a wine that was processed during the Social War. Schmidt (2002) [1980] 252 considers it likely that the wine dates back to a time of peace preceding the Social Wars. L. Morgan (2005) 194 takes it for granted that the wine predates the war.

[89] Nisbet and Rudd (2004) ad loc. point to Juv. 5.31: *calcatamque tenet bellis socialibus uuam*.

[90] Cf. Schmidt (2002) [1980] 251–2, Davis (2007) 212 n.6, Evans (2016) 212–22.

[91] Plb. 3.88 with Thurmond (2017) 226. Cic. *Phil.* 13.11 mentions that Mark Antony emptied Pompey's wine cellar (Tchernia (1986) 117).

[92] Schmidt (2002) [1980] 251 speaks of an 'Erinnerungsfähigkeit' (an ability to remember) of the wine. For the significance of time in other elements of the ode, see Putnam (1996a) 447.

Tasting Language in *Odes* 3.14

As Ellen Oliensis notes, remembering is an odd activity for wine, the proverbial agent of oblivion.[93] In *Odes* 3.14, however, the wine jar remembers the past not just as a fact but even recalls a past style of speech. My first piece of evidence for this must be tentative, as it is based on a doubtful reading in the text. Nisbet raised a number of textual issues in the ode and one of his suggestions was that *uagacem* may be a reasonable alternative for *uagantem* in line 19.[94] While the manuscript evidence supports *uagantem*, the reading *uagacem* is preserved in a quotation of the Horatian line by the grammarian Charisius (*GL* i.66). Although the word is not elsewhere attested in Latin, Nisbet thought that the word, supposedly meaning 'rampageous', might be 'an archaism with a period flavour, or perhaps a whimsical coinage of Horace's own'.[95] This suggestion is attractive. The wine jar then not only remembers historic events, but recalls them in the language of their time, speaking in archaisms. While the fact that *uagacem* has no parallel in Latin may seem to diminish its likelihood, the question *utrum in alterum* offers some support for the reading: it is not unlikely that *uagantem* appeared in the manuscripts as a normalisation of the unusual *uagacem*.[96]

Admittedly it would be shaky scholarship if my argument rested on one doubtful reading, but the passage contains at least one more archaism that is certain (18):[97] *cadum Marsi memorem duelli* ('a cask that remembers the Marsian feud'). The term *duelli* is of course an archaism for *belli*.[98] Ovid, for instance, uses the term

---

[93] Oliensis (1998) 148, pointing to Hor. *C.* 2.7.21: *obliuioso* [...] *Massico*.
[94] Nisbet (1983) 116. Previously suggested by Brink (1971a) 34–5. Klingner (1959) and Shackleton Bailey (2001) mention the reading *uagacem* in the apparatus.
[95] Nisbet (1983) 116.
[96] Cf. Verg. *A.* 11.230, where the archaism *pacem petendum* (gerund with direct object) should be preferred to the alternative manuscript reading *petendam* (Horsfall (2003) *ad loc.*). While the manuscripts are divided between the two readings, the indirect grammatical tradition prefers the archaism.
[97] Is *cadus* another archaism? Brink (1982a) at *Hor. Epist.* 2.2.163 and Muecke at *EO* ii.773 s.v. 'lingua e stile' think so. *Aliter* Nisbet and Rudd (2004) at *C.* 3.29.1–2: 'everyday word'.
[98] L. Morgan (2005) 195 n.20 notes the striking combination of *memorem* with the archaism *duelli*. Cf. Isidorus, *Etymologiae siue Origines* 18.1.9: *bellum antea duellum uocatum* with Maltby (1991) s.v. 'bellum' and *L&S* s.v. 'bellum' I. Horace uses *bellum* forty-eight times and the archaism *duellum* six times (Waltz (1881) 45, Ruckdeschel (1911) 92–3, Bo (1965–6) s.v., Bartalucci at *EO* ii.797 s.v. 'arcaismi', Kießling and Heinze (1961a) at *Epist.* 1.2.7). Axelson (1945) 112 finds fault with Horace's 'Gebrauch der selbst den Epikern zu rostigen Form *duellum*'.

duellum as he talks about a war in Rome's far history (*F.* 6.201). In Horace, the wine 'remembers the Marsian feud', and thus remembers a bygone war as well as a bygone word. The certain presence of the archaism *duelli* offers further support for the reading *uagacem*. Nisbet and Rudd say that *duelli*, 'with its suggestion of "old unhappy far-off things"' makes a contrast with the delights of the symposium.[99] Possibly so, but at least as important is the point that the archaism makes wine a device that brings the past to the symposium. As the wine jar recalls inter-Roman wars, so poet and poem also recall them: as has long been noted, the consulship of Plancus, which Horace mentions at the end of the poem, marks the year of Philippi. Oswyn Murray says that 'the date is carefully placed in the sympotic context, as if it were a mark of vintage'.[100] In this year Horace was fighting under Brutus and Cassius against Octavian, the later Augustus. Horace, much like the curious wine he serves, is a survivor of inter-Roman wars.[101] Before this background of near-death, Horace exhorts to the enjoyment of the present in his *carpe diem* poem.

Odes 3.14 is not alone in recalling wars through old wine and words. In the so-called Cleopatra ode, Horace celebrates Augustus' victory over Mark Antony and the end of the civil wars. After the well-known call to drink, *nunc est bibendum*, Horace says that 'previously it was a sacrilege to bring Caecuban wine from ancestral cellars' (*C.* 1.37.5–6): *antehac nefas depromere Caecubum | cellis auitis*. Horace might be thinking of a wine predating the civil war here, a wine worthy of being opened now. As Horace approaches the 'ancestral cellars', he again brings back not only an old wine but also an old word. The word *antehac* is an archaism, as Roland Mayer notes.[102] Again, in *Epodes* 9, in which Horace also celebrates Augustus' victory at Actium with a banquet, he begins his poem by asking when the time would come to drink 'a Caecuban wine that had been put into storage (*repostum*) for a banquet of celebration' (*Epod.* 9.1).

---

[99] Nisbet and Rudd (2004) *ad loc.* [100] Murray (1985) 47.
[101] In his own account of Philippi, Horace also stresses that he was able to escape the notice of the enemy (*C.* 2.7.13–16). The words *consule Planco* are well discussed by Klingner (1961) [1938] 402–5, Fraenkel (1957) 290, Schmidt (2002) [1994–5] 282–3.
[102] Mayer (2012) *ad loc.*

Tasting Language in Odes 3.14

The word *repostum*, which describes the storage of wine, is another archaism.[103] In *Odes* 2.3, which I discussed above, Horace tells Dellius that he may have made himself happy (*bearis*) with an old Falernian wine with its interior label. The verb *bearis* has been described as an archaism.[104] Finally, as Horace speaks of a 'jar of wine' in the *Epistles* he uses the expression *cadum temeti*, in which *temetum* is an archaism and *cadum* perhaps another one (*Epist.* 2.2.163).[105] The identification of Latin words as archaisms is notoriously difficult, and not every one of my examples might be as clear clear-cut as the example of the wine that remembers the Marsian feud. Nonetheless, the cumulative force of these examples is clear enough – old wine preserves the taste of old words in Horace. Horace's storehouse is not just a thesaurus of wine but also a thesaurus of words. This need perhaps not surprise us; in the *Epistles*, Horace tells us that 'the jar will long keep the fragrance of what it was once steeped in when new'.[106] The link between old wine and old words, styles, and texts is not unique to Horace. Cicero compares the old style of Thucydides' rhetoric to wines of old consular dates, and new oratory to a wine from the preceding year (*Brut.* 287). It is suggestive that Horace finds obsolete words in a storage place: in an influential study, Aleida Assmann identified a cultural phenomenon which she calls 'storage memory' ('Speichergedächtnis').[107] This describes a type of cultural memory that preserves obsolete information, as archives do, for instance. Horace's storage places seem to work in comparable ways.

Wine as a mechanism of remembering past moments is particularly well suited for lyric poetry. One obvious reason is the presence of wine at the symposium, one of the essential spaces for lyric poetry.[108] The other reason, which strikes me as more interesting,

---

[103] Thus L. C. Watson (2003) *ad loc.*
[104] Waltz (1881) 42–3, Nisbet and Hubbard (1978) *ad loc.*
[105] Brink (1982a) *ad loc.* regards both words as archaisms. Fedeli at *EO* ii.262 s.v. 'vino' argues that *temetum* carries the flavour of the rural world. Cf. *OLD* s.v.
[106] *Epist.* 1.2.69–70: *quo semel est inbuta recens seruabit odorem | testa diu.* Horace's jar here preserves the fragrance of Ennius *fr.* 476 Skutsch (Mayer (1994) *ad loc.*): *quom illud quo iam semel est imbuta ueneno.* Also note that Horace frequently employs Grecisms for drinking vessels (Gitner (2012) 114–15).
[107] A. Assmann (2011) [1999] 119–32. [108] See e.g., Murray (1985) for Horace.

is the uniquely timely quality of vintage wines. Wine is a product of the season, since grapes are harvested every autumn and wine is produced. Similarly to flowers or grain, this makes wine an innate part of the natural cycle of the year. Yet, wine is distinct from most other seasonal products in that it can be preserved. Horace's own poetry, too, was always destined to be preserved, as he makes clear in the last poem of the tribiblos, *Exegi monumentum*. As Horace projects a future life of his momentary poems, wine bottles become the ideal vessel for his poetry. While wine is a product of the season and is enjoyed in a particular moment, this seasonal point in time can be preserved for a considerable period.[109] When wine drinkers open a bottle of old wine in our time, they often will have informed themselves previously about how the weather of that year influenced the vintage. Similarly in Martial, even the legendary Opimian, around 200 years old by Martial's time, bears the signs of a fortunate autumn (13.113): *Haec Fundana tulit felix autumnus Opimi. | expressit mustum consul et ipse bibit* ('The fruitful autumn of Opimius has brought forth this wine from Fundi. The consul himself pressed out the must and drank it').[110] Drinking wine can then provide a direct sensory experience of a past season. This flavour of the past leads us back to *Odes* 3.14.

The wine in *Odes* 3.14 is some truly strong stuff from the Marsian war, and the alien, stronger taste is reflected in the archaisms that the wine 'memorises'. In this ode and elsewhere, wine preserves archaisms that have been out of season for decades. The metaphor 'out of season' is indeed appropriate for words in Horace, as he regards the lexical development of words as cyclical, comparable to the seasonal change of leaves (*Ars* 45–72). Horace repeatedly compares words to vines that the poet has to cultivate. Thus, he says in the epistle to Florus (*Epist.* 2.2.122–3): [*sc. poeta*] *luxuriantia conpescet, nimis aspera sano | leuabit cultu, uirtute carentia tollet* ('The aspiring poet will cut back ~~excessive~~ (*otiose!*)

---

[109] Compare and contrast Pindar *O.* 9.48–9, who famously urged to praise 'old wine but the flowers of newer poems'. Horace picks up the saying at *Epist.* 2.1.34–5 (Brink (1982a) *ad loc.*, Spelman (2018) 203–13 and 207 n.68).
[110] The outstanding weather in this year is also noted by Plin. *Nat.* 14.55: *ea caeli temperies fulsit (cocturam uocant), solis opere, natali urbis* DCXXXIII: *durantque adhuc uina ea cc fere annis.*

Tasting Language in *Odes* 3.14

~~foliage~~ verbiage, he will smoothen what is too rough with beneficial attention, and he will uproot those words that lack dignity'). The archaisms in *Odes* 3.14 are words that have not been pruned, and it is fitting that they are preserved by a wine jar. Yet, these thoughts on the seasonal quality of words in Horace are already branching into the next chapter, where I will look in more detail at the eternal cycle of leaves and words in Horace's poetry.

3

GATHERING LEAVES

Horace, Choice of Words, Cyclical Time, and the Production of Presence

This chapter begins where the previous one left off. Horace's choice of words emerged as something noteworthy where his treatment of wine is concerned: old wines frequently bring the taste of old words to the banquet. In the present chapter, I consider how words can evoke the present rather than the past. Horace's *carpe diem* poems thematise present moments, and I will show that within the underlying architecture of a poem even the smallest elements and mosaic pieces, that is, the individual words, contribute to creating a poetry of the present. I am, of course, alluding to Nietzsche's well-known saying, according to which Horace's poems are a 'mosaic of words, in which every unit spreads its power to the left and to the right over the whole, by its sound, by its place in the sentence, and by its meaning'.[1] My interest in this chapter lies in such mosaic pieces and what they can tell us about the mosaic as a whole.

Horace's choice of words was already much-admired in antiquity: Petronius spoke of *Horatii curiosa felicitas* ('Horace's painstaking felicity', Petron. 118.5) and Quintilian characterised him as *uerbis felicissime audax* ('fortuitously bold with his words', *Inst.* 10.96). Horace's phrasing seems strikingly felicitous to ancients and moderns alike (and in turn the phrases of Nietzsche, Petronius, and Quintilian are at least felicitous enough that they will be quoted in any discussion of Horace's choice of words). In this chapter, I will argue that Horace's words are not felicitous for their own sake but underline the message of *carpe diem* poems by producing effects of presence. 'Producing effects

---

[1] Nietzsche (1889) 131 in chapter 12 'Was ich den Alten verdanke' section 1. I take the translation from Anthony Ludovici (= Nietzsche (1911)). Fitzgerald (2016) 70–3 discusses the mosaic metaphor in detail.

of presence' may look like an ironically anachronistic term in a discussion about ancient choice of words. Yet, I will show that there exists a good Horatian model for this expression. What I mean by 'producing presence' is that certain words in Horace's odes evoke the momentary present in which they are set.[2] I will analyse Horace's thoughts about choice of words in his literary epistles as well as his actual choice of words in some *carpe diem* poems.

The chapter has three sections. In the first section, I will look at a well-known passage from Horace's *Ars Poetica* which compares words to leaves, in that they become extinct and return again. I will show that Horace's choice of words as well as his treatment of the *carpe diem* motif obeys a principle of cyclical change. In the second part, I will look at Horace's treatment of choice of words in the *Ars* beyond the leaves simile; while his thoughts engage with the linguistic theories of contemporaneous thinkers, his emphasis on cyclicality is unique to him. In the third part, I will show how Horace puts his theory into practice: in several *carpe diem* poems, certain words evoke the present time.

3.1 Words That Are Green Turn to Brown: Words and Leaves in the *Ars Poetica*

In the *Ars Poetica*, Horace discusses, among other things, a poet's choice of words and also how the vocabulary of a language changes over time. The passage in which he does this is generally admired. Brink called it 'perhaps the most remarkable piece of the *Ars*',[3] and it is arguably the passage that best defies Scaliger's damning verdict on the work, 'de arte sine arte tradita'.[4] In this passage, Horace compares a language's linguistic development to

---

[2] Fitzgerald (1989) offers an interpretation of the pleasure of Horace's text in the tradition of Barthes (1975) [1973]. See, in particular, Fitzgerald (1989) 82 for his take on the Nietzsche quotation and Horace, 92–3 for the Petronius quotation, and 98 for the 'production of aesthetic pleasure'.
[3] Brink (1971a) at 60–72. Thus also Commager (1962) 259: 'perhaps the most exquisite [*sc.* lines] in the *Ars Poetica*'. Dufallo (2005) 89: 'among the most memorably poetic passages'.
[4] Scaliger *Poetices libri septem* vi.7, which can be consulted in the edition of Deitz and Vogt-Spira (1994–2011) v.402–3.

leaves falling from a tree. While some words disappear from usage, old ones return (*Ars* 60–72):[5]

ut siluae foliis pronos mutantur in annos,	(60)
prima cadunt ✶ ✶ ✶ ✶ ✶ ✶ ✶ ✶ ✶ ✶ ✶ ✶ ✶ ✶ ✶ ✶	(61A)
✶ ✶ ✶ ✶ ✶ ✶ ✶ ✶ ita uerborum uetus interit aetas,	(61B)
et iuuenum ritu florent modo nata uigentque.	
debemur morti nos nostraque: siue receptus	
terra Neptunus classes Aquilonibus arcet,	
regis opus, sterilisue diu palus aptaque remis	(65)
uicinas urbes alit et graue sentit aratrum,	
seu cursum mutauit iniquum frugibus amnis	
doctus iter melius: mortalia facta peribunt,	
nedum sermonum stet honos et gratia uiuax.	
multa renascentur quae iam cecidere cadentque	(70)
quae nunc sunt in honore uocabula, si uolet usus,	
quem penes arbitrium est et ius et norma loquendi.	

60 pronos] priuos *Bentley fortasse recte*   **61** *lac. ind. Ribbeck* prima cadunt] priuanturque *Delz* : particulatim *Nisbet*   **68** facta] cuncta ς : saecla *Peerlkamp*   **69** nedum sermonum] sermonum haud *Aldus*

> As trees with their leaves change their appearance as the years slide on, the first leaves fall ✶ ✶ ✶ ✶ ✶ ✶ ✶ ✶ ✶ ✶ ✶ ✶ ✶ ✶, so the old generation of words dies and words that were just born bloom and flourish like young men. We and what is ours are owed to death; whether Neptune's water is made a basin and protects fleets from the North Wind – an achievement worthy of a king – or a swamp, which had long been barren and usable only for boats, now feels the heavy plough and nourishes neighbouring towns, or a river that had harmed the crops learns better ways and changes its course – still, all mortal works will perish, and still less is it true that the prestige and charm of speech could stay alive. Many words that have already fallen out of usage will be reborn, and many words which now have prestige will fall out of usage if convention wants it. Because in the hands of convention lie judgement, authority, and rule of speech.

Horace describes with gentle melancholy the lexical development of language as he likens words to leaves on a tree. Language, humans, and all their possessions are subject to an eternal cycle of death and rebirth. Commentators have noted the unusual tone of

---

[5] I depart from Klingner's text in one point; unlike him, I mark a lacuna in line 61. I discuss my choice on page 111.

Words and Leaves in the *Ars Poetica*

the passage. Thus, Brink discerns the 'lyric intensity of the Odes (say, C. I. 4 or IV. 7)', and Rudd speaks of 'sombre lyrical resonances'.[6] In the pages that follow, I wish to show that this similarity is not merely superficial; rather, the same concept of time that informs the content of Horace's lyric poetry also informs his thoughts on lexical change.[7]

The simile of the leaves goes back, of course, to Homer's *Iliad*, where Glaucus meets Diomedes on the battlefield before Troy and compares generations of men to generations of leaves (6.145–9):[8]

Τυδεΐδη μεγάθυμε, τίη γενεὴν ἐρεείνεις;
οἵη περ φύλλων γενεὴ τοίη δὲ καὶ ἀνδρῶν.
φύλλα τὰ μέν τ' ἄνεμος χαμάδις χέει, ἄλλα δέ θ' ὕλη
τηλεθόωσα φύει, ἔαρος δ' ἐπιγίγνεται ὥρη·
ὣς ἀνδρῶν γενεὴ ἣ μὲν φύει ἣ δ' ἀπολήγει.

Great-hearted son of Tydeus, why are you asking about my ancestry? Just as there are generations of leaves, so there are also generations of men. The wind sheds some leaves to the ground, but the flourishing forest brings forth others when the season of spring is there. So it is also with the generations of men; one generation sprouts, but another passes away.

The Homeric passage can shed some light on a textual issue in Horace's *Ars*. Horace's version includes the first part of the Homeric simile (φύλλα τὰ μέν τ' ἄνεμος χαμάδις χέει ~ *prima cadunt*), but lacks the second part of the simile (ἄλλα δέ [...]). If we assume that Horace modelled the passage on Homer, this lends further support to Ribbeck's diagnosis of a lacuna in line 61. For Ribbeck had noted that the paradosis of Horace's simile illogically compares one thing in the source domain with two things in the target domain: as leaves fall, so do words fall out of usage *and* new ones come about.[9]

---

[6] Brink (1971a) at 60–72, Rudd (1989) 35.
[7] Commager (1962) 258–9 and Grimal (1964) stress the unity in Horace's linguistic thoughts and his outlook on life, that is, in Grimal's words, his 'Art poétique' and his 'art de vivre'. Deschamps (1983) follows Grimal's approach.
[8] Text: van Thiel (1996).
[9] Ribbeck (1869) *ad loc.* Brink (1971a) and Shackleton Bailey (2001) accept that. Housman (1972) [1890] i.155–6 changes the punctuation: *prima cadunt ita uerborum. uetus interit aetas*. This may seem elegant, but the objections of Brink (1971a) *ad loc.* speak against it: the position of *ita* seems wrong and *mutantur* should more naturally mean 'changed with regard to' rather than 'parted from', which is the meaning Housman requires for his solution. Büchner (1980) 485–7 attempts to defend the paradosis.

111

Gathering Leaves

Horace was neither the first nor the last to pluck Homer's leaves. Indeed, even in Homer the simile of the leaves has the appearance of a set piece, as ancients and moderns alike have noted. Thus, ancients claimed that Homer took these lines from Musaeus (*fr.* 5 *DK*), while some modern scholars also thought that Homer's simile was not well integrated.[10] Be that as it may, already in Homer the leaves grow again elsewhere, when Apollo describes the generations of men with the same simile (*Il.* 21.461–7). The self-reference in Homer anticipates the many later adoptions of these lines. Lyric poets in particular were fond of quoting them or alluding to them. What arguably facilitated this lyric appropriation is that the lines already had the appearance of lyric poetry in Homer. Hayden Pelliccia has argued in detail that the leaves simile constitutes a rhetorical device, which the ancients called εἰκάζειν: a rhetorical tool of caricaturing someone by using a comparison, which was a popular game at symposia.[11] Pelliccia says that through the usage of the εἰκάζειν Glaucus 'is identifying himself as a member of symposiastic society, and indeed as an adept of the art of conversational "warfare"'.[12] I doubt that we can go that far. There may have been (proto)symposiasts before Homer, but they lie unknown, overwhelmed by perpetual night, since they lack a sacred bard.[13] In other words, Pelliccia's characterisation of Glaucus as a symposiast is arguably anachronistic. But Greek lyric poets might have looked at the passage in the same manner; to them, too, Glaucus seemed to engage in sympotic banter, and they appropriated the passage accordingly. The leaves of *Omero lirico* would find their appropriate(d) generic place in the lyric *carpe diem* poems of Mimnermus and Simonides in particular, and this *Nachleben* of the Homeric passage is most crucial for the simile's function in Horace:[14] Horace underlines his principle of

---

[10] For example, Fränkel (1921) 40–1, M. L. West (1997) 365, Burgess (2001) 117–26.
[11] Pelliccia (2002) with further examples and references.   [12] Pelliccia (2002) 220.
[13] Following Murray (1983) and others, I thus assume that the Homeric feasts anticipate symposia in many ways but do not yet incorporate the sophisticated sympotic codes that Pelliccia posits. Conversely, Węcowski (2014) 191–247 argues that Homer was part of a symposiastic society and created his 'heroic feasts' as a conscious archaism (further references there).
[14] Homer's appropriation in lyric is analysed by R. L. Fowler (1987) 3–52 (32 on the leaves). And see pages 11–13 in the Introduction of this book. For Homer's leaves and

Words and Leaves in the *Ars Poetica*

word-change with a simile that itself has been reborn again and again and acquired new meaning along the way.

In Horace's *Ars*, the leaves simile is directly followed by a gnome, which alleges that everything is owed to death (63): *debemur morti nos nostraque*. It has long been recognised that this is a translation of a 'Simonidean' epigram, and that the reference to Simonides here suggests that Horace plucked Homer's leaves from Simonides' tree.[15] For Simonides quotes and explains the Homeric image in a *carpe diem* poem (*frr.* 19 + 20):[16]

fr. 19 (Stob. 4.34.28)

ἓν δὲ τὸ κάλλιστον Χῖος ἔειπεν ἀνήρ·
'οἵη περ φύλλων γενεή, τοίη δὲ καὶ ἀνδρῶν'·
παῦροί μιν θνητῶν οὔασι δεξάμενοι
στέρνοις ἐγκατέθεντο· πάρεστι γὰρ ἐλπὶς ἑκάστῳ
ἀνδρῶν, ἥ τε νέων στήθεσιν ἐμφύεται. (5)

fr. 20 (*P.Oxy.* 3965 *fr.* 26 with Stob. 4.34.28 for lines 5–12)

```
              ]ειθο[
              ]ντ[ ... ] . [
          τυτ]θὸν ἐπὶ χρό[νον
    ......]ρλ[ ..... ]ω παρμενο[
```

their *Nachleben*, see Morpurgo (1927), Griffith (1975), Sider (1996), Pelliccia (2002) 229, Rawles (2018) 117–18, and, with a focus on modern poetry, Bloom (1975) 135–7 and Boitani (1989) 99–114. The leaves at Quintus of Smyrna 9.502–4 can be added to the many examples mentioned in these articles. While Boitani's discussion reaches the twentieth century, as he considers the leaves of Giuseppe Ungaretti, W. H. Auden, Robert Frost, and others, Homer's leaves still continue to be reborn again and again, for instance, in the songs of Yves Montand, Simon and Garfunkel, and most recently in a duet by Tom Waits and Keith Richards. Thus, there is at least one thing Quintus of Smyrna and Keith Richards have in common.

[15] *AP* 10.105.2 = [Simonides] 79.2 *FGE* = 46.2 Sider. Whether or not the epigram is genuine matters little. It is sufficient that Horace would have regarded it as Simonidean. This reference to Simonides is discussed by Oates (1932) 104. Sider (1996) 278 makes the point that the reference to Simonides' epigram signals Horace's debt to Simonides' leaves simile in the preceding lines. Besides Oates, important studies on Horace and Simonides include Cataudella (1927–8), Gigante (1994), Barchiesi (1996a; 1996b [1995]), Harrison (2001). In addition, see the older study of Arnold (1891).
[16] I treat the two fragments as deriving from a single poem, in which *fr.* 20 follows *fr.* 19. See Sider (1996) for a detailed discussion, and pages 207–8 in Chapter 5 for Stobaeus' technique of excerpting. I depart from M. L. West's text at *fr.* 20.15, which reads: κοὔ μιν] πανδαμά[τωρ αἱρεῖ χρόνος. But Sider (1996) 264, 272 is right that the reading γ is incompatible with the letter traces on the papyrus. Parsons suggests ὔ]παρ (*exempli gratia*), which is certainly more compatible with the roundish letter shape that the papyrus preserves.

113

Gathering Leaves

θνητῶ⌊ν δ' ὄ⌊φρά τις⌋ ἄνθος ἔχε⌊ι πολυήρατον ἥβης,   (5)
κοῦφο⌊ν ἔχω⌊ν θυμ⌋ὸν πόλλ' ἀτέλεσ⌊τα νοεῖ·
οὔ⌊τε γὰρ ἐλπ⌊ίδ' ἔχ⌋ει γηρασέμεν ⌊οὔτε θανεῖσθαι,
οὐδ', ὑ⌋γιὴς ὅτα⌊ν ᾖ, φ⌋ροντίδ' ἔχει κ⌊αμάτου.
νή⌋πιοι, οἷς ταύ⌊τῃ⌋ κεῖται νόος, ο⌊ὐδὲ ἴσασιν
ὡς χρό⌋νος ἔ⌊σθ' ἥβη⌋ς καὶ βιότοι' ὀλ⌊ίγος   (10)
θνη⌋τοῖς. ἀλλὰ ⌊σὺ⌋ ταῦτα μαθὼν ⌊βιότου ποτὶ τέρμα
ψυχῇ τῶν⌋ ἀγαθῶν τλῆθι χα⌊ριζόμενος.
. . . .(.)] φράζεο δὲ παλα[ιοτέρου λόγον ἀνδρός·
ἢ λήθην] γλώσσης ἔκφυγ' Ὅμηρ[ος
. . . . .]πα.δαμά[(15)
. . . . .(.)]ω ψυδρῆς ε[
. . . . .(.)] ἐν θαλίῃσι [
. . .]ι ἐϋστρέπτων
. . .]ων, ἔνθα καὶ [
.   ]...[(20)

One of the sayings of the man from Chios is the best: 'Just as there are generations of leaves, so there are also generations of men.' Few of the mortals who have heard this take it to heart. For all men have expectations which in their youth sprout in their hearts.

[...] for a short time [...] remain [...] As long as a mortal enjoys the lovely bloom of youth he is light-hearted and devises many things that are impossible to accomplish. For he does not expect to grow old nor to die, and he doesn't think of illnesses when he is healthy. People are fools who think like this and don't know that mortals have a short time of youth and life. But now that you have learned this at the end of your life, endure and pamper your soul with good things. [...] Consider [the account of the man] of old. Homer escaped [the oblivion] of his words. [...] false [...] in feasts [...] well-plaited [...] here and [...].

Horace's application of the leaves simile to words is daring. But David Sider has shown that Horace may develop a thought of Simonides, who already included poetry in his thoughts on mortality and leaves. For Simonides seems to say that Homer's language escaped oblivion (20.14).[17] There is another aspect of Simonides' poem which makes it particularly apt for Horace's purpose in the *Ars*. Richard Rawles recently noted that Simonides uses a high

---

[17] Sider (1996) 276–8. Yet, Sider (2020) now prints *fr.* 20.14 as [λήθην γὰρ] γλώσσης ἒκ φύγ' Ὅμηρ[ος ἑῆς, meaning that Homer escaped oblivion 'as a result of' (ἐκ as a preposition in anastrophe) his words. A poet who follows Horace and applies the image of leaves to the mortality of words is Dante at *Paradiso* 26.136–8 (Boitani (1989) 111, Delz (1995) 12).

Words and Leaves in the *Ars Poetica*

number of archaisms in his poem, that is, he uses a number of expressions which were common in the early Greek hexameter poetry of Homer, Hesiod, and the *Homeric Hymns*, or in the early elegy of Mimnermus, Theognis, and others, but which were no longer common at the time Simonides was writing, in the fifth century BC.[18] Of course, these expressions naturally come with the Homeric quotation: once Homer's seeds are planted, their leaves sprout throughout the poem. Simonides thus describes youth metaphorically as a 'flower' (20.5: ἄνθος), originally a Homeric expression he had plucked from early poetry, perhaps from Mimnermus' poem on the leaves (*fr.* 2.3).[19] Homer's language, his γλῶσσα (20.14), thus does not die: *bits, many bits of Homer dodged all funeral*. Simonides preserves certain Homeric expressions as well as a whole hexameter. But Homer's words have acquired a new context: they are reborn like leaves and now grow on a lyric tree.

It is suggestive that Simonides already made ample use of archaisms in his adaption of Homer's leaves, before Horace in turn would make this simile all about old words that become new again. It is, of course, not certain how many of Simonides' archaisms would have been readily identifiable as such in first-century-BC Rome, but the cumulative force of the evidence surely matters: on the grounds of its content as well as of its expressions, Simonides' poem has the appearance of early poetry.

In Simonides, the archaic words underline the poem's message, which tells its listeners to enjoy the present. Homer's old words survived for centuries and escaped oblivion (or whatever else the supplement in 20.14 might be), while human beings live only for a short time and should enjoy the present. Horace seems to go

---

[18] Rawles (2018) 114–20, and a list on 116–17. Cf. Parsons (2001) 62: 'a nice old-fashioned bow to Mimnermus'.
[19] Rawles (2018) 116 points to *Il.* 13.484, Mimn. *frr.* 1.4, 2.3, 5.3, Thgn. 1007–8, 1069. R. L. Fowler (1987) 45 and 45 n.106 notes that 'the flower of youth' is one of several epic expressions that gains 'particular prominence in lyric because of the subject matter' (cf. Griffith (1975) 79 n.34). Other archaisms Rawles notes in Simonides are στέρνοις ἐγκατέθεντο, πολυήρατος, νήπιοι (in initial position of the hexameter), and lines of thought in combination with certain expressions at 20.5–11 (cf. Thgn. 1007–12), 20.9–12 (cf. Thgn. 483–4), 20.12 (cf. Thgn. 1224). Wilamowitz-Moellendorff (1913) 274–5 notes the epic diction of ἔειπεν, γηρασέμεν, βιότοιο. Such features led, among others, Hubbard (1994: 191–3; 1996) to the conclusion that the poem is in fact an early elegy and should be attributed to Semonides rather than Simonides. I am unconvinced.

a step further. In his account, words are anything but permanent. Words have their seasons. In the *Ars*, language is a consequence of the cyclical change of time and the poet is subject to this change: he chooses his words from a set of current vocabulary, just as he chooses the present moment as a time of merriment. Yet, he also knows that both the present moment and language will change. Horace's *carpe diem* poems are thus works of cyclical time, both in their subject matter and in their theoretical linguistic framework: the cyclical time that is their theme in the description of the seasons is reflected in their vocabulary.

In the *Ars*, Horace's poetry shows some self-awareness of the fleeting, momentary and present nature of its words. Horace's poetry presents a combination of words that can only be fully enjoyed in the present moment, his lifetime, as some words will become extinct later, some will be reused again, and so on. What emerges, then, in Horace is a new poetry of the present moment. While Greek lyric poems were seemingly poems of the present moment by virtue of their occasional nature and their performance in the present, this quality of lyric is lost in Horace's book poetry.[20] Yet, this is supplanted by a linguistic present. Indeed, elsewhere Horace seems to characterise his lyric by its bold and novel choice of words. In the *Epistles*, Horace proudly states his achievement that he was the first who popularised Alcaeus' lyric song in the Latin tongue (*Epist.* 1.19.26–34); he brought 'things untold before' (*inmemorata*) to the Romans. Horace's word-choice, *inmemorata*, neatly underlines the content: just like his lyric, the word itself had been untold before. It is Horace's own coinage, though it is drawn from a Greek source.[21] Both Horace's lyric and his words are strikingly new and yet a repetition of older material.

An ode of Horace becomes the linguistic equivalent to a winter evening at the foot of Mount Soracte: a moment in linguistic time,

---

[20] See Barchiesi (2000) and my Introduction.
[21] Fraenkel (1957) 347, Mayer (1994) *ad loc.*, who suggests ἀμνημόνευτος as a model. This word, however, strikes me as rather prosaic. I was reminded of ἄμνηστος, which appears at Theocritus 16.42 when Theocritus praises the achievement of lyric in general and Simonides in particular to preserve memory. New adjective formations such as *inlacrimabilis* or *inhospitalis*, which render Greek compounds with a privative α, are typical for Horace, as Bartalucci notes at *EO* ii.927–8 s.v. 'arcaismi' (numerous examples at *EO* ii.927).

which is subjected to seasonal word change and therefore can only be fully appreciated in the present. In the future some words will fall out of use, others reappear, and their specific timely quality as neologisms or archaisms will no longer be naturally understood, until philologists gather again the fallen leaves.

3.2 A Linguistic Turn Around and Around: Horace on Semantic Change

Horace's thoughts on lexical development are highly idiosyncratic; they seem to differ from any notable ancient or modern theory that deals with this matter. Neither Aristotle, nor Varro, nor Caesar, nor Cicero thought that lexical development happened in a cyclical fashion. Ancients were aware of linguistic change over time, but they regarded this as a linear development, and so do modern linguists.[22] Indeed, at first sight one may be tempted to dismiss Horace's thoughts as too bizarre to be taken seriously, or one might argue that Horace's prime interest lies in the beauty of the simile of the leaves rather than in linguistic reflections. Yet, I maintain that we should be attentive to Horace's idiosyncratic thoughts in this passage. For if we are attentive, the passage can tell us a lot about Horace's understanding of his own poetry. Even taken at face value, Horace's theory is perhaps not quite as absurd as it may first seem. A significant number of Latin words, which are found in Plautus and Terence, do not then appear in classical Latin, but are present again in late Latin. Such words, Giuseppe Pezzini says, reappeared in Latin through 'revival, recoinage, and reborrowing (normally from Greek)'.[23] This sounds strikingly similar to Horace's ideas of words that are 'revived' (*renascentur*) or that should come 'from a Greek source' (*Graeco fonte*). And the metaphor of word-'coinage' seems to have been coined by Horace anyway (*Ars* 58–9). Of course, Horace could not have known of

---

[22] Dufallo (2005) compares Horace's thoughts with contemporaneous linguistic theory. Uhlfelder (1963) offers an overview on ancient awareness of linguistic change (28–9 deal with lexical change). See D'Alton (1962) 81–3 for an overview on archaisms and neologisms and their acceptance in Roman literary theory. See Fögen (2000) for Roman attitudes to their own language. For an account on semantic change from modern linguistics, see Hock (1991) 280–308.
[23] Pezzini (2016) 14. I owe this reference to Barnaby Taylor.

the linguistic phenomenon that Pezzini describes, but his linguistic reflections are at least not completely absurd. Perhaps more to the point, Aulus Gellius argues in the second century AD that archaisms and neologisms are essentially the same thing, since old, uncommon words have the appearance of neologisms when they appear in modern diction (11.7.2): *noua autem uideri dico etiam ea quae sunt inusitata et desita, tametsi sunt uetusta* ('but I maintain that even these words can seem like new [⁓neologisms] which have been out of use and have become obsolete, although they are in fact old words [⁓archaisms]'). To be sure, Gellius does not sign up to a universal principle of cyclical lexical change, and he goes on to ridicule the habit of some parvenus who use odd archaisms. Nonetheless, it seems that antiquarians took Horace's linguistic thoughts at least to some extent seriously.

Numerous ancient writers besides Horace have considered the subject of choice of words. Horace thus naturally shares some of his categories and terminologies with these other writers. Yet, this should not blind us to the originality and singularity of his thoughts. Though Aristotle discusses the different quality of words, though Cicero speaks of archaisms, neologisms, and metaphors in his discussion of choice of words, and though Varro even compares the appearance and extinction of words to the generations of men,[24] nonetheless, Horace's key idea of lexical cyclicality does not appear in earlier writers. Thus, Varro strongly denies that old words can reappear (*L.* 5.5): *quare illa [sc. uerba] quae iam maioribus nostris ademit obliuio, fugitiua secuta sedulitas Muci et Bruti retrahere nequit* ('therefore when words were already obsolete in the days of our ancestors, their meaning escapes even the diligence of Mucius and Brutus, who cannot capture their nuances though they pursue the matter').[25]

---

[24] Arist. *Po.* 22 1458a–1459a, Cic. *de Orat.* 3.149–58 with Oliensis (1998) 221–2, *Inv.* 1.33 with Norden (1905) 484–5, Var. *L.* 5.5 with Brink (1971a) at *Ars* 60–71. Horace's argument in favour of neologisms seems to be a reaction against Julius Caesar's *De Analogia*, in which Caesar strongly argued against using uncommon words. For Caesar's linguistic theories, see Pezzini (2018) with further references.

[25] I have attempted to mirror Varro's wordplay in my translation. Some nuances are lost, though: Varro compares Mucius and Brutus' hunt for etymologies to the hunt for runaway slaves (Melo (2019) ii.653–4).

Horace on Semantic Change

Horace's linguistic thoughts may even still appear original when we compare them to the theory that is closest to them: Epicurean linguistic thought. Philip Hardie has analysed numerous allusions to the Epicurean poet Lucretius in Horace's lines on choice of words.[26] Lucretius famously wrestled with the poverty of the Latin language (*patrii sermonis egestas* at Lucr. 1.832, 3.260; cf. 1.139) and coined numerous new words in his struggle. Allusions to Lucretius are thus highly appropriate when Horace faces similar issues in the *Ars*. The question remains, though, whether the affinity goes further and Horace actually signs up to an Epicurean understanding of linguistics. Some scholars think so, and argue that Horace as well as the Epicureans Philodemus and Lucretius consider letters to be 'semi-animate entities with a strange faculty of forming realities of their own' – just like atoms.[27] Such a theory would be an ingenious explanation for Horace's claim that language is eternal, yet its components, words, are continuously changed. Cyclicality, however, has no place in Epicurean linguistics, but is crucial to Horace's thoughts.[28] Thus, Horace could have justly said about his linguistic thoughts that in this realm, too, he was the first to plant his footsteps in the void.

The following section immediately precedes the simile of the leaves in the *Ars* and sets out Horace's thoughts on choice of words in some more detail (45–59):[29]

> in uerbis etiam tenuis cautusque serendis (46)
> hoc amet, hoc spernat promissi carminis auctor. (45)
> dixeris egregie, notum si callida uerbum (47)
> reddiderit iunctura nouum. si forte necesse est
> indiciis monstrare recentibus abdita rerum,
> fingere cinctutis non exaudita Cethegis (50)

---

[26] Hardie (2005; 2014: 49–53), pointing in particular to Lucr. 3.964–71.
[27] The expression of Armstrong (1995) 231. The case is made in particular by Oberhelman and Armstrong (1995) 249–54. Cf. Grimal (1968) 91–5, Freudenburg (1993) 119–45, Yona (2018) 146–8. This atomological view, which makes an analogy between letters (*elementa*) and atoms (*elementa*), goes back to P. Friedländer (1941), but is controversially discussed among Lucretian scholars. For an overview, see Volk (2002) 100–105. D. Russell (1973) 41, conversely, argues for Stoic inspiration for choice of words in the *Ars*.
[28] On Epicurean linguistic thought, see, above all, Sedley (1998) 35–49, Taylor (2020).
[29] I depart from Klingner's text in two places; at the end of line 49 I read *rerum* instead of *rerum at*, and in line 51 I place a semicolon instead of a comma after *pudenter*. In these two cases I follow the arguments of Brink (1971a) 140 against Klinger (1940).

continget dabiturque licentia sumpta pudenter;
et noua fictaque nuper habebunt uerba fidem, si
Graeco fonte cadent parce detorta. quid autem
Caecilio Plautoque dabit Romanus ademptum
Vergilio Varioque? ego cur, adquirere pauca   (55)
si possum, inuideor, cum lingua Catonis et Enni
sermonem patrium ditauerit et noua rerum
nomina protulerit? licuit semperque licebit
signatum praesente nota producere nomen.

46 *ante* **45** *transpos. ed. Britannici* 1516 : *post* **45** *codd.* **49** rerum B C K R : rerum et a Ψ V σχ **59** producere nomen] procudere *Aldus* nummum *Luisinus*

> When it comes to stringing words together delicately and carefully, the endeavouring poet should be choosy and embrace one word but ignore another. It is a sign of a distinguished stylist if an ingenious collocation (*callida iunctura*) makes a familiar word new. If it is necessary to explain obscurities with new signifiers, you will have the chance to invent new words which the kilted Cethegi of old had never heard – and you will be granted the right to do so if you make modest use of it. New words that have just been invented will earn trust if they derive from a Greek source (as long as the trickle is moderate). But why did Romans grant to Caecilius and Plautus the privilege that they deny to Vergil and Varius? Why do people begrudge me to acquire a few words where I can, while the language of Cato and Ennius has enriched our ancestors' speech and brought forth new terms for things? It has been and always will be allowed to produce word coinages of present currency.

In this passage, together with the subsequent one on leaves, Horace names three mechanisms through which cyclical lexical change is achieved. The first category is archaisms, words that have fallen out of use and are revived (70–1);[30] the second category is neologisms, new words that are necessary to describe new phenomena (48–59); and the third category is *callidae iuncturae*, the usage of common words in a new context or different setting (47–8, cf. 240–3).[31] In practice, these three categories cannot

---

[30] Bösing (1970) thinks that these lines refer to neologisms rather than archaisms. I am not convinced.

[31] These mechanisms naturally receive due attention in numerous studies on Horace. Thus, Conte (1994) [1987] 311–12 singles out the *callida iunctura* as a hallmark of Horace's lyric style. Muecke at *EO* ii.755–87 s.v. 'lingua e stile' is fundamental and offers a rich bibliography. The following studies are also particularly relevant. *EO* offers rich articles on 'arcaismi' (Bartalucci, ii.797–9), 'neologismi' (Viparelli, ii.925–8), 'callida

always be clearly distinguished, and Horace himself, in fact, conflates them: neologisms are not truly new, as they should ideally derive from a Greek source. Further, though archaisms and *callidae iuncturae* are old words, they have the appearance of new ones. Horace is thus less interested in a careful definition of these three categories, which at any rate do not appear as neatly listed and defined in his work as they do in my discussion here;[32] rather, he stresses the cyclical nature of language change, which a number of interrelated mechanisms bring about.

In the same passage Horace puts this theory into practice. One example is *pronos* in the leaves simile (60): *ut siluae foliis pronos mutantur in annos* ('as trees change in leaf from sliding year to year').[33] Richard Bentley has noted that Romans do not use descriptive epithets for phrases such as *in annos*, *in dies*, or *in horas*, and he thus reads *priuos* instead. A. E. Housman says with characteristic wit: 'I am told that "pronos" is very poetical: I reply, That question does not yet arise. Bentley has not denied that it is poetical; he has denied that it is Latin.'[34] Yet, the problem is, of course, that the word appears in a passage that is precisely about the unstable nature of the Latin language. In the immediately preceding line, Horace claimed for himself the right to innovate

iunctura' (Chersoni, ii.803–8), and 'grecismi' (Ciancaglini, ii.850–6). Waszink (1972) [1964] analyses the passage from the *Ars* and its implication for the *Odes*. See Mayer (1999) and in particular Gitner (2012) on Grecisms, Axelson (1945) 98–113 on unpoetic words, Armstrong (1968), Knox (2013) 538–42 on *callida iunctura* (Ruch (1963) too narrowly defines *callidae iuncturae* as oxymora), Maurach (1995) 83–92 on several of these categories. Also helpful are the categories of 'uocabula noua uel nouata' in the index of Bo (1960) and the categories 'archaisms', 'coinages', and 'colloquial language' in the indices of the commentaries of Mayer (1994) and (2012). Among older studies, there is Rothmaler (1862), Zangemeister (1862), Waltz (1881) 41–137, Ruckdeschel (1911), Brunori (1930) 47–61, 208–9, Immisch (1932) 75–93, Smereka (1935), Cupaiuolo (1942), Leroy (1948). Horace also creates cyclical linguistic dynamics through a device which Maurach (1995) 84 calls 'Rücketymologisierung', that is, Horace uses words in their original, at his time already uncommon meaning, such as *oscula* as 'lips' instead of 'kiss' at *C.* 1.13.15.

[32] Cf. Waszink (1972) [1964] 281, who says that Horace writes here with 'bewußter Vermeidung jeder strengen Systematik'.

[33] The German translation of Delz (1995) 9 for *pronos in annos* is wonderful: 'wenn das Jahr jeweils sich neigt'. The verb 'neigen' describes exactly the movement of *pronos*, while 'sich dem Ende zuneigen' is a natural way of referring to time.

[34] Housman (1972) [1890] i.155, referring to Bentley (1713). Shackleton Bailey (2001) prints *priuos*; Klingner should have mentioned it in his apparatus. The issue really is the combination of *pronus* with *in*. On its own *pronus* can easily qualify time, for example, at Hor. *C.* 4.6.39–40: *pronos* [...] *mensis*.

Latin. And as an innovation in Latin, a *callida iunctura*, the expression *pronos in annos* is effective: each year glides in a downward slope like heavenly bodies, perhaps reminiscent of the downward motion of falling leaves.[35] Some lines earlier, Horace had already said that new words should derive, literally 'fall' (53: *cadent*), from a Greek source. Later, he says that words will reappear that have fallen out of usage, and current words will fall out of usage (70): *cecidere cadentque*. The fall is a universal principle in these lines pertaining to leaves, words, humans, and perhaps also years.

Besides *pronos* or *priuos*, the passage includes a number of other notable expressions which underline its message. Thus, when Horace says that people begrudge him his inventiveness of words, he proves that inventiveness through the usage of a syntactical Grecism that is unparalleled in Latin: *inuideor*, 'I am begrudged'. For the verb *inuideo* normally takes the dative in Latin and the passive construction here follows the Greek φθονοῦμαι.[36] Pointedly, this first-person verb is the only time in the *Ars* when Horace explicitly mentions his own poetry, as Carl Becker has noted.[37] We are thus justified in connecting Horace's theoretical thoughts in these lines with his lyric work – the more so as *inuidia* is a mark of lyric achievement in the sphragis of *Odes* 2.[38] Further striking expressions include *callida iunctura*, which may itself be a *callida iunctura*, as the word *iunctura* was perhaps not used previously in a stylistic context.[39] In the same sentence, the 'known word', *notum uerbum*, is ironically not known at all: the usual word in this context is *usitatum* rather than *notum*.[40] Then, in line 50, when the Cethegi of old times are surprised about

---

[35] Thus Sider (1996) 277 n.24. On the other hand, *priuos* would have welcome Lucretian connotations in a very Lucretian passage (Hardie (2005) 37). Furthermore, *priuos* in the meaning of *singulos* would be an archaism (Brink (1971a) *ad loc.*), which fits the passage rather well.

[36] This is already recognised by the scholiasts. Ps-Acro is particularly attentive to the issue: *mire, dum de fingendis uerbis loquitur, secundum Graecos ipse fincxit 'inuideor'*. Also see Marx (1925) 186–94, Brink (1971a) *ad loc.*, Gitner (2012) 163–4. Cf. *inuidere* at Hor. *S.* 2.6.83–4 with Quintilian *Inst.* 9.3.17, Mayer (1999) 161–2, and Gitner (2012) 133–4.

[37] Becker (1963) 81 n.6.

[38] Becker (1963) 81 n.6 sees the connection to *C.* 2.20.4. Cf. *C.* 4.3.16.

[39] Thus Oberhelman and Armstrong (1995) 252 n.69. Compare and contrast Brink (1971a) *ad loc.*

[40] Hardie (2005: 36; 2014: 50–1), building on observations by Brink (1971a) *ad loc.*

modern words, they would be most surprised about the adjective that qualifies themselves, *cinctutis*, 'kilted', which is a neologism.[41] It seems, though, that perhaps the most remarkable of Horace's wordplays has gone unnoticed. This wordplay can be found at the crucial point at which Horace summarises his thoughts on choice of words in one sentence (68–9): *mortalia facta peribunt, | nedum sermonum stet honos et gratia uiuax* ('still, all mortal works will perish, and still less is it true that the honour and grace of speech could stay alive').[42] Horace's choice of words here is programmatic and wittily underlines the sense. For neither have the word *honos* nor the word *gratia* always stood in honour and favour. The learned Aulus Gellius informs us that *honos* was not at all times an exclusively positive term in Latin, but used to belong to a category of so-called *uocabula ancipitia* (12.9; cf. 11.12). This describes words which can denote a positive as well as a negative quality. *Gratia* is an example for such a word, which Gellius indeed mentions. For *bona gratia* denotes favour, popularity, and esteem, whereas *mala gratia* denotes disfavour and unpopularity.[43] Gellius says that Quintus Metellus Numidicus in the late second century BC spoke of *peior honos*, which supposedly denotes disrespect rather than respect. This meaning of the word was already lost in Horace's day (if it ever existed outside of the inventive minds of antiquarians).[44] Yet, that is precisely the point of the passage: now in the present moment and the present context *honos* and *gratia* enjoy honour and grace, but this has not always been so, nor will it always be so.[45] This is also how Horace describes trees,

[41] Noted by Brink (1971a) *ad loc.* Cf. Hor. *Epist.* 2.2.117: [*sc. uocabula*] *priscis memorata Catonibus atque Cethegis.* Hardie (2005) 37 mentions a connection to Ennius *Ann.* 304–8 Skutsch, where *Cethegus* is a *flos delibatus*, a flower that has long withered. As Hardie says, this possible reference neatly picks up the imagery of the leaves in the simile that follows in the *Ars*.
[42] Cf. Hor. *Epist.* 2.2.112, where Horace says that a good poet should do away with any words that are 'unworthy of honour' (*indigna honore*).
[43] In addition to Gellius, see *OLD* s.v. 'gratia' 5.
[44] *TLL* s.v. says that Metellus simply uses *honos* ironically. For the present purpose it matters little whether or not Gellius is right. It is much more significant that Horace might have thought the same way. Strikingly, Horace uses two out of ten terms in Gellius' list.
[45] Additionally, *honos* is an archaism that receives new honour again in the present passage; Horace also uses *honor* (Muecke at *EO* ii.756 s.v. 'lingua e stile'). In the same sentence, the prosaic word *nedum* also receives new-found poetic honour (Axelson (1945) 85–6, 96, Brink (1971a) *ad loc.*, cf. *autem* in line 53 and Porphyrio

which do not always have their leafage or *honos*.⁴⁶ And this is, of course, also exactly the message of Horace's *carpe diem*. Thus, in one *carpe diem* poem, Maecenas is asked to enjoy the present moment as Fortune's favours (*honores*) are fickle (*C*. 3.29.51–2). In another *carpe diem* poem, Horace tells a certain Quinctius to drink, as spring flowers do not always have the same *honor* (*C*. 2.11.9–10): *non semper idem floribus est honor | uernis*.

The vast majority of the words Horace uses in his poetry may seem unremarkable. These words simply represent the normal diction of Latin in Horace's time.⁴⁷ Yet, the *Ars* asserts that these common words, too, are subject to change, as words in general are shaped by the changing 'usage' (*usus*) of society (*Ars* 71–2).⁴⁸ Thus, even seemingly simple, unadorned words in the *Odes* are an important part of Horace's diction of the present. Certain words, however, evoke present time more emphatically. Such words – again, archaisms, neologisms, *callidae iuncturae* – enrich Horace's diction at crucial points. For instance, when Horace says that archaisms can enrich language, the expression he uses for enrichment, *ditauerit*, is itself an archaism (*Ars* 57).⁴⁹ Horace's attempt to enrich Latin responds to Lucretius' well-known complaint on Latin's paucity (*sermonii patriis egestas*). Horace's solution for this paucity is striking; he is *coining* new words (58–9): *licuit semperque licebit | signatum praesente nota producere nomen* ('It has been and always will be allowed to produce words bearing the mint-mark of the present'). Like coins, words can bear the mark of the time when they were minted.⁵⁰ Words

---

at *Ars* 47). The poetic expression *sermonum haud*, a conjecture in the Aldine edition, is thus unnecessary. Peerlkamp's *saecla* instead of the transmitted *facta* would neatly pick up Homer's γενεή, but is arguably unfounded.

⁴⁶ See *Epod*. 11.5–6, *December* [...] *siluis honorem decutit*, with Delz (1995) 10, Mankin (1995) *ad loc.*, *OLD* s.v. 6b, and cf. Ov. *Met*. 1.565. This meaning of *honos* as 'leafage' may faintly ring at *Ars* 70–1, where natural imagery abounds.

⁴⁷ Thus Muecke at *EO* ii.772 s.v. 'lingua e stile', Klingner (1964) [1951] 443, Waszink (1972) [1964] 290–3, Wilkinson (1959), Nisbet and Hubbard (1970) xxii.

⁴⁸ Brink (1971a) *ad loc.* convincingly argues that *usus* means *consuetudo* here rather than χρεία.

⁴⁹ Noted by Brink (1971a) *ad loc.*

⁵⁰ The metaphor of coinage is already clear enough in the paradosis (signatum *praesente* nota [...] *nomen*), and it is unnecessary to read *procudere* (Aldine edition) instead of *producere*, or *nummum* (Francesco Luisini) instead of *nomen*. Note, though, that Bentley (1713) and Shackleton Bailey (2001) print both these conjectures, which certainly gives added emphasis to the image of coinage. Bentley (1713) *ad loc.* adduces

thus *produce* effects of presence, according to Horace. Serendipitously, Horace's expression '*producing* a word with a present mark' is reborn in our day as literary theory gives new currency to the expression. As Jonathan Culler says, in lyric, uniquely, 'effects of presence are produced'.[51] The expression may sound less natural in English than it does in Latin; Hans Ulrich Gumbrecht, the scholar who coined the expression, stresses that he uses 'production' in the original Latin sense of *producere*.[52] Be that as it may, already Horace theorises about how poetry can produce presence. His answer refers to his choice of words. In the following section, I wish to look at a number of Horatian coinages in more detail and analyse how exactly they produce presence.

3.3 Bags Full of Leaves: Coinages in Horace's *Carpe Diem* Poems (*C.* 4.7, 1.11, 1.36)

Among Horace's books of *Odes*, Book 4 is the collection that is closest in publication date to the *Ars* (though the exact publication dates of both the *Ars* and *Odes* 4 are a matter of debate). *Odes* 4 is also Horace's book of lyric in which scholars have found the highest number of unusual words.[53] One poem in particular, *Odes* 4.7, thematises cyclical time and thus invites comparison with the leaves passage from the *Ars*. I wish to show that the ode is shaped by Horace's ideas about cyclical time with regard to its content as well as its choice of words. Contemplation of the cycle of the seasons leads to insight into human mortality in this *carpe diem* poem:

> Diffugere niues, redeunt iam gramina campis
>   arboribusque comae;
> mutat terra uices, et decrescentia ripas
>   flumina praetereunt.

---

a number of other texts which use the metaphor of coinage for words and writing, all post-dating Horace. Besides the English 'coinage', the German 'Wortprägung' also preserves the metaphor. Cf. Smereka (1935) 73–4, Oliensis (1998) 213–14.
[51] Culler (2015) 37 and *passim*.
[52] Gumbrecht (2004) 16–17 and 17 n.4 (cf. Gumbrecht (2006)).
[53] See, for example, Kießling and Heinze (1961a) at *Epist.* 2.2.115, Rostagni (1930) at *Ars* 70, Collinge (1961) 13–14. Becker (1963) 12 and *passim* makes the case for strong unity in thought in Horace's late work.

Gathering Leaves

Gratia cum Nymphis geminisque sororibus audet (5)
  ducere nuda choros.
inmortalia ne speres, monet annus et almum
  quae rapit hora diem.

frigora mitescunt Zephyris, uer proterit aestas,
  interitura, simul (10)
pomifer autumnus fruges effuderit, et mox
  bruma recurrit iners.

damna tamen celeres reparant caelestia lunae:
  nos ubi decidimus
quo pius Aeneas, quo diues Tullus et Ancus, (15)
  puluis et umbra sumus.

quis scit an adiciant hodiernae crastina summae
  tempora di superi?
cuncta manus auidas fugient heredis, amico
  quae dederis animo. (20)

cum semel occideris et de te splendida Minos
  fecerit arbitria,
non, Torquate, genus, non te facundia, non te
  restituet pietas.

infernis neque enim tenebris Diana pudicum (25)
  liberat Hippolytum
nec Lethaea ualet Theseus abrumpere caro
  uincula Pirithoo.

The snow has fled; now grass is returning to the fields, and leaves to the trees. The earth is going through changes, and rivers are subsiding and flowing between their usual banks. The Grace ventures to lead dances naked together with the nymphs and her twin sisters. Don't hope for immortality; that's the warning that the year gives you and the hour that snatches away the nourishing day. Cold weather is softened by the West Wind; then spring is crushed by summer, which in turn is bound to die as soon as apple-bearing autumn pours forth its fruits, and soon lifeless winter returns.

Yet, the moon quickly recovers its losses in the sky; but in our case, once we have come down where pious Aeneas went and rich Tullus and Ancus, we are dust and shades. Who knows whether the gods above are adding tomorrow's tally to the total of today? All the things that you give to your dear soul will escape the greedy hands of your heir. Once you have died and splendid[54]

---

[54] Thomas (2011) *ad loc.* seems right in arguing that *splendida* is a transferred epithet modelled on Minos' description as Διὸς ἀγλαὸν υἱόν at Hom. *Od.* 11.568. Yet, a literal

Minos has made his judgment, Torquatus, not your lineage, nor your eloquence, nor your piety will bring you back. For not even Diana frees chaste Hippolytus from dark Hades, nor is Theseus strong enough to break the Lethean chains that hold his beloved Pirithous.

The poem urges present enjoyment within the revolving cycle of the seasons. Revolving and repetition work on multiple levels. The poem itself is unusually close to an earlier poem, *Odes* 1.4, and it is universally noted that themes as well as many expressions seem to be revived from this earlier poem.[55] The poem's verbs, too, reflect the cyclical change of nature: *redire* (1), *recurrere* (12), *reparare* (13). Nature is all about revival and recurrence, whereas this is not possible for humans: non, *Torquate, genus,* non *te facundia,* non *te* restituet *pietas* ('Torquatus, *not* your lineage, *nor* your eloquence, *nor* your piety *will bring* you *back*').[56] The third stanza expresses this idea most clearly; it describes the cycle of the seasons with impressive economy.

The meditation on nature's cycle and human mortality in the poem suggests the image of leaves. We all are falling, Horace says (*C.* 4.7.14): *nos* [...] *decidimus*. This unusual verb for dying transfers the fall of leaves to humans.[57] Indeed, the first sentence of the poem has already introduced a connection between leaves and humans. While humans would later fall like leaves, the poem begins by describing leaves as human hairs in the description of their return to trees (1–2): *Diffugere niues, redeunt iam gramina campis | arboribusque* comae ('The snow has fled; now grass is returning to the fields, and leaves [literally: hairs] to the trees').[58]

---

rendering of the transferred epithet sounds unnatural in English (unlike the preceding transferred epithet 'the greedy hands of your heir').

[55] For example, Fraenkel (1957) 419–21, Rudd (1960) 379–83, Woodman (1972), Putnam (1986) 143–4.

[56] For the significance of the verbs with the prefix *re-* and the anaphora of *non*, see, for example, Thomas (2011) at line 1. Syndikus (1972–3) ii.357 n.5 is also good on this. Cyclical and linear time in Horace are amply discussed: Rudd (1960) 380, Commager (1962) 265–91, Davis (1991) 145–88, Lowrie (1997) 50–5. The influence of Catullus 5 on content and diction of the poem is also widely noted (*soles occidere et redire possunt* [...]). For the contrast between human mortality and nature's renewal in Catullus, Horace, and elsewhere, see Fantuzzi (1987), and 104 n.8 on *carpe diem*.

[57] Noted by Davis (1991) 156–7, now widely accepted. Older scholarship saw a connection to falling heavenly bodies, which seems less likely (Rudd (1960) 381, Becker (1963) 150). Still older scholarship thought that *decidere* is a vulgarism here (Smereka (1935) 70).

[58] Becker (1963) 151 n.7 notes another return: the verse ending *gramina campis* is virtually taken from *Ars* 162. Later in Book 4, at *C.* 4.10, *comae* and *decidere* are crucial words

127

Gathering Leaves

The generations of leaves and humans in a *carpe diem* poem – this naturally evokes Simonides. Indeed, scholars have shown the importance of Simonides for the whole ode, and they have identified certain expressions that seem to allude to Simonides directly.[59] What I wish to stress on the following pages is the significance of the choice of words: like the *Ars*, *Odes* 4.7, too, shows an interest in words that fall to the ground and grow again.

In the fifth stanza, Horace tells his addressee, Torquatus, to enjoy the present (17–20):

> quis scit an adiciant hodiernae crastina summae
>   tempora di superi?
> cuncta manus auidas fugient heredis, amico
>   quae dederis animo.

> Who knows whether the gods above are adding tomorrow's tally to the total of today? All the things that you give to your dear soul will escape the greedy hands of your heir.

Some scholars reject the whole stanza as un-Horatian.[60] One of its problems is an expression that is unparalleled in Latin: *amico animo* must equal *animo tuo*, but such a usage of *amicus* is not known elsewhere in Latin. It has long been suggested that Horace is here calquing on the Greek, where expressions such as φίλῳ θυμῷ are natural.[61] Indeed, Kießling and Heinze have wonderfully explained the whole sentence in their commentary; according to them, the expression *dare animo* already introduces a Grecism (~τῇ ψυχῇ δοῦναι) where Latin would prefer *animo obsequi*. As Horace follows Greek texts which urge present enjoyment with the expression 'giving to one's soul', he further heightens the Greek

---

for transience, on which see Commager (1962) 297–8, D. H. Porter (1975) 220–3. For the motif of anthropomorphised trees (and arboreal humans) in Latin literature, see, above all, Nisbet (1987).

[59] See, above all, Barchiesi (1996a) 33–7. Barchiesi includes *C.* 4.7 in a study that argues for Simonides as a key influence for *Odes* 4 as a whole: through Simonides Horace finds new ways to compose lyric praise. The older studies of Cataudella (1927–8) and Oates (1932) 76–90 remain valuable.

[60] Collinge (1961) 111, Becker (1963) 151–8, Günther (2010) 107 (cf. Rudd (1960) 383, who, however, does not go so far as to reject the stanza). Fredricksmeyer (1985) 18–22 praises the lines. Shackleton Bailey (2001) says rightly about these lines: 'a nonnullis sine causa suspecti'.

[61] Already Dacier (1689–97) *ad loc.* suggested the Greek model. In a *carpe diem* context the expression is used at Thgn. 877, 983.

Coinages in Horace's *Carpe Diem* Poems

sense of the line through his use of *amicus*.⁶² Kießling and Heinze also adduce some Greek passages which might have influenced the Horatian expression. Chief among them is this line from Simonides' leaves elegy (*fr.* 20.12): ψυχῇ τῶν ἀγαθῶν τλῆθι χαριζόμενος ('endure and pamper your soul with good things'). Horace's Grecism draws attention to his phrase as a translation from the Greek, something made new. Horace's expression does not mirror Simonides' original very precisely, though. Simonides' model can account neither for *dare* nor *amicus* in Horace. It might be better to say that Horace looks through Simonides at a whole Greek tradition in which the idiom of 'indulging one's soul' is common in a *carpe diem* context. Even a toper could voice this sentiment on his tombstone (*GV* 1368 *apud* Ath. 8.336d, discussed on pages 59–61 of Chapter 1): πιέν, φαγέν καὶ πάντα τᾷ ψυχᾷ δόμεν ('drink, eat, and give everything to your soul').⁶³

The Grecism appears at a crucial moment in Horace's poem: the exhortation to enjoy oneself in the moment, as no one can know if the gods add tomorrow's tally to the total of today (17–18).⁶⁴ In Simonides, the exhortation to gratify one's soul would have been delivered at the symposium. Listeners could have followed the exhortation among music and cups. Simonides' addressee, who is described as old, would have had particularly good reason for urgent enjoyment 'at the end of [his] life'. In reperformances, the implied addressee of the poem would have provided an occasion for urgent enjoyment, even though later audiences might be of various ages. Already in Simonides, addressee and occasion thus go some way towards producing presence rather than simply being

---

⁶² Kießling and Heinze (1966) *ad loc.*
⁶³ This parallel, too, is noted by Kießling and Heinze (1966) *ad loc.*, who also point to Theoc. 16.24. Rawles (2018) 117 thinks that Simonides' poem already reflects earlier ideas such as Thgn. 1224: θυμῷ δειλὰ χαριζομένη. Expressions of this kind are common in Greek *carpe diem*: Mimn. *fr.* 7.1 = Thgn. 795 = *AP* 9.50.1 (σὴν αὐτοῦ φρένα τέρπε; a Homeric expression: for example, *Il.* 1.474, 9.186), *SH* 335.1 (σὸν θυμὸν ἄεξε), [Alexis] *fr.* 25.5 (τὴν ψυχὴν τρέφειν) with the very rich note of Arnott (1996) 825. Persius 5.151 Romanises the expression in a *carpe diem* piece: *indulge genio*. It is curious when the *carpe diem* exhortation of pampering one's soul appears on a Christian epitaph (*SGO* 16/06/01.18 = *GV* 1905.18): τὴν ψυχὴν εὐφραίνετε πάντοτε. Please note that I regularly translate the idiom simply as 'to make oneself happy' or 'to enjoy oneself' in other chapters, where the literal side of the idiom seems less relevant. Also see page 9 in the Introduction on the idiom.
⁶⁴ See Davis (1991) 162–3 on these lines as an 'indirect prescription' of *carpe diem*.

present.⁶⁵ Horace's exhortation in turn conveys a different type of presence.⁶⁶ He uses a strikingly new Latin expression when he exhorts Torquatus to enjoy the present. The words are stamped with the present mark.

The word that is perhaps the most remarkable in the ode is *pomifer*, 'apple-bearing' (11). Horace usually avoids Greek-style compounds of this type.⁶⁷ By contrast, such words are common in Lucretius and Vergil. Indeed, Vergil arguably offers, besides Simonides, the strongest influence on Horace's choice of words in this poem. An expression that would strike even the most superficial reader as Vergilian can be found in line 15: *pius Aeneas*. The less likely *uaria lectio*, which is *pater Aeneas*, is, of course, just as Vergilian. It is thus very much Vergil's Aeneas who offers an example for the universality of death in Horace's poem. Yet, the overt allusion to Vergil only highlights that Horace in fact diverges from Vergil and corrects him: the katabasis of Vergil's Aeneas in Book 6 of the *Aeneid* was a round trip, whereas Horace emphasises that journeys to the underworld are always one-way trips. At the end of the poem, Horace also corrects Vergil's account of the Hippolytus myth and makes his Hippolytus remain in the underworld, whereas Vergil's Hippolytus would be freed.⁶⁸ Horace's *pomifer* is another reference to Vergil, *an oppositio in imitando*:⁶⁹ Vergil uses *malifer* for the same idea, a *hapax legomenon* in the *Aeneid* and Latin literature as a whole (Verg. *A.* 7.740, just preceding the myth of Hippolytus). In the *Ars*, Horace noted that Vergil coins words, while some of his fellow

---

⁶⁵ Horace would use the device of the addressee to mimic occasion, as Citroni (2009) [1983] analysed. Sider (2020) 299 now suggests that the old addressee of Simonides' poem might be the older poet Mimnermus (as in Solon, *fr.* 20). If right, Simonides already creates a fictional addressee who is made present through allusions to his work. Yet, Sider's suggestion is naturally speculative (compare and contrast Rawles (2018) 125–7). See Hose (2008) 204–6 for how Stobaeus (and others) suppress the addressee in lyric excerpts in order to create lyric without 'pragmatics'.
⁶⁶ Again, see Barchiesi (2000) 176 for Horace's poetry in the tradition of reperformance.
⁶⁷ For Horace's restraint in that regard, see Gitner (2012) 27–8; Gitner notes at 66–7 that the Greek *Zephyri* instead of the Roman *Fauonius* further enhance the Greek colouring of the stanza. Paschalis (1995) 182–6 comments on some bilingual wordplay in *C.* 4.7.
⁶⁸ For these Vergilian intertexts, see Traina at *EO* ii.841–50 s.v. 'Ippolito', Thomas (2011) 180, 183. Vergil also adopted Homer's leaves simile (*A.* 6.309–10). Horace's *semel* in line 21 may offer a contrast to Virbius (*uir bis*), the new name of the resurrected Hippolytus in Vergil.
⁶⁹ I take the term from Giangrande (1967), who describes the concept in detail.

Coinages in Horace's *Carpe Diem* Poems

Romans find fault with that (*Ars* 55). Horace's *pomifer* seems to have been coined by himself; the word cannot be found before him.[70] The uncharacteristic word hints at Vergil, and offers a learned allusion to his friend's diction: while Vergil uses twenty-four compound adjectives ending in *-fer*, the word *pomifer* is the only word of this type in Horace.[71] The word *pomifer* also wonderfully illustrates Horace's principle of word change from the *Ars*. The word is old, calqued on Greek καρποφόρος or more likely μηλοφόρος, but is simultaneously reborn and made new.[72] Horace's *pomifer* pointedly evokes the cycle of words in a stanza that is all about time and the cycle of the seasons. Summer is about to die once apple-bearing autumn pours forth its fruits (9–11): *aestas, | interitura, simul | pomifer autumnus fruges effuderit*. The new season is accompanied by a new word; change applies to nature and words. It is also fitting that linguistic change again applies to trees; the generations of apples come and go, each year some apples fall to the ground and new ones grow.

Perhaps the best known of all Horace's *iuncturae* is the expression 'carpe diem' itself. The phrase appears in the poem to Leuconoe (*C.* 1.11):

> Tu ne quaesieris, scire nefas, quem mihi, quem tibi
> finem di dederint, Leuconoe, nec Babylonios
> temptaris numeros. ut melius, quidquid erit, pati.
> seu pluris hiemes seu tribuit Iuppiter ultimam,
> quae nunc oppositis debilitat pumicibus mare   (5)
> Tyrrhenum: sapias, uina liques, et spatio breui

---

[70] The word is first used by Horace at *C.* 3.23.8 qualifying *annus*. Admittedly, one cannot say with certainty whether Horace alluded to Vergil or vice versa. Yet, Vergil's fondness for such words and Horace's restraint in using them strongly suggest that Horace is following Vergil rather than the other way around. For Vergilian coinages of adjectives, see Saccone at *EV* i.54. s.v. 'aggetivazione'. In the present instance Vergil seems to offer an etymological pun on an Indo-European ancestor of 'apple' (O'Hara (2017) 92, 197): *maliferae* [...] *Abellae*. Old words die and grow again...
[71] For the numbers: Ladewig (1870) 13. Traina at *EO* ii.813–15 s.v. 'composti nominali' discusses *pomifer* and notes Vergil's preference for compounds in *-fer* (more references there). Collinge (1961) 111 is wrong when he calls the neologism *pomifer* an 'uninspired epithet'. At any rate, Horace's words inspired Juvenal to his witty take on revolving seasons, *iam letifero cedente pruinis | autumno* (4.56–7), unrecognised apparently by Juvenal's commentators.
[72] Bo (1943–4) 245, no. 32 suggests both καρποφόρος and μηλοφόρος.

spem longam reseces. dum loquimur, fugerit inuida
aetas: carpe diem quam minimum credula postero.

Don't ask Leuconoe what end the gods have decided for me and for you – it's not right to know that. And don't meddle with Babylonian horoscopes. How much better is it to accept whatever will be. Whether Jupiter has granted us other winters or this one is the last one, which is now wearing out the Etruscan Sea against rocks of pumice; either way, be wise, strain the wine, and cut down long-term hopes into a small space. While we are talking, begrudging time will have fled. Pluck the day and put minimal trust in tomorrow.

Though the phrase *carpe diem* has become something of a cliché and is probably most commonly imagined as spoken by the actor Robin Williams, it is in fact a daring and unusual coinage of Horace, as David West pointed out: 'We are brought up with *carpe diem* and cannot see what an astounding phrase it is. Nowhere else in Latin is it used of enjoying a period of time.'[73] Horace combines several expressions and models in this phrase: Pindar already spoke of 'plucking youth' (*P*. 6.48: ἥβαν δρέπων; cf. *fr*. 123.1–2 Maehler); Latin authors applied *carpo* to objects of time at least since Lucilius, though without any implication of enjoyment;[74] yet, plucking fruits is naturally linked to enjoyment (*Epod*. 2.19–20): *ut gaudet insitiua decerpens pira | certantem et uuam purpurae* ('how he [i.e., the happy country-dweller] rejoices as he plucks the pears that he had grafted and the grapes that compete in hue with purple dye'). Horace combines all these connotations in the daring expression *carpe diem*. Each word on its own, *carpe* as well as *diem*, is unremarkable but their combination is a daring *callida iunctura* that gives them splendour and produces presence. Thus, Horace describes in the *Ars* how common words (*de medio sumptis*) can acquire honour or splendour (*honor*) through the usage of a *iunctura* (242–3). In *Odes* 1.11 the

[73] D. West (1967) 58, refuting Collinge (1961) 68: 'Horace does no more than say "carpe diem" in a series of aphorisms piled up in an almost Gilbertian manner.'
[74] Traina (1973) is fundamental for the semantics of the expression 'carpe diem'. Pindar's expression is already noted by Orelli and Baiter (1850) *ad loc*. Pindar's choice of words is daring in its own right and builds on expressions such as ἄνθος ἥβης, which I discussed on pages 11–12, 115 and 115 n.19. Lucilius applied the verb *carpo* to an object of time at *fr*. 917 Marx = 878 Warmington: *hiemem unam quamque carpam* ('let me go through each winter'). For Traina, not Lucilius but Catullus is the first to apply *carpo* to time, as Traina accepts Marx's unlikely conjecture *hieme* in Lucilius (see Dehon (1993)).

iunctura is striking: the day has to be plucked like a fruit in the momentarily fleeting season. The words that describe this also appear as new and gain new honour through a *iunctura* within the seasons of words.[75] If we understand *carpe diem* as a reference to plucking fruits, such as grapes, then this expression is not the only one in the poem that is taken from viticulture. West noted that earlier in the poem Horace already employed expressions from viticulture in his advice to Leuconoe (6–7): *sapias, uina liques, et spatio breui | spem longam reseces* ('be wise, strain the wine, and cut down long-term hopes into a small space'). The tricolon of exhortations blends advice pertaining to Leuconoe's attitude to life with advice pertaining to wine and viticulture. Being wise is a question of her attitude, straining wine is more practical advice, but the third exhortation combines the two spheres. The verb *reseco* describes the pruning of vines and thus belongs to the same imagery as *uina liques*, as West notes.[76] This metaphorical usage of *reseco*, pruning long-term hopes, in turn prepares for the expression *carpe diem*, plucking the day like a grape, according to West.[77] Yet, Horace is not only pruning long-term hopes into a small space (*spatio breui | spem longam reseces*); he is also pruning poetry – none of Horace's odes consists of fewer lines, and the poem is wider than it is long.[78] The poem itself feels pruned to a short

---

[75] Porphyrio: *metaforicos 'primo quoque' inquit 'die fruere'. translatio autem a pomis sumpta est, quae scilicet ideo carpimus, ut fruamur*. Traina (1973) understands the image differently: day after day (*in dies*) should be slowly and continuously harvested from the *aetas*. But *fugerit inuida aetas* suggests speed, which should be countered with one fast plucking action rather than continuous harvesting. The erotic subtext of the ode also suggests urgency (W. S. Anderson (1992) 121): '"Candy is dandy, but liquor is quicker." And his libido says: now!' Horace urges Leuconoe to sleep with him on this day rather than encouraging her to savour every day. Mazzoli (1991) agrees with Traina, but argues that that parts of *dies* are harvested, not parts of *aetas*. Görler (1995) repeats Mazzoli's argument ('pflücke den Tag leer'), apparently unaware of either his article or the response to Mazzoli from Traina (1993).

[76] D. West (1967) 58–64.

[77] Similarly, Seneca at *Epist.* 78.14 would later recommend to 'cut off' (*circumcido*) fears for the future (as well as memories of past ills): *circumcidenda ergo duo sunt, et futuri timor et ueteris incommodi memoria*.

[78] C. 1.38 and 4.10 also consist of only eight lines. Epigrammatic models surely influenced the form of these two poems. Yet, the clipped shape of C. 4.10 also underlines the poem's content, which deals with the cutting of hair. I will return to the idea of cutting *carpe diem* poems in Chapter 5.

space. Its form thus mirrors its content, and its metre furthers this impression: the Greater Asclepiad in this poem confines several phrases in a short space.[79]

Pruning poems as if they were vines is one of Horace's recommendations in his literary letters. Thus, Horace tells the Pisones at *Ars* 291–4 that one should thoroughly 'clip' a poem (*coercuit* and *praesectum*).[80] Later, at *Ars* 445–50, he repeats the advice and says that a good critic, in the fashion of a vinegrower, would check useless growth (*reprehendet inertes*), find fault with too-hard wood (*culpabit duros*), mark untrimmed plants for winter pruning (*incomptis allinet atrum | trauerso calamo signum*), and, in order that the plant receive more light (*parum lucem dare coget*), 'prune pretentious ornamentation' (*ambitiosa recidet | ornamenta*).[81] The image is most developed in the Florus letter. There, Horace says that anyone who wishes to write a proper poem should also take up the spirit of a stern censor and rid his diction of words that are undeserving of honour (*honore indigna*). There follow some lines on choice of words, archaisms and neologisms, which are similar in nature to Horace's later discussion of the issue in the *Ars*. The good poet will also need good pruning skills when it comes to his choice of words (*Epist.* 2.2.115–25):

>obscurata diu populo bonus eruet atque   (115)
>proferet in lucem speciosa uocabula rerum,
>quae priscis memorata Catonibus atque Cethegis
>nunc situs informis premit et deserta uetustas;
>adsciscet noua, quae genitor produxerit usus.
>uemens et liquidus puroque simillimus amni   (120)
>fundet opes Latiumque beabit diuite lingua;
>*luxuriantia conpescet, nimis aspera sano*
>*leuabit cultu, uirtute carentia tollet:*
>ludentis speciem dabit et torquebitur, ut qui
>nunc Satyrum, nunc agrestem Cyclopa mouetur.   (125)

---

[79] Schwindt (2016) 130–1 explains this well. Cf. W. S. Anderson (1992) 120.
[80] See Brink (1971a) *ad loc.* for the pruning metaphor.
[81] I follow D. West (1967) 60 and Rudd (1989) 223–4 here, who argue that the viticulture imagery is sustained throughout *Ars* 445–8 (though intertwined with imagery pertaining to prosecutors, censors, and judges). Brink (1971a) *ad loc.* is more sceptical and only accepts one unambiguous expression as a pruning metaphor: *ambitiosa recidet | ornamenta*.

Coinages in Horace's *Carpe Diem* Poems

He [i.e., someone who wishes to write a good poem] will do well to unearth words that have long been obscure to the people, and he will bring splendid terms to light, which people like Cato or Cethegus of old used to know, but which now lie buried under ugly neglect and desolate old age. And he will admit new words which need has fathered and brought forth. His flow of words will be powerful and clear, and just like the flow of an unpolluted river he will spread prosperity and enrich Latium with the wealth of his language. *He will cut back* ~~excessive~~ *(otiose!) foliage verbiage, he will smoothen what is too rough with beneficial attention, and he will uproot those words that lack dignity.* Although he torments himself, you would think that he moves between registers with playful ease like a dancer who becomes a satyr in one moment and a rustic cyclops in the next one.

There are quite a few different metaphors in play here. Neologisms can enrich the Latin language as a river enriches the countryside (120–1),[82] but old words are also similar to precious metals that are brought to the surface (115–16). Further, Horace compares the ideal poet's effortless motions between different words and registers to a dancer who seamlessly changes from one style to the other as he represents different characters in a pantomime (124–5). Horace's words, then, have the performative quality of momentary dance, as they evoke presence.[83] Other images from this passage would be echoed in the *Ars*. Thus, words are likened to human beings when they are oppressed by old age (118).[84] Finally, Horace again uses imagery taken from vegetation when he says that words need pruning (122–3). *Odes* 1.11 already anticipates in practice Horace's theoretical thoughts.[85] The poem is cut back so that certain striking expressions can shine and are not overshadowed by pretentious ornamentation: *carpe diem quam minimum credula postero* ('pluck the day, and put minimal trust in tomorrow').

In *Odes* 1.36, Horace celebrates the return of Numidia from Spain and describes a drinking party. This is a special day, and Horace says that the day should accordingly be marked with an auspicious white

---

[82] On this passage, see Freudenburg (2018) 142–8.
[83] See Lowrie (2009a) 70 on links between performative discourse and performance media.
[84] Cf. Hor. *C.* 1.4.16: *iam te premet nox fabulaeque Manes.*
[85] D. West (1967) 59–60 already noted that the pruning metaphors at *Ars* 445–8 and *C.* 1.11.6–7 are similar.

mark (*nota*) in the calendar (10): *Cressa ne careat pulcra dies nota* ('don't forget to mark this beautiful day with white chalk [literally: with a Cretan mark]').⁸⁶ As we will see, Horace also marks the present day again with a word coinage that bears the mark (*nota*) of the present (*Ars* 59: *signatum praesente nota producere nomen*; 'to produce words bearing the mint-mark of the present').

The party will include 'long-lived celery' and 'short-lived lily', and this contrast in bloom brings the *carpe diem* motif into the poem (*C.* 1.36.16).⁸⁷ Earlier in the poem, Horace describes the revelry that should take place at the party and says that 'Damalis, that drinker of much neat wine, must not be allowed to beat Bassus at downing the Thracian cup' (*C.* 1.36.13–14): *neu multi Damalis meri | Bassum Threicia uincat amystide*.⁸⁸ The word *amystis* seems to appear here for the first and only time in Latin. The term ἄμυστις can describe both a long draught and a type of large cup that is well suited for heavy drinking.⁸⁹ It has long been recognised that this Grecism points to a well-known passage from Callimachus' *Aetia*, in which the poet is present at a symposium and is delighted to see that another guest also dislikes heavy drinking (*fr.* 178.11–12 Harder):⁹⁰

καὶ γὰρ ὁ Θρηικίην μὲν ἀπέστυγε χανδὸν ἄμυστιν
ζωροποτεῖν, ὀλίγῳ δ' ἥδετο κισσυβίῳ.

For he [i.e., the other guest] also detested drinking neat wine with his mouth wide open in large draughts as the Thracians do; but he liked small cups.

---

⁸⁶ Nisbet and Hubbard (1970) *ad loc.* are convinced that this expression has nothing to do with the 'white day' (ἦμαρ [...] λευκόν) at Callimachus, *Aetia fr.* 178.12 Harder, but Horace makes much of this Callimachean passage in what follows.
⁸⁷ D. West (1995) 179–80.
⁸⁸ T. S. Johnson (2002) suggests *nunc* instead of *neu*, which should be given serious consideration; it makes much more sense if Horace finds it worthy to report that a woman (Damalis) would defeat a man (Bassus) in drinking. One might still agree with Nisbet and Hubbard (1970) *ad loc.*, though, that 'one is reluctant to give up a single *neu*'. At Hedylus 3 *HE apud* Ath. 11.486a a woman engages in a drinking competition, and Hedylus, like Horace, seems to engage with Callimachus, *Aetia fr.* 178 Harder, since some form of the important word ζωρός is almost certainly lurking behind the corrupt †ζωρεσμιτρησι (Hedylus' text is most recently discussed by Ypsilanti (2019) 630–2, who offers the conjecture ζωρὸν κρητῆρσι θυωθέν).
⁸⁹ Porphyrio *ad loc.*, Ath. 11.783d–e, Hilgers (1969) 104, Richard Hunter at Sider (2017) 194.
⁹⁰ Already Orelli and Baiter (1850) *ad loc.* recognised this. I will return to textual issues in the Callimachus passage in Chapter 4.

Coinages in Horace's *Carpe Diem* Poems

Horace reverses the situation and positively encourages heavy drinking. It is clear that Horace's *Threicia amystide* picks up Callimachus' Θρηικίην ἄμυστιν, but Horace's translation is even neater, as the similarities with Callimachus go further. The Grecism *amystide* drenches the whole sentence with Greekness and alerts the reader to further Grecisms. There is indeed another expression in the line which has a Greek feeling to it. The genitive of description, *multi meri*, is mannered, and Horace regularly uses such genitives of description when he renders Greek compounds in Latin.[91] In the present case, the compound ζωροπότης might be lurking behind Horace's *multi meri*. Admittedly, *potor meri* would have been a closer translation of this Greek word than *multi meri*, and Nisbet and Hubbard rather think of πολύοινος as a Greek equivalent of *multi meri*.[92] Nonetheless, ζωροπότης seems the more likely model; πολύοινος is not used in poetry, and it is difficult to see how a random word from Thucydides and other historians would have influenced Horace's diction here. Second, and more importantly, the Callimachean intertext is crucial for the passage; Horace translates Callimachus' striking expression Θρηικίην [...] χανδὸν ἄμυστιν ζωροποτεῖν: multi *Damalis* meri Threicia uincat amystide.

The word ζωροποτεῖν is an important word in the *Aetia* fragment and it would be odd if Horace did not pay attention to it in his allusion to the passage. For the word is modelled on the Homeric *hapax legomenon* ζωρός, which (presumably) means 'neat' and appears at *Iliad* 9.203. In the following chapter, I will look at this term and its usage in some more detail, as I discuss the importance of cups of neat wine and other objects for the poetics of *carpe diem*.[93] For now, I just wish to stress that ζωρός is an important term in *carpe diem* poems from Asclepiades in the third century BC

---

[91] Succinctly explained by Mayer (2012) *ad loc*. See, further, Muecke at *EO* ii.760 s.v. 'lingua e stile', with many examples and references, and my discussion of *aeui breuis* at Hor. *S.* 2.6.97 on pages 200–1 in Chapter 5.
[92] Nisbet and Hubbard (1970) *ad loc*. Also see the detailed discussion of Bo (1943–4) 250, no. 19, who suggests as models both πολύοινος and οἰνοπότης. Mayer (2012) *ad loc*. notes that literary prose prefers an apposition instead of a genitive directly attached to a noun, for example, 'Damalis, puella multi meri'. Then why not 'Damalis, potor multi meri'?
[93] See Chapter 4.1 for references.

to Marcus Argentarius in the first century AD. Horace writes his *carpe diem* poetry into this tradition of drinking wine neat. Horace's choice of words again fits the model of the *Ars*: the new word *amystis* produces presence and lets us imagine a moment at the party when this word is used. And yet, the word is, of course, also old, revived from Callimachus, and much the same is true of *multi meri*, which also points to a Greek source. The words evoke the present moment of Horace's party, but they also evoke other older parties, such as Callimachus despising Thracian drinking rites, and even Achilles pouring wine for his guests in his tent. The words mark a Horatian *now* that exists always again.

Perhaps it is also possible to look at *amystis* from a slightly different angle by considering its register. Adam Gitner observed that many of Horace's Greek terms for drinking vessels belong to an informal register; though such terms may evoke literary precedents, they are essentially colloquial, intimate words, used at drinking parties.[94] Gitner illustrates his case with a wonderful example from English poetry. In his example, Housman pointedly uses the informal word 'can' in the refrain of one of his poems in order to stress the intimate atmosphere: 'Pass me the can, lad.'[95] The term *amystis* is not discussed by Gitner, but, as I noted, this term, too, can describe a drinking vessel as well as a manner of drinking. The unusual word *amystis* would then evoke the intimacy, revelry, and music of the drinking party where people would often simultaneously drink from a large Amystis cup and sing, as Athenaeus informs us in his discussion of cups (Ath. 11.783d–e, quoting the *carpe diem* poem *PMG* 913 *apud* Amipsias *fr.* 21, which mentions the Amystis cup).[96] This discussion of Horace's Thracian cup of song gives some taste of the next chapter, where I will discuss cups in some more detail – yet, before this cup is downed in one draught here, it is perhaps time to finish the present chapter.

---

[94] Gitner (2012) 112–15. For the practice of using Greek words for drinking vessels in Latin, see Macr. 5.21. Cf. Fitzgerald (2021) chapter 4, who argues that the simple, repetitive language of the *Anacreontea* creates the intimate sympotic present.
[95] Gitner (2012) 114, pointing to Housman's 'The chestnut casts his flambeaux' in A. Burnett (1997) 79–80.
[96] For Lyons (2010) 72 this is evidence that Horace's *Odes* were genuinely sung.

Coinages in Horace's *Carpe Diem* Poems

There are a few more leaves left to gather in Horace. A comprehensive treatment of Horatian style which pays careful attention to his choice of words is still a desideratum.[97] In this chapter, I have confined myself to a smaller task – instead of soaring over the whole Horatian forest of words, I have, like a bee, gathered some lovely thyme here and there: I hope to have shown how Horace produces effects of presence through his choice of words. Just as the motif of *carpe diem* is the overarching ethos of the *Odes*, although it is not, of course, included in all of them, so the choice of words in *carpe diem* odes has a particular significance, although similar techniques can also be observed in other odes; but it is in *carpe diem* poems where lyric and linguistic presence programmatically merge. Horace's *carpe diem* poems as well as the individual words of which they consist evoke present moments that occur within the cycle of the seasons.

[97] Thus Muecke at *EO* ii.756 s.v. 'lingua e stile', confirming an assessment of Brink (1971a) x: 'the aspect of style in Horace needs to be opened up afresh, from vocabulary to the structure of sentence and paragraph'.

4

THE PLEASURE OF IMAGES

Epigrams and Objects 100 BC–AD 100

A glass of water that stands in front of someone speaking is a sign that marks this person as a lecturer, but as an object it also has the prosaic function of quenching thirst. With this example, Roland Barthes describes how objects can function as signs.[1] Stern water glasses are naturally of little interest for this chapter; or, as a Greek epigrammatist says: 'our mixing bowl does not welcome water-drinkers' (*AP* 11.20 = Antipater of Thessalonica 20 *GP*). Yet, Barthes' thoughts on objects as signs are worth pursuing: how do we read objects and when does an object become a sign? And, more specifically, how is the *carpe diem* motif expressed through objects and signs? So perhaps it is possible to stay with Barthes' sober image for a little longer before it is time for a stronger mixture. Barthes assigns two different qualities to objects. The first is their function as an object: quenching thirst, in the case of the water glass. The second quality is their function as sign: the sign of the lecturer, in the case of the water glass. In his discussion, Barthes takes the first quality for granted and is primarily interested in this second quality, the object as a sign. The drawback of this approach is that the materiality of the sign goes unappreciated. Hans Ulrich Gumbrecht sees this clearly: 'the purely material signifier ceases to be an object of attention as soon as its underlying meaning has been identified'.[2] In this chapter, my interest lies in both qualities of objects, that is, their materiality as well as their function as signs. I will also analyse how these two qualities interact with each other.

Too theoretical and sober? Time to serve some stronger stuff, then: cups of wine are signs that signify the banquet in the Greco-Roman

---

[1] Barthes (1988) [1966] 183.   [2] Gumbrecht (2004) 81–2.

The Pleasure of Images

world. But what difference does it make if the sign that signifies the banquet is the cup itself, or a song that mentions a cup, or an image that shows a cup, or a book that writes about a cup? In tackling such questions, I will combine two different views. On the one hand, I am interested in the sign and in the curious ways in which cups can oscillate between being objects, texts, and images. We thus hear of someone who is proud to have a famous cup from literature in his collection of physical drinking vessels. Or we read of descriptions of cups so vivid that we seem to see the object cup in front of our eyes. Throughout different media, the cup signifies the banquet. On the other hand, I wish to stress the materiality of the cup and what makes the cup an object. Naturally, presence is an important aspect to this: holding a cup in one's hand, touching it, smelling the wine, tasting the wine – this is different from reading about a cup. This gap is where the *carpe diem* poem is situated as it attempts to evoke the presence of the cup. I have already looked at such a feeling of loss and the attempt to compensate for it in other chapters. In the present chapter, I will show how *carpe diem* poems evoke the presence of objects and how this is crucial for evoking present enjoyment.

The chapter falls into three sections. Cups have already made their presence felt in the preceding two paragraphs, and cups and the banquet will indeed be the focus of the first section. The second section will turn to gems and luxury. The third section will consider a combination of two objects: dining halls and tombs. In terms of texts, most Greek epigrams discussed here are taken from the *Garland of Philip*, while the Latin material comes from Petronius, Pliny, and Martial. The focus of my discussion will thus lie on material between 100 BC and AD 100. From this period a high number of Greek and Latin epitaphs survive that feature the *carpe diem* motif.[3] It is also in particular in this period that artworks express the *carpe diem* motif through the prominent depiction of skulls and skeletons, as Katherine Dunbabin has

---

[3] Galletier (1922) 82 says that the *carpe diem* motif begins to appear on Latin epitaphs in this period. While most surviving *carpe diem* epitaphs were written under the Roman Empire, Bernhardt (2009) 23 cautions us that this is in line with the general epitaphic corpus. On epitaphs and *carpe diem*, see Ameling (1985), and the fuller bibliography provided on page 59 n.66 in Chapter 1.

141

shown in a seminal study.⁴ Finally, we know of some elaborate parties in this period which are wholly centred on *carpe diem*. For instance, we are told that Emperor Domitian hosted a meal in which every single detail could remind his guests of death and funerals: place cards in the form of gravestones bearing the guests' names, black dishes, beautiful slave boys who looked like phantoms, and many more such details. After the dinner, the guests received dishes and other items, perhaps as a form of memento. Domitian's meal juxtaposes death and dining, which is often done as a reminder to enjoy life. Yet, Domitian brings the theme to its limits, and his guests have to envisage their death as a very real possibility, as Catharine Edwards has shown.⁵ Trimalchio's *Cena* from Petronius' *Satyrica* is another banquet from this time that is hardly less elaborate in its staging of the *carpe diem* motif, and I will consider aspects of this banquet later in this chapter. What to make of this seeming prevalence of *carpe diem* in this period? It, arguably, would go too far if one were to conclude that people's minds turned to death in the unstable period following the fall of the Republic.⁶ Rather, the first centuries BC and AD seem to show a particular interest in elaborate, luxurious ways of staging *carpe diem*. We know of numerous ornate objects which express the motif, such as cups, tables, and figurines.⁷

As this chapter analyses the relation between objects and texts, it is only natural that epigrams, which are literally texts 'written onto' objects, become the focus of attention. The relation between objects, art, and epigram has long been recognised as significant, and ekphrasis has consequently been a major theme in discussions of epigrams.⁸ More recently, this field of study has received stimuli from three sides. First, a growing interest in 'material culture' throughout the

---

[4] Dunbabin (1986; also 2003: 32–40).
[5] Edwards (2007) 161–78, analysing Domitian's party at Cassius Dio 67.9.1–4 in some detail, as well as other juxtapositions of death and dining, which she considers a Roman attitude to death at that time. Cf. Erasmo (2008) 19–23.
[6] This is the claim of Döpp (1991) 144–7. Rostovtzeff (1957) i.56 thinks that the *carpe diem* attitude is the result of Augustan peace and prosperity after the civil wars.
[7] One more caveat is that findings from Pompeii, which are naturally part of this period, can distort the evidence.
[8] Epigram and art were already treated in the influential study of P. Friedländer (1912) 55–60. The bibliography for viewing, text, and ekphrasis in Greco-Roman literature is vast. See, in particular, D. P. Fowler (1991), Goldhill (1994), Gutzwiller (2002), Zanker (2003; 2004), Elsner (2007), Tueller (2008) 141–65, Zeitlin (2013), and more sources at Elsner (2014b) 153 n.11. For Greek influence on Roman ekphrasis, see Dufallo (2013).

humanities made scholars consider more carefully the seemingly mundane objects that are thematised in epigrams. Second, both art historians and literary scholars found interest in forms of collections, whether they be collections of artefacts or of literature. Third, an important papyrus find opened up new avenues to understanding the relations between epigrams and objects.[9] Nonetheless, many texts discussed in the present chapter have received little attention, and scholarship is, for example, virtually silent on the epigrams of authors such as Apollonides, Zonas, or Marcus Argentarius that are discussed here. Careful attention to these texts can elucidate how one can read *carpe diem* through objects.[10]

The time investigated here, the Roman Republic and early Empire, means that Greek and Roman evidence must be treated collectively. One Greek writer evidently describes a Roman gem, which he might have encountered while he mixed with the Augustan court. Another Greek epigrammatist describes a Roman *conuiuium* rather than a Greek symposium in one of his poems.[11] A Greek cutter of a gem discussed here may have worked in Rome. In short, any division of this chapter's material along the lines Greek or Roman would be artificial and curtail the exploration of Greco-Roman objects and texts.

4.1 Cups

Cups are fundamental to the symposium. In the ancient world, Athenaeus and Macrobius recognised their significance and wrote learned accounts on various types of cups and their appearances in

---

[9] Material culture: Canevaro (2019) offers a review of material studies and Classics, and Petrovic (2019) offers an introduction. Collecting: Elsner and Cardinal (1994), Pearce (1995). Epigram collections: Gutzwiller (1998). The important papyrus find is the New Posidippus, *P.Mil.Vogl.* VIII 309, edited by Austin and Bastianini (2002). The stimulus of one or more of these three strands can be felt in a number of fascinating studies: Kuttner (2005), Prioux (2007; 2008; 2014; 2015), Männlein-Robert (2007), Squire (2009; 2014), Höschele (2010), Elsner (2014a), along with other articles collected in Gahtan and Pegazzano (2014), and Vout (2018) esp. 39–42.

[10] The motif of *carpe diem* in epigrams has been discussed by Giangrande (1968), and more recently by Sens (2016). Giangrande does away with three epigrams, which I discuss in this chapter, with a sentence about each on page 171 (*AP* 11.25 = Apollonides 27 GP, *AP* 11.28 = Argentarius 30 GP, *AP* 11.38 = Polemon 2 GP).

[11] Höschele (2019) now offers an introduction to Greek epigram in Rome in the first century BC.

literature (Ath. Book 11, Macr. 5.21). Renaud Gagné has recently joined the party of these learned banqueters, and he has discussed in some detail the cup in Greek literature. For Gagné the cup is the 'degree-zero symbol of the symposium'.[12] With this term from Roland Barthes, Gagné underlines the strong semantic role of the cup: any cup anywhere can point to the symposium.[13] The symposium is the natural space for enjoyment, the space that *carpe diem* poems evoke. In sympotic epigrams, published in books and thus separated from the sympotic space, cups are an important sign that can conjure up the symposium. Yet, already early lyric conjured up the presence of cups. A common formula on sixth-century-BC cups is the following call to drinks: χαῖρε καὶ πίει τένδε ('be happy [or: greetings] and drink this').[14] It has been frequently noted that this expression finds a virtually verbatim parallel in one of Alcaeus' sympotic songs (*fr*. 401a and b):[15] (a) χαῖρε καὶ πῶ τάνδε (b) δεῦρο σύμπωθι ((a) 'be happy [or: greetings] and drink this' (b) 'come here and join in the drinking'). Inscriptions as well as Alcaeus' poem refer to a cup with a deictic pronoun: the cup is present. It is tempting to see in Alcaeus' song the song of a momentary now at the symposium: while Alcaeus tells his audience to drink *this* cup, they may indeed hold *this* cup in their hand and look at letters which mirror Alcaeus' song.[16] This, however, is an idealised image. Although cups which mirrored Alcaeus' song in inscriptions might have been common, not every single symposiast would have held such a cup with exactly this writing in his hand for every reperformance to come. Alcaeus already produces

---

[12] Gagné (2016) 208 with further literature.
[13] For degree zero, see Barthes (1968) [1964] 77. The definition here is more helpful than Barthes (1967) [1953], *Writing Degree Zero*, despite the title of the latter work. The zero sign, or Ø, is of course originally a linguistic term, as in zero-morph.
[14] For such cups, see the catalogue of Wachter (2004) 155–9.
[15] See the apparatus of Voigt (1971), Rösler (1980) 265 n.359, Liberman (1999) ii.251, Catoni (2010) 198, Cazzato and Prodi (2016) 6.
[16] Gagné (2016) 221–4 considers cups as words and objects, and makes important points on deixis, presence, and performance. Rösler (1983), in his pragmatic reading of Alcaeus, stressed the function of the deictics, which locate Alcaeus' poetry in the now of the symposium (*demonstratio ad oculos*). For a short critical assessment of deictics and pragmatics in lyric, see D'Alessio (2009) 114–20 with further references. Mundt (2018) 89–115 compares the symposium in Greek lyric (Anacreon), Horace, and the *Anacreontea* through a semiotic lens.

effects of presence rather than simply presence.[17] Epigrammatists would follow this technique.

As we turn our attention to the first centuries BC and AD, we will do well to begin our discussion with actual cups. Among the most spectacular cups from the ancient world are two that are part of the Boscoreale treasure (Figures 4.1–4.2), unearthed in the bay of Naples in 1895 and now in the Louvre (Louvre Bj 1923, 1924).[18]

Figure 4.1(a, b, c) Silver cup with skeletons (Cup A)
Cup A from the Boscoreale treasure, Paris, Louvre Bj 1923

---

[17] I follow the important analysis of materiality and reperformance in Alcaeus of Fearn (2018). Cf. the first chapter of Hobden (2013), Clay (2016).
[18] For a description and interpretation of the cups, see, above all, Dunbabin (1986) 224–30 with further references.

The Pleasure of Images

Figure 4.2(a, b, c) Silver cup with skeletons (Cup B)
Cup B from the Boscoreale treasure, Paris, Louvre Bj 1924

Dated to the Augustan-Tiberian era, the two silver cups urge viewers to *carpe diem* qua the depiction of skeletons. Garlands that are embossed below the rims of the cup set a sympotic scene throughout, and several skeletons engage in sympotic activity: on Cup A, one skeleton is playing a lyre; another puts a garland on his head; yet another looks at a skull. Other activities on the two cups are not sympotic, though they also stress the *carpe diem* message, and we will encounter them again in this chapter. Thus, one skeleton holds a butterfly in his hand, which is labelled ψυχίον ('little soul'), and a purse labelled φθόνοι ('envy') in the other hand. Yet another skeleton pours a libation over an unburied mangled skeleton that lies on the ground on Cup B. Beside the skeletons that are anonymous revellers, other skeletons are identified by inscriptions as philosophers and poets. This includes, on Cup A, Sophocles, Moschion, Zeno, and Epicurus, and, on Cup B, Menander, Archilochus, and Monimus. The cups combine several concepts of 'the thought and art of Graeco-Roman society of the first centuries B.C. to A.D.', as Katherine Dunbabin has shown,[19] for in this period skeletons and skulls widely express the *carpe diem* motif in the form of figurines and on cups, gems, mosaics, tombs, and earthenware. The depiction of dramatists as skeletons reflects the idea of life as a stage, and the skeleton-philosophers point to sentiments about the universality of death, which even philosophers, for all their wisdom, cannot avoid.

One skeleton whose role has not been sufficiently explained is the one of Archilochus playing the lyre on Cup B (Figure 4.2(b)). Of course, this could just be an extension of the theme 'everyone dies, even famous philosophers and poets', as Dunbabin suggests.[20] But there may be more to it; as the cups are sympotic objects, which depict sympotic scenes, Archilochus might have been shown here as a sympotic poet. As a poet who famously drinks reclining on his spear (*fr.* 2) and who is characterised as 'wine-stricken' by Callimachus, he is an appropriate subject for a cup (*fr.* 544 Pfeiffer: μεθυπλῆγος). Moreover, some fragments of Archilochus have been interpreted as *carpe diem* pieces.[21] On Cup A, there is a corresponding skeleton playing a lyre (Figure 4.1(b)). While it is anonymous, Dunbabin has convincingly proposed that the parallel between the two cups suggests that this was also meant to be a well-known poet.[22] Above this skeleton's lyre is written τέρπε ζῶν σεα[υ]τόν ('while you are alive, enjoy yourself'). The position of these words, placed directly over the lyre, suggests that they represent a song that arises from the instrument.[23] Perhaps this line of song would have indicated the identity of the poet to an ancient viewer. At least given the attention to detail that the cups display, this seems

[19] Dunbabin (1986) 228. Cf. Gigante (1979) 103–12, 114–22.
[20] Dunbabin (1986) 230.   [21] Archil. *frr.* 2, 4, 11, 13 with Davis (2010b) 109–11.
[22] Dunbabin (1986) 228 n.156.
[23] For any discussion of sympotic imagery and depictions of songs on cups, Lissarrague (1990) [1987] is fundamental, though he deals with a very different period, archaic and classical Greece.

The Pleasure of Images

a more likely deduction than to simply assume with Dunbabin that the artist had forgotten to include the poet's name.[24] The Boscoreale cups include more phrases which represent sympotic song. Thus, on Cup B, the following words are placed above two smaller skeletons representing slaves, of which one plays pipes and the other one a lyre (visible on Figures 4.2(a) and 4.2(b)): εὐφραίνου ὄν ζῆς χρόνον ('enjoy the time that you are alive').[25] Finally, Cup A shows a third exhortation: ζῶν μετάλαβε· τὸ γὰρ αὔριον ἄδηλον ἐστι ('take a share in life; for tomorrow is uncertain'). This sentence is written below a Hamlet-like skeleton who looks at a skull (Figure 4.1(a)). Indeed, at first one may entertain the possibility that these sentences should be attributed to our Hamlet skeleton. The exhortation, however, makes little sense when spoken to a skull; it should be addressed to the living (or the quasi-living skeletons). Yet, it is equally difficult to imagine that the skull voices this sentence. It is thus most natural to assume that this exhortation, too, represents song and should be attributed to the small skeleton clapping his hands below the letters. The parallel between the two cups supports this interpretation: Cup B shows a song in corresponding position above two small skeletons. Consistency also seems to demand this conclusion: all three exhortations on the cups are represented as song.

That the Boscoreale cups are signs of the banquet is clear enough, but the complexity in their use of motifs and media is striking, and perhaps most so in their evocation of song. In addition to the inscribed songs, the structure of the cups also helps to evoke music: the garlands at the upper rim and the small dancing skeletons at the lower end of the cup give a rhythmic sympotic feeling to the whole scene. As the cups evoke music, they can

[24] Dunbabin (1986) 228 n.156. Somewhat similar is the expression σῆν αὐτοῦ φρένα τέρπε at Mimn. fr. 7.1 = Thgn. 795 = AP 9.50.1, but the parallel is arguably too loose and the wording too conventional to make much of it (cf. Il. 1.474, 9.186 and page 129 n.63 in Chapter 3).

[25] The words are similar to the song of Seikilos, which I discussed in the Introduction, as Marx (1906) 146 noted: ὅσον ζῆς, φαίνου. Another parallel can be found in a funerary poem for a performer of Homeric songs, which urges to *carpe diem* (*SGO* 10/05/04.1–2): χήροις ὦ παροδεῖτ᾽, ὅσσον δ᾽ ἐσορᾷς φάος ἠοῦς, | εὔφραινν᾽ ἐν θαλίαισιν ἐὴν φρένα, τέρπε σεαυτόν. It is tempting to assume that similar, metrical expressions are lurking behind the prose of the Boscoreale cups.

reinforce the musical enjoyment at the banquet and truly create present enjoyment: touching the cups, feeling the skeletons and the silver material, and tasting wine from them creates enjoyment. And yet, these cups also express a sentiment of loss and nostalgia for a lost ideal of early lyric song: Archilochus plays the lyre and urges banqueters to live it up, but Archilochus has already been dead for centuries and he as well as his fellow banqueters are skeletons. Song is not so present after all. The cups thus raise a key question that will concern us in this chapter: how do we read objects instead of listen to songs, in the context of *carpe diem*?[26]

As we turn to texts, let us begin with an epigram that stresses the materiality of the cup – though clay instead of the silver of the Boscoreale cups. The epigram, included in the *Garland of Philip*, is attributed to Zonas, an epigrammatist of whom little is known unless he is to be identified with Diodorus Zonas, an influential orator around the time of the Mithridatic Wars in the first century BC.[27] In the epigram, a speaker talks of a clay cup (*AP* 11.43 = Zonas 9 *GP*):

δός μοι τοὐκ γαίης πεπονημένον ἁδὺ κύπελλον,
ἇς γενόμην καὶ ὑφ' ᾇ κείσομ' ἀποφθίμενος.

Give me the sweet cup made from earthenware, earth from where I came and under which I will lie again when I am dead.

The epigram seems to have eluded critical attention. It falls into two parts. In the hexameter, a symposiast asks someone for a sweet cup. This is the sympotic gesture par excellence, the call for drinks.[28] The command in this line thus evokes a scene at the banquet, and a reader places both the speaker and his addressee at the symposium. The hexameter, then, lets us listen to the chatter of sympotic dialogue, and we can find a parallel for such a piece of casual dialogue in the words of a thirsty slave in comedy (Ar. *Eq.*

---

[26] Another well-known cup, which conveys a *carpe diem* message, is the *kto chro* cup, which shows a skeleton, objects of the symposium, two dancers, and the inscription κτῶ χρῶ, 'aquire and use'. See Zahn (1923), Dunbabin (1986) 199–203 with further parallels. For the formula κτῶ χρῶ, see Robert (1936) 136–7.
[27] For a discussion of the identity of Zonas, see Reitzenstein at *RE* v.1. col. 660–1 s.v. 'Diodorus' no. 35, Gow and Page (1968) 263–4.
[28] See Cazzato and Prodi (2016) 6–10, Gagné (2016) 226–7. For commands of this kind, see Hutchinson (2016) 269, no. 123. Ath. 11.482e–483a discusses κύπελλον cups.

120, and similar again in 123): δός μοι, δὸς τὸ ποτήριον ταχύ ('give me, quickly give me the cup').²⁹ The pentameter evokes a different image. Two relative clauses offer more information on the cup's material, earthenware. The speaker says that like the cup he comes from the earth and will lie again under the earth when he is dead.³⁰ The language in the pentameter is evocative of epitaphs. In particular the first-person verb κείσομαι points to funerary epigrams, in which κεῖμαι is an extremely common, formulaic expression.³¹ The epitaphic heritage of the genre is inscribed into the DNA of the Zonas' epigram. Exhortation to present enjoyment and insight into human mortality are expressed through a line of sympotic dialogue that clashes with a line evocative of funerary epigram.³² The implicit lesson of the epigram is *carpe diem* – drink from earthenware now before the same material will surround you in death. The sweet cup acts as a sign for the pleasures of the symposium, but the cup shares its material with the earth that will entomb us. Within a single elegiac couplet, we listen to pleasant sympotic chatter and read of death. The poem evokes both the tactile presence of an earthenware cup at the banquet and the letters on an epitaph; in doing so, it oscillates between presence and meaning. It is precisely in this interaction of materiality and reading, of object and sign, of sympotic dialogue and funerary epigram, where we find the *carpe diem* motif. As we seem to touch the cup's earthenware material, taste its sweetness, and as we interpret the cup as a sympotic sign and discern the letters of the epigram evocative of inscriptions, we read *carpe diem*.

An epigram of Apollonides raises further questions on how one can read cups. Apollonides was a Greek poet who wrote in the first

---

[29] Another command of this kind appears in a comedic fragment of Anaxandrides (*fr.* 33): δὸς δὴ τὸν χοᾶ | αὐτῷ σύ, Κῶμε, καὶ τὸ κυμβίον φέρων.

[30] The poem also plays with the common identification of cups as humans, which can be found in the form of anthropomorphic cups as well. On such cups, see Gagné (2016) 215 with bibliography at 215 n.56 and n.57.

[31] For κεῖμαι as a convention and marker of sepulchral epigram, see, for example, Tueller (2008) 46–8, 95–6. Also cf. forms of κεῖμαι below in this chapter at *AP* 11.28 = Argentarius 30 *GP*, *AP* 9.439 = Crinagoras 47 *GP*. Zonas is far from being the only epigrammatist who played with the generic conventions of κεῖμαι. See, for example, *AP* 5.85.4 = Asclepiades 2.4 *HE* with Sens (2011) *ad loc.*

[32] Cf. *AP* 7.452 = Leonidas 67 *HE* for a similar technique, discussed on pages 16–17 in the Introduction. For Zonas' general debt to Leonidas, see Gow and Page (1968) 413.

Cups

century AD in the Roman Empire and may have lived in Asia, as two of his epigrams possibly mention pro-consuls of Asia.[33] In the following epigram, Apollonides describes how someone is asleep at the symposium and his cup calls him back to action (*AP* 11.25 = 27 *GP*):[34]

ὑπνώεις, ὦ 'ταῖρε, τὸ δὲ σκύφος αὐτὸ βοᾷ σε·	(1)
ἔγρεο, μὴ τέρπου μοιριδίῃ μελέτῃ.	
μὴ φείσῃ, Διόδωρε, λάβρος δ' εἰς Βάκχον ὀλισθών	
ἄχρις ἐπὶ σφαλεροῦ ζωροπότει γόνατος.	
ἔσσεθ' ὅτ' οὐ πιόμεσθα πολὺς πολύς· ἀλλ' ἄγ' ἐπείγου·	(5)
ἡ συνετὴ κροτάφων ἅπτεται ἡμετέρων.	

You are sleeping, my friend, but the cup itself is shouting for you: wake up and don't enjoy practising for death. Don't be sparing, Diodorus, but rather slip greedily into Bacchus' wine and drink it neat until the legs give way. There will be a time – a long, long time – when we will not be drinking. But come get up. Sober old age is already touching our temples.

Although this poem is praised by Gow and Page as 'perhaps the best'[35] of Apollonides' epigrams, it has like many of the epigrams from the *Garland of Philip* received no critical attention. This is a pity, for the poem elegantly combines features of inscribed epigram and Hellenistic literature with the fashion of the early Empire.

The first line sets the scene: someone addressed in the second person is asleep at the symposium and his cup 'is shouting' (βοᾷ) at him. The following line is set in quotation marks by Gow and Page as the content of the cup's speech:[36] ἔγρεο, μὴ τέρπου μοιριδίῃ μελέτῃ ('wake up and don't enjoy practising for death'). The cup admonishes the sleepy symposiast to wake up and not to enjoy his sleep, here wittily called a 'practice for death' (μοιριδίῃ μελέτῃ). It is

[33] Gow and Page (1968) ii.147–8 and Reitzenstein at *RE* ii.1 col. 119 s.v. 'Apollonides' no. 26.
[34] The word ἔγρεο appears at the beginning of the first pentameter of an epigram with a *carpe diem* theme here as well as at *AP* 5.118.2 = Argentarius 11.2 *GP*. Also cf. the expression σφάλλομαι ἀκρήτῳ μεμεθυσμένος at *AP* 11.26.1 = Argentarius 27.1 *GP* with line 4 of the Apollonides' epigram here. The intertextual relation between Apollonides and Argentarius deserves further exploration.
[35] Gow and Page (1968) ii.148. In general, though, Apollonides is described as a 'competent but undistinguished composer'. *Aliter* Reitzenstein at *RE* ii.1 col. 119 s.v. 'Apollonides' no. 26.
[36] Gow and Page (1968). The same punctuation is used at Beckby (1957–8) iii.556 and in the translation (though not the text) of the Loeb edition of Paton (1916–18). Jacobs (1794–1814) ii.132 does not use any quotation marks.

151

interesting if the admonition comes from the cup. To be sure, we can also find a talkative wine vessel in a charming epigram by Apollonides' contemporary Marcus Argentarius, who calls a flagon (λάγυνος) 'sweet-talking, soft laughing, large lipped, long-throated', clearly punning on the shape of the vessel and its function at the symposium (*AP* 9.229 = 24 *GP*). Furthermore, a cup that was passed around at a symposium and indicated who was singing was itself called ᾠδός ('singer').[37] Thus, wine-vessels as symbols of the symposium can act like symposiasts, chatting and singing. The case of the cup in Apollonides' epigram, however, is arguably different. For the shout of the cup might be best understood as a reference to an inscription on a cup, as the epigram plays with the heritage of the epigrammatic genre in inscriptions. Words of verbal action are regularly used for inscriptions on epigrams and blur the lines between speaking and writing,[38] but perhaps more specifically relevant is a cup in a satyr play which is said to 'call' (καλεῖ) someone 'by showing its inscription'.[39] This neatly shows how an inscription on a cup can simultaneously function as an inscription and as a verbal action. Irmgard Männlein-Robert says about epigrams of similar form that the voice of the epigram only becomes articulate once the reader lends his own voice to the epigram as he reads the text aloud.[40] Indeed, in our present case we can see such a reception in action, as the speaker of the epigram reads out the inscription of the cup to the sleeping Diodorus, thus giving a voice to the epigram.

If the 'shout' of the cup is understood as an inscription on a cup, the question arises whether this speech or inscription is really just limited to one line, as most editions mark it. The exhortation in the following line suggests otherwise: μὴ φείσῃ, Διόδωρε ('don't be sparing, Diodorus'). This negated imperative closely follows μὴ τέρπου ('don't enjoy'), and it is most natural to assume that both

---

[37] See Antiphanes *fr.* 85 with Liberman (2016) 43 and Gagné (2016) 220 and 220 n.79.
[38] See, for example, Männlein-Robert (2007) 157–67 with several examples for what she calls a 'Mediendifferenz'. The idea of epigrams as the voice of the object is as old as epigrams themselves (*SGO* 01/12/05 = *CEG* 429): αὐδὴ τεχνήεσσα λίθο.
[39] Achaeus *Omphale TrGF* 33 *apud* Ath. 11.466e–f: ὁ δὲ σκύφος με τοῦ θεοῦ καλεῖ πάλαι τό γράμμα φαίνων. The inscription is then spelled out, as the individual letters are mentioned, thus highlighting the written nature. On the fragment, see Lämmle (2013) 111–12, Gagné (2016) 212.
[40] Männlein-Robert (2007) 158: 'die Stimme, i.e. das Epigramm, muss durch die Stimme des Lesers beim lauten Lesen konkret zum Klingen gebracht werden'.

imperatives are said by the same speaker, the cup. Furthermore, this exhortation displays the most typical features of inscriptions on cups: an indication of the owner and an exhortation to drink. I thus suggest that lines 2–4 should be placed into quotation marks as being spoken by the cup.[41] The device of the speaking cup is noteworthy, and the verb βοᾷ ('the cup is shouting to you'), which introduces the speech of the cup, encapsulates issues of presence and absence. The loudly shouted imperatives evoke presence and the exuberant space of the banquet. And yet, this shout turns out to be an inscription on a cup, something read rather than sung.

Apollonides' epigram stages the act of reading *carpe diem*. The epigram displays self-consciousness about its status as a text and about the role of the reader. It may therefore be unsurprising that the epigram also includes a sophisticated philological note. One of what I take to be the cup's exhortations is the imperative ζωροπότει ('drink neat wine!'). Gow and Page do not comment on this word, though this rare compound-word might be the most marked one in the epigram. In Chapter 3 on Horace's choice of words, it was already possible to take a sip from this neat wine of words; now it is time to down it properly. The verb ζωροποτέω derives from the adjective ζωρός, a Homeric *hapax legomenon*, which appears at *Iliad* 9.203. There, Odysseus, Ajax, and Phoenix visit Achilles in his tent, who tells Patroclus to bring a larger mixing bowl and to mix something ζωρότερον. The meaning of this word was subject to much debate in the ancient world: some considered it to refer to old wine, others took it to mean 'quicker', yet others thought it to signify 'hot' or 'boiling' wine, but most accepted the meaning 'neat' or 'unmixed'. Such philological debates were themselves regularly set at symposia and suited the self-referential sympotic space: at the literary symposia of Plutarch and Athenaeus the question about the meaning of ζωρότερον is a sympotic question in more than one sense (Plu. *Moralia* 677c–678b, Ath. 10.423d–424a).[42]

---

[41] Lines 5–6 should again be assigned to the speaker of the epigram. For both the first-person-plural verb οὐ πιόμεσθα and the first-person-plural possessive pronoun ἡμετέρων can hardly be assigned to the cup.

[42] Sens (2011) 107 mentions other discussions concerning the meaning of ζωρός, among which Arist. *Po.* 25 1461a 14 and Hdt. 6.84.3 are perhaps particularly worth mentioning. For further uses of the term, see Magnelli (1997) 456.

It is in particular Callimachus' use of ζωροποτέω in the *Aetia*, quoted in Chapter 3, which strongly influenced later literature (*fr.* 178.12 Harder, page 136 in this book).[43] Indeed, Paul Maas had already suggested that Apollonides took ζωροποτεῖν from Callimachus.[44] Callimachus notably rejects the fashion of drinking neat wine, but many poets would write polemic allusions to this passage. This is, in particular, the case with *carpe diem* poems, as we have seen in Horace's case (*C.* 1.36.13–14, pages 135–8 in Chapter 3). In epigrams it becomes difficult to tell if poets are more intoxicated from the neat wine they describe or from the philological fascination that this term entails. Thus, Hedylus begins an epigram with the resounding noun ζωροπόται ('drinkers of neat wine'), which helps him to characterise his poetic programme in contrast to Callimachus, as Sens has analysed in detail (4 *HE apud* Ath. 11.497d).[45] Even much later, in sixth-century-AD Byzantium, Callimachus' passage still invited allusive games among epigrammatists. Thus, Macedonius begins a poem with the *hapax legomenon* χανδοπόται (*AP* 11.59), perhaps modelled on Hedylus' *incipit*, but almost certainly alluding to Callimachus' striking expression χανδὸν ἄμυστιν ζωροποτεῖν ('*drinking* neat wine *with the mouth wide open* in large draughts').[46] Terms around ζωρο- would also act as a tool for cross-referencing and editing when Meleager compiled his collection of epigrams. For as he found ζωρός in a *carpe diem* poem of Asclepiades (*AP* 12.50 = 16 *HE*), Meleager placed a poem of his own before this, which he introduced with the verb ζωροπότει (*AP* 12.49 = 113 *HE*).[47]

---

[43] Although the papyrus *P.Oxy.* 1362 supports the reading οἰνοποτεῖν from Ath. 10.442f, 11.781d for Callimachus *fr.* 178.12 Harder, I agree with Merkelbach (1967), Massimilla (1996) 408, Hollis (1972), and Harder (2012) 971 (further literature there) that ζωροποτεῖν from Ath. 11.477c and Macrob. 5.21.12 is the correct reading. For Callimachus' poetic programme in this passage, see Hunter (1996a), reprinted with revisions at Fantuzzi and Hunter (2004) 76–83.
[44] At Pfeiffer (1949–53) i.504.
[45] Sens (2015), esp. 501. Gow and Page (1965) at Hedylus 4.1 did perhaps not choose their words wisely when saying that 'there is no special point in ζωρο-'. Nor does Giangrande (1968) 131 n.2 give full justice to the word by calling it a 'jocular "Schimpfwort"'. Cf. page 136 n.88 for a likely form of ζωρός in a corrupt line of Hedylus 3 *HE apud* Ath. 11.486a.
[46] Another sixth-century-AD allusion: οὔτε ζωροτέρῳ μείζονι κισσυβίῳ at *AP* 5.289.4 (Agathias) with Hollis (1972).
[47] Gutzwiller (1997) 172–5 analyses how Meleager's editing might have shaped the sequence here. The connection between the two epigrams was recognised by Wifstrand (1926) 20.

Cups

Cross-referencing is perhaps not something that many people associate with hard drinking. Yet this peculiar double nature of the word ζωρός goes some way towards explaining the dynamics of reading *carpe diem*. The one side in Apollonides' epigram is the emphatic imperative ζωροπότει; this is much stronger stuff than would have commonly been drunk (mixing measurements are exhaustively discussed at Ath. 10.426b–427d). Such a call for drinks attempts to mirror and even surpass an exuberantly drinking lyric poet like Alcaeus: really living it up *now*. Then again, the Homeric hapax and all the philological baggage that comes with it underlines the written medium of the poem: this is emphatically a poem of reading and writing rather than singing symposiasts.

Apollonides was not the only one who made much of the word ζωρός in the first centuries BC and AD. His contemporary Marcus Argentarius exhorts in a *carpe diem* poem to taking a 'neat cup of wine' (Βάκχου ζωρὸν δέπας). Set in a decidedly Roman setting, in which a wife can take part in a banquet, the epigram gives us a literary version of the sentiment of the Boscoreale cups. Let us enjoy ourselves; all philosophy amounts to nothing as even famous philosophers die (*AP* 11.28 = 30 *GP*):

πέντε θανὼν κείσῃ κατέχων πόδας, οὐδὲ τὰ τερπνά (1)
ζωῆς οὐδ᾽ αὐγὰς ὄψεαι ἠελίου·
ὥστε λαβὼν Βάκχου ζωρὸν δέπας ἕλκε γεγηθώς,
Κίγκιε, καλλίστην ἀγκὰς ἔχων ἄλοχον.
εἰ δέ σοι ἀθανάτος σοφίης νόος, ἴσθι Κλεάνθης (5)
καὶ Ζήνων Ἀίδην τὸν βαθὺν ὡς ἔμολον.

When you lie dead you'll have five feet of land, and you will not see the pleasures of life or the rays of the sun. Therefore, grab *a neat cup of Bacchus' wine*, down it, and be happy, Cincius, with your beautiful wife in your arms. But if you think that the mind of wisdom is immortal (?), keep in mind that Cleanthes and Zeno went down to deep Hades.

Marcus Argentarius alludes to a *carpe diem* epigram of Asclepiades, as he substitutes Asclepiades' Βάκχου ζωρὸν πόμα for Βάκχου ζωρὸν δέπας in the same metrical *sedes* ('neat drink [or "cup" in the other case] of Bacchus' wine').[48] Argentarius also

---

[48] Noted by Small (1951) 141 pointing to *AP* 12.50.5 = Asclepiades 16.5 *HE*. Apollonides uses the adjective ζωρός in describing the sacrifice of a cup of neat wine at *AP* 6.105.3 = 1.3 *GP*.

155

follows Asclepiades' lead in making an etymological pun on the Homeric ζωρός. In his epigram, the exhortation to drink Βάκχου ζωρὸν δέπας is a direct result (ὥστε) of the insight that after death one is unable to see the 'pleasures of life' anymore (τὰ τερπνὰ ζωῆς). The 'neat wine' (ζωρός) thus equates to 'life' (ζωή) and, by suggesting this equation, Argentarius follows Homeric scholia, which define ζωρότερον in *Iliad* 9 as ἀκρατότερον, παρὰ τὸ ζῆν ('unmixed, deriving from living').[49] Argentarius takes this witty etymological play from Asclepiades, where Richard Hunter has already identified the same learned allusion to Homeric scholarship (*AP* 12.50.4–5 = 16.4–5 *HE*):[50] τί ζῶν ἐν σποδιῇ τίθεσαι; | πίνωμεν Βάκχου ζωρὸν πόμα ('why are you lying in ash, although you are *alive*? Let's drink the *neat* drink of Bacchus' wine'). Perhaps Asclepiades and Argentarius still wish to live it up and drink like Homer's feasting hero, but this manner of drinking now needs glossing. The etymology of a Homeric crux makes ζωρός a crucial term for *carpe diem*. For if the study of Homer shows that unmixed wine is related to life, then we can truly say with Trimalchio, *uinum uita est* (Petron. 34.7), and indulge in the idea of *carpe diem*.

The etymology of ζωρότερον was still known to Martial. In one of his epigrams, a Roman snob boasts that his collection of old drinking vessels contains, among other items, also the cup of Nestor and the very cup of Achilles from *Iliad* 9 (8.6.11–12): *hic scyphus est in quo misceri iussit amicis | largius Aeacides uiuidiusque merum* ('this is the cup in which Aeacus' grandson Achilles told his friends to mix a more generous and neater mixture, a veritable eau de vie'). In Martial, *largius* translates Homer's μείζονα, while *merum* translates ζωρότερον. As has been recognised, Martial, too, like the Greek epigrammatists, glosses the supposed etymology of ζωρότερον from ζῆν by associating 'unmixed wine' (*merum*) with a 'livelier' mixture (*uiuidius*).[51] Achilles' drinking vessel becomes,

---

[49] The scholion can be consulted at Erbse (1971) ii.441.
[50] Hunter (2010) 287 and 287 n.58. Asclepiades' epigram in turn rewrites Alcaeus, *fr.* 346 (Hunter (2010) 284–8, Sens (2011) 102–4 in detail with further literature). O'Hara (2017) 21–42 offers a summary of Alexandrian etymological thinking with numerous examples and references.
[51] Scriverius (1619) *ad loc.* recognised the allusion to the *Iliad*, which helped him to defend the correct manuscript reading *uiuidiusque merum* (previously printed in the

at least in the imagination of Martial's snob, a physical object that is present at the banquet.[52] Though the collection of Martial's snob is absurd, it seems that there existed people in the ancient world who imagined that they owned physical drinking vessels of Homeric heroes. Thus, the learned Athenaeus tells us that the people of Capua in Campania believed that they had the genuine cup of Homer's Nestor in their city – a cup that Martial's collector of course owns as well (Mart. 8.6.9–10).[53] In his treatment of Achilles' cup, Martial's collector shows some interest in Homeric scholarship, but he does little to live up to the Homeric ideal: instead of Achilles' strong mixture, he serves some unimpressive young wine in his precious cups. This is most emphatically not the idea of *carpe diem*. Martial points to some dissonance between the object as an object and as a sign: while Achilles' cup is suggestive of a splendid symposium from the past, it has become a dusty object in a collection. It works as a signifier but has lost its function as an object.

While Martial's snob claims that his collection also includes a krater that was damaged in the battle of Lapiths and centaurs (8.6.7–8), Pliny the Elder tells us of a different and particularly fascinating broken cup in a collection of precious vessels (*Nat.* 37.19). In a section on Myrrhine vessels, Pliny notes their exceptional value, saying that one single cup of this material was valued at 70,000 sesterces.[54] An ex-consul was particularly fond of these vessels, and after Nero had confiscated the collection of cups from this man's children he displayed them in a private theatre in the

Aldine edition) against *bibit usque* (v.l. *ipse*) of the *recentiores*. I find the alternative suggestion of P. A. Watson (1998) 38, according to which the owner of the cups confuses the right reading ζωρότερον with ζωότερον, ingenious but less likely. P. A. Watson (1998) 37 and Watson and Watson (2003) 207 seem wrong in claiming that *merum* is simply a poetic synonym of *uinum*. It surely means 'unmixed wine' here, being a neat translation of the Homeric ζωρότερον.

[52] P. A. Watson (1998) 37 suggests that Martial's snob is misremembering Homer, as Achilles asks for a 'mixing bowl' (κρητῆρα), while Martial mentions a 'cup' (*skyphus*). Perhaps so, but Martial conflates the two types of vessels by saying that wine was mixed in the cup.

[53] Athenaeus mentions the cup in Capua at 11.489b, and discusses the cup of Nestor in detail at 11.487f–494b, on which subject, see Gaunt (2017) 102–7.

[54] Most discussions focus on the nature of the material, which Romans called 'myrrhine'. While this material may have been fluor-spar or agate, its nature is not relevant to the present discussion. Stein-Hölkeskamp (2005) 156–8 discusses cups made from this material.

The Pleasure of Images

horti Neronis. There Nero would sing in front of a large audience when he was rehearsing his performances, which were designated for an even larger audience at the theatre of Pompey. Pliny says that he himself saw that even the pieces of a broken cup were added to the collection and presented like a corpse, so that it might show the 'sorrows of the age and the ill-will of Fortune' (*Nat.* 37.19):[55]

uidi tunc adnumerari unius scyphi fracti membra, quae in dolorem, credo, saeculi inuidiamque Fortunae tamquam Alexandri Magni corpus in conditorio seruari, ut ostentarentur, placebat.

At this time, I saw the pieces of a single broken cup added to the exhibition. I believe it was decided to keep these pieces for display in a coffin – just like the body of Alexander the Great – as signs of the sorrows of the age and the ill-will of Fortune.

It seems that Pliny was among the spectators of one of Nero's performances, as he presents the story as an eye-witness account of himself.[56] Pliny tells us not only what he sees, but he also informs us of the motifs behind the display of the odd object. It is difficult to ascertain to what extent this actually represents Nero's motivation or merely Pliny's imaginative interpretation. The qualification *credo* may hint at some guesswork of Pliny. Yet, whether we can discern Nero's staging of cups or Pliny's reception, either way we gain valuable insights into first-century views on cups.

Ida Gilda Mastrorosa thinks that Pliny wishes to underline Nero's decadence and the extravagant form of his collection.[57] The object is indeed most unusual and makes for a unique collection: why would one want to display shards of a cup? Yet, what

---

[55] I follow Eichholz's translation of *adnumerari* as 'added' (*sc.* to the exhibition). In contrast, R. König (1994) translates *adnumerari* with 'man zählte', following *OLD* s.v. *adnumero* 2 and *TLL* s.v., where this passage is listed as an example for the meaning 'to enumerate, run through, count'. I struggle to make sense of this; surely the point cannot be that someone counted the pieces of the cup and found out whether they were ten or a hundred, but rather that even the pieces of a cup were 'added' (*OLD* s.v. 3) to the spectacular collection of cups in Nero's theatre. I therefore agree with Eicholz's 'included in the exhibition' as well as with the translation in the Budé edition of Saint-Denis (1972), 'mis au nombre des objets exposés'.

[56] For Nero as performer, see Leigh (2017). Pliny criticises the *carpe diem* attitude at *Nat.* 14.142.

[57] Mastrorosa (2010) 106. Bounia (2004) 198 here sees a 'fetishisation of the artefact'.

Cups

Nero does here (or what Pliny ascribes to him) is rather witty and only understandable through the practice of displaying skeleton figurines at the symposium, as Trimalchio does in the *Satyrica* (Petron. 34.8).[58] The coffin also belongs to this motif, but instead of a human skeleton we find a broken cup inside. As a sign for enjoyment and drinking, its likening to a human being is a strong reminder to enjoy life while one can. Such an object is well placed in a performative space, in which Nero played the lyre. All this makes for rather exciting evidence: at least if we can trust Pliny, Nero, like Domitian, was another ruler of the first century AD who staged *carpe diem* (see the next section of this chapter for a *carpe diem* epigram of the Roman client king Polemon).

Though the broken cup of Nero's collection is unique, there is at least one piece that comes close to it and offers further support for seeing a *carpe diem* motif in this cup. For in Petronius' *Satyrica* we can also find a broken wine vessel in a funerary context. When Trimalchio describes his future tomb, he wishes it to feature sealed amphorae containing wine, and a carving of one of them broken, with a crying boy weeping over it (Petron. 71.11: *amphoras copiosas gypsatas, ne effluant uinum. et unam licet fractam sculpas, et super eam puerum plorantem*).[59] While Pliny describes a broken wine cup in a coffin, Trimalchio wants to have a carving of a broken amphora in his tomb. The message is arguably the same in Trimalchio's case – one should drink wine while one can (that is, while one is alive or as long as the amphora is intact). Thus, Trimalchio's lesson from the extended description of his last will and tomb is to live it up (Petron. 72.2): *ergo* [...] *cum sciamus nos morituros esse, quare non uiuamus?* ('so, as we know that we will die, why shouldn't we live it up?').[60]

---

[58] For material evidence and further references on skeleton figurines, see Dunbabin (1986) 185–212. García Baracco (2020) offers an introduction of Dunbabin's theme to the general reader, and one may profit from the rich illustrations of skeletons (at 53–65) as well as from the inclusion of a recent find of a mosaic with a skeleton that was naturally not known to Dunbabin (49 and her figure 20 at 50; the find caused a media sensation and was first published by Pamir and Sezgin (2016)).

[59] The paradosis *unam* is preferable to Jacob Gronovius' *urnam*. The conjecture tells us more about Gronovius's time than about the text. Thus, in the generation before Gronovius, Fortunio Liceti, interpreting a gem, misidentified an amphora placed next to a skeleton as a funerary urn (Liceti (1653) 158–9: 'urna rogum').

[60] Cf. *CIL* xii 4548: *amici dum uiuimus uiuamus*. I do not wish to go into a discussion of Trimalchio as a Nero figure. The parallel underlines the fashion of the age rather than any individual traits. According to Plin. *Nat.* 37.20, Titus Petronius, who may be the

Perhaps Nero's shattered cup best exemplifies Barthes' 'semantization of the object';[61] for the shattered cup has no practical function anymore and is still framed as a sign for the banquet (this is similar to the sign system of musical notes on the Seikilos epitaph discussed in the Introduction). Even without function the cup evokes luxury, revelry, and pleasure. The functionless cup is a proper zero-degree symbol; if within the semantics of cups a cup's morpheme is that one can drink from it, then Nero's zero-degree cup has lost its morpheme, but still creates meaning as part of a system of signs. At the same time, Pliny's account puts a strong emphasis on the cup's material: though the cup has lost its form, its precious material still evokes luxury.

4.2 Gems

Nero's broken cup from the last section is included in a book on gems and stones in Pliny's *Natural History*, since it was made from myrrhine. There is an interesting overlap between gems and cups. For example, epigrams on gemmed cups are also included in the section λιθικά ('stones') in a collection of Posidippus' epigrams (2, 3 Austin and Bastianini). Indeed, the papyrus discovery of the New Posidippus and its epigrams about stones also changes how we interpret other epigrams on gems. Notably, Évelyne Prioux has fruitfully interpreted Posidippus' λιθικά as a precious collection of epigrams, which mirrors real gem collections that Ptolemaic rulers may have possessed, and Prioux has applied some of the lessons from the New Posidippus to epigrams of other authors.[62] The following section will look at gems and epigrams from the late Hellenistic period and the Roman Principate which include the *carpe diem* motif. Taking into account the importance of epigrams about stones, which we learned from the New Posidippus, I will analyse how epigrams respond to artworks on gems and how the

---

author of the *Satyrica*, broke a particularly precious myrrhine vessel before his death in order that Nero might not have it.

[61] Barthes (1988) [1966] 182.
[62] Prioux (2008; 2014; 2015). Also see Kuttner (2005), Höschele (2010) 148–70, Elsner (2014b), and, on the λιθικά and the New Posidippus in general, see the articles collected in Acosta-Hughes, Kosmetatou, and Baumbach (2004), Gutzwiller (2005).

carpe diem motif becomes treated as a luxury and simultaneously a justification for luxury in these media.⁶³ Crinagoras, whose epigrams are included in *The Garland of Philip*, was an influential citizen from Mytilene, who served as an envoy to Rome on at least three occasions.⁶⁴ Two of these embassies approached Julius Caesar, the third one Augustus in Spain in 25 BC. It seems that Crinagoras spent substantial time in Rome after his third embassy and was an intimate friend of the family of the Princeps, as attested to by epigrams for Antonia (*AP* 9.239 = 7 *GP*, *AP* 6.244 = 12 *GP*) and Marcellus (*AP* 6.161 = 10 *GP*, *AP* 9.545 = 11 *GP*). Crinagoras' epigrams thus offer a fascinating Greek voice from the circle around the Princeps, which is too often ignored when scholarship focusses on the likes of Horace and Vergil.

The following epigram of Crinagoras leads from a description of a skull on the wayside to a *carpe diem* exhortation (*AP* 9.439 = Crinagoras 47 *GP*):⁶⁵

βρέγμα πάλαι λαχναῖον ἐρημαῖόν τε κέλυφος (1)
ὄμματος ἀγλώσσου θ' ἁρμονίη στόματος,
ψυχῆς ἀσθενὲς ἔρκος, ἀτυμβεύτου θανάτοιο
λείψανον, εἰνόδιον δάκρυ παρερχομένων,
κεῖσο κατὰ πρέμνοιο παρ' ἀτραπόν, ὄφρα <μάθῃ τις> (5)
ἀθρήσας, τί πλέον φειδομένῳ βιότου.

---

⁶³ For the *realia* of gems and other stones, see Plin. *Nat.* 36–7, Rossbach at *RE* vii col. 1052–115 s.v. 'Gemmen', Zwierlein-Diehl (2007), and Casagrande-Kim (2018) for gem collections in Rome. Gems and other luxurious objects are curiously absent from Horace's *carpe diem* poems. The reason may be found in Horace's general avoidance of extended descriptions and luxury in his lyric work, as analysed by Hardie (1993) 121–4, pointing to Hor. *Epist.* 1.6.17–18, 2.2.180–2, where Horace rejects gems and other luxury.

⁶⁴ For Crinagoras' life, see the commentary of Ypsilanti (2018) 1–14. Crinagoras' embassies are known from inscriptions (*IG* xii² 35), which record a decree, letter, and treaty from the embassies and were published by Cichorius (1888), who analyses the implications for Crinagoras at 47–61.

⁶⁵ See Gow and Page (1968) ii.257–8, Ypsilanti (2018) 466–7 for arguments why the attribution to Crinagoras is most likely correct and the attribution to Antiphilus in *Pl* an error. Rubensohn (1888) 32, 58 argues for the opposing view, largely on metrical grounds. As Gow and Page (1968) note *ad loc.*, either πέλας or κατά from the paradosis should be deleted, and the deletion of πέλας might be preferable. Jacobs's supplementation of the line ending *exempli gratia* seems close to the truth. Although Gow and Page strongly argue in favour of these readings, they do not put them into their text. I accept them here, and provide a more generous apparatus, which also includes Griffiths' recent supplementation for the penultimate line.

5 κεῖσο κατά Sternbach : κεῖσο πέλας κατά PPl   παρ' ἀτραπόν P : παρὰ πρόπον Pl   μάθῃ τις suppl. Jacobs : τις εἴπῃ suppl. Griffiths

> Skull that was hairy long ago, deserted shell of the eye, frame of a mouth without a tongue, weak fence of the soul, remains of an unburied dead, cause for tears of passers-by at the wayside, lie there under the tree stump beside the path that <one> may look at you and <learn> what gain there is for someone who is sparing of his means.

There is not a single finite verb in the first four lines; instead, there is a list of nouns that describe the skull. Crinagoras employs some recondite words and metaphors, but he essentially draws an anatomy of a skull, consisting of cranium (without hair), eye sockets (without eyes), joint of the jaws (without tongue), and teeth (without soul). Constantly, this anatomy underlines what the skull is not: a living human. The descriptive nature of the epigram is further underlined by the participle ἀθρήσας ('looking on') in line 6: the sight of the skull is focalised through someone who looks at it. The descriptive style of the epigram, which draws the scene featuring skull, tree-stump, path, and passer-by who looks at the skull and cries, seems to ask for parallels in art. Indeed, Nikolaus Himmelmann has pointed to the parallels between this epigram and a number of second- and first-century-BC Roman-Etruscan gems which show shepherds looking at a skull on the wayside in an exhortation to *carpe diem*.[66] As Himmelmann has shown in detail, these gems may have inspired the imagery of Guercino's famous painting *Et in Arcadia ego*, and for this intriguing insight alone the article surely deserves more readership.[67] While Crinagoras' epigram describes a lifeless skull, this image is contrasted with the material that we are arguably invited to imagine: a gem that may be gleaming with inner life.[68] Image and material constitute an antithesis, then, of death and life, poverty and luxury.

---

[66] Himmelmann (1980) 95–6 with table 37c, and in more detail Himmelmann-Wildschütz (1973) with further references. Cf. Dunbabin (1986) 212. Himmelman's work is apparently not known to the Crinagoras commentary of Ypsilanti (2018) 464–72, which shows neither awareness of gems nor of the ekphrastic nature of the epigram.

[67] Himmelmann-Wildschütz (1973). *Et in Arcadia ego* has been an important subject in art history, treated in a well-known article by Panofsky (1963).

[68] Philip Hardie pointed out to me that gems were often ascribed life in the ancient world. Plin. *Nat.* 37.66 offers an example for gems that evoke life.

Gems

Figure 4.3 Berlin Gem with shepherd and skull
AGD ii Berlin 138, no. 349, table 64 (= Berlin, Antikensammlung, Inv. FG 417)

Crinagoras' epigram describes numerous features which can be found on gems (Figures 4.3–4.5): naturally, the skull itself and the chance wanderer who looks at it. But even the details are paralleled on gems; thus, gems regularly show the skull below a tree-trunk (Figures 4.4 and 4.5(a) and (b)),[69] and one gem shows a shepherd raising his head, which Himmelmann interprets as gesture that shows shock and sadness (Figure 4.3).[70] In the

---

[69] See *AGD* i.2 Munich 33, no. 729, table 84 (= Munich, Staatliche Münzsammlung, Inv. A 1700); Copenhagen, Thorvaldsen Museum, Inv. 1204.
[70] Himmelmann-Wildschütz (1973) 230, pointing to *AGD* ii Berlin 138, no. 349, table 64 (= Berlin, Antikensammlung, Inv. FG 417).

163

Figure 4.4 Munich Gem with shepherd and skull
AGD i.2 Munich 33, no. 729, table 84 (= Munich, Staatliche Münzsammlung, Inv. A 1700). Photo taken from imprint

epigram, such a reaction is implied in the description of the skull as a 'cause for tears of passers-by at the wayside'. Finally, gems sometimes depict a bee, fly, or butterfly over the skull, which represents the soul (Figures 4.5(a) and (b)).[71] The epigram describes the skull, or perhaps more specifically its mouth and teeth, as 'weak fence of the soul' (ψυχῆς ἀσθενὲς ἕρκος). The word ψυχή can mean butterfly or moth as well as soul.[72] Thus the idea of a weak fence of the soul may also evoke the image of a butterfly which easily escapes from the skull, as can be seen on some gems. It should be clear by now that the epigram is indeed a description of a gem, or more specifically of an Italian gem, which Crinagoras probably saw during one of his

---

[71] Copenhagen, Thorvaldsen Museum, Inv. 1204; Wien, Kunsthistorisches Museum, Inv. IX no. 237.
[72] *LSJ* s.v. III and VI. The word ἕρκος for teeth is, of course, Homeric, and Gow and Page (1968) *ad loc.* point to *Il.* 9.408, where the soul leaves the ἕρκος ὀδόντων.

Figure 4.5(a) Copenhagen Gem with shepherd and skull
Copenhagen, Thorvaldsen Museum, inv. no. 11204.

embassies in Rome.[73] Indeed, we know from Pliny that Marcellus, with whom Crinagoras conversed in Rome, owned a gem collection, which he dedicated to the temple of Apollo on the Palatine (*Nat.* 37.11).[74]

Several epigrams of Crinagoras are literary accompaniments of little luxurious gifts, similar in fashion to the *Apophoreta* of Martial (see Crinagoras 3–7 *GP*). These epigrams on objects such as a silver pen, an Indian bronze oil flask, or book editions of Anacreon and Callimachus can give us an impression of fashionable luxury objects at the Augustan court. This is also true for the epigram on the wayside skull. The circle around Augustus would have recognised a description of a gem in this epigram, and Marcellus perhaps even possessed

---

[73] Apart from Crinagoras' epigram, the motif seems to be largely confined to art. Perhaps the closest literary parallel is the *carpe diem* skolion *P.Oxy.* 1795.25–6 (at *CA* 199–200), which imagines the possibility of a passer-by stumbling upon a corpse: νεκρὸν ἐάν ποθ' ἴδῃς καὶ μνήματα κωφὰ παράγῃς, | κοινὸν ἔσοπτρον ὁρᾷς· ὁ θανὼν οὕτως προσεδόκα. At Theoc. 23.29–40, a *carpe diem* message is juxtaposed with the image of someone stumbling on the corpse of a shepherd. But the juxtaposition is arguably too loose to make much of. Other epigrams on wayside skulls mentioned in the commentaries, such as *AP* 7.472 = Leonidas 77 *HE*, show some similarities but have nothing to do with *carpe diem*.

[74] On the gem collections of Marcellus and other Romans, see Micheli (2016) 82–4, Casagrande-Kim (2018). On Crinagoras and Marcellus, see Höschele (2019) 475–83.

The Pleasure of Images

Figure 4.5(b) Copenhagen Gem with shepherd and skull (imprint) Copenhagen, Thorvaldsen Museum, inv. no. I1204. Photo taken from imprint

such a gem. In the last line, the epigram asks what good it is to be thrifty: τί πλέον φειδομένῳ βιότου. The sentence is strikingly similar to the first words of a *carpe diem* poem of Asclepiades, as Maria Ypsilanti notes (*AP* 5.85 = 2 *HE*):[75] φείδῃ παρθενίης. καὶ τί πλέον; ('you are saving your virginity. But what is there to gain?'). The allusion strengthens the *carpe diem* motif in Crinagoras' epigram. Indeed, the word φείδομαι ('to spare') is common in *carpe diem* poems, which tell their addressees not to be sparing with their money, their wine, their sexual favours, and so on.[76] These different

---

[75] Ypsilanti (2018) *ad loc.*, following Guichard (2004) in his Asclepiades commentary *ad loc.*
[76] On pages 99–100 in Chapter 2, I analysed the Latin equivalent *parco* at Hor. *C.* 3.28.7. The Greek φείδομαι is also used in the *carpe diem* songs *PMG* 913 and *P.Oxy.* 1795.3 (at *CA* 199–200, if restored correctly).

categories are easily conflated, and Crinagoras' epigram seems to warn against both attaching too much importance to one's life and being too thrifty with one's means.[77] If we consider again that this epigram represents a luxurious gem, the question also reinforces a message that the purposed material already gives – anyone who owns such a precious piece knows very well how not to be thrifty but spend money on precious objects.

Another epigram, attributed to Polemon II, a Roman client king of Pontus, makes the ekphrastic connection between a gem and an epigram explicit, by describing a gem that shows a loaf and flagon, a garland, a skull, and an inscribed *carpe diem* message (*AP* 11.38 = Polemon 2 *GP*):

ἡ πτωχῶν χαρίεσσα πανοπλίη ἀρτολάγυνος (1)
αὕτη καὶ δροσερῶν ἐκ πετάλων στέφανος
καὶ τοῦτο φθιμένοιο προάστιον ἱερὸν ὀστεῦν
ἐγκεφάλου, ψυχῆς φρούριον ἀκρότατον.
'πῖνε', λέγει τὸ γλύμμα, 'καὶ ἔσθιε καὶ περίκεισο (5)
ἄνθεα· τοιοῦτοι γινόμεθ' ἐξαπίνης'.

Here is the welcome equipment of beggars, their bread and flagon, and here is a garland of dewy leaves, and here is a sacred bone, the suburb of the dead brain, the highest citadel of the soul. 'Drink', the engraving says, 'and eat and garland yourself with flowers; suddenly we will be like this'.

Like Crinagoras' epigram on the wayside skull, the first four lines of this epigram also consist of a list of nouns without any finite verb, describing an artwork, before again the third couplet provides a *carpe diem* message as an interpretation of the artwork. The first four lines are described by Gow and Page as 'pompous and insipid'.[78] But what exactly do these lines describe? Évelyne Prioux says that this epigram is 'the description of a sardonyx engraved with the typical belongings of a beggar'.[79] Yet, neither garlands nor skulls can be considered typical possessions of beggars. Rather, the epigram describes three different sets of items, and presents them as thesis,

---

[77] Being too frugal with both one's 'life' and one's 'means of living' (*LSJ* s.v. βίοτος I and II). For the first meaning, see Gow and Page (1968) *ad loc.*: 'what is gained by one who takes too much care of himself'. For the second meaning, see Beckby (1957–8) ii.275, who translates 'was ihm Geizen im Leben erbringt' (cf. Jacobs (1794–1814) viii.408). Note that a *carpe diem* epitaph set below a relief with a skull urges readers to make use of their means (*SGO* 05/01/62.3 = *GV* 1364.3): βιότῳ χρῆσαι.
[78] Gow and Page (1968) ii.400.   [79] Prioux (2015) 69.

antithesis, and synthesis. The word ἀρτολάγυνος – whether this is a 'bag with bread and bottle' (so *LSJ*) or 'equipment comprising loaf and flagon' (so Gow and Page) – basically describes a beggar's banquet, and ἡ πτωχῶν χαρίεσσα πανοπλίη only refers to this item.[80] The next item, the 'garland of dewy leaves', stands for a contrasting type of banquet, a luxurious symposium. The third item, the skull, shows that, either way, one will be dead, whether one lives sparingly or in luxury. A well-known magnificent mosaic, set in a table at a Pompeian *triclinium*, makes very much the same statement.[81] It shows a skull, which sits on a wheel of fortune and over which two sets of items are balanced. One consists of a king's sceptre, diadem, and purple, the other one of a beggar's staff, pouch, and ragged cloth. Nonetheless, Polemon is not associating himself with beggars or foregrounding 'the Cynic motif of the beggar', as Prioux wants it.[82] Rather, Polemon makes very clear which of the two dinners – beggar's banquet or garlanded symposium – one should choose by exhorting the reader to go for garlands (περίκεισο ἄνθεα).

The last couplet can also be found on a now-lost gem, illustrated by Antonio Gori (Figure 4.6), which shows a skull above the epigram and a table below it (*CIG* 7298 = Kaibel 1129).[83] Prioux argued that the gem might be a modern forgery inspired by Polemon's epigram, as the gem was not known before the seventeenth century and as its loss makes it impossible to determine its authenticity with certainty.[84] But if a forger was inspired by the *Greek Anthology*, would he not rather have chosen to depict the items mentioned in the epigram (bread, bottle, garland, skull), instead of a table? Following Robert Zahn and Katherine Dunbabin,[85] I think it is more likely that the gem is authentic. Indeed, the authentic Leiden gem, discussed below,

---

[80] The mention of beggars is thus necessary and Gow and Page (1968) are not wise in saying *ad loc.* that 'it is hard to see the point of saying so'.

[81] Museo Archeologico Nazionale di Napoli, Inv. no. 78289, also adduced by Prioux (2015) 70. See the seminal paper on the mosaic by Brendel (1934) as well as Dunbabin (1986) 213–14. This equalising force of death can also be found in *carpe diem* poems of Horace, such as *S.* 2.6.95, *C.* 1.4.13–14, 2.3.21–4, 2.14.9–12 with the discussion of Davis (1991) 163–7.

[82] Prioux (2015) 70. To be sure, a number of Cynic epigrams begin with lists of beggars' possessions (*AP* 7.65–8, Ausonius *Epigrams* 55 Green), but Polemon's epigram does not extol Cynic philosophy (on the relation between *carpe diem* and cynic imagery, see Brendel (1934) 170–3).

[83] Gori (1726–43) iii, appendix 21, no. 25. [84] Prioux (2015) 69–70.

[85] Zahn (1923) 11 and 11 n.44, Dunbabin (1986) 215 n.118.

Figure 4.6 Lost gem with skull, table, and inscription
Gori (1726–43) iii, appendix 21, no. 25; *CIG* 7298 = Kaibel 1129

offers a parallel for a similar phrase that is put on a gem along with an image. There are several other gems that show similar motifs to the ones described in Polemon's epigram.[86] One gem, which depicts a skeleton, a butterfly, a jug, and a loaf or a patera, also features the inscription κτῶ χρῶ ('acquire and use').[87] Such simple, inscribed gems may have been the source for the more elaborate epigrams discussed in this chapter. The same idea is also expressed on a very

---

[86] See *AGD* i.2 Munich 230, no. 2168 (= Munich, Staatliche Münzsammlung, Inv. A. 2805) and a gem formerly in the Odam collection at Furtwängler (1900) i table 46, no. 24, description at ii.222, no. 24, with Dunbabin (1986) 214–15.

[87] The gem itself is lost, but an eighteenth-century engraving survives; see Zahn (1923) 10–11 and his plate 1, Robert (1943) 182, and, in particular, Dunbabin (1986) 204 for more parallels and literature.

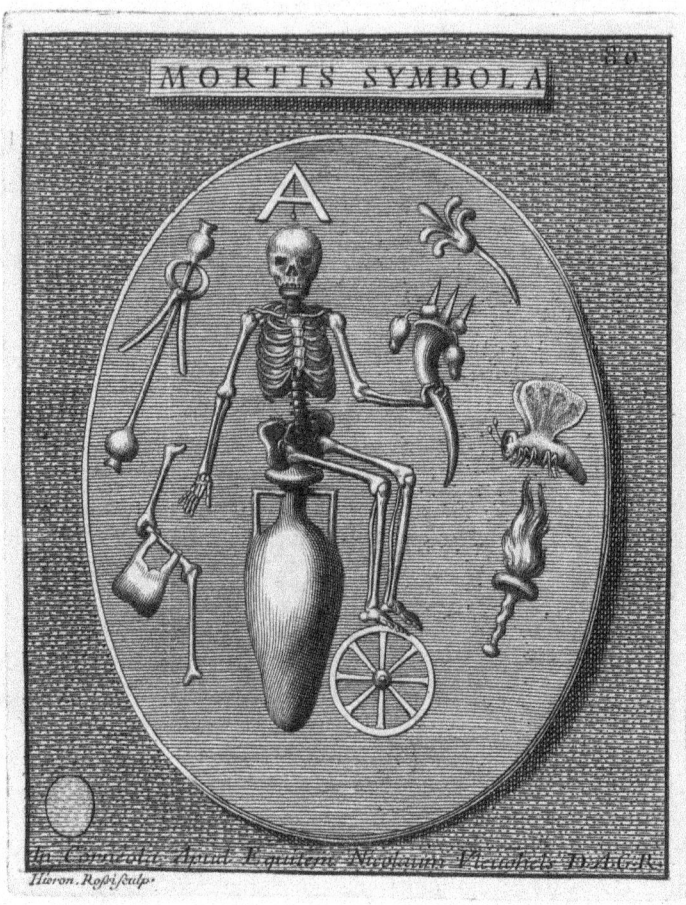

Figure 4.7 Lost gem with skeleton
Venuti and Boriani (1736) table 80

curious gem that is now lost, though there exists an etching by Antonio Boriani with a commentary by Rodulphino Venuti (Figure 4.7).[88] Venuti claims that the gem included an inscription of a

---

[88] Venuti and Boriani (1736) table 80 and 56–8. Their heading 'Mortis symbola' is wrong and part of the common misconception of identifying skeletons in ancient art with Mors or Thanatos, on which see Dunbabin (1986) 186–8.

proverbial saying from Cicero, in which Cicero says that the best soothsayer is the one whose guesswork is best (*De Div.* 2.12; same saying in Greek at E. *TrGF* 973). If the gem actually included this inscription (presumably on its back), it would make for exciting evidence: Epicurus' distrust in divination was well known (*frr.* 15, 212 Arrighetti), and it is easy to see how such a sentiment could appeal to the idea of *carpe diem* in popular Epicureanism. Indeed, we can see similar statements in Horace's *carpe diem* poems (*C.* 1.11.1– 2, 3.29.29–32; also *AP* 11.23.1–2 = Antipater of Thessalonica 38.1–2 *GP*). Yet, it is also easily conceivable that a proverbial quotation of perhaps the most canonical author of antiquity might be a modern addition, and as the gem is lost it is not possible to examine the inscription itself.[89]

In Polemon's epigram, the last couplet is the inscription proper and marked as such (λέγει τὸ γλύμμα; 'the engraving says'),[90] whereas the two previous couplets offer a description of the gem's visual features. These two couplets are redundant on the gem of Gori, where images are present and need no description. This may help to explain the 'marked contrast between the bombast of the first four lines and the forceful simplicity of the last two', which Gow and Page notice.[91] The simplicity of the last lines points to its heritage in inscribed epigrams on *carpe diem*. The first two couplets, however, do not reflect the language of inscribed epigrams, but with their affected bombast perhaps attempt to mirror the luxury and value of the artwork with rare words. As the epigram represents both images and inscription by words, it chooses a jewelled style for the representation of the gem's visual features. It thus contrasts the descriptive nouns that lack verbs in the first four lines with the urgent sequence of three verbs in the

---

[89] Brendel (1934) 175 n.1 is perhaps rightly sceptical about the inscription, which was a well-known proverb in the Renaissance, included by Erasmus in his *Adagia* at ii.iii.78. Brendel (1934) 174–8 and Dunbabin (1986) 224 n.150 can, however, explain some puzzling features of the gem's imagery and thus make a strong case for the authenticity at least of the image.

[90] Cf. *APl* 89.4 = Gallus 2.4 *FGE*, 'πῖνε', λέγει τὸ τόρευμα, noted by Gow and Page (1968) *ad loc.* (v.l. τὸ γλύμμα printed at *FGE*, though I do not see from where Page takes the reading γλύμμα. It is neither mentioned by Jacobs nor Beckby). Page (1981) 62 excludes too quickly the possibility that λέγει signifies an inscription in Gallus' epigram (*aliter* Jacobs (1794–1814) ii.106).

[91] Gow and Page (1968) 402.

The Pleasure of Images

imperative in the fifth line: πῖνε [...] καὶ ἔσθιε καὶ περίκεισο ἄνθεα ('drink [...] and eat and garland yourself with flowers').[92]

The epigrams of Crinagoras and Polemon and the gems that depict the same subjects thematise luxury. To be sure, not all ancient gems are equally luxurious. Some ancient gems were glass pastes. Yet, the gem Polemon describes is most naturally imagined to belong to his royal gem collection and be highly valuable. Gori's lost gem that includes part of Polemo's epigram is a sard. Among the first-century-BC Roman gems that inspired Crinagoras' epigram we also find sard or carneol, the most common gem in antiquity.[93] In the next paragraph, we will encounter an agate, a stone that used to be of great value, but was apparently not anymore in Pliny's time (*Nat.* 37.139). Though the precise value of individual gems may vary, then, texts and gems in this chapter all argue in favour of spending while one is alive and take gems as a sign for luxury.[94] In the first centuries BC and AD, *carpe diem* was a motif fashionable enough to be treated through luxurious objects, such as gems, cups, and dinner tables, and epigrams interact with these objects. *Carpe diem* even becomes the justification for the existence of such objects; the gems are minute pieces with maximum price tags, zero-degree signs of luxury, so to say, but this extreme form of spending is justified by the admonitions that there is no use in thriftiness after death. Life is short, so spend and don't be greedy! When gems proclaim this, the exhortation's success is almost guaranteed. The reader, most likely the owner of the gem, did in fact spent a fortune on a little stone and holds this very stone in his hand as he reads the inscription. Epigrams, in describing such gems, aim to evoke luxury of this kind by means of ekphrasis.

The final example in this section will again combine several media: it is an extant gem, which features both an image and a text

---

[92] For this triad of merriment, see pages 8–9 in the Introduction and Chapter 1 *passim* on the Sardanapallus epitaph.

[93] See Zwierlein-Diehl (2007) 307–8.

[94] For Polemon's epigram and its relation to royal gem collections, see Prioux (2015) 69–70. Micheli (2016) argues for gem collections as symbols of luxury. For the luxury of gems, real ones as well as epigrammatic ones, see Kuttner (2005) 159–61 and *passim*. Posidippus 16 Austin and Bastianini plays with the idea that some gems are undervalued, though they look luxurious. Gems naturally take pride of place in a list of luxurious objects at Hor. *Epist.* 2.2.180: *gemmas, marmor, ebur* [...].

(Figure 4.8). The late Hellenistic gem, plausibly dated to the first century BC and now in Leiden, shows both an engraving that exhorts to *carpe diem* and an image that underlines this message. The Leiden gem, an agate, has the following inscription in its upper part (Leiden, Rijksmuseum van Oudheden, Inv. GS-01 172 = *CIG* 7299):[95]

Πάρδαλα, πεῖ|νε, τρύφα, περιλά|μβανε. θανεῖν σε | δεῖ. ὁ γὰρ χρόνος | ὀλίγος.

Leopard, drink, live in luxury, hug! You must die; for time is short.

The lower part of the gem shows two men having intercourse on a couch, and below this image the text reads:

Ἀχαιέ, ζήσαις.

Greek man, may you live it up!

In a fascinating analysis of the gem, John Clarke observed that the penis of the penetrated man is large and erect, which finds no parallel in artistic representations of intercourse between two men.[96] Clarke goes on to show that the perspective of the image is even designed to highlight this unique detail, and he assumes that this gem is a custom-made piece, which allows us a rare look into the love life of an individual couple from the ancient world: it shows love and tenderness between two men of similar age rather than Hellenistic cultural constructions of roles in man-to-man intercourse.

Compared to the unique image, the text of the *carpe diem* exhortations first seems commonplace. Several parallels can be found in literary epigrams, more in inscribed epitaphs.[97] One inscription offers the same sequence of imperatives (*SGO* 02/09/32.5):[98]

---

[95] Cf. Maaskant-Kleibrink (1978) i.186–7, no. 1172, ii.372. On grounds of artistic technique, Maaskant-Kleibrink (1978) ii.372 argues for a second- to first-century-BC date and regards the later time as more likely. She thinks the artist might have been from Asia Minor and worked either there or in/around Rome.
[96] Clarke (1998) 38–42.
[97] See the epitaphs in Ameling (1985) and further sources cited on page 59 n.66 in Chapter 1.
[98] Maaskant-Kleibrink (1978) ii.372 notes that a parallel to the inscription of the Leiden gem was known to Henri Seyrig but that she was unable to find it. *SGO* 02/09/32 might be the inscription in question. The following epigram is also very close (*SGO* 18/01/19.9–10): πεῖνε, τρύφα, τέρπου δώροις χρυσῆς Ἀφροδείτης. The underlined exhortation offers a gloss

173

Figure 4.8 Gem with image of lovers and inscription
Leiden, Rijksmuseum van Oudheden, Inv. GS-01172 (= *CIG* 7299)

ὡς ζῇς εὐφραίνου, ἔσθιε, <u>πεῖνε, τρύφα, περιλάμβανε</u>·

While you live, enjoy yourself, eat, *drink, live in luxury, hug*!

on περιλάμβανε on the Leiden gem, which also refers to sexual activity. Similarly: πίε, φάγε, τρύφησον, ἀφροδισίασον (*IK* Kios 138–9, no. 78). The note at *CIG* 7299 is wrong, as has been seen by Robert (1965) 188–9. The imperative περιλάμβανε is an exhortation to intercourse and has nothing to do with grasping garlands, as Fritz says *ad loc.* ('ad uerbum περιλάμβανε intellegi τὸν στέφανον').

Furthermore, the sentence θανεῖν σε δεῖ on the Leiden gem finds a parallel in an epitaph (*GV* 1016.5),[99] and the observation that time is short can be found very similarly expressed in a fragment of Amphis (*fr.* 8: ὀλίγος οὐπὶ γῇ χρόνος; 'time on earth is short'), all in the context of *carpe diem*. But rather than the text itself, which is conventional, the engagement between text, image, and material on the Leiden gem is fascinating. Thus, Ann Kuttner has ingeniously suggested that the 'oval, banded agate glosses the nickname "Leopard" by resembling the animal's spots'.[100] Indeed, it can be added to Kuttner's suggestion that Pliny tells us of certain agates that are said to resemble lions' skin (Plin. *Nat.* 37.142). Two of the three imperatives on the Leiden gem also relate to material and image. For the exhortation to live in luxury (τρύφα) points to the luxury of the gem, and the admonition to hug (περιλάμβανε) refers to the activity on the image.

Clarke prints the inscription as a continuous text. But perhaps more attention should be paid to the arrangement of text and image on the gem, which, in fact, presents the text above and below the image. This arrangement makes an old suggestion of D'Ansse de Villoison from 1801 attractive, who understood the text as a dialogue between two lovers, respectively addressed as Πάρδαλα and Ἀχαιέ.[101] The change of addressee within three sentences makes it unlikely that they are all spoken by the same person and addressed to a single addressee. Indeed, the two vocatives which stand at the beginning of each text section highlight the change of addressee. Therefore, the upper part of the text is most naturally assumed to be spoken by the man who is lying on top of the other one. Then the man lying below answers him, and his answer is written below him. The arrangement of above and below does not only apply to the text and the lovers' bodies but also to the very material of the gem: a lighter stripe of the agate separates two darker

---

[99] Cf. *Anacreont.* 45.5: θανεῖν με δεῖ.
[100] Kuttner (2005) 161 n.87. For stones with such an illustrating function in the *lithika* of Posidippus, see Gutzwiller (1995) 386 and M. Smith (2004). On agates, see Zwierlein-Diehl (2007) 308.
[101] D'Ansse de Villoison (1801) 463 (462–8 offer several inscriptional and literary parallels for the *carpe diem* motif). The dialogic nature is accepted at *CIG* 7299.

parts above and below.¹⁰² The gem supplies one more hint that supports the interpretation of this as a dialogue. Clarke stresses that the mutual gaze of the two male lovers during intercourse is rather exceptional in art.¹⁰³ This striking gesture also becomes better understandable if we see the two lovers speaking to each other.

To some extent, the Leiden gem allows us a glance at the sort of artwork the epigrams of Crinagoras and Polemon are mimicking. Here, the imperative τρύφα ('live in luxury') is written on a luxurious gem as part of a *carpe diem* exhortation, and whoever owned and read the gem could perceive the presence of luxury whenever he read the exhortation.¹⁰⁴ But the implications of the gem go further still. For the gem also shows us how texts can give a closer rendition of present enjoyment when they interact with visual art. Together, text and image show a dialogue of two lovers in the very act of utmost enjoyment. It can be assumed that the owner of the gem felt aroused whenever he looked at it. Materiality, imagery, and text of the gem reinforce one another: as the gem exhorts to present enjoyment it evokes the presence of an ecstatic moment. Image and material help a rather hackneyed text to bridge the gap to present enjoyment.

4.3 Dining Halls and Tombs

In the past two sections, I have looked at individual objects, cups and gems respectively, and I have considered their quality as signs. In the section that follows, I will look at combinations of objects. Roland Barthes notes that the syntax of objects, their syntagma, is comparatively simple; it consists of the parataxis of objects, that is, some objects are juxtaposed.¹⁰⁵ The two objects that interest me here are dining halls and tombs. I will analyse what happens when we find these two objects in close spatial proximity, either in the city space or on the page of a book. I will analyse how the parataxis of objects can evoke the *carpe diem* motif.

---

[102] Philip Hardie pointed this out to me.   [103] Clarke (1998) 41.
[104] On τρυφή in Greek epitaphs on *carpe diem*, see Kajanto (1969) 361.
[105] Barthes (1988) [1966] 186–7.

Dining Halls and Tombs

The following epigram of Martial purports to be an inscription of a dining hall. The sight of Augustus' mausoleum from the dining hall leads to an exhortation of *carpe diem* (2.59).[106]

Mica uocor: quid sim cernis, cenatio parva:
ex me Caesareum prospicis ecce tholum.
frange toros, pete uina, rosas cape, tinguere nardo:
ipse iubet mortis te meminisse deus.

I am called 'the Crumb'. You can see what I am: a small dining hall. Look! From me you look out on the dome of the Caesars' mausoleum. Throw yourself upon the cushions of the couches, ask for wine, get roses, soak in nard. The god himself asks you to remember death.

By now the structure of such epigrams looks rather familiar; again, a description (here consisting of one couplet) is followed by an exhortation and a lesson in the next and final couplet.[107] As in Crinagoras' and Polemon's epigrams, the first couplet marks Martial's epigram as literary. For the description, *quid sim cernis, cenatio parua* ('you can see what I am: a small dining hall'), would have been superfluous in an inscribed epigram. In this description, Martial conjures up the sight of the two objects: he wants us to 'see' (*cernis*) the dining hall, and he wants us – 'look!' (*ecce*) – to 'look out' (*prospicis*) on the mausoleum of Augustus; the two objects materialise before our eyes. The third line, in contrast, constitutes the inscription proper of the epigram; inscribed parallels can easily be found, and one could indeed imagine such a line inscribed on the wall of a dining hall (which is, of course, not the same as assuming that the epigram was in fact inscribed). This type of inscription would be equally appropriate for tombs and dining halls, two vastly different places, which are juxtaposed in Martial's epigram.

---

[106] See Heilmann (1998) and Rimell (2008) 51–93 on the juxtaposition of living and dying in Martial. Blake (2008) analyses Martial's *Xenia* and *Apohoreta* from the perspective of material culture.

[107] Cf. C. A. Williams (2004) 199 on the structure. The similarity of this epigram to Greek epigrams has been analysed by Prinz (1911) 14–15. For Martial and Greek epigram in general, Mindt (2013) 502 n.3 offers further references.

177

Juxtaposition was identified as an important element of Martial's epigram books by William Fitzgerald.[108] Adducing nineteenth-century developments such as the newspaper or the figure of the flâneur, Fitzgerald sees Martial's technique of authorial juxtaposition as a mirror of a varied urban landscape.[109] Though Fitzgerald himself admits that juxtaposition as an authorial decision is a concept as difficult to prove as it is to disprove, there is much to say in favour of this theory. Indeed, if it can be shown that Martial also juxtaposes contrasting topographical features of the city within the same epigram, this might add further weight to Fitzgerald's argument. Or, in other words, are there epigrams of Martial which describe the city-space as a combination of differences, similar to the arcades or department stores of nineteenth-century Paris, which consisted of a combination of different shops or objects?[110] One category of juxtaposition in Martial, which Fitzgerald highlights, is the juxtaposition of social orders.[111] An example where this juxtaposition of social orders is mirrored by a juxtaposition of places is *Epigrams* 2.57. This is a biting social commentary, which first presents a parvenu strolling through the Saepta Julia, a 'favourite strolling ground and social showcase',[112] but in the end shows him in a pawnshop, at Cladus' counter (*Cladi mensam*).[113] Fashionable strolling grounds and pawnshops are spaces that are closely juxtaposed in Rome, and as Martial shows the parvenu first in one place and then in the other, we move through different social orders, as we move through the city.[114]

The concept of topographical juxtaposition also applies to Martial 2.59 on the *mica*; it tells of two places, a mausoleum and a dining hall. Their proximity in the urban landscape and their contrast in function brings about the message in the second couplet. A flâneur could pass the two sights in quick succession and

---

[108] Fitzgerald (2007) 106–38.
[109] Fitzgerald (2007) 4–13, building on the interpretation of Charles Baudelaire's poetry by Walter Benjamin (1973) [1969], in particular chapter 2.
[110] Benjamin (1973) [1969] chapter 2.   [111] Fitzgerald (2007) 121–38.
[112] C. A. Williams (2004) *ad loc.*
[113] The paradosis *claudi* is unmetrical; Salmasius' *Cladi* seems right.
[114] Cf. Rimell (2008) 7–8: Martial's 'poetry *is* Rome, both the city itself (a mass of streets, buildings, monuments and people) and Rome as concept and dream'. The concept of the 'city as text' is explored at Rimell (2008) 19–50. Textual approaches to the city of Rome are also the focus of Edwards (1996).

develop thoughts similar to Martial's, or he could save himself the bodily exercise and actually see the mausoleum already from the dining hall. When the cityscape offers juxtapositions of tombs and dining halls, of death and booming life, and when such sights also feature epigrams, then the city itself already constitutes a text of juxtaposed epigrams, and all Martial has to do is *transcribe* Rome, as it is already *inscribed*.[115]

Scholars have long seen the similarity to another epigram of Martial, in which the mausoleum of Augustus again invites thoughts of *carpe diem* (5.64):

> Sextantes, Calliste, duos infunde Falerni,
>   tu super aestiuas, Alcime, solue niues,
> pinguescat nimio madidus mihi crinis amomo
>   lassenturque rosis tempora sutilibus.
> tam uicina iubent nos uiuere Mausolea, (5)
>   cum doceant ipsos posse perire deos.
>
> Callistus, fill two large cups with Falernian wine. Alcimus, melt summer snow over the cups. My hair should become oily and wet with too much perfume, and my temples should become exhausted with the weight of stitched roses. The mausoleum, which is very close, tells us to live it up, as it teaches that even the gods themselves can die.

Though here only one topographical marker is explicitly mentioned, namely the mausoleum, the presence of the dining hall is implied in the setting of the first four lines. Indeed, Fitzgerald has alerted us to the significance of the word *uicinus* in Martial's epigrams,[116] which here once more highlights a juxtaposition: 'the mausoleum, which is *very close*, tells us to *live* it up, as it teaches that even the gods themselves can *die*'. Life and death are neatly juxtaposed in one neighbourhood.

It is significant that Martial makes the *carpe diem* argument through a combination of objects, namely of a dining hall and a tomb. This combination can be described as juxtaposition in Fitzgerald's term or as parataxis and syntagma, in the terms of

---

[115] The epigram caused topographical trouble, though: which is the *cenatio* in question? L. Friedländer (1886) *ad loc.* confidently identifies it with *mica aurea* of Domitian, whereas C. A. Williams (2004) *ad loc.* says that this structure did not offer any views of Augustus' mausoleum. See also Rodríguez Almeida (2014) 493–4.

[116] Fitzgerald (2007) 5, and 5 n.9 referring to Pailler (1981) 87 n.30.

Barthes. Juxtaposition here creates spatial closeness between semantically contrasting objects. Or, simply put, the juxtaposition says: 'A dining hall is not a tomb.' This might seem obvious, but it shows how objects act as signs. Both signs have different meanings, and the simple combination of two signs or objects with contrasting meaning creates the *carpe diem* motif: because dining halls are not tombs, we have to enjoy the present moment.

Sometimes the juxtaposition of dining halls and tombs expresses identity between the two objects, resulting in a sentence that stresses the opposite: 'a tomb is a dining hall'. This is, for example, the case with the tomb of Cornelius Vibrius Saturnius, found in Pompeii. His tomb features an impressive funerary triclinium, which along with similar monuments points to beliefs that the dead could still drink – a belief that was commonly expressed through the *Totenmahl* motif in the ancient world.[117] Not only did Cornelius Vibrius Saturnius find the thought of a tomb as a dining hall appealing, but Petronius' Trimalchio, too, envisages a tomb for himself that will feature dining halls (*triclinia*). Indeed, the *Cena Trimalchionis* offers a particularly detailed juxtaposition of tomb and dining hall. This juxtaposition begins long before Trimalchio's ekphrasis of his tomb. For already before the dinner starts, a wall painting in Trimalchio's house has the appearance of the type of wall painting one would find in a tomb (Petron. 29).[118] But, just as Trimalchio's house already looks much like a tomb (Herzog: 'Totenhaus'), the detailed ekphrasis of the tomb that Trimalchio planned for himself makes the tomb look much like a dining hall. In this ekphrasis, Trimalchio describes features of his tomb, including his own statue, several other statues, the tomb's size,

---

[117] For this and similar monuments, see Dunbabin (2003) 126–9, and see her chapter 4 on the *Totenmahl* motif in general (with further references). For epitaphs engaging with this motif, see Brelich (1937) 51–3. Cf. Jensen (2008), and several articles in Draycott and Stamatopoulou (2016). Murray (1988) argues that an equation of rather than a contrast between death and dining is not known in the Greek archaic and classical period, but may appear in other limited periods and areas, on which see also Dunbabin (2003) 137–9.

[118] This has been observed by Herzog (1989) 125–6. Also see Döpp (1991), who notes that the architecture of Trimalchio's house resembles the structure of the underworld in Book 6 of Vergil's *Aeneid*. Whitehead (1993) analyses Trimalchio's tomb in some detail.

Dining Halls and Tombs

the surrounding orchard and vineyard, a relief that shows a dining scene, a sundial, and two inscriptions (Petron. 71.5-12). In this passage, the juxtaposition of dining hall and tomb becomes most marked. Trimalchio asks, for example, that his tomb may also depict dining halls (71.10):[119] *faciantur, si tibi uidetur, et triclinia. facias et totum populum sibi suauiter facientem* ('and also make some dining halls (if that seems good to you). And show all the people having a great time').[120]

As soon as Trimalchio had finished his speech, he, his wife, Habinnas, and his household 'filled the dining hall with lamentation, as if invited to a funeral' (Petron. 72.1): *haec ut dixit Trimalchio, flere coepit ubertim. flebat et Fortunata, flebat et Habinnas, tota denique familia, tamquam in funus rogata, lamentatione triclinium impleuit.* As the dining hall (*triclinium*) becomes a funeral space, and as the tomb features a dining space (*triclinia*), the architecture of the two spaces is thoroughly confused:[121] the dining hall becomes tomb and vice versa. What needs stressing is how the ekphrasis recreates the materiality of the tomb: as Trimalchio quotes the epigrams that will be written on his tomb, and as he describes numerous architectural features, the words that describe his tomb become an object. And though Trimalchio's ekphrases elsewhere might be considered notorious rather than impressive (Petron. 52.1), in the present case he might very well succeed in creating an object through words, as the dinner participants already have such an object before their eyes: sitting in Trimalchio's *Totenhaus* makes it easy to see a tomb in front of you. Through the ekphrasis and the setting of the dinner, Trimalchio thus also shows us a combination of two objects: dining hall and tomb. And while he certainly underlines the similarity and, indeed, interchangeability of the two objects and thus seems to pronounce that a 'dining hall is a tomb', Trimalchio ultimately wants to have it both ways; for, in the end, the careful

---

[119] Cf. Dunbabin (2003) 88-9.
[120] The plural *triclinia* is difficult: it has been variously taken to mean 'dining halls' or 'dining tables' (Donahue (1999) 73). Either way, reference is made to the dining space, the *triclinium*, so that the difference does not, I believe, affect the present discussion.
[121] Panayotakis (1995) 104-5 notes that other features of the tomb, such as dogs, garlands, perfumes, and so on, have antecedents at the *Cena*. Rimell (2002) 38-9 argues that as Trimalchio composes his own memorial he becomes an author figure for the *Cena*.

staging of objects leads to an exhortation of *carpe diem*, which implies that a tomb in the end is not quite like a dining hall after all (Petron. 72.2): *ergo* [...] *cum sciamus nos morituros esse, quare non uiuamus?* ('so, as we know that we will die, why shouldn't we live it up?').

5
AS IS THE GENERATION OF LEAVES, SO ARE THE GENERATIONS OF COWS, MICE, AND GIGOLOS

Excerpe Diem! *or Excerpts of* Carpe Diem

In 1752, the German poet Christoph Martin Wieland wrote *Anti-Ovid, or the Art of Loving*. In this response to Ovid's *Ars Amatoria*, Wieland attempted to show that true love, by contrast with lust, always includes virtue.[1] The prefaces of later editions express Wieland's dissatisfaction with his juvenilia and note the extensive changes made later.[2] Indeed, in the preface of his collected works, Wieland says that the *Anti-Ovid* became a frock whose original colour is not discernible anymore, because it only consists of patches.[3] One passage or patch that Wieland included in all editions shows the Greek lyric poet Anacreon appearing in the first canto and singing a *carpe diem* song: 'Genießt und liebt, weil euch die Jugend winkt, | Sie wird verblühn, genießt und liebt, und trinkt' ('Enjoy yourselves and love because you are young and youth will wither; enjoy yourselves and love and drink'). The insertion of an Anacreontic song within an anti-Ovidian poem is interesting. To be sure, the hedonistic attitude of the two ancient poets can easily be linked ('verführerische Sittenlehre'; 'seductive teachings'), and Ovid himself recommends reading Anacreon at *Ars Amatoria* 3.30. But on a formal level it is striking to see a piece of lyric appearing inside a work of didactic poetry.[4] Is it the case that Wieland, the great expert in ancient literature, knew that such inserted lyric excerpts of *carpe diem* are also a notable feature of ancient texts – the more so as he published a translation of Horace's

---

[1] Wieland (1752). [2] Wieland (1776: 137–8; 1798: 7–8). [3] Wieland (1798) 7–8.
[4] Formally, the piece would have sat more comfortably among the eight Anacreontic lyric poems in the appendix of Wieland's work.

Sermones which includes a similar excerpt?⁵ This and other excerpts of *carpe diem* will be the topic of this chapter.

The previous chapters of this book have all dealt with short texts on the *carpe diem* theme. All of these, whether they are epigrams or lyric poems, can justly be called '*carpe diem* poems'. The topic of this chapter is longer texts which are not primarily about *carpe diem*, but which contain shorter sections dedicated to this motif. These 'sections' are characterised by three traits (though not all traits necessarily apply to every passage): they are clearly demarcated units within a longer surrounding text, they are self-contained, and they constitute (apparent) quotations or will in turn be quoted. Thus, in Wieland's *Anti-Ovid* the *carpe diem* section is demarcated through a different diction, and a separate speaker. As a poem on its own, it is clearly self-contained, and it at least pretends to be a work of Anacreon, not Wieland. Such demarcated and self-contained passages can also be found in ancient literature. Indeed, Horace's *Ars Poetica* provides us with a neat image for such passages. For not just Wieland refers to texts as patches – Horace criticises poets who make use of 'purple patches' (*purpureus pannus*; *Ars* 14–23), rhetorical set pieces that stick out as alien elements.⁶ Though their material is precious, they are all too well known and do not fit into the surrounding text. In looking at such 'purple patches' of *carpe diem*, I am interested in these seemingly conflicting dynamics: the natural splendour of the material (purple) and its reduction to a small piece in poor surroundings (patch). What is particularly notable is how the natural splendour of the purple material of *carpe diem* passages keeps attracting readers, so that the same patches are repeatedly removed and continuously sewn onto new clothes in anthologies, *florilegia*, and commonplace-books. The purple patch then becomes an independent textual object, completely removed from its original context, a cliché or a pure excerpt.

The term 'excerpts' perhaps requires some explanation. This is the word I will use to refer to sections of *carpe diem* in this chapter, a term with several interpretative benefits. In my use of the term,

---

⁵ Wieland (1813) 436–7 (see page 199 in this chapter).
⁶ Wieland translated, of course, also the *Ars Poetica*, where he rendered the purple patch thus: 'einen Purpurstreifen angeflickt' (Wieland (1816) 211).

Excerpts of *Carpe Diem*

I note its primary meaning from the Latin verb *excerpere*, 'to pick out' or 'select'. Seneca, for example, uses *excerpta* to refer to literary extracts (Sen. *Epist.* 33.3).[7] While I will consider some excerpts in Seneca and Athenaeus according to the ancient meaning of the term, I ultimately wish to add a broader meaning. Let us again consider the Wieland passage. The *carpe diem* song is presented as an excerpt from Anacreon, but this is, of course, a pastiche by Wieland himself, who is evidently inspired by the *Anacreontea*, which are in turn themselves pastiches of Anacreon's poetry. A further source for Wieland is a *carpe diem* ode of Horace (*C.* 1.4.16–20), which provides him with an ending for his poem, and the name Phyllis in Wieland's poem also appears in several Augustan poets. Additionally, Wieland here parodies the fashion of Anacreontic poetry, which was in full bloom in Germany when he published the *Anti-Ovid*.[8] Thus, the distinctions between real quotations and pseudo-quotations are hopelessly blurred. It, therefore, seems much more fruitful to broaden the meaning of the term 'excerpt', in order to analyse the specific intertextual dynamics that combine quoting, abridging, and imitating.[9] Referring to this intertextual overlap as 'excerpt', I wish to explore the rhetorical scope of purple passages of *carpe diem*, which – whether actual quotations or pastiches – draw on the *auctoritas* of a purple model. This broader view on 'excerpts' relates to work on textual dynamics beyond Classics. Thus, the slavist Gary Saul Morson wrote a book on quotations, in which he analysed among other things something he called 'quotationality': 'Sometimes we do not cite specific words but rather conjure the *aura* of a quotation' (original emphasis).[10] There exists one more reason why 'excerpt' is an appropriate term for the phenomenon discussed here. The semantics of the word *excerptum* already point to how the concept of *carpe diem* is treated

---

[7] *L&S* s.v.
[8] The 'German Anacreon' Johann Wilhelm Ludwig Gleim published his Anacreontic *Versuch in Scherzhaften Liedern* in 1740, and Anacreontic poetry became an 'infectious plague', in the words of a contemporary, as noted by Höschele (2014) 201 n.14.
[9] An important theoretical article of the Romanist Wolfgang Raible (1995) distinguishes three modes of intertextuality: amplification of texts (e.g., commentaries), abridgment (e.g., epitomes), parallel texts (e.g., pastiches). The combination of the latter two categories is the theme of this chapter. For cutting and excerpting lyric, see, in particular, Hose (2008).
[10] Morson (2011) 37. I owe this reference to Henry Spelman.

in longer texts; bits of poems or patches are *cut out* and 'flowery purple passages' (*flosculi*; see Sen. *Epist.* 33.1, 33.7) are *plucked out*.[11] Indeed, when one author encourages 'plucking sweet things' (*carpamus dulcia*; Pers. 5.151), we cannot tell whether this is just an exhortation to enjoyment, or a metaliterary comment on plucking sweet poetry. My interpretation of excerpts develops some thoughts on allusions as physical, pluckable textual objects, put forward by Philip Hardie, and engages with Gian Biagio Conte's thoughts on the rhetorical scope of intertextuality.[12] In short, I am arguing that it is no coincidence that the motif of *carpe diem* is particularly prone to being excerpted.[13]

Naturally, not every excerpt of *carpe diem* can be discussed in this chapter. Rather, mirroring my material, I will gather some of the choicest examples. The selection here focusses in particular on textual developments towards and during the Roman Empire, and pays close attention to their later reception in quotations, *florilegia*, and anthologies. While two texts that are discussed here, Vergil's *Georgics* and Horace's *Sermones* 2, still look towards the Empire, other texts are firmly placed within this period. By focusing on the Empire, I am, however, not claiming that such excerpting is a purely late phenomenon. Indeed, one of the earliest *carpe diem* poems we possess, Mimnermus, *fr.* 2, can fruitfully be linked to excerpting, as Mimnermus excerpts and decontextualises material from a Homeric purple passage on leaves (*Il.* 6.146–9).[14] The Theognidean corpus, featuring many short 'snippets' on *carpe diem*, may also invite this concept. And perhaps one of the best-known and most elaborate *carpe diem* set-texts is the speech of drunken Heracles in Euripides' *Alcestis* (780–802), a text that would in turn become much excerpted.[15] Nonetheless, the focus on the Roman Empire is not arbitrarily chosen. For, as David

---

[11] On the flower imagery in miscellanies, see, in particular, Fitzgerald (2016) 153–4.
[12] Hardie (2012) 229–38, Conte (1986).
[13] This has been suggested to me by Emily Gowers.
[14] On Mimnermus, *fr.* 2, see, for example, Griffith (1975), Sider (1996), and pages 11–13 in the Introduction.
[15] In his Valedictory Lecture as Regius Professor of Greek at Cambridge, titled 'I Think I Should Probably Go Now' (accessible at www.classics.cam.ac.uk/file/valedictoryweb sitepdf), Richard Hunter has reminded us that Heracles' *carpe diem* argument was excerpted by Plu. *Moralia* 107b–c (the perhaps spurious *Consolatio ad Apollonium*), Stobaeus 4.51.13, as well as by the fifth-century-AD grammarian Orion at *Anthologion*

Konstan says in relation to excerpts in Stobaeus, while excerpts have always been a part of Greco-Roman literature, they become increasingly important in the Empire.[16] This period, and in particular its anthologies and satires, which are stuffed full with other genres, seem the richest meadows for gathering my flowers.

The chapter falls into four different parts, each one dedicated to a case study of excerpting. In the first part, I will look at Vergil's *Georgics* 3 and discuss how purple passages from archaic poetry are used to convey an independent voice of wisdom. The other focus of this section is how the natural splendour of a purple passage leads to later excerption. The topic of my second section is the tale of the town and the country mouse in Horace, *Sermones* 2.6. Here, I am concerned with how a section on *carpe diem* can appear as an intrusive voice of high-style poetry in the pedestrian context of the *Sermones*. The third section deals with Trimalchio's poems in Petronius' *Satyrica*. I will analyse these excerpts as a product of rhetorical education which treats literature as a series of patterns. The other theme I am interested in here is how Trimalchio's recitation of poetic scraps demonstrates an especially 'sympotic' preference for extracting lyric (as in Athenaeus' *Deipnosophistae*). Finally, in the last part of this chapter, I will look at Juvenal, *Satires* 9. I will show how excerpting and re-excerpting has created a cliché that can be inserted just about anywhere, so that the musings of a Roman male prostitute ended up in a letter to Charles IV, the emperor of the Holy Roman Empire and self-proclaimed descendant of saints.

5.1 Plucking Grass: Cows, Flocks, Vergil, *Georgics* 3, and Seneca

A passage that was considered a purple passage in antiquity and adapted by numerous authors is Hesiod's description of a summer day in the *Works and Days*, where the poet advises his addressee to enjoy the season by sitting in the shade and having a good meal with wine (*Op.* 582–96):[17]

8.4.2. Lines 782–93 on *carpe diem* are also preserved by *P.Oxy.* 5486, which may be from the same column as *P.Oxy.* 4547, which preserves lines 772–9 (cf. Chepel (2016)).
[16] Konstan (2011). Cf. Jacob (2000) 104–6, König and Whitmarsh (2007b).
[17] Text: West (1978).

Excerpts of *Carpe Diem*

ἦμος δὲ σκόλυμός τ' ἀνθεῖ καὶ ἠχέτα τέττιξ
δενδρέῳ ἐφεζόμενος λιγυρὴν καταχεύετ' ἀοιδὴν
πυκνὸν ὑπὸ πτερύγων θέρεος καματώδεος ὥρῃ,
τῆμος πιόταταί τ' αἶγες καὶ οἶνος ἄριστος, (585)
μαχλόταται δὲ γυναῖκες, ἀφαυρότατοι δέ τοι ἄνδρες
εἰσίν, ἐπεὶ κεφαλὴν καὶ γούνατα Σείριος ἄζει,
αὐαλέος δέ τε χρὼς ὑπὸ καύματος· ἀλλὰ τότ' ἤδη
εἴη πετραίη τε σκιὴ καὶ Βίβλινος οἶνος
μᾶζά τ' ἀμολγαίη γάλα τ' αἰγῶν σβεννυμενάων (590)
καὶ βοὸς ὑλοφάγοιο κρέας μή πω τετοκυίης
πρωτογόνων τ' ἐρίφων· ἐπὶ δ' αἴθοπα πινέμεν οἶνον
ἐν σκιῇ ἑζόμενον, κεκορημένον ἦτορ ἐδωδῆς,
ἀντίον ἀκραέος Ζεφύρου τρέψαντα πρόσωπα·
κρήνης δ' αἰενάου καὶ ἀπορρύτου, ἥ τ' ἀθόλωτος, (595)
τρὶς ὕδατος προχέειν, τὸ δὲ τέτρατον ἱέμεν οἴνου.

When the golden thistle blooms and the chirping cicada sits in a tree and ceaselessly pours out its shrill song from under its wings in the season of toilsome summer, then the goats are fattest and wine is best, the women most lustful and the men at their weakest, because Sirius burns their heads and knees, and the skin is dry from the heat. But then make sure that there's some shade from a rock and Bibline wine, a milk cake, the milk of goats which are drying up, the meat of a forest-grazing cow that has not yet given birth, and the meat of newly born kids. Also, drink gleaming wine, while you are sitting in the shade, when you've fulfilled your desire for food, with your face turned towards the fresh west wind. Pour in three measures of water from a spring that's ever-flowing, running and unmuddied, and put in a fourth measure of wine.

These lines are repeatedly quoted when authors wish to speak in Hesiod's authoritative voice, and already in archaic lyric Alcaeus used this voice in an exhortation to heavy drinking, as Richard Hunter has shown (*fr.* 347):[18]

Τέγγε πλεύμονας οἴνῳ, τὸ γὰρ ἄστρον περιτέλλεται,
ἀ δ' ὥρα χαλέπα, πάντα δὲ δίψαισ' ὐπὰ καύματος,
ἄχει δ' ἐκ πετάλων ἄδεα τέττιξ . . .
ἄνθει δὲ σκόλυμος, νῦν δὲ γύναικες μιαρώταται
λέπτοι δ' ἄνδρες, ἐπεὶ ⟨ ⟩ κεφάλαν καὶ γόνα Σείριος
ἄσδει

---

[18] Hunter (2014) 123–66 with further bibliography. For Alcaeus' fragment, its history, and further sources, see Budelmann (2018) 110–13, Ponzio (2001).

Cows, Flocks, Vergil, *Georgics* 3, and Seneca

Drench your lungs in wine, because the star is revolving and the season is harsh; everything is thirsty under the heat, and the cicada sings sweetly from the leaves … the golden thistle blooms; now women are at their most repulsive and men are feeble, because Sirius burns their heads and knees

We do not know the context of Alcaeus' fragment, but a *carpe diem* context may be at least suspected. Not only would this be in line with other poems of Alcaeus (see *frr.* 38, 335, 346), but it would also fit the reception of this fragment: Horace adapts the idea of drinking in a warm season in *Odes* 3.29.18–20 as well as in 4.12, where the *carpe diem* motif is strongly present in each case,[19] and the same can be said about the pseudo-Vergilian *Copa* (in particular lines 25–38).[20] Moreover, when Athenaeus quotes part of this fragment, he does so within a sequence of drinking exhortations of Alcaeus of which some have a definite *carpe diem* context and others have a possible one.[21] Though this cumulative evidence makes a *carpe diem* context in Alcaeus not unlikely, it is more fruitful to look at Alcaeus' poem through the lens of its reception: we can see that the passage came to be treated as a model for '*carpe diem* in summer'. This is something not yet present in Hesiod, but linked to the reception of Alcaeus' poem, which became an oft-quoted excerpt in its own right.[22] Indeed, whether this is an instance of misquotation or of reperformance, Alcaeus *fr.* 352 shows close verbal resemblance

---

[19] For the Alcaean reference at Hor. *C.* 3.29.18–20, see Davis (1991) 175 and 175 n.26.
[20] For *carpe diem* in the *Copa*, see J. Henderson (2002) 261–4, and see page 20 in the Introduction. If the puzzling expression *tangomenas faciamus*, which Trimalchio uses at Petron. 34.7 and 73.6, indeed refers to Alcaeus' τέγγε πλεύμονας οἴνῳ, as has been suggested (see, e.g., Alessio (1960–1) 353–4, Setaioli (2011) 101 n.61 and 102 n.62, Schmeling (2011) *ad loc.*), then there is yet another work that associates Alcaeus' poem with *carpe diem*. Moreover, *P.Oxy.* 3724.iv.20, perhaps an epigram of Philodemus, has the *incipit* ζωροπότην ὤρη(ι?) or ὤρη() (perhaps: 'It is the season for the man who drinks his wine straight for [...]', following Sider (1997) 203–5, 214, and see pages 153–7 in Chapter 4 on ζωροποτεῖν and *carpe diem*). Though this has to remain speculation, I am tempted to see in this *incipit* a reference to Alcaeus drinking in the summer heat, the more so as Philodemus quotes Alcaeus' image of wetting the lungs with wine elsewhere (*AP* 11.34.7 = Philodemus 6.7 Sider).
[21] Ath. 10.430a–d, where *fr.* 335 and 346 make the motif explicit, and *frr.* 338 and 367 have been received as *carpe diem* poetry respectively through Hor. *C.* 1.9, 1.4/4.7.
[22] For verbal quotations of Alc. *fr.* 347, see Voigt (1971) *ad loc.* Also note the allusions to Alcaeus' poem at *Anacreont.* 18.1–4, and 60.32–6 with Most (2014) 146–9, though neither poem employs the *carpe diem* motif.

to *fr.* 347 and is a case in point for its status as a purple passage.²³

In Vergil's *Georgics*, both Hesiod and Alcaeus are used as models for a description of summer heat. The one gives the passage didactic authority; the other adds a sense of humour and sympotic dimension to *carpe diem*, as Vergil explains how one should take care of flocks in the summer (Verg. *G.* 3.323–38):

> at uero Zephyris cum laeta uocantibus aestas
> in saltus utrumque gregem atque in pascua mittet,
> Luciferi primo cum sidere frigida rura
> carpamus, dum mane nouum, dum gramina canent, (325)
> et ros in tenera pecori gratissimus herba.
> inde ubi quarta sitim caeli collegerit hora
> et cantu querulae rumpent arbusta cicadae,
> ad puteos aut alta greges ad stagna iubebo
> currentem ilignis potare canalibus undam; (330)
> aestibus at mediis umbrosam exquirere uallem,
> sicubi magna Iouis antiquo robore quercus
> ingentis tendat ramos, aut sicubi nigrum
> ilicibus crebris sacra nemus accubet umbra;
> tum tenuis dare rursus aquas et pascere rursus (335)
> solis ad occasum, cum frigidus aëra Vesper
> temperat, et saltus reficit iam roscida luna,
> litoraque alcyonen resonant, acalanthida dumi.

But when the Zephyrs are calling and joyous summer sends the flocks of sheep and goats to the woodland pastures and the meadows, then let us take to the cool fields at the rise of the morning star, while the morning is young, while hoar frost whitens the grass, and the dew in the tender grass is most welcome to cattle. Then, when the fourth celestial hour has brought thirst and the song of shrill cicadas bursts through the thickets, I will ask the flocks to drink the water that runs through wooden channels at the side of wells or deep pools. But in the midday sun look for a shaded valley where the great oak of Jupiter with its old trunk stretches out its huge branches or where a grove, dark with many holms, lies with hallowed shade. Then, give them again trickling water and feed them again until sunset, when the cool evening star chills the air and the moon refreshes the woodland pastures by dropping dew now, and the shores resound with the song of the halcyon and the thickets echo the song of the finch.

---

[23] *Fr.* 352: Πώνωμεν, τὸ γὰρ ἄστρον περιτέλλεται. See Rösler (1983) 19–20, Budelmann (2018) 111.

Hesiod and Alcaeus have lent purple splendour to a topic that does perhaps not possess it by nature: the feeding and drinking schedule of flocks. The structure of the summer day in these lines and the prescriptions are taken from an agricultural treatise: Richard Thomas has shown in detail how Vergil here adopts a section of Varro's *Res rustica*.[24] Vergil changes, however, the tone of 'some of the most functional and mundane prose of ancient literature',[25] as Thomas points out. I argue that Vergil achieves that as he combines Varro's text with other models: dry technical instructions on farming are turned into a Hesiodic purple passage and are made to echo the sound of Alcaeus' lyric. Thus, some features of the passage, such as the zephyr winds and the chirping cicada, are clear references to Hesiod.[26] Shade and drinking can also be found in Hesiod's description of the summer day, though they do appear in Varro as well. A reference to Hesiod naturally befits Vergil's *Ascraeum carmen* (Verg. *G.* 2.176), but there might be more in play here. As Richard Hunter has shown, the rich history of allusions to this specific passage from Hesiod makes it a typical Hesiodic 'excerpt', exactly the type of passage an author cites whenever he wishes to speak with Hesiodic authority.[27]

By nodding to both Hesiod and Alcaeus, Vergil shows some awareness of the quotation history of the text. Alcaeus' influence on the passage seems not to have been noted so far. Two lines of the passage strongly recall the lyric poet (327–8): *inde ubi quarta sitim caeli collegerit hora | et cantu querulae rumpent arbusta cicadae* ('then when the fourth celestial hour has brought thirst and the song of shrill cicadas bursts through the thickets'). These lines evoke ἀ δ' ὤρα χαλέπα, πάντα δὲ δίψαισ' ὐπὰ καύματος, | ἄχει δ ἐκ πετάλων ἄδεα τέττιξ ('the season is harsh, everything is thirsty under the heat, and the cicada sings sweetly from the leaves'). The train of thought that moves from thirst in one line to a singing cicada in the next one is the same in both poets, whereas Hesiod

---

[24] Thomas (1987) 233–5 referring to Varro *R.* 2.2.10–11.   [25] Thomas (1987) 230.
[26] The Hesiodic influence has been noted by Heyne (1826) and Erren (2003) *ad loc.*, Hunter (2014) 145 n.58, and see this chapter, page 192 n.29 for the discussion of another Hesiodic feature in the *Georgics* passage.
[27] Hunter (2014) 123–66. For Hesiod's poem as a sequence of self-contained passages that invite excerpting, see Canevaro (2015).

Excerpts of *Carpe Diem*

first mentions the cicada and burning heat later. While this could still be explained as a coincidence, another feature within these lines is crucial: the motif of thirst. This is not mentioned by Hesiod, whereas Alcaeus makes thirst the theme of his poem (at least from how the fragmentary state of the poem allows us to judge). Picking up the thirst motif, Vergil makes *hora* the agent of thirst, which may be an interlingual pun on Alcaeus' ὥρα.[28] We are hearing Alcaeus' lyric voice, a sound effect that transcends meaning. In a way, Vergil speaks of even heavier drinking than Alcaeus. Whereas Alcaeus speaks of 'drenching the lungs', in Vergil the drinking vessels are massive troughs.[29] The difference is, of course, that Vergil does not speak of wine for men but of water for flocks. The evocation of Alcaeus creates a drinking-party for flocks: whereas in Hesiod and Alcaeus humans are asked to enjoy the season, in Vergil's world of humanised animals the flocks do that and even beat Alcaeus at drinking. The combined reference to more than one model is characteristic of Vergil's 'art of reference',[30] and it is almost certain in the present case when we know that ancient commentators were already well aware of the Alcaean reference to Hesiod.[31] Vergil, here, continues dynamics of excerpting that are already present in archaic literature: Hesiod creates a self-contained purple passage, Alcaeus excerpts it, and Vergil's version points to this textual history.

---

[28] The etymology of *hora* from ὥρα was well known to the Augustans, and Horace played with the original Greek sense of the word at *C.* 1.12.16, as Gitner (2012) 25 notes. Also cf. Maltby (1991) s.v. 'hora'. Admittedly, thirst is also present at Varro *R.* 2.2: *sole exorto potum propellunt*; but the word *hora* does not appear in Varro, while Alcaeus owes ὥρα to Hes. *Op.* 584. In another passage influenced by Alcaeus, Hor. *C.* 4.12.13, already adduced by Heyne (1826) *ad loc.*, the seasons bring thirst: *adduxere sitim tempora, Vergili*. The line addresses Vergil, as if to say that he, too, has translated this Alcaeus passage (for the vexed question of who the Vergilius in the ode is, see, e.g., Thomas (2011) 226–8 with further bibliography and recently Tarrant (2015a)).

[29] Thomas (1988) and Mynors (1990) at Verg. *G.* 3.330 say that *ilignis canalibus* must refer to troughs. Thomas notes that *currentem undam* is difficult to square with troughs, but the expression is arguably an attempt to instil some Hesiodic wisdom into the poem, translating κρήνης ἀποῤῥύτου of the purple model at Hes. *Op.* 595.

[30] Thomas (1986). Also see Thomas (1988) *passim*.

[31] Proclus quotes the Alcaeus fragment in his Hesiod commentary, noting: τοιαῦτα δὲ καὶ τὸν Ἀλκαῖον ᾄδειν. The fact that Proclus does not include Alcaeus' half-line on thirst in his quotation (Marzillo (2010) 214, 354) also indicates that this has no parallel in Hesiod.

Vergil's flocks enjoy the summer day with ample drink and shade. Yet, there is some haste implied and the danger that enjoyment does not last forever (324–5): *frigida rura | carpamus, dum mane nouum, dum gramina canent* ('let us take to the cool fields, while the morning is young, while hoar frost whitens the grass'). This is a difficult sentence, as the meaning of *carpo* is not clear. To appropriate the meaning of the sentence, we can adduce a comparable passage from Tibullus (2.5.56): *carpite nunc, tauri, de septem montibus herbas, | dum licet: hic magnae iam locus urbis erit* ('now, bulls, graze on the grass of the seven hills while you may; soon here will be the site of a great city'). Tibullus exhorts steers to graze (*carpite*) on the future site of Rome, while they still can (*dum licet*). The enjoyable time for steers will pass and the tag *dum licet* strongly points to *carpe diem*.[32] In Vergil, the limiting factor introduced by an anaphora of *dum* is the freshness of the meadow in the morning, which will not last. Ironically, here whiteness marks a time of enjoyment, whereas in the context of *carpe diem* it usually signifies oppressive old age.[33] But what to make of *carpamus*? The *dum* clause about the appeal of morning fields to flocks points to the meaning 'grazing' for *carpamus*. Yet, the first-person plural is somewhat surprising and suggests that, unlike in Tibullus, this does not describe flocks 'grazing' the fields, but humans 'taking to' the fields. Perhaps in a book that uses *carpo* in both these meanings, we should exclude neither option.[34] The first-person plural then expresses exuberance and shows humans taking part in the enjoyment of animals.[35] *Carpere* with a sense of enjoyment includes, once more, references to 'plucking' the products of the seasons (here: dewy grass), as I have discussed in Chapter 3. Horace would, of course, apply a much bolder object to *carpere* in the *Odes* by joining it with *dies*.

---

[32] For *dum licet* as a part of *carpe diem*, see Hor. *C.* 2.11.16, 4.12.26, *S.* 2.6.96, *Epist.* 1.11.20, as well as Petron. 34.10, discussed on pages 205–10 of this chapter. Cf. Sen. *Dial.* 10.19.2, and page 9 n.28 in the Introduction.
[33] For example, Hor. *C.* 1.9.17.
[34] See Verg. *G.* 3.142 and 3.347 for walking and 3.465 for grazing. For *carpo* in Vergil, see, in particular, Traina at *EV* i.676–7 s.v. 'carpo'.
[35] Mynors (1990) *ad loc.* suggests a notion of enjoyment in *carpo*, Thomas (1988) *ad loc.* says that the first person implies exuberance. Already Heyne (1826) *ad loc.* noted the ambiguity of *carpamus*.

Excerpts of *Carpe Diem*

We have seen how a purple passage from Hesiod and in turn one of Alcaeus become excerpted and re-excerpted, while in their new contexts they still always point back to the archaic originals and their advice. In the discussion of the next passage, the sense of detachment of the statement will become clearer. Here, Vergil exhorts the farmer to haste when it comes to cattle-breeding. As Vergil humanises his animals once more, he says that cattle only enjoy a fleeting time of happy youth, before old age and death overcome them (Verg. *G.* 3.63–71):

> interea, superat gregibus dum laeta iuuentas,
> solue mares; mitte in Venerem pecuaria primus,
> atque aliam ex alia generando suffice prolem.   (65)
> optima quaeque dies miseris mortalibus aeui
> prima fugit; subeunt morbi tristisque senectus
> et labor, et durae rapit inclementia mortis.
> semper erunt quarum mutari corpora malis:
> semper enim refice ac, ne post amissa requiras,   (70)
> ante ueni et subolem armento sortire quotannis.

> In the meantime, while the cattle have joyful youth in abundance, let loose the males; be first to send the cattle to Venus, and by breeding supply generation upon generation. All life's best days flee first for unhappy mortals; diseases come about and gloomy old age and suffering, and the harshness of stern death snatches them away. Always there will be cattle whose shape you want to change. Yes, always renew them; stay ahead so that you don't regret your losses afterwards, and every year choose new stock for the herd.

As in the previous section, Vergil creates a *carpe diem* for animals. At first sight the placement of such a *carpe diem* section in *Georgics* 3 may seem natural enough; the urgent tone that the farmers had better make good use of their cattle's short period of fertility is solid animal husbandry (modern farming manuals also stress that a key factor for cattle breeding is the critical time of the cows' oestrus). Formally, the motif of *carpe diem* also seems to work well within a didactic poem. After all, the motif of *carpe diem* is naturally instructive: it supposedly expresses advice, imperatives are prominent, an authoritative speaker is required, and so is an addressee who

Cows, Flocks, Vergil, *Georgics* 3, and Seneca

will profit from the advice.[36] Thus, we have seen in the previous section how Vergil successfully blends Hesiodic wisdom with Alcaean largesse in creating a heavy drink. Yet, when Vergil applies the motif to cattle-breeding he takes the instructive nature of *carpe diem* to its limits and possibly beyond. The traditional lyric advice on the human condition constitutes a contrast to the technicalities of cattle-breeding. Vergil's style in these lines is a far cry from the precision and technicality usual in treatments of cattle-breeding.[37] The misplacement of this purple patch in the *Georgics* is reflected in its reception. Lines 66 to 68, in particular, have proved popular with posterity: Seneca discussed them at length at *Epistulae* 108.24–9 and *De breuitate uitae* 9.2, and Samuel Johnson is said to have recited the passage 'with great pathos'.[38] For Seneca, Johnson, and many besides them, these lines encapsulate the human condition. And yet the lines appear in a section on cattle-breeding, a context that is widely ignored.[39] This detachment of the passage from its context of cattle is suggestive. In other words, I do not so much wish to emphasise the fault of Seneca and others who ignore the context of the passage as I wish to show how

---

[36] See pages 23–4 in the Introduction on *carpe diem* and didactic poetry.
[37] Cf. Varro *R.* 2.2.18, Pliny *Nat.* 8.176–7. This involves precision with dates, such as *coitus a delphini exortu a. d. pr. non. Ianuarias diebus triginta, aliquis et autumno* at *Nat.* 8.177 or the technical term *ineo* ('to tup') for the mating of animals in both texts. On *ineo*, see Adams (1990) 190, 206. Vergil avoids such explicit vocabulary that would almost seem obscene for his humanised cows.
[38] Boswell's *Life*, under 1770 (Hill and Powell (1934) ii.129), as noted by Parry (1972) 41, Mynors (1990) *ad loc.* Pointedly, we encounter this passage, too, excerpted and collected through Rev. Dr Maxwell's *Collectanea* of Johnson's witticisms. The humanist Rodolphus Agricola also ignored the context of the Vergilian passage in his *De formando studio*.
[39] Della Corte (1986) at 68 speaks of 'vita umana'. Mynors (1990) *ad loc.*: 'the transition to human beings is made quite without warning'. Erren (2003) at 66 comments, 'unerbittliche Vergänglichkeit ist *den Menschen* von Natur auferlegt' (my emphasis). Mazzoli (1970) 217 characterises the Vergilian quote in Seneca thus: 'versi altamente commossi, che cantano e profetizzano la perenne tragedia del *destino umano*' (my emphasis). Gummere (1917–25) translates the passage at Sen. *Epist.* 108.24–9: 'hapless human life' (though, to his credit, this is also how Seneca arguably understands the passage). Some scholars note the original context of cattle: Krauß (1957) 33, W. Richter (1957) *ad loc.*, Klingner (1967) 285, Putnam (1979) 176, Thomas (1988) *ad loc.* G. D. Williams (2003) 172 points out at Sen. *Dial.* 10.9.2 that the lines in Vergil are 'quite different in tone and emphasis', as they deal with 'cattle, not human beings'.

Excerpts of *Carpe Diem*

their reception makes us see more clearly that the passage is already detached in the *Georgics*. Even there the passage feels separated from the rest of the text, as it does not quite fit into the context of cattle-breeding. Indeed, Samuel Johnson may have a point that the *carpe diem* sentiments are more naturally at home at the dinner table than in discussions about mating cows and bulls.

It is arguably one expression in particular that seems an ill match for cattle and invited readers from Seneca onwards to see in these lines a statement on the human condition, namely *miseris mortalibus* ('unhappy mortals', Verg. *G.* 3.66). This expression is naturally evocative of human affairs, not cattle. Servius may have felt the mismatch, as he insisted that we should not limit the passage to cattle, but understand it as referring to everything: *ista sententia non solum ad animalia pertinent, sed generaliter ad omnia*.[40] When Vergil applies the term *miseris mortalibus* to cattle, the expression seems to resist this application. The expression *miseris mortalibus* is taken from Lucretius 5.944. Monica Gale has shown that the anthropomorphic features of Vergil's animals in *Georgics* 3 owe much to Lucretius, who already blurred the lines between humans and beasts.[41] Indeed, when Lucretius uses the term *miseris mortalibus*, he does so in a description of prehistoric humans who behave much like beasts.[42] The Lucretian model might have suggested itself for Vergil's humanised animals. Elsewhere, Vergil also applies the term *mortalis* to animals; before Mezentius meets Aeneas in battle, he speaks to his horse Rhaebus and includes it along with humans among the *mortales*, in a passage in a similar tone to the one in the *Georgics* (Verg.

[40] Parry (1972) 41 is characteristically sensitive to the tone of the passage: 'The limits of the proper age for breeding, a practical matter of animal husbandry, is transformed by Virgil's quick thought into a melancholy reflexion on the transience of happiness and life itself'. Cf. Knox (1992) 47: 'with the phrase *miseris mortalibus* Virgil throws off the pretense that he is writing only of animals'.

[41] Gale (1991). Vergil humanises animals throughout *Georgics* 3, for example, in closest proximity to the passage of interest here Verg. *G.* 3.60–1: *aetas Lucinam iustosque pati hymenaeos | desinit ante decem, post quattuor incipit annos*. Also see Liebeschuetz (1965) and, in particular, the examples collected at 64–5.

[42] Lucr. 5.925–47; see, in particular, 932: *uolgiuago uitam tractabant more ferarum* and in 947 the comparison of humans with *saecla ferarum*. See the reading of G. Campbell (2003) 204: 'This coarse fodder was *quite sufficient* for these tough bestial early humans'. Cf. Gale (1991) 417.

A. 10.861–2):⁴³ *Rhaebe, diu, res si qua diu mortalibus ulla est,* | *uiximus* ('Rhaebus, we have lived for a long time, if anything lasts long for mortals').

Vergil uses the word *mortalis* for animals but, when he does so, he is aware that this is a term which *carpe diem* poems use to describe the human condition.⁴⁴ This is what Heracles does in Euripides' *Alcestis* when he mentions 'all mortals' in the context of *carpe diem* (βροτοῖς ἅπασι, line 782), and a character from a lost play directs his *carpe diem* advice to 'all mortals' (πᾶσιν δὲ θνητοῖς, *TrGF Adespota* 95.1 *apud* Ath. 8.336b–c).⁴⁵ As Vergil turns this description of the human condition into a description of cows and uses almost entirely human terms, the passage becomes detached from the surrounding text, a detachment that can be felt in its reception. Conte described this effect of allusion in his *Rhetoric of Imitation* thus: 'the foreign body remains distinct from, and hostile to, the coherent design of the whole work within which it "refuses" to be integrated'.⁴⁶ This refusal to be integrated characterises the excerpts of *carpe diem* in this chapter. Thus, the passage in the *Georgics* has the appearance of a lyric purple patch stitched onto the fabric of the *Georgics*; whether we think of Horace, *Odes* 2.14.1–4 here, which Richard Thomas speculates may have been influenced by Vergil, or about Mimnermus, *fr.* 1, we are reminded of lyric poetry, which bears little relation to cattle-breeding.

When Seneca takes the passage out of context and quotes it misleadingly, he gets away with it, because the passage is already detached from the rest of the text in the *Georgics*.⁴⁷ Seneca introduces the passage in *De breuitate uitae*, as if Vergil, half-lyric sage, half-prophet, were standing in front of him performing a song (9.2): *clamat ecce maximus uates et uelut diuino ore*

---

⁴³ Cf. Harrison (1991) *ad loc.* For the very similar case of *mortalis animas* referring to mice at Hor. *S.* 2.6.93–5, see Chapter 5.2. Vergil also uses the variation *mortalibus aegris* (e.g., *A.* 12.850 with Tarrant (2012) *ad loc*).
⁴⁴ Cf. Thomas (1988) at Verg. *G.* 3.66, who calls these terms 'wholly human'.
⁴⁵ Also see Thgn. 1007, *GV* 1978.16, and the slightly different but still generalising Choerilus *SH* 335.1 (discussed in detail in Chapter 1.2), Amphis, *Ialemus fr.* 21.1, Lucr. 3.912–15, Petron. 34.10.
⁴⁶ Conte (1986) 88. Cf. Hardie (2012) 229–38.
⁴⁷ For Seneca's technique of taking Vergilian passages out of context, see Krauß (1957), Setaioli (1965), Tischer (2017).

Excerpts of *Carpe Diem*

instinctus salutare carmen canit ('look, the greatest poet shouts out and as if inspired with divine utterance he sings a saving song'). This is hardly a good characterisation of Vergil's voice, talking of cattle-breeding in the *Georgics*, but we will see throughout this chapter the prevalent association of the *carpe diem* motif with song and lyric: Seneca quotes a passage of text, but for him the passage is evocative of song and performance. Seneca invites us then to see Vergil as if he were present in front of us (*ecce*). And, perhaps appropriately, Seneca virtually lets us see Vergil's words presently performed on the stage when he uses the Vergilian expression *optimos uitae dies* ('life's best days') in a *carpe diem* section of one of his plays (*Phaed.* 450). His introduction of Vergil's line in *De breuitate uitae* also shows us how excerpts of *carpe diem* were commonly received: we will encounter throughout this chapter readers who admire the *carpe diem* motif as if it were the purest form of poetry and wisdom, even if it reappears in as base a context as cattle-breeding. This reception is part of the culture of excerpting; enduring admiration for the motif leads to further excerpting and so a cliché is created. Vergil's exhortation for constant renewal proves as true for poetic excerpts as it does for cows: *semper enim refice* ('yes, always renew them').[48]

5.2 Plucking the Road, or Of Mice and Muses: Horace, *Sermones* 2.6

In Horace's *Sermones* 2.6, the *carpe diem* motif is again applied to animals, in this case mice. The rustic Cervius tells a fable of a town and a country mouse. Though the country mouse does his utmost to offer a good dinner to the town mouse during his visit, the latter is displeased with the rustic meal and uses the idea of *carpe diem* as an argument for preferring the luxurious life in the city to impoverished simplicity in the countryside (Hor. *S.* 2.6.90–7):

> tandem urbanus ad hunc 'quid te iuuat' inquit, 'amice,   (90)
> praerupti nemoris patientem uiuere dorso?
> uis tu homines urbemque feris praeponere siluis?

---

[48] Cf. J. Henderson (1996) 129–30 n.11 on Vergil's 'careful selection' of cows and poetry here.

Horace, *Sermones* 2.6

carpe uiam, mihi crede, comes, terrestria quando
mortalis animas uiuunt sortita neque ulla est
aut magno aut paruo leti fuga: quo, bone, circa, (95)
dum licet, in rebus iucundis uiue beatus,
uiue memor, quam sis aeui breuis.'

Finally, the town mouse said to him [i.e., the country mouse]: 'How can it please you, my friend, to endure a life on the ridge of a rugged forest? Why don't you prefer people and the town to the savage forests? Trust me, my friend, seize the way, since terrestrial beings live with mortal souls as their lot, and neither the great nor the small can escape death; therefore, my good fellow, while you may, live a happy life among pleasures; live and keep in mind how short-lived you are.'

There is something enticing about the presence of a passage on *carpe diem* already in the *Sermones*, before Horace made this one of the most important themes of his poetry in the *Odes*.[49] Indeed, *carpe uiam* in the passage from the *Sermones* already seems to look forward to the daring lyric expression *carpe diem* of *Odes* 1.11. Andrea Cucchiarelli speculates that this ode had already been written and published separately, but as there is no evidence for this it seems more likely that in this case the humorous usage of an expression precedes the serious one.[50] Wieland might have recognised the connection, as he included in his translation of the passage from the satire the phrase 'so sei du weise' ('be wise'), which has no direct equivalent in the Latin of *Sermones* 2.6, but is an excerpt from the *carpe diem* ode, 1.11, where Horace writes *sapias* ('be wise').[51] The similarity between the speech of the *urbanus mus* and *Odes* 1.11 is arguably not accidental. Indeed, I will argue that the section in *Sermones* 2.6 is poignantly different

---

[49] Horace has treated the theme in *Epod.* 13, published around the same time as *Sermones* 2 (see Chapter 2.1).
[50] Cucchiarelli (2001) 165 n.177. Cf. Commager (1962) 121, Harrison (2007b) 237. The expression *carpe uiam* would be reused by the Sibyl at Verg. *A.* 6.629 and several times by Ovid. A well-known example of an expression which first appears in a humorous context before it is re-used in a serious one is *inuita, o regina, tuo de uertice cessi* at Cat. 66.39, adopted with slight changes at Verg. *A.* 6.460, on which see Conte (1986) 88–90. An example from Horace's *Sermones* is the kitchen fire at 1.5.73–4, which Vergil may imitate in a more serious context in his description of the fires of Troy (*A.* 2.310–2), on which see Gowers (2012) 204–5.
[51] Wieland (1813) 437. The usage of *sapias* at Ov. *Am.* 1.4.29 with McKeown (1987–) *ad loc.* suggests that this was a recognisable Horatian expression. Veyne (1967) 106 notes the usage of *sapias* at Pers. 5.167.

Excerpts of *Carpe Diem*

from its surroundings and sticks out as an excerpt of lyric poetry within the humble mouse tale. Horace's foray into lyric poetry risks crossing the generic boundaries of satire.[52] On the following pages, I will analyse how the purple patch (cf. *Ars* 14–23) stands out among the surrounding clothes, or how the lyric *carpe diem* excerpt intrudes on the satirical fable of mice.[53]

Numerous features of the town mouse's speech display a much loftier style than befits Horace's pedestrian muse, and show the mouse's aspiration to being *urbanus* in every sense.[54] Thus, commentators have long noted the rare tmesis of *quocirca* in line 95, the mannered *uiuunt sortita* instead of *sortiti sunt in uita*, and the elevated register of *letum*, which Horace elsewhere only uses in the *Odes*, as well as the high register of *aeuum*.[55] The last one is part of the expression *sis aeui breuis*, which deserves closer

---

[52] I follow the important thoughts on generic play in *Sermones* 2.6 of Cucchiarelli (2001) 162–8 and Freudenburg (2006), who already described Horace as 'playing at lyric's boundaries'. On the fable in general, see, above all, Fraenkel (1957) 138–44, Brink (1965), Rudd (1966) 243–57, D. West (1974), Harrison (2013) 164–6; also Seel (1972), Barbieri (1976), Warmuth (1992) 119–25, Hopkins (1993), Leach (1993) 285–7, Fedeli (1994a) 289–97, Schmidt (1997) 56–73, Oliensis (1998) 46–51, and Knorr (2004) 207–14.

[53] In a satire that uniquely refers to itself as *carmen* (22), this is not the only foray into lyric. Earlier, Horace already began to sing a hymn (16–23), as has been analysed by Fraenkel (1957) 139–40, Cucchiarelli (2001) 165–6, and Freudenburg (2006). It might be added that this hymn, too, possesses the characteristics of an excerpt. When Horace excerpts lyric poetry in the *Odes*, he most notably does so with 'mottoes' taken from *incipit*s under which poems were catalogued (Pasquali (1964) [1920] 9, Feeney (1993) 44, Cavarzere (1996)). Horace's hymn in *S.* 2.6 also begins with a Pindaric motto in line 17, *quid prius inlustrem saturis musaque pedestri?* (cf. Pi. *O.* 2.1–2, *fr.* 89a Maehler, Hor. *C.* 1.12.1–3 with Fraenkel (1957) 139–40). This 'pompous beginning' of a purple patch (*inceptis gravibus*, *Ars* 14) is soon contrasted with the cacophony of satiric interjections (on interjections, see Rudd (1966) 243–57, Thomas (2010)). A similar cacophonic return to satire will also be observed after the *carpe diem* excerpt.

[54] On *urbanitas*, see Ramage (1973) and, in particular, 77–86 on Horace.

[55] Orelli and Baiter (1850) *ad loc.* on *quo* [...] *circa*: 'tmesis rarissima'. See Fedeli (1994b) *ad loc.* on *uiuunt sortita*, and Kießling and Heinze (1961b) *ad loc.* on *letum*. Persius in his *Satires* tellingly uses *letum* only in another parodic passage on *carpe diem* (Pers. 5.153; quoted on page 217 in this chapter). On *aeuum*, see Ruckdeschel (1911) 37–8, Smereka (1935) 68, Brink (1982a) at Hor. *Epist.* 2.1.159, and, in particular, Mayer (1994) at Hor. *Epist.* 1.3.8 and (2012) at Hor. *C.* 1.12.45. It does not seem to be recognised that Housman excerpted Horace's *mortalis animas sortita* for his dedication of the Manilius edition to Moses Jackson, where he wrote *fataque sortitas non immortalia mentes* (at A. Burnett (1997) 289–91). The mock grandiloquence of Horace's words suits Housman's ironic and melancholic preface well, which he directs to the love of his youth, the 'scorner of these studies' (for Housman's preface, see Harrison (2002), and page 33 n.138 in the Introduction).

attention. Kießling and Heinze, here, see a translation of the Greek βραχύβιος, while the Homeric ὠκύμορος is also used in the context of *carpe diem* at *AP* 11.23 (= Antipater of Thessalonica 38 *GP*) and the epitaph *SGO* 05/01/62.4 (= *GV* 1364.4); but, arguably, Paul Lejay, who thinks of ὀλιγοχρόνιος, hits the mark.[56] Though Adam Gitner does not discuss this expression in his dissertation on Grecisms in Horace, his analysis of a different expression seems valuable for the present passage. Gitner says of Horace's periphrastic expression *seri studiorum* ('late learners') at *Sermones* 1.10.21, translating Greek ὀψιμαθεῖς, that 'it serves to draw attention to the translation as a translation, so that one feels the Greek moving beneath it'.[57] In *Sermones* 2.6, the *urbanus mus*, who misses a certain *je ne sais quoi* at the rustic dinner, is eager to show off his cosmopolitism and *urbanitas*. His Grecism draws attention to this passage as a set piece of Greek-style lyric poetry. In this genre ὀλιγοχρόνιος indeed appears in a *carpe diem* poem (Mimn. *fr.* 5.5 *apud* Stob. 4.50.69 = Thgn. 1020).[58] Further, a Hellenistic *carpe diem* epigram ascribed to Plato ends on a very similar note to the little speech of Horace's mouse: σκέψαι τὴν ὥρην ὡς ὀλιγοχρόνιος ('consider how short-lived youth is', *AP* 5.79 = [Plato] 4 *FGE*). The town mouse seems to ask the country mouse to remember (97: *memor*) poetry of this kind as well as to remember the sentiment.[59] Indeed, Persius would in turn answer Horace's call and remember the passage: at *Satire* 5.153, he uses the Horatian expression *uiue memor leti* in a *carpe diem* context.[60]

---

[56] Kießling and Heinze (1961b) and Lejay (1966) [1911] *ad loc*. However, βραχύβιος is not attested in poetry, and ὠκύμορος is rendered by Horace as *cita mors* at *S*. 1.1.8, C. 2.16.29 with Nisbet and Hubbard (1978) *ad loc*. Landolfi (1995) 231 notes that Sallust uses *aeui breuis* in the first sentence of the *Bellum Iugurthinum* in a statement on the human condition. It is possible that this sentence influenced Horace, but alternatively the parallel may point to a shared interest of Sallust and Horace in archaisms and the like.
[57] Gitner (2012) 234–5. The link with ὀψιμαθεῖς had already been recognised by Porphyrio. Kießling and Heinze (1961b) at Hor. *S*. 1.1.33 note on *magni formica laboris* that a genitive of quality often substitutes Greek compound adjectives as at Hor. *C*. 1.36.13, 3.9.7. Cf. Muecke at *EO* ii.760 s.v. 'Lingua e stile' with further examples and references.
[58] Lejay (1966) [1911] *ad loc*.
[59] I owe this point to Thomas J. Nelson, who suggested to me that *memor* may function here as an intertextual marker.
[60] See Hooley (1997) 109–10, and page 217 in this chapter.

Excerpts of *Carpe Diem*

Moreover, Horace himself uses a comparable expression in one of his *carpe diem* poems. For in *Odes* 2.14, the Postumus ode, Horace describes Postumus as a 'shortlived master', *breuis dominus* (*C.* 2.14.24).[61] When Kießling and Heinze say about this expression 'noch kühner gesagt' ('an even bolder expression'), their note almost sounds like a German translation of Quintilian's characterisation of Horace (*uerbis felicissime audax*; 'fortuitously bold with his words', *Inst.* 10.96).[62] Indeed, such a *callida iunctura* formed *ex Graeco fonte* is characteristic of Horace's project of writing Greek lyric in Latin (see Hor. *Ars* 45–71, discussed in Chapter 3.1 and 3.2). It is thus rather apt that Brink discerns a 'sudden lyric touch', when Horace uses the expression *aeui breuis* again in the *Epistles* in the context of *carpe diem* (*Epist.* 2.1.144).[63] In *Sermones* 2.6, however, the marked translation and the high register show that the town mouse's speech is inserted here from a different language, a different genre, and a different dinner. Indeed, when a mouse uses the expression *aeui breuis*, one cannot but think of the mouse's 'short' stature.[64] So much for the purple patch, but what about the surrounding clothing, the story of the mice?

While few conversation topics are more sympotic than *carpe diem*, fables on mice are the opposite of elegant dinner conversation.[65] Indeed, mice have certain characteristics that link them with small-scale writing such as fables and satire.[66] Thus, in the *Ars Poetica*, Horace criticises writers of epic, who promise too much and come up with too little, by referring to

---

[61] Glossed as δεσπότης ὀλιγοχρόνιος by Orelli and Baiter (1850) *ad loc.*, an expression used at Lucian *Nigr.* 26, as Nisbet and Hubbard (1978) note *ad loc.* Also cf. the noun-adjective combination ὀλίγος χρόνος in the *carpe diem* poems Simon. *fr.* 20.10, *AP* 10.100 = Antiphanes 7 *GP*. In comparison, the antonym *longus* is a leitmotif of mortality in Horace (Davis (1991) 157–9).
[62] Kießling and Heinze (1966) *ad loc.*
[63] Brink (1982a) *ad loc.* Already Porphyrio's comment here paraphrases the *carpe diem* motif.
[64] Ov. *F.* 2.574 applies the adjective *breuis* to *mus.* Cf. Freudenburg (2021) at Hor. *S.* 2.6.97, who notes that a mouse's life lasts only five to six months, and his note at 2.6.95 on *magno et paruo*.
[65] A case in point is Ar. *V.* 1181–5, where the boorish Philocleon is rebuked by his son for wishing to tell a fable of a mouse and a weasel at a symposium ('Once there was a mouse and a weasel').
[66] Cf. the *Batrachomyomachia*, adduced by Cucchiarelli (2001) 166 n.178.

a Greek proverb that involves a mouse (Hor. *Ars* 139): *parturient montes, nascetur ridiculus mus* ('mountains are in labour and give birth to – a ridiculous mouse').[67] This poetic embarrassment, the tiny single-syllabic *mus* ending the hexameter, is contrasted with Homer, who gets epic right, perhaps by adding just one letter to *mus*: *dic mihi, Musa, uirum* ('tell me, Muse, of the man'; Hor. *Ars* 141). Rather than in epic, mice find their appropriate generic place in Cervius's *fabella* in *Sermones* 2.6, where the diminutive makes the fable look almost as small as its subject matter. The fable arises as a cognate of Horace's *Sermones* at the countryside dinner (2.6.71): *sermo oritur* ('a chat begins').[68] There is one other thing that links mice and satire. Horace describes the style of his satires in *Sermones* 2.6 with the oxymoron *Musa pedestris* (2.6.17; cf. Hor. *Ars* 95 *sermone pedestri*). And what could be better suited to a 'muse that goes on a foot' or is even 'crawling on the ground' (*sermones* [...] *repentes per humum, Epist.* 2.1.250–1) than mice, who are 'terrestrial beings' (*terrestria*, 2.6.93) and 'crawl' over the ground (*urbis auentes | moenia nocturni* subrepere; 'eager to *creep* under the walls of the town at night', 2.6.99–100)?[69] Indeed, ancient etymologies link *mus* with *humus*, the natural territory for Horace's satires, as he claims in the *Epistles*.[70] Yet Horace's pedestrian m(o)use most risks leaving the humble path when the talk turns to *carpe diem*.[71] It does not come that far, though: the mice are soon to find out that they are too 'terrestrial' and that the danger of death can materialise for the 'small' much faster than for the 'great'. The excerpt is parodic and cannot be simply cut out and pasted in the *Odes*.

Few poets who appeal to the *carpe diem* motif really think that there is a genuine chance that actually 'tomorrow we die'. For the two mice, however, this does almost materialise, when they can

---

[67] Cf. Cucchiarelli (2001) 165–6, Calboli (2002). Phaedr. 4.24 adopts the proverb.
[68] Harrison (2013) 165, Freudenburg (2021) 229.
[69] On *Musa pedestris*, see Freudenburg (1993: 183–4; 2021: *ad loc.*), Cucchiarelli (2001) 57–66, Gowers (2005) 53, L. Morgan (2010) 334–45, and, in particular, Gowers (1993a) for an analysis of the journey to Brundisium at *Sermones* 1.5, which shows the 'walking Muse' in action.
[70] See Maltby (1991) s.v. 'mus' quoting Isidorus, *Etymologiae siue Origines* 12.3.1.
[71] Though in the fable we have already seen high style pouring through, as epic diction is used in the description of the mice. See D. West (1974) 70 and Muecke (1993) at 2.6.97.

scarcely escape the Molossian dogs that break into their luxurious city dinner (2.6.110–15):

> ille cubans gaudet mutata sorte bonisque (110)
> rebus agit laetum conuiuam, cum subito ingens
> ualuarum strepitus lectis excussit utrumque.
> currere per totum pauidi conclaue magisque
> exanimes trepidare, simul domus alta Molossis
> personuit canibus. (115)

> The country mouse was reclining and enjoyed his changed lot and played the guest delighting in all the good things, when suddenly loud dashing of the doors made them both tumble from their couches. Panicked, they ran through the whole room and they were even more terrified – more dead than alive – when the lofty house rang with the barking of Molossian dogs.

This scene quickly finds the mice's lofty ambitions cut short and sees them close to the ground, running on their feet again (*currere*).[72] The scene also literalises the pretensions of the earlier lyric excerpt; there, the *urbanus* asserted that there is no 'flight from death' (*leti fuga*) but, once a danger of death materialises, he quickly forgets his sentiment and flees. Finally, the scene also lets us hear the last, barking sound of this satire (before the closing words of the country mouse): the Molossian dogs are exclusively perceived as a barking sound. Certainly, this is sufficient to restrain the ambitions of the country mouse, who looks for simple fare again instead of lavish symposia. But maybe the barking is a call to order in more than one sense. The barking dogs are probably an invention of Horace, which is neither present in Aesop's, nor Babrius', nor Phaedrus' version of the fable (Aesop 314 Hausrath and Hunger, Babrius 108, Phaedrus *fabulae nouae* 9 Postgate).[73] Moreover, the sound of barking dogs has been associated with the sharp sound of satire since Lucilius, who repeatedly portrays himself as a barking dog.[74] So possibly in *Sermones* 2.6,

---

[72] Cf. Graverini (2011–12) 165–6 on how mice cannot reach the lofty regions of Horace's lyric, such as *C.* 2.20.
[73] For the reconstructed version of Phaedrus, see Holzberg (1991). Babrius 60 includes another mouse that voices a *carpe diem* sentiment; see page 57 n.60 in Chapter 1.
[74] See Lucilius' self-stylisation as a wild dog at *fr.* 2 M(arx) = 3–4 W(armington), *fr.* 377–80 M = 389–92 W, *fr.* 1095–6 M = 1000–1 W with Haß (2007) 90–1, Persius' characterisation of the sound of satire as *canina littera* at 1.109–10 with W. S. Anderson (1958) and Bramble (1974) 151–2 against Kißel (1990) *ad loc.*, and

which is ranging between low and high style and is in acute danger of leaning towards the latter – maybe here Lucilius' barking sound of satire calls not just the mice to order but also Horace the satirist. As it is not the time yet to turn to lyric, the chaotic canine cacophony offers an appropriately satirical ending, reminiscent of the similar scene that ended *Sermones* 1.2.[75] The country mouse happily lay on 'purple coverlets' (*purpurea ueste*, 2.6.106) at the town dinner until the barking frightened him. Yet, if anyone should know the danger of an unfitting purple patch it is, of course, Horace, and the Molossian guard dogs of genre make sure that he does not forget it.

5.3 Butchering Poetry: Trimalchio, Petronius' *Satyrica*, and Athenaeus

In the person of Trimalchio in Petronius' *Satyrica* we find another would-be-*urbanus*, who attempts to stage recitals of literary and not-so-literary works, which are supposed to show his sophistication.[76] In the following section, I will look at Trimalchio's epigrams on *carpe diem* and analyse how their aesthetics are shaped by cutting and fragmentation. As Trimalchio's poems can be compared to carefully (or perhaps not-so-carefully) cut-up portions of food, we can witness a debased version of the quotation culture of Athenaeus' *Deipnosophistae*. But the comparison of texts with delicate bits of food links Trimalchio's epigrams not only with Athenaeus' fragmented quotations but also with over-seasoned rhetorical *sententiae*, such as the schools of rhetoric teach. An exploration of this rhetorical scope of Trimalchio's epigrams is the other focus of this section.

Towards the beginning of the meal, Trimalchio decides to serve some Opimian wine which he alleges is 100 years old. The

---

Horace's self-stylisation as a dog at *S.* 2.1.85, *Epod.* 6. Further sources for dog imagery can be found at, for example, Freudenburg (1993) 77–80, Cucchiarelli (2001) 127–9, L. C. Watson (2003) 251–6, Hawkins (2014). Cucchiarelli (2001) 162–8 notes the originality of the barking dogs in *S.* 2.6, but interprets them as an iambic voice from the *Epodes* in contrast to a satirical voice in one of several generic 'intersezioni' he discusses in the *Sermones* (152–68).
[75] Cf. Lejay (1966) [1911] at *S.* 2.6.114. Also see the barking ending at Hor. *S.* 2.1.85.
[76] For *urbanitas* as Trimalchio's aspiration, see Petron. 36.7, 39.6, 48.5, 52.7.

combined sight of the wine and a skeleton puppet makes Trimalchio think of human transience, a topic that occupies him throughout the dinner, and he expresses his thoughts in a *carpe diem* poem (Petron. 34.10):[77]

> 'eheu nos miseros, quam totus homuncio nil est!
> sic erimus cuncti, postquam nos auferet Orcus.
> ergo uiuamus, dum licet esse bene.'
>
> 'Poor us! The life of human creatures amounts to nothing! We'll all end up like this, after Orcus has carried us off. So, let's live it up while we may.'

The 100-year-old wine raises the expectation of a poem that emulates and surpasses Horace, who frequently links his *carpe diem* poems with vintage wines – though none as old as Trimalchio's (see Chapter 2). Yet, where Horace masters most difficult Greek metres, Trimalchio falls short of elegiacs. For the metrical form of his poem is unusual: although there are parallels for a sequence of hexameters followed by a pentameter in inscriptions, it is surprising when encountered in a book.[78] The unusual metrical form makes the poem seem compressed; but, even though one pentameter line seems to be missing, there are enough *carpe diem* expressions for four lines crammed into three lines. The word *homuncio*, for example, bears some resemblance to *homullus*, which Lucretius uses in a similar context at *De rerum natura* 3.914;[79] *uiuere* with the pregnant sense of 'enjoying life' is used in this context by Catullus and Horace, among others, and so is *dum licet*.[80] Trimalchio crams all these well-known expressions into three lines. The result is a poem that seems almost cut and pasted.

---

[77] On death and dining at the *Cena Trimalchionis*, see Arrowsmith (1966), Grondona (1980), Gagliardi (1989), Herzog (1989), Dunbabin (1986: 194–5, *passim*; 2003: 132–7). For other instances of the *carpe diem* motif in Petronius, see 64.3 with Schmeling (2011) *ad loc.*, 99.1, 111.12 featuring an excerpt of Verg. *A.* 4.34, and 114.9.

[78] See Aldo Setaioli at Schmeling (2011) *ad loc.*, who cites *CLE* 1105, 1179, 1260, 1292. Cf. Setaioli (2011) 99–100.

[79] Aldo Setaioli at Schmeling (2011) *ad loc.*

[80] For *uiuo*, see Cat. 5.1, Hor. *S.* 2.6.96–7 and further sources at Aldo Setaioli at Schmeling (2011) *ad loc.* and Setaioli (2011) 106. Petronius uses *dum licet* again in the same context at 114.9 The expression is a regular feature of Horatian *carpe diem*: *C.* 2.11.16, 4.12.26, *S.* 2.6.96, *Epist.* 1.11.20. Cf. page 9 n.25 and n.28 in the Introduction for both expressions. The importance of the Horatian references here have been described by, for example, Cugusi (1967) 90, Gagliardi (1989) 14 n.6, Stucchi (2002) 215–16, and recently stressed again by Setaioli (2011) 101.

Gregson Davis says that 'it is this bare skeleton [*sc.* of the Horatian *carpe diem* ode] that Petronius, a demonstrably percipient reader of Horace, parodies'.[81] Indeed, I described above how Horace, *Odes* 1.11 already seems to play with its form, as the exhortation to 'cut back long-term hopes' (*spatio breui | spem longam reseces*) is voiced in a poem that, extraordinarily in the *Odes*, is wider than it is long and thus seems itself pruned or cut back (see pages 131–5 in Chapter 3). Trimalchio's epigram goes further still; it has the appearance of a lyric excerpt, something cut out and cut back from familiar motifs, a pseudo-quotation that attempts to evoke a lyric atmosphere, albeit with one missing line.[82] A comparable case is perhaps Simonides' *carpe diem* poem that adapts Homer's image of the generations of leaves (*frr.* 19 + 20; also see pages 113–16 and 128–30 in Chapter 3); in Stobaeus, Simonides' elegy begins with a pentameter, so that a preceding hexameter seems to have been cut out (Stob. 4.34.28). Otherwise, the poem seemed complete, until papyrus evidence revealed that Stobaeus had additionally omitted a central section and the ending in order to create a condensed *carpe diem* poem (*P.Oxy.* 3965 *fr.* 26).[83] This condensed poem fits well into the section title of Stobaeus, περὶ τοῦ βίου ὅτι βραχύς ('On the brevity of life'). Trimalchio's three lines are no less condensed, but the difference is that Stobaeus' (or his intermediary's) surgical knife fooled us for centuries: it created a neat little poem, and without the papyrus evidence no one would have ever suspected that a central section is missing. Trimalchio's butchering is rather different from Stobaeus' surgical approach, and his poem has never found much favour.

---

[81] Davis (1991) 147, who also speaks of a 'witty Petronian travesty' of a 'Horatian exemplar'. For a revival of Horace's poetry under Nero, see Mayer (1982).

[82] Cf. Bakhtin (1981) 70 on the *Cena Cypriani*, a parodic text from late antiquity or the Middle Ages, in which 'the entire Bible, the entire Gospel was as it were cut up into little scraps, and these scraps were then arranged in such a way that a picture emerged of a grand feast at which all the personages of sacred history from Adam and Eve to Christ and his Apostles eat, drink and make merry'.

[83] This is how Bowie (2010) 599–601 describes Stobaeus' technique of cutting here, whose view I follow. *Aliter* Sider (1996) 269, who argues that Stobaeus might have excerpted two passages from Simonides' poem, one under the lemma Σιμωνίδου, the other one under the lemma ἐν τῷ αὐτῷ. Once the second lemma got lost, the two excerpts would have been combined in the manuscript tradition. On excerpting and Stobaeus, see Konstan (2011). For the aesthetics of cutting lyric in Stobaeus, see Hose (2008) 304–5.

Excerpts of *Carpe Diem*

The method, however, is the same – both readers prune poetry in order to create a highly condensed *carpe diem* piece.

Trimalchio, of course, would protest against my characterisation of his mediocre cutting skills. For if anyone truly cares about the art of cutting it is Trimalchio. At his dinner, it is not only in the realms of poetry that cutting is treated as an art and poems become ex-cerpts (*carpere*), but cutting meat is also a form of art for Trimalchio. Thus, at one point a slave dressed as the Homeric hero Ajax attacks a boiled calf as if he is mad, cuts it, and presents the pieces to the guests (Petron. 59). This spectacle of cutting is closely connected with Trimalchio butchering Homer. For Trimalchio introduces this Ajax while he summarises Homer's *Iliad* and creates arguably the worst epitome of this epic: Agamemnon kidnaps Helen, who is the sister of Diomedes and Ganymedes and so on and so forth. Cutting meat and poetry are strongly entwined; the literary digest and the digestible are connected. Elsewhere, cutting up food is a spectacle not unlike gladiatorial games (Petron. 36.6):[84] *'Carpe'* [sc. Trimalchio] *inquit. processit statim scissor et ad symphoniam gesticulatus ita lacerauit obsonium, ut putares essedarium hydraule cantante pugnare* ('"Cut", said Trimalchio. Immediately the meat-cutter came forth and cut the dish, moving in rhythm to the music; you would have thought that a gladiator in a chariot was fighting to the sound of the water organ'). Trimalchio highlights the importance of cutting with an exhortation that puns on the name of the carver (*Carpus*) and the exhortation to cut (*carpe!*) (Petron. 36.7): *'Carpe, Carpe'*. Even before the narrator learns the meaning of the pun, he suspects that here again Trimalchio aspires to *urbanitas* (Petron. 36.7): *ego suspicatus ad aliquam urbanitatem totiens iteratam uocem pertinere* ('I suspected that the frequent repetition of the word aimed at some sort of urbane witticism').

Poems and meat-cutting alike rely on staged repetitions, but a gag that depends on the repetition of one word becomes stale when the whole gag is repeated all over again and old dinner

---

[84] See Rosati (1999) [1983] 88. Cf. Juv. 5.120–4 with Braund (1996) *ad loc.* Just as Roman writers increasingly learn their trait in the rhetorical schools, the meat-carver is also taught by a *magister* (Juv. 5.122), or he is the *discipulus* of a *doctor* (Juv. 11.137). Also see Schnurbusch (2011) 103–4 on the meat-carver in Rome. For Carpus as the name of one of Nero's cutters, see Grimal (1941). For food and literature in Rome, see Gowers (1993b).

guests know it all too well (Petron. 36.8). I can only tentatively suggest that the parallels between the meat-cutting incident and Trimalchio's poems may go further still. Though Horace's expression 'carpe diem' might not have had quite the proverbial meaning in Petronius' time that it would later acquire in English, Ovid, as well as Petronius' probable contemporary Persius, used *carpere* in a *carpe diem* context (Ov. *Ars* 3.79; Pers. 5.151). Furthermore, this chapter has shown two instances in Vergil and Horace where *carpo* already expresses urgency and enjoyment in exhortations of *carpe diem*, before the *Odes* were written. Thus, it is possible that in a dinner that relies as heavily on the idea of *carpe diem* as Trimalchio's, the repeated *Carpe, Carpe!* also points to the idea of enjoyment. At any rate, Trimalchio's dinner indulges in excerpts: both poems and meat are more or less artfully cut up and the excerpt becomes a spectacle. Trimalchio's poems were in turn also excerpted and collected in the *Florilegium Gallicum*.[85] There, his little *carpe diem* poem received the moralising heading *Quod uiuendum sit bene dum licet* ('Why we must live it up while we may'). No doubt, Trimalchio would have been pleased. Once more a purple passage seems to call for its future excerption.

Aesthetics of excerpting, of 'sampling' older culture, may also help to explain what is going on with the peculiar wine Trimalchio serves. Its label praises it as 100-year-old Opimian (*Falernum Opimianum annorum centum*; Petron. 34.6) and it inspires Trimalchio to his thoughts on *carpe diem*. In an ingenious article, Barry Baldwin suggested that Trimalchio's faux pas in this scene consists of serving a wine so old that it was only used as a bitter by his time.[86] Thus, Pliny tells us that by his time Opimian was reduced to a thick liquid, with which younger wines were spiced (*Nat.* 14.55). When Trimalchio serves this wine at his dinner and responds to it with his *carpe diem*

---

[85] On the *Florilegium Gallicum*, see the text of Brandis and Ehlers (1974), and the notes of Ullman (1930) and Reeve (1983). For florilegia and their relation to anthologies, see Chadwick (1969).

[86] Baldwin (1967). This is more convincing than the theory of Bicknell (1968), who argues that the wine is a forgery, since wines from 121 BC did not mention their provenance on the label, according to Pliny *Nat.* 14.94. Pliny, however, is wrong, as *CIL* i^2 2929 (= Rigato and Mongardi (2016) 108, no. 1) shows, a label of a Falernian wine from 160 BC (also mentioned by Cic. *Brut.* 287). Apparently this wine label is not known to Tchernia (1986), in the seminal account of wine in Rome. Thus, Tchernia's *terminus ante quam* for the appearance of 'grand crus' in Rome and provenances on wine labels is set not early enough.

Excerpts of *Carpe Diem*

poetry, he seems to act in the tradition of Horace (see Chapter 2), but the samples of the past he serves, whether wine or poetry, are too condensed and leave a stale taste in his guests' mouths.[87] Literature as over-spiced dish, pastiche of repeated and all-too-well-known motifs – this is something that is not only an important theme of Trimalchio's poems but also of the *Satyrica* as a whole and Neronian literature in general.[88] At some point, Petronius even alludes to Horace's purple patch (Petron. 118.5).[89] In the opening of the novel as it has been handed down, Encolpius blames the schools of rhetoric for this type of literature (Petron. 1–5). Gian Biagio Conte in *The Hidden Author* says of this section: 'In Petronius' eyes the great myths of literature have become simply patterns, forms of expression, collections of memorable gestures.'[90] This rhetorical approach to literature also characterises Trimalchio's poems, which treat *carpe diem* as such a pattern.[91] It is thus not surprising that 'Encolpius' image of clichéd *sententiae* as "honey-balls of phrases, every word and act sprinkled with poppy-seed and sesame" (1.15) gets served up by [...] Trimalchio'[92] (31.10). Trimalchio's poems are all about *loci communes* and rhetorical imitation.

In his *Rhetoric of Imitation*, Conte distinguishes between two different types of allusion, both linked to rhetorical devices: 'integrative allusions', which can be compared to metaphors and harmonise the voices of two poets, and 'reflective allusions', which can be compared to similes and contrast the voices of two poets.[93] Earlier in this chapter, I showed how Vergil's *carpe diem* for cows

---

[87] Perhaps a misguided attempt to offer *aliquid decoctius* (Pers. 1.25 with Gowers (1994))? Cf. Rimell (2002) 185–7.

[88] For the *Satyrica* as a treatment of Neronian culture, whatever its creation date may be, see Vout (2009). For the *Satyrica* as a parody of Greek and Latin literature, see Conte (1996), Connors (1998), and, more recently, Panayotakis (2009). For Trimalchio and 'uses of literacy', see Horsfall (1989a), and, more pertinently, (1989b) 197–200.

[89] Noted by Brink (1971a) 96. Brink also points to Quint. *Inst.* 8.5.28, which mentions the purple patch. For the purple patch in late antiquity, see Pelttari (2016).

[90] Conte (1996) 47. The entire second chapter of Conte's book is relevant for the present discussion.

[91] Already Holzberg (1998) in his review of Conte (1996) noted that we could also apply Conte's findings to Trimalchio's literary output.

[92] Rimell (2007) 119. Also see Rimell (2002) 132 and Kißel (1978) 312–13 on rhetorical over-spicing.

[93] Conte (1986) 52–69.

Trimalchio, Petronius' *Satyrica*, and Athenaeus

in *Georgics* 3 is an example of a reflective allusion: the allusion to lyric poetry is not integrated in its present context of cattle-breeding and feels detached. Through the analysis of Trimalchio's poetry, this assessment of excerpts can be further modified. The lyric scraps that are inserted in the texts of this chapter feel detached, are treated as quotations, but are often not specific allusions to a single source. Thus, they do not fit easily into the categories that Gian Biagio Conte and Richard Thomas introduce in their studies of ancient allusion.[94] As the excerpts of *carpe diem* evoke purple passages of a whole genre of poetry and can be adduced in various contexts, I propose to compare them to yet another rhetorical figure: the *exemplum*. Like *exempla*, Trimalchio's *carpe diem* excerpts are recasts of old models, rooted in rhetoric and attempting to convey the paradigms and *auctoritas* of old wisdom, when occasions such as the serving of old wine require a literary response.

The epigram of Trimalchio that has concerned us so far is not the only one that seems incomplete and patched together. When an acrobat falls down during his performance and injures Trimalchio slightly, he marks this event with another epigram (Petron. 55.3):

'quod non expectes, ex transuerso fit, [...]
et supra nos Fortuna negotia curat.
quare da nobis uina Falerna, puer'.

'What you don't expect hits you from the other side, ... and above us Fortune controls our affairs. So bring us Falernian wine, slave.'

The lines do not scan. Though this can be solved with Heinsius' *ubique* | *nostra* filling the gap at lines 1–2, emendation is probably unnecessary, and in this one point my text differs from Müller's Teubner edition. As Aldo Setaioli discussed in detail, the failing arguably derives from the improvised nature of the poem: Trimalchio could not know that the acrobat falls, so that he has to improvise his composition and fails.[95] Inspired by the sudden *fall* of

---

[94] Conte (1986; with the arguments recently revisited in 2017), Thomas (1986). Cf. D. P. Fowler (1997), Hinds (1998).
[95] Setaioli (2011) 109–10 with further sources at 109 n.104 and 110 n.105. The opinion that the metrical shortcomings of the poem are intended by Petronius goes back to Walsh (1970) 128; yet, recent arguments in favour of an engineered incident can be found at Rimell (2002) 191–4, Schwindt (2004a); also see Huxley (1970), Woodall (1971), Slater (1990) 161 n.11. Yeh (2007) 95–7 argues that the poems at Petron. 34 and 55 form one single poem. I am

the acrobat, the poem presents quite literally oc-*cas*-ional poetry, and the falling artist already foreshadows Trimalchio's failing artistry.[96] But besides its obvious failure and its improvised nature, these verses again point to the status of Trimalchio's poetry as excerpts that are cut up and pieced together. The one line Trimalchio gets right is *quare da nobis uina Falerna, puer* ('so bring us Falernian wine, slave'). It is telling that this line does not have a direct relation to the occasion, but was probably a line Trimalchio always had in store, so that he could add it to various poems. This is supported by the fact that Trimalchio uses variations of this command in prose at Petronius 34.7, *quare tangomenas faciamus*, and Petronius 73.6, *itaque tangomenas faciamus* ('so let's do some deep drinking'). Such a command is, of course, extremely common in sympotic poetry.[97]

Trimalchio is not the only symposiast who chops up lyric. The effect of reading Trimalchio's parodic lyric scraps is similar to that of reading the fragments of early Greek lyric on the *carpe diem* theme. The similarity may not be accidental. Of course, I am not suggesting that authors such as Petronius only knew fragments of early Greek poetry. Nor am I implying that the quality of all these poems is similar. Rather, I am saying that early Greek poetry came to be treated as prime material for excerpts, which could be quoted at fitting occasions. This is, for example, what happens in Athenaeus. In similar fashion to Trimalchio, the Deipnosophist Ulpian also exhorts a slave to bring more drinks and he does so with a literary excerpt, though here one from Middle Comedy rather than lyric (Ath. 10.426b quoting Xenarchus *Twins fr.* 3.1): πίμπλα σὺ μὲν ἐμοί, σοὶ δ' ἐγὼ δώσω πιεῖν ('fill my cup and I'll return the favour'). Perhaps this literary allusiveness even in the most pedestrian conversation is something Trimalchio also aspires to with the riddling phrase *quare tangomenas faciamus* ('so let's

---

unconvinced. For the poem as a 'perversion' of Horace's *carpe diem*, see Vogt-Spira (2002) 203–4.

[96] On the pun of *casus* and more words related to 'falling' in this section, see Connors (1998) 53, Schwindt (2004a). For similarities with the falling tapestries at the *Cena Nasidieni* at Hor. *S.* 2.8, see Schmeling (2011) at Petron. 54.1, 55.2. At the *Cena Nasidieni*, the diners also respond to the incident with platitudes on the nature of fate (*S.* 2.8.61–74).

[97] For example, Alc. *fr.* 346.4–6, Anacr. *fr.* 356, *Anacreont.* 48.8, Hor. *Epod.* 9.33–6, *C.* 1.9.5–12. For further commands, see Hutchinson (2016) 269, no. 123.

do some deep drinking'), which may or may not be an allusion to Alcaeus. In Athenaeus, the Deipnosophists heap up literary excerpts, which, as Christian Jacob has analysed, are as carefully prepared as the food at the dinner: food and texts alike are artfully cut up and rearranged into delicate little portions.[98] When we read early Greek lyric, we often read it as fragments through Athenaeus' perspective. This sympotic filter is similar to the filter of Trimalchio, as fragmentary texts interact with sympotic activity. At one point, for example, the Deipnosophist Democritus first drinks and then quotes a long list of texts that show how Alcaeus is drinking in every season (ταῦτ' εἰπὼν ὁ Δημόκριτος καὶ πιὼν ἔφη; 'Democritus finished his point, drank and said', 10.429f). This list also includes Alcaeus *fr.* 335 at Athenaeus 10.430c:

Οὐ χρῆ κάκοισι θῦμον ἐπιτρέπην.
προκόψομεν γὰρ οὐδὲν ἀσάμενοι,
ὦ Βύκχι, φάρμακον δ' ἄριστον
οἶνον ἐνεικαμένοις μεθύσθην

We must not surrender our hearts to misfortunes for we won't achieve anything if we are troubled, Bycchis. The best medicine is to get wine and get drunk.

As it is handed down, the text quickly proceeds from the condition of misery in human life to the exhortation to drink, just as Trimalchio's epigrams do. Again, this is not to say that Alcaeus and Trimalchio are two poets of comparable quality. Rather, it shows how the imperial symposium acts as the filter through which we look at *carpe diem* poems as excerpts, whether they are Alcaeus' or Trimalchio's. The phenotype of the poetry at the two very different symposia is comparable, as they result from cutting lyric up to smallest excerpts that resemble little delicacies. Readers have quite literally *shaped* the texts they received; we look at the *carpe diem* motif of early Greek lyric, filtered through Athenaeus, as a sequence of similar gnomic expressions, which can be cut up and heaped up in a similar way to Trimalchio's epigrams (see Ath. 8.335d–336f, 10.430a–d). The fragmentation

---

[98] Jacob (2004) 167: 'les extraits de textes, comme les plats cuisinés, participent du même processus de préparation et de présentation, entre l'art et la technique, par découpage, conditionnement, assemblage, et assaisonnement du matières premières, naturelles ou linguistiques'. Cf. Jacob (2000) 104–10, J. König (2012) 94–106.

of *carpe diem*, the thematic arrangement of these fragments, and their treatment as rhetorical patterns create excerpted objects, which are commonly known and can be inserted just about anywhere. In the next section, I will turn to an excerpt that appears in most unusual surroundings.

5.4 Plucking Flowers: Naevolus in Juvenal 9

Once more, Juvenal pumps up the volume.[99] Already in *Satire* 1, he professes that he has received a glut of rhetorical education and has *exempla* and purple passages at his fingertips (Juv. 1.7–14).[100] It is thus hardly surprising that in Juvenal, too, we can identify a rhetorical re-patching of a lyric purple passage. In his ninth satire, Naevolus, a bisexual male prostitute, struggles with his impotence, his profession, and his poverty (all problems that are somewhat intertwined). After some lengthy complaints from Naevolus, his interlocutor advises him to live a good life (Juv. 9.118–23):

> uiuendum recte, cum propter plurima, tum est his
> [idcirco ut possis linguam contemnere serui]
> praecipue causis, ut linguas mancipiorum   (120)
> contemnas; nam lingua mali pars pessima serui.
> [deterior tamen hic qui liber non erit illis
> quorum animas et farre suo custodit et aere.]

119 *post* 118 *ponunt PA, post* 123 Φ, *om. Vat. Ottob.* 2885, *Vat. Pal.* 1700, *del. Pithoeus*   **122–3** *del. Pinzger*

> You must live a proper live for many reasons [for that reason so you can ignore the tongue of your slave] but chiefly because of this, namely that you may ignore the tongues of your slaves. For the tongue is the worst part of a bad slave. [Still worse off is the man who will not be free from those he keeps up with his bread and money.]

The gist of the narrator's advice is the recommendation of a proper lifestyle, *uiuendum recte* (119). As has regularly been noted, the

---

[99] The expression is taken from J. Henderson (1996). The entire article on Juvenal's treatment of rhetorical set-pieces is relevant for the present discussion.
[100] See J. Henderson (1996). Juv. 1.7–14 seems to engage with Horace's purple patch at *Ars* 14–23 (Brink (1971a) *ad loc.*).

Naevolus in Juvenal 9

advice seems to come straight from Horace, who used this expression a number of times.[101] Naevolus, however, finds that the Horatian commonplace is too trite to offer useful advice,[102] and he does not understand how it can help him, when his time of youth is quickly passing by (Juv. 9.124–9):[103]

> 'utile consilium modo, sed commune, dedisti.
> nunc mihi quid suades post damnum temporis et spes   (125)
> deceptas? festinat enim decurrere uelox
> flosculus angustae miseraeque breuissima uitae
> portio; dum bibimus, dum serta, unguenta, puellas
> poscimus, obrepit non intellecta senectus.'

126–7 uelox ... breuissima *del. Ruperti*

'You've just given me some good advice, but it's a bit trite. Can you tell me what to do now after my time has been wasted and my hopes deceived? The fleeting flower, you know, the shortest portion of our brief and miserable life, hurries to run its course; while we are drinking, while we are asking for garlands, perfumes, and girls, old age stealthily creeps up.

This passage contains a textual problem in lines 126–127. The text seems to offer an odd mixture of metaphors, which involves the description of a flower as 'running'. Various solutions have been proposed. Wakefield, for instance, places a comma before *uelox flosculus*, so that it stands in apposition to *breuissima portio angustae miseraeque uitae*.[104] Housman, too, puts *uelox flosculus* into apposition by placing it within commas, and Courtney recommends this in his commentary.[105] This solution disentangles the mixed metaphor and neatly makes *portio uitae* the subject of

---

[101] Bellandi (2021) *ad loc.* discusses the Horatian flavour of the expression in detail (Hor. *C.* 2.20.1, *Epist.* 1.2.41, 2.2.213) and offers a rich bibliography.
[102] There is an issue with interpolations at Juv. 9.118–23, as lines 120–1 are a repetition of line 119. Yet, the expression *uiuendum recte* should be retained, as this represents the trite advice Naevolus criticises in his answer (*utile consilium* [...] *sed commune*; see Bellandi (2021) at line 124). Willis (1997) goes too far in deleting lines 118–23 in total (following Ribbeck (1865) 112–13). Sensible solutions can be found in Clausen (1959) (deletion of lines 120–3) and Clausen (1992) (deletion of lines 119 and 122–3, printed above). The discussion of Courtney (1980a) *ad loc.* is very valuable (also Courtney (1975) 149–50).
[103] Clausen (1992) does not mention Ruperti's claim of an interpolation in his apparatus. I add this here.
[104] Wakefield (1789–95) v.153.
[105] Housman (1931), Courtney (1980a) *ad loc.*, whereas Clausen (1992), Knoche (1950), and L. Friedländer (1895) do not use any punctuation within the sentence.

festinat, while the apposition *uelox flosculus* offers an image of comparison. But does this really solve all issues? Susanna Braund points out that *uelox,* the attribute of *flosculus,* signifies speed and thus goes rather well with the verb *festinat decurrere.* Moreover, she argues that *portio uitae* is no less bold a choice as the subject of a verb of running, so that we have to accept the metaphorical language anyway.[106] Subsequently, Braund opts for a different solution in her Loeb text and places a comma after *flosculus,* effectively putting *angustae miseraeque breuissima uitae portio* in apposition. She renders the sentence, then, thus: 'The fleeting blossom, you know, the briefest part of our limited and unhappy life, is speeding to an end.'[107] This seems satisfactory (I have adopted Braund's solution in my translation above). But a more radical solution has also been suggested: Ruperti argued for a deletion from *uelox* to *breuissima,* which Nisbet applauded and Willis printed.[108] Certainly this solves the problems with the odd word order and deletes one of the metaphors, so that the remaining one appears rather clear:[109] *festinat enim decurrere uitae portio* ('a portion of our life hurries to run its course'). Essentially the problem comes down to the *Gretchenfrage* of Juvenalian textual criticism: how much is interpolated? Here is not the place to repeat the arguments of this hotly contested debate,[110] but rather I wish to show that in this passage the question of interpolation is closely linked to the poetics of *carpe diem.*

Naevolus' first reaction to the interlocutor's advice, according to which he should live a good life, is the complaint that this advice may be good but is too 'general' or 'trite' (*commune*; Juv. 9.124). Ironically, the generic *carpe diem* piece that follows is even more trite than anything the interlocutor had mentioned before. This is, of course, a technique Juvenal uses elsewhere in the satire, when

---

[106] Braund (1988) 154 n.122. Is the last argument fully convincing? The metaphor of life as a run or torch run is common enough, and Sen. *Dial.* 10.8.5 has *uita festinat,* Sen. *Her. F.* 179 has *properat cursu uita citato.*

[107] Braund (2004) 360.   [108] Ruperti (1818), Nisbet (1962) 236, Willis (1997).

[109] As Braund (1988) 133–4 notes, the usage of diminutives is characteristic for Naevolus, whose own name is a diminutive. This may make the deletion of *flosculus* undesirable. Bellandi (2021) *ad loc.* now argues strongly against deletion and says that mixed metaphors are not uncommon in Juvenal.

[110] See Ribbeck (1865), Housman (1931) xxxi–xxxvi, Nisbet (1962) 233–6, Reeve (1970), Högg (1971), Courtney (1975), Willis (1989; and the preface of his Teubner (1997)).

Naevolus displays the same self-defeating rhetoric.[111] Naevolus thus already flags up the triteness of his statement beforehand, and the heaped-up images of *carpe diem* strengthen the appearance of these lines as an excerpt, the half-quotation of a half-educated gigolo.[112] Indeed, the beginning of the satire characterises Naevolus as a formerly 'elegant dinner guest' (*conuiua facetus*), whose witticisms full of *urbanitas* were 'bred within the city limits' (Juv. 9.9–11).[113] Naevolus' little *carpe diem* piece would befit such conversation at a dinner, just as Horace's mouse and Petronius' Trimalchio attempted to show their *urbanitas* through the *carpe diem* motif at dinner. Thus, Braund points to Trimalchio's speech in Petronius *Satyrica* 34.10 as a parallel for similar 'pretentious and fatuous utterances' on *carpe diem*.[114] Possibly even closer in genre is a passage from Persius (5.151–3).[115]

> indulge genio, carpamus dulcia, nostrum est
> quod uiuis, cinis et manes et fabula fies,
> uiue memor leti, fugit hora, hoc quod loquor inde est.
>
> Enjoy yourself, let's seize our pleasures, just our life is ours; you'll be dust and shades, a mere story. Live and keep in mind that you are mortal. The hour is fleeting – even the time that I'm speaking right now.

The rapid asyndetic style is similar to the passage in Juvenal, and when some commentators find fault with Horace for mixing upperworld and underworld concepts in saying at *Odes* 4.7.16 *puluis et umbra sumus* ('we are dust and shades'), Persius here easily tops this with three metaphors, saying: *cinis et manes et fabula fies* ('you'll be dust and shades, a mere story').[116]

---

[111] See Juv. 9.96–7 with Braund (1988) 152, where Naevolus complains about his patron's lack of trust and in the same instance reveals his patron's secrets (note the counterfactual subjunctive): *qui modo secretum commiserat, ardet et odit, | tamquam prodiderim quicquid scio*.
[112] Braund (1988) 154 compares the other literary allusions at Juv. 9.37, 9.64–5, and 9.69, and calls the present one 'the most marked'.
[113] On these lines, see Bellandi (2008).   [114] Braund (1988) 154 n.123.
[115] Text: Clausen (1992).
[116] Thomas (2011) at Hor. *C.* 4.7.16 calls the mixing of upper- (*puluis*) and underworld (*umbra*) concepts an 'oddity' and regards Soph. *El.* 1158–9 as the only parallel. Yet, Pers. 5.152 may not be too dissimilar, as Kißel (1990) *ad loc.* notes. For Persius' general indebtness to Horace, see, for example, Hooley (1997). Unlike Thomas, Ausonius liked the Horatian expression and used it at *Epitaphia heroum* 17.2 Green, as Green (1991) notes *ad loc.*

Excerpts of *Carpe Diem*

Naevolus' mixture of metaphors tops this yet again. The dialogic nature of Persius' fifth *Satire* may have further contributed to the attractiveness of this passage for the dialogic *Satire* 9, a form that is exceptional in Juvenal, but much less so in Persius.[117] In Naevolus' speech, some ideas that may remind us in particular of Horace are crudely crammed together in a few lines voiced by a bisexual gigolo, who is complaining about the brief time of sexual potency before pale impotence approaches with *aequo uel forsitan inaequo pede*.[118] Yet, though we should understand Naevolus' fleeting youth primarily as the fleeting youth of his *membrum*, this is not explicit in the text (just as in Vergil, *Georgics* 3.63–71, the *carpe diem* passage treats the fertility of cattle in rather oblique terms); the *carpe diem* passage is demarcated and self-contained and one could – if one so wished – take it out of context and quote it, in the spirit of Seneca and Johnson, with pathos at the dinner table.[119] In fact, it is not even necessary to imagine such fictional situations (*non est cantandum, res uera agitur!*), for Ausonius actually did this very thing and quoted Naevolus' speech at *Epigrams* 14.1–3:[120]

> Dicebam tibi, 'Galla, senescimus: effugit aetas.
>   utere uere tuo; casta puella anus est.'
> spreuisti, *obrepsit non intellecta senectus*
>
> I used to tell you: 'Galla, we are growing old. Time flies. Enjoy your youth. A chaste girl is an old woman.' You turned me down. *Old age has stealthily crept up.*

---

[117] Noted by Highet (1954) 274. Also see Braund (1988) 130.

[118] Among the categories of Juvenal's humour that Schmitz (2000) offers, this probably fits best into 'imitation and parody' at 169–207. Then again, if it were possible to put humour systematically into four categories, thirteen sub-categories, twenty-six sub-sub-categories, and fourteen sub-sub-sub-categories, as Schmitz does, German humour would probably be 'more of a thing'. On parody in Juvenal, also see Lelièvre (1958). For the specific Horatian allusions, see Bellandi 2009 [1974] 479 and 479 n.16, Braund (1988) 154 n.122, Keane (2015) 111 and 111 n.43.

[119] One should remember that failing potency is the issue that Naevolus first mentions as the cause for his misery at Juv. 9.32–7. The interlocutor also clearly understands the *carpe diem* passage as referring to potency, since his following advice attempts to offer a remedy for this (Juv. 9.134/134A): *tu tantum erucis inprime dentem*. Despite the grave textual issues in these lines, the reference to an aphrodisiac is quite clear. For impotence and *carpe diem*, also see *AP* 10.100 (= Antiphanes 7 *GP*) and 11.30 (= Philodemus 19 Sider).

[120] I take the numeration and text from Green (1999).

The last words of line 3 adopt Naevolus' *obrepit non intellecta senectus* ('old age stealthily creeps up'), as Robert Colton has noted.[121] Yet, the setting in a poem of persuasion of love in the tradition of *AP* 5.21 (Rufinus) is much more respectable than Naevolus' professional concerns about his waning sexual powers.[122] In a way, Ausonius pre-emptively responded to Gilbert Highet's rather naïve wish that the 'beautiful poetry of 9.126–9 is worthy of a better setting, and once more shows the peculiar character of Juvenal, who, like Swift, had a soft heart inside his armour of cynicism'.[123] Highet here fell for the purple splendour of one of Juvenal's rhetorical set-pieces. This is a typical technique of Juvenal: pumping up the volume by throwing purple passages and excerpts into strange surroundings. This is also what he does, for example, in *Satire* 3, when he throws the description of a cave, a set-piece promised in *Satire* 1, into the gutter of Rome.[124] Such rhetorical set-pieces are isolated textual objects, purple patches, which can be cut. Philip Hardie has described how certain allusions to locks of hair become pluckable textual objects in their own right.[125] In *Satire* 9, *flosculus*, the Juvenalian term suspected of interpolation, is ironically also a 'rhetorical ornament' (= *flosculus*), plucked from lyric poetry, though it is not entirely certain who plucked it. What we do know is that this flower is plucked from Horace, and, quite appropriately for a short excerpt, it is made smaller through a diminutive: *Odes* 2.3.13–14, *nimium* breuis | flores *amoenae* [. . .] *rosae* ('the all too *brief bloom* of the lovely rose').[126]

As an excerpt, a lyric set-piece in elevated tone, these are not truly Naevolus' words. This brings us back to the question that first concerned us in terms of textual criticism: who is talking? Is it Juvenal's Naevolus overdoing it with his short lyric piece or an interpolator who recognised the *carpe diem* motif and added one more image of his own to the line? This question involves

---

[121] Colton (1973) 49.   [122] Cf. Colton (1973) 49.
[123] Highet (1954) 274; also see 118.   [124] J. Henderson (1996) 128.
[125] Hardie (2012) 229–38.
[126] For the rose as a Horatian symbol of *carpe diem*, see Gold (1993).

considering the role of interpolation in Latin poetry. Traditionally, textual critics would have described interpolators as dismissively as Robin Nisbet did in his notes on Juvenal: 'one cannot assume that the interpolator, fool though he was, always wrote gibberish'.[127] Recently, however, Richard Tarrant offered some stimulating thoughts on interpolation that markedly differ from Nisbet's portrayal of the interpolator as a μέγα νήπιος.[128] According to Tarrant, it might be fruitful to look at interpolations as creative work on the text. Tarrant proposes the term 'collaboration' for an 'imaginative response to a text that enhances or amplifies it'.[129] Here, the interpolator is perhaps amplifying Juvenal's already-pumped-up volume. He may be someone who is appreciating Juvenal's poetry and is giving his best go at being Juvenal. Naturally, this explanation does not work for interpolations that are versified glosses, but is arguably fruitful for the present case. If we accept Ruperti's assumption of an interpolation, an interpolator would have recognised the *carpe diem* motif and enriched it with the *carpe diem* buzzwords *uelox*, *flosculus*, *angustus*, *breuis*. We can then see an interpolator who is shaped by the education of his time, knows his Horace, and can insert flowers from *Odes* 2.3.[130] For the interpolator, the motif of *carpe diem* was then all too well-known (*commune*), and he could join Naevolus' imitation game by adding further motifs and making the passage even more absurd than it was before. Of course, this is not a necessary conclusion, and I find it at least as likely that Juvenal wrote the lines as they have been handed down, and that he himself attributed the mix of metaphors and buzzwords to Naevolus. But the important point to note, I think, is that we cannot tell for certain whether Juvenal or an interpolator inserted this motif.[131] The poetic meadows were well explored and the schools had taught

---

[127] Nisbet (1962) 233–4.
[128] Tarrant (2016) 85–104. For objections against this view, see 88 n.8.
[129] Tarrant (2016) 88.
[130] If the line is an interpolation, it is surely an ancient one, as it is present in the entire manuscript tradition. Cf. Tarrant (2016) 88–9 on ancient interpolations and 88 on the reflection of the cultural milieu of the time in interpolations.
[131] Excerpts become increasingly more important in the Empire. Yet, even in the case of Alcaeus' archaic lyric, we have been unable to say whether a *carpe diem* fragment was genuinely Alcaean or an imitation that came with reperformance (*fr.* 352).

everyone how to pluck flowers there. When Mimnermus replanted Homer's leaves, this was daring, and perhaps already a little less so when Simonides followed him. By the time Juvenal was writing, the simile of Homer's leaves was a writing exercise at school.[132] Everyone plucked the flowers of *carpe diem*. One reader who was particularly aware of the semantics of plucking was the Renaissance poet Petrarch, who as a young man would look around the 'meadows of poets' (*auctorum pratis*) and excerpt or pluck the flowers of poetry (*haec* [...] *decerpsisti*; 'I plucked these'; also *flosculos decerpere*; 'to pluck little flowers', *Epistolae Familiares* (henceforth *Fam.*) 24.1).[133] Later, in the *Canzoniere*, too, Petrarch describes himself plucking rhymes and verses as well as herbs and flowers (thus effectively glossing *flosculus*): 'or rime et versi, or colgo herbette et fiori' (*Canzoniere* 114.6). Quite pointedly, Petrarch describes Horace in very much the same way: [*sc. Horatium*] *carpentem riguo gramine flosculos* ('Horace was plucking little flowers on a well-watered meadow', *Fam.* 24.10.118–25).[134] Here, Horace's *breuis flores rosae* ('all too brief bloom of the rose') from *Odes* 2.3 becomes a small excerpt, a *flosculus*, which brings us back to Juvenal. For the passage from Juvenal 9.124–9 is itself also such a little flower plucked by Petrarch and noted in his reading. Petrarch would then quote the Juvenal passage in a letter to Emperor Charles IV (*Fam.* 23.2.13).[135] And one can only hope that Charles, who boasted two saints among his ancestors, was unaware of its original context. Petrarch quoted the same passage again in a letter to his patron Philippe de Cabassole, the Bishop of Cavaillon (*Fam.* 24.1.4). In both letters, the passage appears in a sequence of excerpts from Latin literature, all of which deal with transience. Thus, in the letter to Philippe, lines from the usual suspects, Horace's *carpe diem* poems such as *Odes* 1.4, 1.11, 2.11, 2.14, are quoted. But here and in the letter to Charles IV, we also meet Vergil's cows again. Evidently, Petrarch picked up the Vergilian quotation from Seneca, as he

---

[132] *P.Oxy.* 761 from the first century AD with Cribiore (1994).
[133] For plucking flowers in miscellanies and anthologies, see Fitzgerald (2016) 153–4.
[134] Houghton (2009) 165 already compared the two passages, albeit with a different focus.
[135] As noted by Highet (1954) 316. On the theme of transience in Petrarch's letter to Horace (*Fam.* 24.10), see Houghton (2009) 166–7 with further bibliography. *Fam.* 24.10.88–93 summarises Horatian *carpe diem*.

introduces it in almost the same way.[136] Vergil's cows, Juvenal's gigolo, and Horace's *Odes* all make it into the same list of excerpts, as the passages have lost their context and are isolated objects, which can be collected and re-arranged as a collection of little flowers. Indeed, Petrarch notes in a letter how he eagerly marked passages dealing with the transience of human life in his editions and was genuinely moved (*Fam.* 24.1). This practice helped Petrarch to imitate a classical style and similar techniques were advanced in the Renaissance in the form of commonplace-books, which were collections of *loci communes* from classical literature. These collections, based on marginal notes, gave authors a toolbox of ancient models, of purple patches full of *auctoritas*.[137] But when we encounter a list of topoi based on Petrarch's reading in one of his letters, it almost reads like an *inanis strepitus uerborum*, a sequence of marginal notes with no corresponding text; his list shows purple threads below the patches and turns the motif of *carpe diem* into a sequence of completely isolated excerpts (*Fam.* 24.1):

miserae scilicet uitae huius angustias, breuitatem, uelocitatem, festinationem, lapsum, cursum, uolatum, occultasque fallacias, tempus irreparabile, caducum et mutabilem uitae florem, rosei oris fluxum decus, irrediturae iuuentutis effraenam fugem, et tacitae obrepentis insidias senectutis, ad extremum rugas et morbos et tristitiam et laborem et indomitae mortis inclementiam implacabilemque duritiem.

The distress and brevity of this miserable life, its speed and haste, its tumbling course, flight, and hidden deceits, time's irrevocability, the perishable and changing flower of life, the fugitive beauty of a rosy face, the frantic flight of unreturning youth, the traps of old age stealthily creeping up, and, finally, the wrinkles, diseases, gloominess, suffering, and the harshness of indomitable death and its stern implacability.[138]

---

[136] Petrarch *Fam.* 24.1: *audiebam diuino clamantem ore Vergilium.* Cf. Sen. *Dial.* 10.9.2 discussed on pages 195–8 of this chapter: *clamat ecce maximus uates et uelut diuino ore instinctus salutare carmen canit.* Petrarch also follows Seneca in quoting two more texts from Vergil in sequence. The same quotation technique can arguably be observed in Otto Vaenius' *Emblemata Horatiana*, a collection of famous sayings from Horace, which accompany Vaenius' illustrations and are supplemented by sayings from other authors, discussed in detail by Mayer (2009). Vaenius, too, combines quotations of Horace's *Odes*, Seneca's *De breuitate uitae*, and Vergil's cows. Cf. Mindt (2017) 332–3.

[137] See Moss (1996). Serendipitously, Porphyrio paraphrases Horace's 'purple patch' as *loci communes*. Cf. the reception of Horatian quotations as described by Most (2010) 459–60, Ziolkowski (2005) 183–5, Holzberg (2009) 11–15, and Dinter (2009).

[138] Translation: Bernardo (1975–85), adapted.

Naevolus in Juvenal 9

The possibility of an interpolator inserting an additional image to the *carpe diem* piece of an impotent gigolo, which in turn is inserted into a letter to the self-proclaimed descendant of saints, brings me to a natural close: Juvenal 9 shows the most extreme context for a *carpe diem* excerpt and after this it hardly seems possible to go further. Over the course of this chapter, we have witnessed the ongoing fascination with the *carpe diem* motif, as it was excerpted and re-excerpted. These dynamics of excerpting would continue, as generations of poets would pluck the flower of *carpe diem*. Plucking flowers thus became an important motif of French poetry in the sixteenth century, and perhaps the most Horatian *iunctura* in this time is offered by the Pléiade poet Ronsard, who speaks of gathering the youth ('cueillez, cueillez votre jeunesse'; 'pluck your youth, pluck it'). Yet, such later poems of Ronsard or also Herrick's well-known *Gather ye rosebuds* are beyond the scope of this study.[139] Rather, I wish to stress that when Ronsard and others weave their garlands, they gather their flowers from the same meadows which have been explored by humanists and ancient writers. Indeed, other humanists who followed Petrarch's lead used excerpts of Latin poetry in their compositions. Beside many other motifs, the expression *carpe diem* itself was also adopted; Angelo Poliziano wrote *carpamus uolucrem diem* ('let's pluck the winged day') in a *carpe diem* poem, and probably just two years later Erasmus of Rotterdam finished his *Elegia de mutabilitate temporum* with the following couplet: *utamur, ne frustra abeat torpentibus, aeuo | carpamus primos, dulcis amice, dies* ('let's make use of our time (if we are idle, time's lost); let's pluck the days of our youth, my sweet friend').[140] Yet, as Erasmus himself tells us, it lies in the nature of the commonplace imagery of *carpe diem* that it can also be

[139] On the reception of ancient *carpe diem* in these and other poems, see Race (1988) 118–41, Hyman (2019).
[140] For Poliziano and *carpe diem* poem, see Gaisser (2017) 122, and see pages 120–5 on *carpe diem* in Latin Renaissance poems. For Horace and Erasmus, see Schäfer (1970), in particular 57 on *carpamus*. The short encyclopaedia article of Braden (2010) looks at the phrase 'carpe diem' in the classical tradition. In ancient poetry after Horace's *Odes*, the expression *carpe* appears in the context of *carpe diem* at Ov. *Ars* 3.79 (*carpite florem*), Pers. 5.151 (*carpamus dulcia*), Mart. 7.47.11 (*gaudia carpe*), and an epitaph at Courtney (1995) 186–7, no. 199 (*flores ama Veneris, Cereris bona munera carpe*). *De ros. nasc.* also admonishes to gather flowers (*colligo, uirgo, rosas*). In the Middle Ages,

Excerpts of *Carpe Diem*

employed for the opposite cause.[141] And thus, in a later poem Erasmus would attribute every possible *carpe diem* image and expression to an interlocutor whose hedonistic arguments he refutes in his reply – if time is short, we should dedicate our life to learning (*Elegia in iuuenem luxuria defluentem atque mortis admonitio*). Erasmus indeed also followed a similar strategy in his great collection of proverbs, the *Adagia*, successors of commonplace-books: when he explains a Horatian idiom on the shortness of time from a *carpe diem* poem, he says that we should dedicate our lives to study as time is short.[142] In the light of Erasmus' interest in commonplaces, it is not surprising that his *carpe diem* poems read like a collection of pseudo-quotations from Horace and others woven into a new garland. Indeed, one of the images of his *Elegia de mutabilitate temporum* again evokes the language of Juvenal's gigolo: *sic, sic flos aeui, sic, dulcis amice, iuuentus | heu properante cadit irreparata pede* ('just so, sweet friend, the flowering bloom of our lifetime, our youth, hastens and dies, never to be recovered'). Here, too, we encounter the odd mixed metaphor of a surprisingly speedy flower. This, however, is just one of many images in a poem pieced together from ancient motifs and phrases, which Erasmus, as he said elsewhere, gathered (*carpo*) like a Matine bee in an image itself gathered from Horace (*C.* 4.2.27–32).[143]

It is easy to smile about Gilbert Highet's naïve wish to have Naevolus' short poem excerpted, and we can see through Seneca's manipulative quotation strategies. Yet, their treatment of the *carpe*

---

a poem in the *Carmina Burana* begins thus: *Omittamus studia | dulce est desipere | et carpamus dulcia | iuuentutis tenere!* This neatly combines Hor. *C.* 4.12.28 with Pers. 5.151. Besides *carpe diem* poems, other poems regularly use the phrase *carpere uitam* to express enjoyment, for example, several epitaphs, including Christian ones, such as *CLE* 706.10 from the sixth century AD: *aeternam fisus Christo cum carpere uitam*.

[141] Vredeveld (1993) i.xxxix–xlii notes that Erasmus says in his *Ecclesiastes* that Horace's *carpe diem* argument on the shortness of life can easily be reversed. Vredeveld also shows how Erasmus puts this into practice in his poetry. In the present paragraph, I follow Vredeveld's argument.

[142] Erasmus *Adagia* iv.iv.21 on *dum uirent genua* from Hor. *Epod.* 13.4. The *Adagia* were also the predecessors of the collection of Roman *Sprichwörter* by Otto (1962) [1890]; see esp. *utere temporibus*, under which *carpe diem* is subsumed (*tempus* 2), and *fugit irreparabile dies* (*dies* 1).

[143] *De senectute carmen* 96–8: *dum sedulus per omne | authorum uoluor genus impiger, undique carpo | apis in modum Matinae.* Cf. Schäfer (1970) 59.

diem theme points to something inherently fascinating about the motif. Jonathan Culler argues that one fundamental characteristic of lyric is something he calls after Baudelaire 'lyric hyperbole': in lyric, seemingly trivial observations are characterised as extremely significant, whether it is the fall of a leaf or the withering of a rose.[144] Such lyric images succeed in becoming commonplaces – or at least Baudelaire described these dynamics as a success in a passage adduced by Culler: 'to create a cliché is genius. I must create a cliché.'[145] *Carpe diem*, then, is a quintessentially lyric motif, not despite but because it easily becomes a cliché: as phrases and images are repeated again and again, they paradoxically become solidified as gestures for a momentary now.[146] The passages of this chapter indulge in such lyric hyperboles and clichés, and believe in their splendour. Excerptors strive to catch the hyperbolic essence of lyric. Yet, once the passages are excerpted, we often see clearly the triviality of the hyperbolic statements. On the one hand, *carpe diem* continues to be treated as a lyric motif par excellence, displaying *urbanitas*. It is adduced in excerpts, which present the motif as some poetic or vatic wisdom, a wisdom that is properly expressed through lyric rather than philosophy. Whoever adduces this motif, even if he hardly manages to scramble two or three lines together, believes that he has reached the Parnassus and has become an Alcaeus or Horace, as he has said something quintessentially lyric. On the other hand, excerpting creates a cliché, a text removed from its proper context and occasion, textual objects that are compared to little flowers, dinner delicacies and purple patches. Indeed, the two contrasting sides of *carpe diem* can be understood through its status as a purple patch: the shine of its purple material keeps attracting people who remove the patch and stitch it on ever more

---

[144] Culler (2015) 258–63. Cf. the stimulating thoughts of Payne (2006) 182 on Pindar's gnomic statements: 'gnomic lyric [...] presupposes its own transhistorical reception by addressing abstract formulations to a universal subject created by its own pronominal structures'.

[145] Culler (2015) 131 quoting from the collected works of Baudelaire at Pichois (1975–6) i.662.

[146] Cf. Fitzgerald (2021) chapter 4, who analyses how the *Anacreontea* and Leconte de Lisle in his Horatian *Études Latines* aspire 'to distill an ancient poet to a few verbal gestures whose simplicity produces the maximum of resonance'. The result, as Fitzgerald describes it, is a neoclassical aesthetics that revels in clichés.

clothes. As a patch or excerpt, the *carpe diem* motif is a textual object: small, cut up, removable, always displaying its noble material, even if it is just a scrap of this material on shabby clothes. The image of the purple patch and the rhetorical scope that is behind it offer further justification for treating the passages in these sections as 'excerpts', even when they are no direct quotation; for the purple material has to come from somewhere and always looks all-too-well-known, even if it is an imitation rather than a quotation. As textual objects, the excerpts of this chapter are removed from present occasion to the extent that the *carpe diem* motif is applied to cows, mice, and a gigolo. It is thus perhaps not altogether unfitting when, in our own day, we encounter another decontextualised excerpt, utterly removed from its original context: on a T-shirt that screams 'Carpe that fucking diem!'[147]

---

[147] For example, numerous versions at www.redbubble.com. 'Carpe that f*cking diem' is also the title of a collection of 'quotes and mottoes for making the most of life', as the blurb wants it, published by Summersdale in 2018.

EPILOGUE
Echoes of Carpe Diem

What do we hear when it is all over? What do we hear when the music stops? Applause or silence, perhaps? Eventually one or the other, but before that we hear the music again reverberating, resonating, resounding, re-echoing. In this Epilogue, too, we will hear exactly this: a last echo of *carpe diem*, which sounds forth in late antiquity, succeeding the time frame under investigation in this book. Listening to this later echo, we can hear once more some of the leitmotifs of this book reflected from the page of the text. The text in question is *De aduentu ueris* of Pentadius, a poet variously dated between the third and sixth century AD (*Anthologia Latina* i.235 Riese = 227 Shackleton Bailey, whose text I print):[1]

Sentio, fugit hiems, Zephyrisque animantibus orbem
iam tepet Eurus aquis. sentio, fugit hiems.
parturit omnis ager, persentit terra calores
germinibusque nouis parturit omnis ager.
laeta uirecta tument, foliis sese induit arbor;   (5)
uallibus apricis laeta uirecta tument.
iam Philomela gemit modulis; Ityn impia mater
oblatum mensis iam Philomela gemit.
monte tumultus aquae properat per leuia saxa
et late resonat monte tumultus aquae.   (10)
floribus innumeris pingit sola flatus Eoi
tempeaque exhalant floribus innumeris.
per caua saxa sonat pecudum mugitibus Echo
uoxque repulsa iugis per caua saxa sonat.
uitea musta tument uicinas iuncta per ulmos;   (15)
fronde maritata uitea musta tument.

---

[1] In line 9, Shackleton Bailey (1982) prints *resonat* instead of *properat*, which is printed in all other editions. As neither Shackleton Bailey's own apparatus nor the apparatus of any other edition mentions the reading *resonat* in line 9, I assume that this is a mistake rather than a conjecture, and I print *properat*. Oddly enough, Paolucci (2016) prints Riese's text but in her discussion refers to the alleged reading *resonat* in line 9 (page 23 n.85).

Epilogue: Echoes of *Carpe Diem*

nota tigilla linit iam garrula luce chelidon;
dum recolit nidos, nota tigilla linit.
sub platano uiridi iucunda⟨t⟩ somnus in umbra
sertaque texuntur sub platano uiridi.   (20)
nunc quoque dulce mori, nunc, fila, recurrite fusis;
inter et amplexus nunc quoque dulce mori.

19 iucundat *Meyer* : iucunda *codd*. **21–2** nunc *Shackleton Bailey ter scripsit* : tunc *codd*.

> I feel winter has fled. While the Zephyrs breathe new life into the world, Eurus already grows warm on the water. I feel winter has fled. Every field is in labour. The earth feels the warmth, and with new buds every field is in labour. Grass bursts forth joyously. The tree dresses itself with leaves. In sunny valleys grass bursts forth joyously. Philomela now laments melodiously. For Itys, who was served at the table, the impious mother Philomela now laments. From the mountain the roaring water rushes through smooth stones, and widely there resounds from the mountain the roaring water. With innumerable flowers the breeze of the Eastern wind paints the ground, and the valleys are fragrant with innumerable flowers. Through hollow rocks resounds Echo with the mooing of the cattle, and the voice reverberated by the hills through hollow rocks resounds. Clusters of the vine swell that have been joined to neighbouring elm trees. As their leafage is married clusters of the vine swell. The familiar roof timber is being smeared with mud already at daybreak by the twittering swallow. As she repairs her nest, the familiar roof timber is being smeared with mud. Under the green plane-tree sleep is pleasing in the shade, and garlands are woven under the green plane-tree. Now it is also sweet to die, now threads of fate, run back on the spindles. Among embraces now it is also sweet to die.

Surely the most immediately striking feature of this poem is its repetitiveness: each elegiac couplet repeats the words of the first half of the hexameter in the second half of the pentameter. Indeed, if Pentadius is known for anything (and this is perhaps a big 'if'), then it is this type of metre, which he uses in three out of the six poems that are attributed to him (*AL* i.234–5, i.265–8 Riese = 226–7, 259–62 Shackleton Bailey).[2] As the metre makes us rehear *carpe diem* again and again, I wish to show how this feature prompts us to recall the leitmotifs we have encountered in this book. The metre in

---

[2] Kenney and Clausen (1982) 694 note the metrical peculiarities and then drily remark: 'Pentadius' sole virtue is neatness'. *DNP* and *OCD* s.v. stress the characteristic metre, but arguably go too far in doubting Pentadius' authorship for three poems that do not follow this scheme.

Epilogue: Echoes of *Carpe Diem*

Pentadius' poem is variously called epanaleptic, serpentine, echoic, or *uersus recurrens*.[3] While Ovid makes occasional use of this device, Pentadius makes it the main feature of three poems, and a number of other poems of late antiquity seem to have followed him.[4] What needs stressing though is that in each case the peculiarly repetitive elegiacs fit the subject matter of Pentadius' poem (or, rather, one is tempted to think that Pentadius looked for any subject that might have suited the metre).[5] His poem on the mutability of fortune programmatically states in the first couplet that the same constantly returns as changed (i.234 Riese = 226 Shackleton Bailey): *res eadem adsidue momento uoluitur uno | atque redit dispar res eadem adsidue* ('constantly the same thing rolls around in one motion, and there *returns* in altered state constantly the same thing'). This return of the same in changed fashion is as true for the works of fortune that the poem describes as it is for the metre of the poem, in which the same words constantly return anew. Such unity of metre and subject matter also holds true for Pentadius' poem on Narcissus, in which the words reflect and mirror themselves (i.265 Riese = 259 Shackleton Bailey).[6] Finally, the repetitive metre also has some connection to the subject matter in our present poem.

Pentadius' echoic elegiacs allow us to hear the soundscape of spring as a series of repetitions: as sounds that constitute repetitions, as sounds that return each year, and as sounds that are echoes of other spring poems. Now it is spring and now Philomela, the nightingale, laments for Itys (7–8):[7]

> iam Philomela gemit modulis; Ityn impia mater
> oblatum mensis iam Philomela gemit.

---

[3] Guaglianone (1984) 155–72, Cristóbal (1985), Wills (1996) 430–5, Paolucci (2016) 19–20.

[4] Paolucci (2016) 17–27 (also in Italian as Paolucci (2015a; 2015b) points to Ov. *Am.* 1.9.1–2, 3.2.27–8, *Epist.* 5.117–18, *Rem.* 71–2, Mart. 9.97. All of these examples and many more are naturally discussed by Wills (1996) 430–5 (page 433 n.85 notes the feature in Pentadius). In the context of *carpe diem*, the device also appears on the epitaph *CLE* 1499 = *CIL* vi 15258.5–8 (Wills (1996) 434). Pentadius' technique influenced the *Anonymi uersus serpentini* in the Salmasian anthology and Christian authors in late antiquity and the Middle Ages (Schetter (1986) 231–3, Paolucci (2016) 20 with further sources and references). On the ludic nature of such devices, see McGill (2005) 73–4.

[5] Arcaz Pozo (1989) 168–9 makes this important point.   [6] Elsner (2017) 198.

[7] For confusion of Philomela and Procne in some Latin writers, see Arnott (2007) s.v. 'aēdwn', Thomas (2011) 229–30. See Plin. *Nat.* 10.81–5 for the musicality of the song of the nightingale.

Epilogue: Echoes of *Carpe Diem*

Philomela now laments melodiously. For Itys, who was served at the table, the impious mother Philomela now laments.

The nightingale sings melodiously in musical measures (*modulis*) and Pentadius' text strives to mimic this song through repetitive sounds. The repeated hemiepes *iam Philomela gemit* is the most obvious marker of repetition. Yet, repetition occurs also at the level of letters. Five letters in sequence make 'i' sounds, mimicking and amplifying the inherently repetitive and onomatopoeic birdsong '*Ityn Ityn*' by chirping, tweeting, singing it: *modulis; Ityn impia.*[8] As we seem to hear the song of the nightingale and seem to perceive its presence, so the poem tells us that this is happening *now* (*iam*). And yet the very term that marks the present moment, *iam*, is repeated as we are listening not only to momentary song but also to its delayed echo (and note the preceding *iam* in line 2, and then again in line 17). The word *iam* also points to a whole literary history of moments when it was *now already* spring in Greek epigrams, in Catullus' poetry, and in Horace's poetry, which all marked this time with ἤδη and *iam*, often in repetitions.[9] It is *always already* spring. Indeed, *iam* encapsulates the temporal quality of *carpe diem* poems, which evoke presence and lament its loss, as the counterpart of 'now' (*iam*) is 'no longer' (*non iam*);[10] thus, Horace begins one *carpe diem* poem set in spring time with an anaphora of *iam*, saying that *now* the spring breeze arises and that *no longer* the meadows are stiff with frost (*C.* 4.12.1–4).[11] *Iam*, then, which marks the momentary arrival of spring in Pentadius, is a convention in spring poems, and so are many other features of Pentadius' poem, such as the arrival of the west winds, the beginning of the seafaring season, the swallow, the loosening of the earth, and the new flowers.[12] Indeed, Pentadius'

---

[8] An echo of a nightingale from Horace? Syndikus (1972–3) ii.399 finds a similar technique employed at Hor. *C.* 4.12.5.
[9] Nisbet and Hubbard (1970) 59 pointing to *AP* 10.1.2 = Leonides 85.2 *HE*, numerous more epigrams following Leonidas' model at the beginning of *AP* 10, Cat. 46.1–2, 7–8, Hor. *C.* 1.4.5, 4.7.1, 4.12.1–4.
[10] I wish to thank William Fitzgerald for suggesting this to me.
[11] For the importance of *iam* in *carpe diem* poems, also see page 9 n.28 in the Introduction.
[12] For these features, see Pasquali (1964) [1920] 715–16, Nisbet and Hubbard (1970) 59, Woodman (1972) 753–5, Giovini (2005). In addition to the spring poems cited above at note 9, the following passages should perhaps also be noted: *AP* 9.363 (Meleager,

Epilogue: Echoes of *Carpe Diem*

west winds carry a breeze of Greek poetry to the poem; they are Greek Zephyrs rather than the Roman Favonius, and as they 'breathe new life into the world' and 'animate' it (*animantibus*) they offer an etymological pun on the Greek word for wind, ἄνεμος.[13] The Greek spirit here underlines the recurrent quality of spring, which always comes again.[14] While spring marks the return of nature, such return is not possible for humans. This is the lesson of *carpe diem*, as we have encountered it before in this book in Horace, *Odes* 4.7, a poem not less replete with words that mark return and reversal (see pages 125–31 in Chapter 3). Pentadius turns to the *carpe diem* motif at the end of his poem (21): he wishes that his youth may return and the threads of fate roll back on their spindles. The very futility of this wish brings the *carpe diem* motif to the poem: youth will never return for humans, but death will come instead. Pentadius thus says that it is sweet to die at that time. To be sure, the train of thought in the last couplet is rather less clear than in Horace's *carpe diem* poems set in spring, but the juxtaposition of spring and death, the contrast between the return of nature, and the impossibility of such circularity for man together express the *carpe diem* motif. It is in this motif that we can hear echoes of Horace's poetry.[15] Indeed, we are able to hear these echoes even more clearly if we agree with Shackleton Bailey, who thought that Pentadius followed Horace, *Odes* 1.4 and described the spring with an anaphora of *nunc* (rather than the transmitted *tunc* in lines 21–2):

> nunc quoque dulce mori, nunc, fila, recurrite fusis;
> inter et amplexus nunc quoque dulce mori.

> Now it is also sweet to die, now threads of fate, run back on the spindles.
> Among embraces now it is also sweet to die.

excluded in *HE*), Lucr. 5.737–47, Verg. *G.* 2.323–45, Ov. *F.* 4.125–32, the *Pervigilium Veneris*.
[13] Maltby (1991) s.v. 'anima' lists a number of late antique writers who point to the etymology with ἄνεμος: Lactantius, *De opificio dei* 17.2, Servius at Verg. *A.* 8.403, Isidorus, *Etymologiae siue Origines* 11.1.7. For a wordplay of this kind in a similar context, cf. Hor. *C.* 4.12.2 *animae* [...] *Thraciae* with Thomas (2011) *ad loc*.
[14] Cf. Gitner (2012) 66–7, who makes a similar point on the Greek lexical influence in the description of the west winds and spring at Hor. *C.* 4.7.9–12.
[15] Cf. Grimal (1978) 271–2, Arcaz Pozo (1989) 167–8, Giovini (2005) 105–6.

231

Epilogue: Echoes of *Carpe Diem*

It would be only too fitting if, at the end of this overtly repetitive poem, repetitions of *nunc* not only describe this very moment of enjoyment but also bring back moments of enjoyment from Horace. On more practical grounds, the confusion of *tunc* and *nunc* is palaeographically easy enough and the imperative *recurrite* goes well with *nunc*. Nonetheless, the conjecture will not convince everyone and some readers may suspect that this is one of the cases in which Shackleton Bailey 'caught the authors napping rather than the scribes'.[16] Be that as it may, even readers who prefer the paradosis will see Horace's poetry reflected in Pentadius' poem, for though spring poems are common enough in ancient literature, the combination of spring and *carpe diem* is characteristic of Horace's poetry. In fact, we do not possess any ancient poems which combined these two themes before Horace. It is tempting to assume with Nisbet and Hubbard that Greek models for such poems have been lost, and fragments of Alcaeus include indeed some tantalising references to spring, drinking, and death (*frr.* 286, 367).[17] Yet, once more in this book we hear in later poetry what might very well be the echoes or re-echoes of early Greek lyric, but cannot with certainty identify the source of the sound.

Perhaps appropriately to its very nature, the echo arrives with some delay at the analysis of this poem. Surely the poem's content reflects its repetitive metre most strongly and programmatically in the description of the echo (13–14):[18]

> per caua saxa sonat pecudum mugitibus Echo
> uoxque repulsa iugis per caua saxa sonat.

---

[16] Reeve (1985) 178 in his review of the edition, commenting on the ingenuity of some of Shackleton-Bailey's conjectures. Indeed, in his apparatus, Shackleton Bailey says that he might also prefer *mihi* twice instead of *quoque* in the last couplet. This seems rather unlikely.

[17] Nisbet and Hubbard (1970) 58–61, and see page 13 and 13 n.47 as well as 19 in the Introduction. Evans (2016) 101 n.148 compares Horace's spring poems with *AP* 9.412 = Philodemus 29 Sider, on which see page 20 n.83 in the Introduction. Davis (1991) 159 rejects the appellation 'spring poems' for Horace and argues that spring is merely a pretext for *carpe diem*, easily interchangeable with other seasons. The point is well taken, but this should not blind us to the influence of spring poems of Catullus and the *Greek Anthology* on such poems of Horace.

[18] Thus also Arcaz Pozo (1989) 168–9, Paolucci (2016) 22–3. For the technique of mimicking the sound of echo through the repetitions of half a hexameter, cf. Bion, *Epitaphius Adonis* 37–8 with Wills (1996) 346–7.

Epilogue: Echoes of *Carpe Diem*

Through hollow rocks resounds Echo with the mooing of the cattle, and the voice reverberated by the hills through hollow rocks resounds.

The echo resounding through the hollow rocks again and again exemplifies, of course, what the poem has been about all long: a *uox repulsa*, a reverberated voice, audible already in the repetitive song of the nightingale, audible, too, in the resonating rush of water from the mountains (10: *et late resonat monte tumultus aquae*). Echoes can travel over long distances as they carry sound. The echo in Pentadius' poem in late antiquity has traversed a particularly long distance: it reflects the sounds of spring, Horace, and perhaps even a re-echo of Alcaeus, and allows us to hear, sonorously and amplified, certain issues we have encountered before in this book. The echo also allows us to revisit the concepts of textuality, performance, and evocation of present time, which have been at the heart of this book. Indeed, several studies have fruitfully linked the echo to such concepts. Thus, Michèle Lowrie has shown how an ode of Horace, which tells of echoing applause for Maecenas, is itself such an echo (*C.* 1.20): the poem does not itself offer praises, but rather repeats praises; the written page of Horace's lyric reflects events with some delay.[19] Lowrie also notes that 'the word chosen for echo, "imago" (image), bridges the aural and the visual, the respective domains of performativity and writing'.[20] Yet, repetition and delay are features of the lyric voice that precede book-lyric: through reperformance early Greek lyric can already be heard as a cascade of echoing sounds, always reflecting an original event that we cannot hear any more, as Pauline LeVen has shown.[21] At the same time, echoes are the oldest recording device in history, which make sounds present, as Shane Butler has argued.[22] This is precisely the issue for Narcissus in the well-known treatment of the myth of Echo in Ovid's *Metamorphoses* (3.334–510): Narcissus does not consider

---

[19] Lowrie (2009a) 66–71. Compare and contrast Gramps (2021) 78–84 on echo and presence in the same ode. For the echo as a carrier of allusion from Milton onwards, see Hollander (1981).
[20] Lowrie (2009a) 70.
[21] LeVen (2018). For the echo as a concept for reperformance, see also Phillips (2016) 217–35 on Echo in Pi. *O.* 14.
[22] Butler (2015) 59–87. Cf. LeVen (2021) 107–35 on Echo and different forms of listening in Ovid (and Longus).

that his own voice is repeated with delay, but he readily believes that someone talks to him in the moment.

The double nature of the echo is crucial for Pentadius' poem in particular and *carpe diem* in general. On the one hand, the sound of the echo is always delayed, only a replication of the event; on the other hand, we are under the impression that we are listening to the event now, in the moment. Though the echo is never in the moment, it is always about the moment, replicating the moment. Pentadius' poem lets us hear the sound of the moment, the soundscape of a spring day. As half-lines are repeated again and again, the poem transcends meaning and instead produces effects of presence. That is to say, the repetitions of half-lines do not offer the reader any new information, and instead privilege the effects of prosody and repetitive sound patterns: we seem to hear melodious sounds and songs rather than meaningful words.[23] The echo, then, brings the delay of song as well as the presence of song.

As the echo both delays vanished sounds and makes them present, so we have seen in this book how *carpe diem* poems both stress and compensate for a perceived loss of song. Over the course of five chapters, we have seen how *carpe diem* texts are neither solely performative nor textual: they evoke present song but always with a delay.[24] Perhaps in the manner of Pentadius' serpentine poem, my discussion has returned to where it took off in the Introduction, when we listened to Housman's echo of Horace's spring poem, *Ode* 4.7. Other parts of this book also resonate with Pentadius' soundboard. Thus, we were able to hear the words of the legendary Assyrian king Sardanapallus in present tense, long after he had voiced them (Chapter 1). We have tasted Horace's wines, as wine storage in his poetry allows for delayed experience of the seasons: opening an old bottle of wine, one can still taste the warm weather of the year (Chapter 2). Horace's choice of words, his neologisms and archaisms, allow us to feel the atmosphere of

---

[23] For such effects of repetitions, I am drawing on Butler (2015) 59–87 and in particular on Trimble (2018) 38–40, who analyses the refrain of Catullus 64 (to which I shall return presently). 'Effects of presence' and prosody naturally refer to Gumbrecht (2004) and Culler (2015), the studies of whom I have raised in the Introduction.

[24] It is needless to stress again that in this regard textual exhortations of *carpe diem* take their cue from reperformances of lyric *carpe diem* songs, in which momentary enjoyment was already designed to be repeatable.

Epilogue: Echoes of *Carpe Diem*

the moment long after they were coined (Chapter 3). Epigrams that write about objects such as cups, gems, and dining halls conjure up such objects and stress the medial distance to them. Again, sensory experiences are mediated as writing evokes the taste and touch of cups and the visual splendour of gems (Chapter 4). Finally, even excerpts of *carpe diem* that are inserted into the most unlikely surroundings still seem to evoke lyric song (Chapter 5).

This book, then, has proposed ways of understanding *carpe diem* that have aimed to break new ground. The outcomes are threefold. First, against the prevalence of treating the *carpe diem* motif as trite, this book has demonstrated the significance of the motif. *Carpe diem* poems have been shown to be crucial texts for questions of textuality, performance, and presence. Texts of this kind strive to transcend writing and the page of the book, so that they become truly present. How texts wrestle with this ambition, how they approach this ideal, or consciously fall short of it, is central for understanding how poetry writes *now*. This is of particular importance to lyric: a type of poetry that always looks back to an idealised notion of momentary original performance, and does so most notably in its reception of the *carpe diem* motif.

Second, readers and the activity of reading have been central for the poetics of *carpe diem*. Reading *carpe diem* has been shown to be an activity with two sides to it. On the one hand, this is an activity that puts a strong stress on the textuality of poems. Thus, readers indulge in the art of variation that comes with epigram collections, they read certain philologically marked terms as cross-references, and they cut up texts and excerpt them. On the other hand, reading *carpe diem* is an activity that attempts to go beyond reading as an interpretative act of understanding: texts seem to sing, resounding echoes seem to arise from the page, neologisms seem to scream 'now', some words evoke the taste of past seasons. Often, both these sides of reading *carpe diem* are in play, as texts oscillate between meaning and presence effects.

Third, this book has demonstrated throughout the value of analysing poetry alongside other forms of cultural production. The book shares this interest in the presence of things with studies in disciplines beyond Classics, and in particular with Hans Ulrich

Epilogue: Echoes of *Carpe Diem*

Gumbrecht's book *In 1926: Living at the Edge of Time*.[25] In alphabetically ordered articles ranging from 'Airplanes' and 'Americans in Paris' to 'Telephone' and 'Wireless Communication', Gumbrecht writes curious crossings between dictionary entries, research notes, and streams of consciousness, which all describe aspects of the year 1926. By describing parts of the everyday world, such as objects, leisure activities, art forms, technologies, and ideas, Gumbrecht aims to make 1926 present, rather than to interpret events of this year. Readers are invited to feel the atmosphere of the year and to 'forget [...] that they are *not* living in 1926'.[26] When Horace asks for a vintage wine of a certain year, here, too, we are invited to soak up the atmosphere of the year; the calendar year with its oenological texture, its political associations, and its private memory is meant to affect our senses. And yet, I have argued that wines in Horace do more than make the atmosphere of a single year present. Rather, this book has shown that texts and things have an ability to evoke presence which goes beyond a certain historical date: the moment the wine is sealed, the moment it is opened, and the moment that the poetry book is opened all merge. Despite these differences, I share with Gumbrecht an interest in the potential of things to evoke presence, and I have attempted to cast a similarly wide net: musical notation, tombs, inscriptions, calendars, wine labels, wine cellars, cups, gems, dining halls, present tenses, imperatives, and the atmosphere of neologisms and archaisms have all been shown to evoke presence. *Carpe diem* poems attempt to transcend the page of the book, and so we have followed their lead and looked at the materials such texts evoked. As literature studies beyond Classics are concerned with the questions at the heart of this book – textuality, performance, and presence – the wider-reaching approach of this book may also offer an angle of investigation for other disciplines: Classics, which has long included the study of epigraphy, art history, or linguistics alongside philology, may point to the tools to tackle the problem of presence in literature.

Let us for a last time pick up the thread of Pentadius and return to his poem. In the final couplet, Pentadius addresses the threads of

---

[25] Gumbrecht (1997).
[26] Gumbrecht (1997) x. Cf. pages 31–5 in the Introduction for a discussion of Gumbrecht (2004), which also argues that interpretation should not be privileged over presence.

Epilogue: Echoes of *Carpe Diem*

fate and tells them to run back on the spindles (21): *nunc, fila, recurrite fusis* ('now threads of fate, run back on the spindles'). This sentence is crucial for the poem's texture, for the way the poem weaves together text, song, and repetitions. It is clear that the phrase alludes to the well-known refrain of the song of the Fates in Catullus 64: *currite ducentes subtegmina, currite, fusi* ('run threads, drawing out the weft, run on').[27] As Pentadius *re*uses Catullus, so he notes that now the spindles are *re*run rather than simply run (*recurrite*). The poetic echo is marked as such. Yet, the dynamics of echoing go further; when Pentadius evokes Catullus' song, a polyphony of echoes arises, since Catullus' words come with their own echoes. In Catullus 64, the repetitiveness of the refrain mimics song. It is arguably this very repetitiveness which suggested itself to Pentadius' poem that is all about repetitions evoking song. The last couplet comments on the repetitive metre of the poem: 'Re-run back on the spindles, you threads' – rerunning verses is what this poem has been doing all along, and *uersus recurrentes* describe a type of repetitive metre that is closely related to the serpentine verses in Pentadius' poem.[28] Another expression in this last couplet also comments on the poem's shape: *inter et amplexus*. For 'embracing' or 'surrounding' is an appropriate description of a metre in which two identical parts embrace the centre. It is indeed above all through the peculiar metre that Pentadius attempts to rerun time and bring back an ever-so-elusive present that is always in the past. And although he cannot succeed in bringing back his youth, the repetitive metre seems to make time go backwards, as the end of the pentameter brings us back to the beginning of the hexameter. The metre thus

---

[27] In Catullus 64, the line is repeated numerous times: Cat. 64.327 = 333, 337, 342, 347, 352, 356, 361, 365, 371, 375, [378], 381. On the Catullan refrain here and modes of echoing and reflection, see above all, Trimble (2018). The Catullan line is also echoed at Verg. *Ecl.* 4.46–7, as Macrobius 6.1.41 notes. Macrobius' observation points to the interest in this line in late antiquity. Lemaire (1824) 323 notes the possible Vergilian echo in Pentadius; Arcaz Pozo (1989) 168 notes the Catullan echo.

[28] See Sidonius *Epist.* 8.11.5: [*sc. Lampridius faciebat*] *elegos uero nunc echoicos nunc recurrentes, nunc per anadiplosin fine principiisque conexos*. The context (here and at *Epist.* 9.14.4) makes clear that *uersus recurrentes* are palindromic verses. Sidonius' third category might describe Pentadius' serpentine verses (Wills (1996) 434). While Wills (1996) 432 calls Pentadius' serpentine metre *uersus recurrentes*, I can find no evidence that this appellation was used in antiquity.

Epilogue: Echoes of *Carpe Diem*

evokes a timeless present. In this, the poem both differs and conforms with Catullus 64. Whereas the song of the Fates ran onwards to the future as it described the final fate of Achilles dying at Troy, Pentadius' song sounds forth always now. Yet, the repetitions through which Pentadius' poem evokes presence and music owe much to Catullus. Concerning the refrain of Catullus 64, Gail Trimble has recently argued that 'the pattern of sounds that the reader hears becomes more important than the meaning that the words convey'.[29] As Pentadius reruns his song, he makes time stand still and makes us listen to the sound of the now. Yet, as the last sound fades away, as we are urged to seize the day one last time, and as we seem to hear a song that tells us to do so here and now, we realise that while we have been searching for the present, it is only the echoes of songs that we hear reverberating through time.

---

[29] Trimble (2018) 38. Cf. the repetitive refrain of the *Pervigilium Veneris*, which like Pentadius' poem describes the arrival of spring and mimics song (Catlow (1980) 51). On refrains in Latin poetry, see Wills (1996) 96–9. Emily Gowers points out to me that William Dunbar's poem *Lament for the Makers* also uses a Latin refrain in a poem that is all about time and transience.

BIBLIOGRAPHY

Acosta-Hughes, B., E. Kosmetatou, and M. Baumbach, eds. 2004. *Labored in papyrus leaves. Perspectives on an epigram collection attributed to Posidippus (P.Mil.Vogl. VIII 309)*. Cambridge, MA.
Acosta-Hughes, B. and S. A. Stephens. 2012. *Callimachus in context. From Plato to the Augustan Poets*. Cambridge.
Adams, J. N. 1990. *The Latin sexual vocabulary*. London.
Adams, J. N. and N. Vincent, eds. 2016. *Early and late Latin. Continuity or change?* Cambridge.
Albrecht, M. von. 1993. 'Musik und Dichtung bei Horaz'. In *Bimillenario della morte di Q. Orazio Flacco, Atti del convegno di Venosa (1992)*, 75–100. Venosa.
Alessio, G. 1960–1. *Hapax legomena ed altre cruces in Petronio*. Naples.
Alföldy, G., T. Hölscher, R. Kettemann, and H. Petersmann, eds. 1995. *Römische Lebenskunst. Interdisziplinäres Kolloquium zum 85. Geburtstag von Viktor Pöschl*. Heidelberg.
Algra, K., J. Barnes, J. Mansfeld, and M. Schofield, eds. 1999. *The Cambridge history of Hellenistic philosophy*. Cambridge.
Alster, B. 2005. *Wisdom of ancient Sumer*. Bethesda, MD.
Ameling, W. 1985. 'Φάγωμεν καὶ πίωμεν. Griechische Parallelen zu zwei Stellen aus dem Neuen Testament'. *ZPE* 60: 35–43.
Ancona, R. 1994. *Time and the erotic in Horace's Odes*. Durham, NC and London.
Anderson, B. and F. Rojas, eds. 2017. *Antiquarianisms. Contact, conflict, comparison*. Oxford and Philadelphia, PA.
Anderson, W. D. 1994. *Music and musicians in ancient Greece*. Ithaca, NY.
Anderson, W. S. 1958. 'Persius 1. 107–10'. *CQ* 8: 195–7.
Anderson, W. S. 1992. 'Horace's different recommenders of "carpe diem" in C. 1.4, 7, 9, 11'. *CJ* 88: 115–22.
Apperson, G. L. 1905. 'The wines of Horace'. *The Antiquary* 1: 298–301.
Arcaz Pozo, J. L. 1989. 'En torno al *De adventu veris* de Pentadio'. *CFC(L)* 23: 157–69.
Armstrong, D. 1968. *Toward a theory of structure in Horace*. Diss. University of Texas at Austin.
Armstrong, D. 1995. 'The impossibility of metathesis. Philodemus and Lucretius on form and content in poetry'. In Obbink, D., ed. 1995: 210–32.
Arnold, T. 1891. *Die griechischen Studien des Horaz*. Edited by W. Fries. Halle a. S. Original edition 1855–6.

Bibliography

Arnott, W. G. 1955. 'The *Asotodidaskalos* attributed to Alexis'. *CQ* 5: 210–16.
Arnott, W. G. 1970. 'Studies in comedy, II. Toothless wine'. *GRBS* 11: 43–7.
Arnott, W. G. 1996. *Alexis. The fragments*. Cambridge.
Arnott, W. G. 2007. *Birds in the ancient world from A to Z*. London.
Arrighetti, G. 1973. *Epicuro. Opere.* 2nd ed. Turin.
Arrowsmith, W. 1966. 'Luxury and death in the *Satyricon*'. *Arion* 5: 304–31.
Assmann, A. 1999. *Erinnerungsräume. Formen und Wandlungen des kulturellen Gedächtnisses.* 3rd ed. Munich [tr.= (2011)]
Assmann, A. 2011. *Cultural memory and Western civilization. Functions, media, archives.* Cambridge.
Assmann, J. 1977. 'Feste des Augenblicks – Verheißung der Dauer. Die Kontroverse der ägyptischen Harfnerlieder'. In Assmann, J., E. Feucht, and R. Grieshammer, eds. 1977: 55–84.
Assmann, J. 1989. 'Der schöne Tag. Sinnlichkeit und Vergänglichkeit im altägytischen Fest'. In Haug, W. and R. Warning, eds. 1989: 3–28.
Assmann, J., E. Feucht, and R. Grieshammer, eds. 1977. *Fragen an die altägyptische Literatur. Studien zum Gedenken an Eberhard Otto.* Wiesbaden.
Assmann, J. and B. Gladigo, eds. 1995. *Text und Kommentar. Archäologie der literarischen Kommunikation IV.* Munich.
Austin, C. and G. Bastianini. 2002. *Posidippi Pellaei quae supersunt omnia.* Milan.
Austin, J. L. 1962. *How to do things with words.* Oxford.
Axelson, B. 1945. *Unpoetische Wörter.* Lund.
Babcock, C. L. 1978. 'Horace, *Epodes* 13. Some comments on language and meaning'. In Riechel, D. C., ed. 1978: 107–18.
Bain, D. 1991. 'Six Greek verbs of sexual congress'. *CQ* 41: 51–77.
Bakhtin, M. 1981. 'From the prehistory of novelistic discourse'. In *The dialogic imagination.* Translated by C. Emerson and M. Holquist. Austin, TX, and London.
Baldwin, B. 1967. 'Opimian wine'. *AJPh* 88: 173–5.
Barber, D. 2014. 'Presence and the future tense in Horace's *Odes*'. *CJ* 109: 333–61.
Barbieri, A. 1976. 'A proposito della *Satira* II, 6 di Orazio'. *RAL* 31: 479–507.
Barchiesi, A. 1995. 'Simonide e Orazio sulla morte di Achille'. *ZPE* 107: 33–8.
Barchiesi, A. 1996a. 'Poetry, praise, and patronage. Simonides in Book 4 of Horace's *Odes*'. *ClAnt* 15: 5–47.
Barchiesi, A. 1996b. 'Simonides and Horace on the death of Achilles'. In *The New Simonides*, edited by D. Boedeker and D. Sider, *Arethusa* 29.2: 247–53 [= Boedeker and Sider (2001) 255–60]
Barchiesi, A. 2000. 'Rituals in ink. Horace on the Greek lyric tradition'. In Depew, M. and D. Obbink, eds. 2000: 167–82 [= Lowrie (2009b) 418–40]
Barchiesi, A. 2005. 'Lane-switching and jughandles in contemporary interpretations of Roman poetry'. *TAPhA* 135: 135–62.

Bibliography

Barchiesi, A. 2007. 'Carmina. Odes and Carmen Saeculare'. In Harrison, S. J., ed. 2007a: 144–62.
Barchiesi, A. 2009. 'Lyric in Rome'. In Budelmann, F., ed. 2009a: 319–35.
Barchiesi, A. and W. Scheidel, eds. 2010. The Oxford handbook of Roman studies. Oxford.
Bardon, H. 1944. 'Carpe diem'. REA 46: 345–55.
Barigazzi, A. 1975. 'Saghe sicule e beotiche nel simposio delle Muse di Callimaco'. Prometheus 1: 5–26.
Barigazzi, A. 1981. 'Fenice di Colofone e il Giambo di Nino'. Prometheus 7: 22–34.
Barker, A. 1995. 'Heterophonia and poikilia. Accompaniments to Greek melody'. In Gentili, B. and F. Perusino, eds. 1995: 41–60.
Barthes, R. 1953. Le degré zéro de l'écriture. Paris. [tr. = (1967)]
Barthes, R. 1964. 'Éléments de sémiologie'. Communications 4: 91–135. [tr. = (1968)]
Barthes, R. 1966. 'Sémantique de l'objet'. In Nardi, P., ed. 1966. [tr. = (1988)]
Barthes, R. 1967. Writing degree zero. Translated by A. Lavers and C. Smith. London.
Barthes, R. 1968. Elements of semiology. Translated by A. Lavers and C. Smith. New York.
Barthes, R. 1973. Le plaisir de texte. Paris. [tr. = (1975)]
Barthes, R. 1975. The pleasure of the text. Translated by R. Miller. New York.
Barthes, R. 1988. 'Semantics of the object'. In The semiotic challenge, 179–90. Oxford.
Baumbach, M., A. Petrovic, and I. Petrovic, eds. 2010. Archaic and classical Greek epigram. Cambridge.
Baumbach, M. and N. Dümmler, eds. 2014. Imitate Anacreon! Mimesis, poiesis and the poetic inspiration in the Carmina Anacreontea. Berlin and Boston, MA.
Beard, M. 1987. 'A complex of times. No more sheep on Romulus' birthday'. PCPhS 33: 1–15.
Beckby, H. 1957–8. Anthologia Graeca. 4 vols. Munich.
Becker, C. 1963. Das Spätwerk des Horaz. Göttingen.
Bellandi, F. 1974. 'Naevolus cliens'. Maia 26: 279–99. [tr. = (2009)]
Bellandi, F. 2008. 'Buffoni e cavalieri (A proposito di Iuv. 9, 9 ss.: agebas vernam equitem)'. MD 60: 205–17.
Bellandi, F. 2009. 'Naevolus cliens'. In Plaza, M., ed. 2009: 469–505.
Bellandi, F. 2021. Giovenale. Satira 9. Berlin and Boston, MA.
Ben-Dov, J. and L. Doering, eds. 2017. The construction of time in antiquity. Cambridge.
Benjamin, W. 1969. Charles Baudelaire. Ein Lyriker im Zeitalter des Hochkapitalismus. Zwei Fragmente. Edited by R. Tiedemann. Frankfurt. [tr. = (1973)]

Bibliography

Benjamin, W. 1973. *Charles Baudelaire. A lyric poet in the era of high capitalism*. Translated by H. Zohn. London.
Bentley, R. 1713. *Q. Horatius Flaccus*. 2nd ed. Amsterdam.
Bernardo, A. S. 1975–85. *Letters on familiar matters = Rerum familiarium libri. Francesco Petrarca*. 3 vols. Albany, NY.
Bernays, L. 1996. 'Zur Interpretation der Horaz-Ode 4.11'. *Prometheus* 22: 35–42.
Bernhardt, R. 2009. 'Sardanapal. Urbild des lasterhaften orientalischen Despoten. Entstehung, Bedeutung für die griechisch-römische Welt und Nachwirkung'. *Tyche* 24: 1–25.
Bernsdorff, H. 2020. *Anacreon of Teos. Testimonia and fragments*. 2 vols. Oxford.
Bettenworth, A. 2016. *Hoc satis in titulo . . . Studien zu den Inschriften in der römischen Elegie*. Münster.
Bettini, M. 1988. *Antropologia e cultura romana. Parentela, tempo, immagini dell'anima*. Rome. [tr. = (1991)]
Bettini, M. 1991. *Anthropology and Roman culture. Kinship, time, images of the soul*. Translated by J. Van Sickle. Baltimore, MD.
Bibauw, J., ed. 1969. *Hommages à Marcel Renard*. 3 vols. Brussels.
Bicknell, P. 1968. 'Opimian bitters or "Opimian" wine'. *AJPh* 89: 347–9.
Bignone, E. 1936. *L'Aristotele perduto*. 2 vols. Florence.
Binder, G. and B. Effe, eds. 1991. *Tod und Jenseits im Altertum*. Trier.
Bing, P. 1995. 'Ergänzungsspiel in the epigrams of Callimachus'. *A&A* 41: 115–31. [= (2009) 85–105]
Bing, P. 1998. 'Between literature and the monuments'. In Harder, M. A., R. F. Regtuit, and G. C. Wakker, eds. 1998: 21–43. [= (2009) 194–216]
Bing, P. 2002. 'The un-read muse? Inscribed epigram and its readers in antiquity'. In Harder, M. A., R. F. Regtuit, and G. C. Wakker, eds. 2002: 39–66. [= (2009) 116–46]
Bing, P. 2009. *The scroll and the marble*. Ann Arbor, MI.
Bing, P. and J. S. Bruss, eds. 2007a. *Brill's companion to Hellenistic epigram*. Leiden and Boston, MA.
Bing, P. and J. S. Bruss. 2007b. 'Introduction'. In Bing, P. and J. S. Bruss, eds. 2007a: 1–26.
Birrell, A. 1993. *Popular songs and ballads of Han China*. 2nd ed. Honolulu.
Blake, S. H. 2008. *Writing materials. Things in the literature of Flavian Rome*. Diss. University of Southern California.
Bloom, H. 1975. *A map of misreading*. Oxford and New York.
Blümner, H. 1911. *Die römischen Privataltertümer*. Munich.
Bo, D. 1943–4. 'Gli epiteti della lirica oraziana in relazione a quelli dei modelli greci'. *RIL* 77: 233–58.
Bo, D. 1960. *De Horati poetico eloquio. Indices nominum propriorum, metricarum rerum, prosodiacarum grammaticarumque*. Turin.
Bo, D., ed. 1965–6. *Lexicon Horatianum*. 2 vols. Hildesheim.
Boardman, J. 2002. *The archaeology of nostalgia. How the Greeks re-created their mythical past*. London.

Bibliography

Bodel, J. 1995. 'Chronology and succession 2. Notes on some consular lists on stone'. *ZPE* 105: 279–96.

Boedeker, D. and D. Sider, eds. 2001. *The New Simonides. Contexts of praise and desire.* Oxford.

Boitani, P. 1989. *The tragic and the sublime in medieval literature.* Cambridge.

Bollack, J. and A. Laks, eds. 1976. *Études sur L'Épicurisme antique.* Lille.

Bonavia-Hunt, N. A. 1969. *Horace the minstrel. A practical and aesthetic study of his aeolic verse.* Kineton.

Boncquet, J. 1987. *Diodorus Siculus (II, 1–34) over Mesopotamië. Een historische kommentaar.* Brussels.

Borchhardt, J. 1996–7. 'Zur Politik der Dynasten Trbbênimi und Perikle von Zêmuri'. *Lykia* 3: 1–23.

Bösing, L. 1970. '*Multa renascentur* (Hor. *Ars* 70–72)'. *RhM* 113: 246–61.

Bosworth, A. B. 1980–95. *A historical commentary on Arrian's history of Alexander.* 2 vols. Oxford.

Bounia, A. 2004. *The nature of classical collecting. Collectors and collections, 100 BCE–100 CE.* Aldershot and Burlington, VA.

Bowie, E. L. 1986. 'Early Greek elegy, symposium and public festival'. *JHS* 106: 13–35.

Bowie, E. L. 2007. 'From archaic elegy to Hellenistic sympotic epigram?' In Bing, P. and J. S. Bruss, eds. 2007a: 95–112.

Bowie, E. L. 2010. 'Stobaeus and early Greek lyric, elegiac and iambic poetry'. In Horster, M. and C. Reitz, eds. 2010: 587–617.

Bowie, E. L. 2012. 'Unnatural selection. Expurgation of Greek melic, elegiac and iambic poetry'. In Harrison, S. J. and C. Stray, eds. 2012: 9–24.

Braden, G. 2010. 'Carpe diem'. In Grafton, A., G. W. Most, and S. Settis, eds. 2010: 169–70.

Bramble, J. C. 1974. *Persius and the programmatic satire. A study in form and imagery.* Cambridge.

Brandis, T. and W.-W. Ehlers. 1974. 'Zu den Petronexzerpten des *Florilegium Gallicum*'. *Philologus* 118: 85.

Braund, P. and J. Wilkins, eds. 2000. *Athenaeus and his world.* Exeter.

Braund, S. M. 1988. *Beyond anger. A study of Juvenal's Third Book of Satires.* Cambridge.

Braund, S. M. 1996. *Juvenal. Satires Book I.* Cambridge.

Braund, S. M. 2004. *Juvenal and Persius.* Cambridge, MA, and London.

Breed, B. W. 2006. *Pastoral inscriptions. Reading and writing Virgil's Eclogues.* London.

Brelich, A. 1937. *Aspetti della morte nelle iscrizioni sepolcrali dell'impero romano.* Diss. Budapest.

Brendel, O. 1934. 'Untersuchungen zur Allegorie des pompejanischen Totenkopf-Mosaiks'. *MDAI(R)* 49: 157–79.

Brink, C. O. 1965. *On reading a Horatian satire. An interpretation of Sermones II 6.* Sydney.

Bibliography

Brink, C. O. 1971a. *Horace on poetry. The Ars Poetica*. Cambridge.
Brink, C. O. 1971b. 'Horatian notes II. Despised readings in the manuscripts of the *Odes*, Book II'. *PCPhS* 197: 17–29.
Brink, C. O. 1982a. *Horace on poetry. Epistles, Book 2. The letters to Augustus and Florus*. Cambridge.
Brink, C. O. 1982b. 'Horatian notes III. Despised readings in the manuscripts of the *Epodes* and a passage of *Odes* Book 3'. *PCPhS* 28: 30–56.
Brink, L. and D. A. Green, eds. 2008. *Commemmorating the dead. Texts and artifacts in context*. Berlin and New York.
Broccia, G. 2006. 'Appunti sul tema del vino in Orazio'. *Maia* 58: 25–32.
Broccia, G. 2007. *La rappresentazione del tempo nell'opera di Orazio*. Rome.
Brun, J.-P., M. Poux, and A. Tchernia, eds. 2004. *Le vin. Nectar des dieux, génie des hommes*. Strasbourg.
Brunori, G. 1930. *La lingua d'Orazio*. Florence.
Brunt, P. A. 2009. 'On historical fragments and epitomes'. *CQ* 30: 477–94.
Bruss, J. S. 2005. *Hidden presences. Monuments, gravesites, and corpses in Greek funerary epigram*. Leuven.
Bruss, J. S. 2010. 'Ecphrasis in fits and starts? Down to 300 BC'. In Baumbach, M., A. Petrovic, and I. Petrovic, eds. 2010: 385–403.
Büchner, K. 1980. 'Bentley, Brink und Horazens *Ars poetica*'. *Hermes* 108: 476–91.
Budelmann, F., ed. 2009a. *The Cambridge companion to Greek lyric*. Cambridge.
Budelmann, F. 2009b. 'Introducing Greek lyric'. In Budelmann, F., ed. 2009a: 1–18.
Budelmann, F. 2018. *Greek lyric. A selection*. Cambridge.
Budelmann, F. and T. Phillips, eds. 2018. *Textual events. Performance and the lyric in early Greece*. Oxford.
Budelmann, F. and T. Power. 2013. 'The inbetweenness of sympotic elegy'. *JHS* 133: 1–19.
Buora, M. and S. Magnani, eds. 2016. *Le iscrizioni con funzione didascalico-esplicativa. Committente, destinatario, contenuto e descrizione dell'oggetto nell'instrumentum inscriptum. Atti del VI incontro Instrumenta inscripta*. Trieste.
Burgess, J. S. 2001. *The tradition of the Trojan War in Homer and the epic cycle*. Baltimore, MD, and London.
Burkert, W. 1991. 'Oriental symposia. Contrasts and parallels'. In Slater, W. J., ed. 1991: 7–24.
Burkert, W. 2009. 'Sardanapal zwischen Mythos und Realität. Das Grab in Kilikien'. In Dill, U. and C. Walde, eds. 2009: 502–15.
Burnett, A. 1997. *The poems of A.E. Housman*. Oxford.
Burnett, A. P. 1983. *Three Archaic poets. Archilochus, Alcaeus, Sappho*. London.
Busch, S. 1999. *Versus balnearum. Die antike Dichtung über Bäder und Baden im Römischen Reich*. Stuttgart and Leipzig.
Busine, A. 2012. 'The discovery of inscriptions and the legitimation of new cults'. In Dignas, B. and R. R. R. Smith, eds. 2012: 241–56.

Bibliography

Butler, S. 2015. *The ancient phonograph*. New York.
Butler, S. and S. Nooter, eds. 2019. *Sound and the ancient senses*. London and New York.
Cairns, D., ed. 2005. *Body language in the Greek and Roman worlds*. Swansea.
Cairns, F. 1982. 'Horace *Odes* 3,22. Genre and sources'. *Philologus* 126: 227–46. [= (2012) 441–61]
Cairns, F. 1992. 'The power of implication. Horace's invitation to Maecenas (*Odes* 1.20)'. In Woodman, A. J. and J. Powell, eds. 1992: 84–109. [= (2012) 213–43]
Cairns, F. 2012. *Roman lyric. Collected papers on Catullus and Horace*. Berlin and Boston, MA.
Cairns, F. 2016. *Hellenistic epigrams. Contexts of exploration*. Cambridge.
Calame, C. 1977. *Les chœurs de jeunes filles en Grèce archaïque I. Morphologie, fonction religieuse et sociale*. Rome. [tr. = (1997)]
Calame, C. 1997. *Choruses of young women in ancient Greece. Their morphology, religious role and social function*. Translated by D. Collins and J. Orion. Lanham, MD, and London.
Calboli, G. 2002. 'On Horace's *Ars Poetica* 139. *Parturient montes, nascetur ridiculus mus*'. In Sawicki, L. and D. Shalev, eds. 2002: 65–76.
Calder, W. M., U. K. Goldsmith, and P. B. Kenevan, eds. 1985. *Hypatia. Essays in Classics, comparative literature and philosophy presented to Hazel E. Barnes*. Boulder, CO.
Callender, M. H. 1965. *Roman amphorae with an index of stamps*. London.
Cameron, A. 1995. *Callimachus and his critics*. Princeton, NJ.
Campbell, D. A. 1989. 'Going up? ἀναβῆναι in Anacreon 395 (Page)'. *EMC* 33: 49–50.
Campbell, G. 2003. *Lucretius on creation and evolution*. Oxford.
Cannatà Fera, M. and G. B. D'Alessio, eds. 2001. *I lirici greci. Forme della comunicazione e storia del testo*. Messina.
Canevaro, L. G. 2015. *Hesiod's Works and days. How to teach self-sufficiency*. Oxford.
Canevaro, L. G. 2019. 'Materiality and Classics. (Re)turning to the material'. *JHS* 139: 1–11.
Carpino, A. A., T. D'Angelo, M. Muratov, and D. Saunders, eds. 2018. *Collecting and collectors from antiquity to modernity*. Boston, MA.
Casagrande-Kim, R. 2018. 'Collecting gems in ancient Rome'. In Carpino, A. A., T. D'Angelo, M. Muratov, and D. Saunders, eds. 2018: 99–112.
Castagna, L. and G. Vogt-Spira, eds. 2002. *Pervertere. Ästhetik der Verkehrung. Literatur und Kultur neronischer Zeit und ihre Rezeption*. Munich.
Cataudella, Q. 1927–8. 'L'elegia di Semonide e l'ode di Orazio IV 7'. *Bollettino di filologia classica* 34: 229–32.
Catlow, L. 1980. *Pervigilium Veneris*. Brussels.
Catoni, M.-L. 2010. *Bere vino puro*. Milan.
Cavarzere, A. 1992. *Orazio. Il libro degli Epodi*. Venice.

Bibliography

Cavarzere, A. 1996. *Sul limitare. Il 'motto' e la poesia di Orazio*. Bologna.
Cazzato, V. 2016. 'Symposia *en plein air* in Alcaeus and others'. In Cazzato, V., D. Obbink, and E. E. Prodi, eds. 2016: 184–206.
Cazzato, V. and A. P. M. H. Lardinois, eds. 2016. *The look of lyric. Greek song and the visual*. Leiden and Boston, MA.
Cazzato, V., D. Obbink, and E. E. Prodi, eds. 2016. *The cup of song. Studies on poetry and the symposion*. Oxford.
Cazzato, V. and E. E. Prodi. 2016. 'Introduction. Continuity in the sympotic tradition'. In Cazzato, V., D. Obbink, and E. E. Prodi, eds. 2016: 184–206.
Chadwick, H. 1969. 'Florilegium'. In *Reallexikon für Antike und Christentum*, edited by T. Klauser, 1131–60. Stuttgart.
Chepel, E. 2016. 'Alcestis' daily bread. The meaning of vv. 788–9 and a new Oxyrhynchus papyrus'. *ZPE* 200: 86–7.
Cichorius, C. 1888. *Rom und Mytilene*. Leipzig.
Citroni, M. 1983. 'Occasione e piani di destinazione nella lirica di Orazio'. *MD* 10–11: 133–214. [tr. = (2009)]
Citroni, M. 1995. *Poesia e lettori in Roma antica. Forme della comunicazione letteraria*. Rome and Bari.
Citroni, M. 2009. 'Occasion and level of address in Horatian lyric'. In M. Lowrie, ed. 2009b: 72–105.
Citroni, M. 2017. 'Heinze, Fraenkel e altre voci. Contributi sparsi alla storia e al significato del dibattito su occasione e destinatario in Orazio lirico'. *Dictynna* 14.
Citti, F. 2000. *Studi oraziani. Tematica e intertestualità*. Bologna.
Clarke, J. R. 1998. *Looking at lovemaking. Constructions of sexuality in Roman art 100 B.C.–A.D. 250*. Berkeley and Los Angeles, CA, and London.
Clausen, W. V. 1959. *A. Persi Flacci et D. Iuni Iuuenalis Saturae*. Oxford.
Clausen, W. V. 1992. *A. Persi Flacci et D. Iuni Iuuenalis Saturae*. 2nd ed. Oxford.
Clausen, W.V., F. R. D. Goodyear, E. J. Kenney, and J. A. Richmond. 1966. *Appendix Vergiliana*. Oxford.
Clauss, J. J. and M. Cuypers, eds. 2010. *A companion to Hellenistic literature*. Malden, MA, Oxford, and Chichester.
Clay, J. S. 2010. 'Horace and Lesbian lyric'. In Davis, G., ed. 2010a: 128–46.
Clay, J. S. 2016. 'How to construct a sympotic space with words'. In Cazzato, V. and A. P. M. H. Lardinois, eds. 2016: 204–16.
Clayman, D. L. 2007. 'Philosophers and philosophy in Greek epigram'. In Bing, P. and J. S. Bruss, eds. 2007a: 497–517.
Cohen, M. E., D. C. Snell, and D. B. Weisberg, eds. 1993. *The tablet and the scroll. Near Eastern studies in honor of William W. Hallo*. Bethesda, MD.
Collinge, N. E. 1961. *The structure of Horace's Odes*. Oxford.
Colton, R. E. 1973. 'Ausonius and Juvenal'. *CJ* 69: 41–51.
Commager, S. 1957. 'The function of wine in Horace's *Odes*'. *TAPhA* 88: 68–80. [= Lowrie (2009b) 33–49]

Bibliography

Commager, S. 1962. *The Odes of Horace. A critical study*. New Haven, CT, and London.
Comotti, G. 1988. 'I problemi dei valori ritmici'. In Gentili, B. and R. Pretagostini, eds. 1988: 17–25.
Comotti, G. 1989. *Music in Greek and Roman culture*. Translated by R. V. Munson. Baltimore, MD and London.
Connors, C. 1998. *Petronius the poet. Verse and literary tradition in the Satyricon*. Cambridge.
Conte, G. B. 1986. *The rhetoric of imitation*. Translated by C. Segal. Ithaca, NY, and London.
Conte, G. B. 1987. *Letteratura latina. Manuale storico dalle origini alla fine dell'Impero romano*. Florence.
Conte, G. B. 1994. *Latin literature. A history*. Translated by J. B. Solodow. Baltimore, MD and London.
Conte, G. B. 1996. *The hidden author*. Translated by E. Fantham. Berkeley and Los Angeles, CA, and London.
Conte, G. B. 2017. *Stealing the club from Hercules. On imitation in Latin poetry*. Berlin and Boston, MA.
Courtney, E. 1975. 'The interpolations in Juvenal'. *BICS* 22: 147–62.
Courtney, E. 1980a. *A commentary to the Satires of Juvenal*. London.
Courtney, E. 1980b. 'Observations on the *Latin anthology*.' *Hermathena* 129: 37–50.
Courtney, E. 1995. *Musa lapidaria. A selection of Latin verse inscriptions*. Atlanta, GA.
Courtney, E. 2001. *A companion to Petronius*. Oxford.
Costa, C. D. N., ed. 1973. *Horace*. London.
Crawford, M. H. 2012. 'From vintage to *mise en amphore*?' *ZPE* 183: 282.
Cribiore, R. 1994. 'A Homeric writing exercise and reading Homer in school'. *Tyche* 9: 1–9.
Cristóbal, V. 1985. 'Los versos ecoicos de Pentadio y sus implicaciones métricas'. *CFC(L)* 19: 157–67.
Cucchiarelli, A. 2001. *La satira e il poeta. Orazio tra Epodi e Sermones*. Pisa.
Cugusi, P. 1967. 'Nota petroniana (*Sat.* 93, 2, v. 4)'. *RCCM* 9: 86–94.
Culler, J. D. 1981. *The pursuit of signs. Semiotics, literature, deconstruction*. Ithaca, NY.
Culler, J. D. 2015. *Theory of the lyric*. Cambridge, MA, and London.
Cupaiuolo, F. 1942. *A proposito della callida iunctura oraziana*. Naples.
Curtis, L. 2017. *Imagining the chorus in Augustan poetry*. Cambridge.
Dacier, A. 1689–97. *Les œuvres d'Horace*. 10 vols. Paris.
Dahlmann, H. 1983–7. *Zu Fragmenten römischer Dichter*. 3 vols. Wiesbaden and Stuttgart.
D'Alessio, G. B. 2009. 'Language and pragmatics'. In Budelmann, F., ed. 2009a: 114–29.
D'Alessio, G. B. 2018. 'Fiction and pragmatics in ancient Greek lyric. The case of Sappho'. In Budelmann, F. and T. Phillips, eds. 2018: 31–62.

Bibliography

Dalley, S. 1999. 'Sennacherib and Tarsus'. *AS* 49: 73–80.
D'Alton, J. F. 1962. *Roman literary theory and criticism*. New York.
D'Angour, A. 2018. 'The musical setting of ancient Greek texts'. In Phillips, T. and A. D'Angour, eds. 2018: 47–72.
D'Angour, A. 2019. 'Hearing ancient sounds through modern ears'. In Butler, S. and S. Nooter, eds. 2019: 31–43.
D'Anna, G. 1979. 'Ancora sul motivo oraziano del "carpe diem"'. *AMArc* 7: 103–15.
D'Ansse de Villoison, J.-B. G. 1801. 'Palæographie'. *Magasin encyclopédique, ou journal des sciences, des lettres et des arts* 7: 451–509.
Darbo-Peschanski, C., ed. 2004. *La citation dans l'antiquité*. Grenoble.
Davis, G. 1991. *Polyhymnia. The rhetoric of Horatian lyric discourse*. Berkeley and Los Angeles, CA, and Oxford.
Davis, G. 2007. 'Wine and the symposium'. In Harrison S. J., ed. 2007a: 207–20.
Davis, G., ed. 2010a. *A companion to Horace*. Malden, MA, Oxford, and Chichester.
Davis, G. 2010b. 'Defining a lyric ethos. Archilochus lyricus and Horatian melos'. In Davis, G., ed. 2010a: 105–27.
Day, J. W. 2007. 'Poems on stone. The inscribed antecedents of Hellenistic epigram'. In Bing, P. and J. S. Bruss, eds. 2007a: 29–47.
Day, J. W. 2010. *Archaic Greek epigram and dedication. Representation and reperformance*. Cambridge.
Day, J. W. 2019. 'Reading inscriptions in literary epigram'. In Kanellou, M., I. Petrovic, and C. Carey, eds. 2019: 19–34.
Dehon, P.-J. 1993. 'Note sur le sens de *carpo* dans Lucilius, *fragment* 828 (Krenkel)'. *TAPhA* 114: 557–9.
Deitz, L. and G. Vogt-Spira. 1994–2011. *Julius Caesar Scaliger. Poetices libri septem. Sieben Bücher über die Dichtkunst*. 6 vols. Stuttgart.
de Jong, I. J. F. and J. P. Sullivan, eds. 1994. *Modern critical theroy and classical literature*. Leiden, New York, and Cologne.
Delignon, B. 2017. 'Dîner avec Mécène'. In Delignon, B., N. Dauvois, and L. Cottegnies, eds. 2017: 77–90.
Delignon, B., N. Dauvois, and L. Cottegnies, eds. 2017. *L'invention de la vie privée et le modèle d'Horace*. Paris.
Della Corte, F. 1986. *Le Georgiche di Virgilio. Libri III-IV*. Genoa.
Delz, J. 1995. 'Wie die Blätter am Baum, so wechseln die Wörter'. In Krömer, D., ed. 1995: 1–12.
Dentzer, J-.M. 1982. *Le motif du banquet couché dans le Proche-Orient et le monde grec du VIIe au IVe siècle avant J.C.* Rome.
Depew, M. and D. Obbink, eds. 2000. *Matrices of genre*. Cambridge, MA.
Derrida, J. 1980a. 'La loi du genre'. *Glyph* 7: 176–201. [tr. = (1980b)]
Derrida, J. 1980b. 'The law of genre'. Translated by Avital Ronell. *Critical Inquiry* 7: 55–81.
Desbat, A. 2004. 'Marques et images de marques'. In Brun, J.-P., M. Poux, and A. Tchernia, eds. 2004: 305–15.

Bibliography

Deschamps, L. 1983. 'Il tempo in Orazio'. *Orpheus* 4: 195–214.
Dickey, E. and A. Chahoud, eds. 2010. *Colloqiual and literary Latin*. Oxford.
Dihle, A., ed. 1968. *L'épigramme grecque*. Geneva.
Diels, H. 1901. *Poetarum philosophorum fragmenta*. Berlin.
Dignas, B. and R. R. R. Smith, eds. 2012. *Historical and religious memory in the ancient world*. Oxford.
Dill, U. and C. Walde, eds. 2009. *Antike Mythen. Medien, Transformationen und Konstruktionen*. Berlin.
Dinter, M. 2005. 'Epic and epigram. Minor heroes in Virgil's *Aeneid*'. *CQ* 55: 153–69.
Dinter, M. 2009. 'Laying down the law. Horace's reflection in his *sententiae*'. In Houghton, L. B. T. and M. Wyke, eds. 2009: 96–108.
Dodds, E. R. 1960. *Euripides. Bacchae*. 2nd ed. Oxford.
Donahue, J. F. 1999. 'Euergetic self-representation and the inscriptions at *Satyricon* 71.10'. *CPh* 94: 69–74.
Donahue, J. F. 2004. *The Roman community at table during the Principate*. Ann Arbor, MI.
Döpp, S. 1991. '"Leben und Tod" in Petrons *Satyrica*'. In Binder, G. and B. Effe, eds. 1991: 144–66.
Dornseiff, F. 1929. 'Dareios und Sardanapal'. *Hermes* 64: 270–1.
Draycott, C. M. and M. Stamatopoulou, eds. 2016. *Dining and death. Interdisciplinary perspectives on the funerary banquet in ancient art, burial and belief*. Leuven.
Dressel, H. 1878. 'Ricerche sul monte Testaccio'. *Annali dell'Istituto di corrispondenza archeologica* 50: 118–92.
Drews, R. 1970. 'Herodotus' other *logoi*'. *AJPh* 91: 181–91.
DuBois, P. 1995. *Sappho is burning*. Chicago, IL.
Du Quesnay, I. M. Le M. 1995. 'Horace, *Odes* 4.5. Pro Reditu Imperatoris Caesaris Divi Filii Augusti'. In Harrison, S. J., ed. 1995: 128–87. [= Lowrie (2009b) 271–336]
Du Quesnay, I. M. Le M. and A. J. Woodman, eds. 2012. *Catullus. Poems, books, readers*. Cambridge.
Dufallo, B. 2005. 'Words born and made. Horace's defense of neologisms and the cultural poetics of Latin'. *Arethusa* 36: 89–101.
Dufallo, B. 2013. *The captor's image. Greek culture in Roman ecphrasis*. Oxford.
Dunbabin, K. 1986. 'Sic erimus cuncti ... The skeleton in Graeco-Roman art'. *JDAI* 101: 185–255.
Dunbabin, K. 2003. *The Roman banquet. Images of conviviality*. Cambridge.
Durbec, Y. and F. Trajber, eds. 2017. *Traditions épiques et poésie épigrammatique*. Leuven.
Ecker, U. 1990. *Grabmal und Epigramm. Studien zur frühgriechischen Sepulkraldichtung*. Stuttgart.
Edmunds, L. 1992. *From a Sabine jar. Reading Horace, Odes 1.9*. Chapel Hill, NC.

Bibliography

Edmunds, L. 2001. *Intertextuality and the reading of Roman poetry*. Baltimore, MD, and London.
Edmunds, L. 2010. 'The reception of Horace's *Odes*'. In Davis, G., ed. 2010a: 337–66.
Edwards, C. 1996. *Writing Rome. Textual approaches to the city*. Cambridge.
Edwards, C. 2007. *Death in ancient Rome*. New Haven, CT and London.
Elsner, J. 1994. 'From the pyramids to Pausanias and Piglet. Monuments, travel and writing'. In Goldhill, S. and R. Osborne, eds. 1994: 224–54.
Elsner, J. 2007. *Roman eyes. Visuality and subjectivity in art and text*. Princeton, NJ.
Elsner, J. 2014a. 'Afterword. Framing knowledge. Collecting objects, collecting texts'. In Gahtan, M. W. and D. Pegazzano, eds. 2014: 156–62.
Elsner, J. 2014b. 'Lithic poetics. Posidippus and his stones'. *Ramus* 43: 152–72.
Elsner, J. 2017. 'Late Narcissus'. In Elsner, J. and J. Hernández Lobato, eds. 2017: 176–204.
Elsner, J. and R. Cardinal, eds. 1994. *The cultures of collecting*. London.
Elsner, J. and J. Hernández Lobato, eds. 2017. *The poetics of late Latin literature*. Oxford and New York.
Elsner, J. and J. Masters, eds. 1994. *Reflections of Nero*. London.
Ensor, E. 1902. 'On Horace II.17 and I.20'. *CR* 16: 209–11.
Erasmo, M. 2008. *Reading death in ancient Rome*. Columbus, OH.
Erbse, H. 1971. *Scholia Graeca in Homeri Iliadem*. Berlin.
Erler, M. 2012. 'Schmerzfreiheit als Lust. Traditionelles in Epikurs Hedonekonzept'. In Erler, M. and W. Rother, eds. 2012: 53–69. [tr. = (2015)]
Erler, M. 2015. 'Hedonê in the poets and Epicurus'. In King, R. A. H., ed. 2015: 303–18.
Erler, M. and W. Rother, eds. 2012. *Philosophie der Lust. Studien zum Hedonismus*. Basel.
Erler, M. and M. Schofield. 1999. 'Epicurean ethics'. In Algra, K., J. Barnes, J. Mansfeld, and M. Schofield, eds. 1999: 642–74.
Erren, M. 2003. *P. Vergilius Maro. Georgica*. Heidelberg.
Evans, C. 2016. *Time in the Odes of Horace*. Diss. University of Virginia.
Fantuzzi, M. 1987. 'Caducità dell'uomo ed eternità della natura. Variazioni di un motivo letterario'. *QUCC* 26: 101–10.
Fantuzzi, M. 2010. 'Typologies of variation on a theme in archaic and classical metrical inscriptions'. In Baumbach, M., A. Petrovic, and I. Petrovic, eds. 2010: 289–310.
Fantuzzi, M. and R. L. Hunter. 2004. *Tradition and innovation in Hellenistic poetry*. Cambridge.
Fassino, M. and L. Prauscello. 2001. 'Memoria ritmica e memoria poetica. Saffo e Alceo in Teocrito *Idilli* 28–30 tra ἀρχαιολογία metrica e innovazione alessandrina'. *MD* 46: 9–37.
Fearn, D. 2017. *Pindar's eyes. Visual and material culture in epinician poetry*. Oxford.

Bibliography

Fearn, D. 2018. 'Materialities of political commitment? Textual events, material culture, and metaliterarity in Alcaeus'. In Budelmann, F. and T. Phillips, eds. 2018: 93–113.
Fearn, D. 2020. *Greek lyric of the archaic and classical periods. From the past to the future of the lyric subject*. Leiden and Boston, MA.
Fedeli, P. 1994a. 'Commentare Orazio'. In *Atti dei convegni di Venosa, Napoli, Roma. Novembre 1993*, 287–98. Venosa.
Fedeli, P. 1994b. *Q. Orazio Flacco. Le opere. Le satire*. Rome.
Fedeli, P. and I. Ciccarelli. 2008. *Q. Horatii Flacci Carmina liber IV*. Florence.
Feeney, D. C. 1993. 'Horace and the Greek lyric poets'. In Rudd, N., ed. 1993: 41–63. [= (2021) ii.64–90 = Lowrie (2009b) 202–31]
Feeney, D. C. 1998. *Literature and religion at Rome. Cultures, contexts, and beliefs*. Cambridge.
Feeney, D. C. 2007. *Caesar's calendar*. Berkeley and Los Angeles, CA.
Feeney, D. C. 2021. *Explorations in Latin Literature*. 2 vols. Cambridge.
Fehr, B. 1971. *Orientalische und griechische Gelage*. Bonn.
Feldherr, A. 2010. *Playing gods. Ovid's Metamorphoses and the politics of fiction*. Princeton, NJ, and Oxford.
Felski, R. 2015. *The limits of critique*. Chicago, IL.
Fermor, P. L. 2002. *A time of gifts*. Original edition, 1977. London.
Fink, S. 2014. 'Sardanapal. Ein Hedonist aus Mesopotamien?' In Gaspa, S., A. Greco, D. Morandi Bonacossi, S. Ponchia, and R. Rollinger, eds. 2014: 239–50.
Fischer, S. 1996. *Die Aufforderung zur Lebensfreude im Buch Kohelet und seine Rezeption der ägyptischen Harfnerlieder*. Diss. University of South Africa.
Fish, S. E. 1976. 'Interpreting the "Variorum"'. *Critical Inquiry* 2: 465–85.
Fitzgerald, W. 1989. 'Horace, pleasure and the text'. *Arethusa* 22: 81–104.
Fitzgerald, W. 2007. *Martial. The world of the epigram*. Chicago, IL and London.
Fitzgerald, W. 2016. *Variety. The life of a Roman concept*. Chicago, IL and London.
Fitzgerald, W. 2021. *The living death of antiquity. Neoclassical aesthetics*. Oxford.
Flashar, H. and K. Gaiser, eds. 1965. *Synusia. Festgabe für Wolfgang Schadewaldt*. Pfullingen.
Floridi, L. 2007. *Stratone di Sardi*. Alessandria.
Fögen, T. 2000. *Patrii sermonis egestas. Einstellungen lateinischer Autoren zu ihrer Muttersprache. Ein Beitrag zum Sprachbewusstsein in der römischen Antike*. Munich.
Foster, M., L. Kurke, and N. Weiss, eds. 2019a. *Genre in archaic and classical Greek poetry. Theories and models*. Leiden.
Foster, M., L. Kurke, and N. Weiss. 2019b. 'Introduction'. In Foster, M., L. Kurke, and N. Weiss, eds. 2019a: 1–28.
Ford, A. 2002. 'From letters to literature. Reading the "song culture" of classical Greece'. In Yunis, H., ed. 2002: 15–37.

Bibliography

Forsberg, S. 1995. *Near Eastern destruction datings as sources for Greek and Near Eastern Iron Age chronology. Archaeological and historical studies. The Cases of Samaria (722 B.C.) and Tarsus (696 B.C.)*. 2nd ed. Uppsala.

Foucault, M. 1969. *L'archéologie du savoir*. Paris. [tr. = (1972)]

Foucault, M. 1972. *The archaeology of knowledge*. Translated by A. M. Sheridan Smith. London.

Fowler, D. P. 1991. 'Narrate and describe. The problem of ecphrasis'. *JRS* 81: 25–35. [= (2000) 64–85]

Fowler, D. P. 1994. 'Postmodernism, romantic irony, and classical closure'. In de Jong, I. J. F. and J. P. Sullivan, eds. 1994: 231–56. [= (2000) 5–33]

Fowler, D. P. 1997. 'On the shoulders of giants. Intertextuality and classical studies'. *MD* 39: 13–34. [= (2000) 115–37]

Fowler, D. P. 2000. *Roman constructions. Readings in postmodern Latin*. Oxford.

Fowler, R. L. 1987. *The nature of the early Greek lyric. Three preliminary studies*. Toronto, ON, Buffalo, NY, and London.

Fraenkel, E. 1957. *Horace*. Oxford.

Frahm, E. 2003. 'Images of Ashurbanipal in later tradition'. *Eretz Israel* 27: 37–48.

Frahm, E., ed. 2017. *A companion to Assyria*. Malden, MA, Oxford, and Chichester.

Frangoulidis, S., S .J. Harrison, and T. D. Papanghelis, eds. 2018. *Intratextuality and Latin Literature*. Berlin and Boston, MA.

Fränkel, H. 1921. *Die homerischen Gleichnisse*. Göttingen.

Fränkel, H. 1962. *Dichtung und Philosophie des frühen Griechentums*. 2nd ed. Munich. [tr. = (1975)]

Fränkel, H. 1975. *Early Greek poetry and philosophy. A history of Greek epic, lyric, and prose to the middle of the fifth century*. Translated by M. Hadas and J. Willis. Oxford.

Franz, J. 1840. *Elementa epigraphices Graecae*. Berlin.

Fredricksmeyer, E. A. 1985. 'Horace Odes 4.7. The most beautiful poem in ancient literature?' In Calder, W. M., U. K. Goldsmith, and P. B. Kenevan, eds. 1985: 15–26.

Freudenburg, K. 1993. *The walking muse. Horace on the theory of satire*. Princeton, NJ.

Freudenburg, K., ed. 2005. *The Cambridge companion to Roman satire*. Cambridge.

Freudenburg, K. 2006. 'Playing at lyric's boundaries. Dreaming forward in Book Two of Horace's *Sermones*'. *Dictynna* 3.

Freudenburg, K., ed. 2009. *Horace. Satires and Epistles. Oxford readings in classical studies*. Oxford.

Freudenburg, K. 2018. 'Satire's censorial waters in Horace and Juvenal'. *JRS* 108: 141–55.

Freudenburg, K. 2021. *Horace. Satires Book II*. Cambridge.

Friedländer, L. 1886. *M. Valerii Martialis Epigrammaton libri*. Leipzig.

Bibliography

Friedländer, L. 1895. *D. Junii Juvenalis Saturarum libri V.* Leipzig.
Friedländer, L. 1923. *Darstellungen aus der Sittengeschichte Roms*. 10th ed. 4 vols. Leipzig.
Friedländer, P. 1912. *Johannes von Gaza und Paulus Silentiarius. Kunstbeschreibungen Justinianischer Zeit*. Leipzig and Berlin.
Friedländer, P. 1941. 'Pattern of sound and atomistic theory in Lucretius'. *AJPh* 62: 16–34.
Frieman, R. L. 1972. 'Wine and politics in Horace'. *EMC* 16: 84–91.
Froning, H., T. Hölscher, and H. Mielsch, eds. 1992. *Kotinos. Festschrift für Erika Simon*. Mainz.
Fulkerson, L. 2017. *A literary commentary on the elegies of the Appendix Tibulliana*. Oxford.
Furlani, G. 1927. 'Di un supposto gesto precatorio assiro'. *RAL* 3: 234–72.
Furtwängler, A. 1900. *Die antiken Gemmen. Geschichte der Steinschneidekunst im klassischen Altertum*. 3 vols. Leipzig and Berlin.
Gabba, E., ed. 1983. *Tria corda. Scritti in onore di Arnaldo Momigliano*. Como.
Gagliardi, D. 1975–6. 'Temporalità e angoscia nella lirica oraziana'. *AAPel* 53: 37–44.
Gagliardi, D. 1989. 'Il tema della morte nella cena petroniana'. *Orpheus* 10: 13–25.
Gagné, R. 2016. 'The world in a cup'. In Cazzato, V., D. Obbink, and E. E. Prodi, eds. 2016: 207–29.
Gahtan, M. W. and D. Pegazzano, eds. 2014. *Museum archetypes and collecting in the ancient world*. Boston, MA, and Leiden.
Gaisser, J. H. 2017. 'Lyric'. In Moul, V., ed. 2017: 113–30.
Gale, M. R. 1991. 'Man and beast in Lucretius and the *Georgics*'. *CQ* 41: 414–26.
Galletier, E. 1922. *Étude sur la poésie funéraire romaine*. Paris.
García Baracco, M. E. 2020. *Larvae convivales. Gli scheletri da banchetto dell'antica Roma*. Rome.
Gaspa, S., A. Greco, D. Morandi Bonacossi, S. Ponchia, and R. Rollinger, eds. 2014. *From source to history. Studies on ancient Near Eastern worlds and beyond. Dedicated to Giovanni Battista Lanfranchi on the occasion of his 65th birthday on June 23, 2014*. Münster.
Gaunt, J. 2017. 'Nestor's cup and its reception'. In Slater, N. W., ed. 2017: 92–120.
Gemoll, W. 1892. *Die Realien bei Horaz*. Berlin.
Genette, G. 1987. *Seuils*. Paris. [tr. = (1997)]
Genette, G. 1997. *Paratexts. Thresholds of interpretation*. Translated by J. E. Lewin. Cambridge.
Gentili, B. 1984. *Poesia e pubblico nella Grecia antica da Omero al V secolo*. Rome and Bari. [tr. = (1988)]
Gentili, B. 1988. *Poetry and its public in ancient Greece. From Homer to the fifth century*. Translated by A. T. Cole. Baltimore, MD.
Gentili, B. 1990. 'Die pragmatischen Aspekte der archaischen griechischen Dichtung'. *A&A* 36: 1–17.

Bibliography

Gentili, B. and F. Perusino, eds. 1995. *Mousike. Metrica ritmica e musica greca in memoria di Giovanni Comotti*. Pisa and Rome.

Gentili, B. and R. Pretagostini, eds. 1988. *La musica in Grecia*. Rome and Bari.

Giangrande, G. 1967. '"Arte allusiva" and Alexandrian epic poetry'. *CQ* 17: 85–97.

Giangrande, G. 1968. 'Sympotic literature and epigram'. In Dihle, A., ed. 1968: 91–175.

Gigante, M. 1979. *Civiltà delle forme letterarie nell'antica Pompei*. Naples.

Gigante, M. 1994. 'Orazio tra Simonide e Posidippo'. *AAT Supplemento al* vol. 128: 55–71. [= (2006) 369–85]

Gigante, M. 2006. *Scritti sulla poesia greca e latina*. Naples.

Gilbert, P. 1946. 'Horace et l'Egypte aux sources du *carpe diem*'. *Latomus* 5: 61–74.

Gildenhard, I., U. Gotter, W. Havener, and L. Hodgson, eds. 2019. *Augustus and the destruction of history. The Politics of the past in early Imperial Rome*. Cambridge.

Giovini, M. 2005. '"Lo sento, l'inverno è fuggito". Pentadio e le simbologie primaverili dal mondo antico a Valafrido Strabone (con un postilla su Eliot)'. *FuturAntico* 2: 85–119.

Gitner, A. 2012. *Horace and the Greek language. Aspects of literary bilingualism*. Diss. Princeton University.

Gold, B. K. 1993. '*Mitte sectari, rosa quo locorum sera moretur*. Time and nature in Horace's *Odes*'. *CPh* 88: 16–31.

Goldhill, S. 1994. 'The naïve and knowing eye. Ekphrasis and the culture of viewing in the Hellenistic world'. In Goldhill, S. and R. Osborne, eds. 1994: 197–223.

Goldhill, S. 2017. 'Is this reperformance?' In Hunter, R. L. and A. Uhlig, eds. 2017: 283–301.

Goldhill, S. and R. Osborne, eds. 1994. *Art and text in ancient Greek culture*. Cambridge.

Goodyear, F. R. D. 1977. 'The *Copa*. A text and commentary'. *BICS* 24: 117–31.

Gordon, P. 2012. *The invention and gendering of Epicurus*. Ann Arbor, MI.

Gori, A. F. 1726–43. *Inscriptiones antiquae in Etruriae urbibus exstantes*. 3 vols. Florence.

Görler, W. 1995. '*Carpere, capere, rapere*. Lexikalisches und Philosophisches zum Lob der Gegenwart bei lateinischen Dichtern'. In Alföldy, G., T. Hölscher, R. Kettemann, and H. Petersmann, eds. 1995: 47–56.

Gow, A. S. F. and D. L. Page. 1965. *The Greek Anthology. Hellenistic epigrams*. 2 vols. Cambridge.

Gow, A. S. F. and D. L. Page. 1968. *The Greek Anthology. The Garland of Philip, and some contemporary epigrams*. 2 vols. Cambridge.

Gowers, E. 1993a. 'Horace, *Satires* 1.5. An inconsequential journey'. *PCPhS* 39: 48–66.

Gowers, E. 1993b. *The loaded table. Representations of food in Roman literature*. Oxford.

Bibliography

Gowers, E. 1994. 'Persius and the decoction of Nero'. In Elsner, J. and J. Masters, eds. 1994: 131–50. [= Plaza (2009) 173–98]
Gowers, E. 2005. 'Horace, *Satires* 1 and 2'. In Freudenburg, K., ed. 2005: 48–61.
Gowers, E. 2012. *Horace. Satires Book I.* Cambridge.
Grafton, A., G. W. Most, and S. Settis, eds. 2010. *The classical tradition.* Cambridge, MA, and London.
Gramps, A. 2021. *The fiction of occasion in Hellenistic and Roman poetry.* Berlin and Boston, MD.
Graverini, L. 2011–12. '"Of mice and poets". Callimaco e Virgilio in Orazio, *Sat.* II 6'. *Incontri di filologia classica* 11: 151–70.
Graziosi, B. 2009. 'Horace, Suetonius, and the lives of Greek poets'. In Houghton, L. B. T. and M. Wyke, eds. 2009: 140–60.
Grazzini, S. 2011–18. *Scholia in Iuuenalem recentiora.* 2 vols. Pisa.
Green, R. P. H. 1991. *The works of Ausonius.* Oxford.
Green, R. P. H. 1999. *Ausoni opera.* Oxford.
Grewing, F., ed. 1998. *Toto notus in orbe.* Stuttgart.
Griffin, J. 1985. *Latin poets and Roman life.* London.
Griffin, J. 1997. 'Cult and personality in Horace'. *JRS* 87: 54–69.
Griffith, M. 1975. 'Man and the leaves. A study of Mimnermos *fr.* 2'. *ClAnt* 8: 73–88.
Griffith, M. 2009. 'Greek lyric and the place of humans in the world'. In Budelmann, F., ed. 2009a: 72–94.
Grillo, L. and C. B. Krebs, eds. 2018. *The Cambridge companion to the writings of Julius Caesar.* Cambridge.
Grimal, P. 1941. 'Note à Pétrone, *Satiricon*, XXVI'. *RPh* 15: 19–20.
Grimal, P. 1964. 'Horace. De l'art de vivre à *l'Art poétique*'. *BAGB* 23: 436–47.
Grimal, P. 1968. *Essai sur l'Art poétique d'Horace.* Paris.
Grimal, P. 1978. *Le lyrisme à Rome.* Paris.
Grondona, M. 1980. *La religione e la superstizione nella Cena Trimalchionis di Petronio.* Brussels.
Groningen, B. A. van. 1960. *Pindare au banquet. Les fragments des scolies.* Leiden.
Grottanelli, C. 1995. 'Wine and death. East and west'. In Murray, O. and M. Tecuşan, eds. 1995: 62–89.
Guaglianone, A., ed. 1984. *Pentadio. Le sue elegie e i suoi epigrammi.* Padua.
Guichard, L. A. 2004. *Asclepíades de Samos. Epigramas y fragmentos.* Bern.
Guichard, L. A. 2017. 'From school to desacralisation, or how Palladas read Homer'. In Durbec, Y. and F. Trajber, eds. 2017: 157–70.
Gumbrecht, H. U. 1997. *In 1926. Living at the edge of time.* Cambridge, MA and London.
Gumbrecht, H. U. 2004. *Production of presence. What meaning cannot convey.* Stanford, CA.
Gumbrecht, H. U. 2006. 'Presence achieved in language (with special attention given to the presence of the past)'. *H&T* 45: 317–27.

255

Bibliography

Gumbrecht, H. U. 2011. *Stimmungen lesen*. Munich. [tr. = (2012)]
Gumbrecht, H. U. 2012. *Atmosphere, mood, Stimmung. On a hidden potential of literature*. Translated by E. Butler. Stanford, CA.
Gummere, R. M. 1917–25. *Seneca. Ad Lucilium Epistulae morales*. 3 vols. Cambridge, MA and London.
Günther, H.-C. 2010. *Die Ästhetik der augusteischen Dichtung. Eine Ästhetik des Verzichts. Überlegungen zum Spätwerk des Horaz*. Leiden.
Günther, H.-C., ed. 2013. *Brill's companion to Horace*. Leiden and Boston, MA.
Günther, H.-C., ed. 2015. *Virgilian studies. A miscellany dedicated to the memory of Mario Geymonat*. Nordhausen.
Gutzwiller, K. 1995. 'Cleopatra's ring'. *GRBS* 36: 383–98.
Gutzwiller, K. 1997. 'The poetics of editing in *Meleager's Garland*'. *TAPhA* 127: 169–200.
Gutzwiller, K. 1998. *Poetic garlands. Hellenistic epigrams in context*. Berkeley and Los Angeles, CA.
Gutzwiller, K. 2002. 'Art's echo. The tradition of Hellenistic ecphrastic epigram'. In Harder, M. A., R. F. Regtuit, and G. C. Wakker, eds. 2002: 85–112.
Gutzwiller, K., ed. 2005. *The new Posidippus. A Hellenistic poetry book*. Oxford.
Gutzwiller, K. 2010. 'Heroic epitaphs of the classical age. The Aristotelian Peplos and beyond'. In Baumbach, M., A. Petrovic, and I. Petrovic, eds. 2010: 219–49.
Habinek, T. N. 2005. *The world of Roman song. From ritualized speech to social order*. Baltimore, MD and London.
Hadot, P. 1981. *Exercices spirituels et philosophie antique*. Paris. [tr. = (1995)]
Hadot, P. 1995. *Philosophy as a way of life. Spiritual exercises from Socrates to Foucault*. Oxford.
Hagel, S. 2010. *Ancient Greek music. A new technical history*. Cambridge.
Hall, E. 1991. *Inventing the barbarian. Greek self-definition through tragedy*. Oxford.
Halliwell, S. 2008. *Greek laughter. A study of cultural psychology from Homer to early Christianity*. Cambridge.
Harder, M. A. 2012. *Callimachus. Aetia*. 2 vols. Oxford.
Harder, M. A., R. F. Regtuit, and G. C. Wakker, eds. 1993. *Callimachus*. Leuven.
Harder, M. A., R. F. Regtuit, and G. C. Wakker, eds. 1998. *Genre in Hellenistic poetry*. Leuven.
Harder, M. A., R. F. Regtuit, and G. C. Wakker, eds. 2002. *Hellenistic epigrams*. Leuven.
Hardie, P. R. 1993. '*Ut pictura poesis*? Horace and the visual arts'. In Rudd, N., ed. 1993: 120–39.
Hardie, P. R. 2005. 'Time in Lucretius and the Augustan poets. Freedom and innovation'. In Schwindt, J. P., ed. 2005a: 19–42. [= (2009) 41–64]
Hardie, P. R. 2009. *Lucretian receptions*. Cambridge.
Hardie, P. R. 2012. 'Virgil's Catullan plots'. In Du Quesnay, I. M. Le M. and A. J. Woodman, eds. 2012: 212–38.

Bibliography

Hardie, P. R. 2014. 'The *Ars Poetica* and the poetics of didactic'. In *New approaches to Horace's Ars poetica*, edited by A. Ferenczi and P. R. Hardie, *MD* 72: 43–54.
Hardie, P. R., ed. 2016. *Augustan poetry and the irrational*. Oxford.
Harrison, S. J. 1991. *Vergil. Aeneid 10*. Oxford.
Harrison, S. J., ed. 1995. *Homage to Horace. A bimillenary celebration*. Oxford.
Harrison, S. J., ed. 1999. *Oxford readings in the Roman novel*. Oxford.
Harrison, S. J. 2001. 'Simonides and Horace'. In Boedeker, D. and D. Sider, eds. 2001: 261–71.
Harrison, S. J. 2002. 'A. E. Housman's Latin elegy to Moses Jackson'. *TAPhA* 132: 209–13.
Harrison, S. J., ed. 2007a. *The Cambridge companion to Horace*. Cambridge.
Harrison, S. J. 2007b. 'Town and country'. In Harrison, S. J., ed. 2007a: 235–47.
Harrison, S. J. 2013. 'Author and speaker(s) in Horace's *Satires* 2'. In Marmodoro, A. and J. Hill, eds. 2013: 153–71.
Harrison, S. J. 2017. *Horace. Odes Book II*. Cambridge.
Harrison, S. J. and C. Stray, eds. 2012. *Expurgating the Classics. Editing out in Greek and Latin*. London.
Hartmann, A. 2013. '*Cui vetustas fidem faciat*. Inscriptions and other material relics of the past in Graeco-Roman antiquity'. In Liddel, P. P. and P. Low, eds. 2013: 33–54.
Haß, K. 2007. *Lucilius und der Beginn der Persönlichkeitsdichtung in Rom*. Stuttgart.
Haubold, J. 2013. 'Berossus'. In Whitmarsh, T. and S. Thomson, eds. 2013: 105–16.
Haug, W. and R. Warning, eds. 1989. *Das Fest*. Munich.
Hausrath, A. and H. Hunger. 1959. *Corpus fabularum Aesopicarum*. 2nd ed. Leipzig.
Hawkins, J. N. 2014. 'The barking cure. Horace's "anatomy of rage" in *Epodes* 1, 6, and 16'. *AJPh* 135: 57–85.
Heberdey, R. and A. Wilhelm. 1896. *Reisen in Kilikien*. Vienna.
Heilmann, W. 1998. 'Epigramme Martials über Leben und Tod'. In Grewing, F., ed. 1998: 205–19.
Heinze, R. 1918. 'Die lyrischen Verse des Horaz'. *Berichte über die Verhandlungen der Sächsischen Gesellschaft der Wissenschaften zu Leipzig, philologisch-historische Klasse* 70. [= (1960) 227–94]
Heinze, R. 1923. 'Die horazische Ode'. *Neue Jahrbücher* 51: 153–68. [= (1960) 172–89; tr. = (2009)]
Heinze, R. 1960. *Vom Geist des Römertums*. Edited by E. Burch. Stuttgart.
Heinze, R. 2009. 'The Horatian ode'. In Lowrie (2009b): 11–23.
Henderson, J. 1995. 'Horace, *Odes* 3.22, and the life of meaning'. *Ramus* 24: 103–51. [= (1999) 114–44]
Henderson, J. 1996. 'Pump up the volume. Juvenal, *Satires* 1.1–21'. *PCPhS* 41: 101–37. [= (1999) 249–73]

Bibliography

Henderson, J. 1999. *Writing down Rome. Satire, comedy and other offences in Latin poetry*. Oxford.
Henderson, J. 2002. 'Corny Copa, the motel muse'. In Spentzou, E. and D. P. Fowler, eds. 2002: 253–78.
Henderson, W. J. 1995. 'Mimnermus' images of youth and age'. *Akroterion* 40: 98–105.
Henderson, W. J. 2010. '"This is life". Transience and *carpe diem* in Palladas of Alexandria'. *Ekklesiastikos Pharos* 92: 243–63.
Henriksén, C., ed. 2019. *A companion to ancient epigram*. Hoboken, NJ.
Herington, C. J. 1985. *Poetry into drama. Early tragedy and the Greek poetic tradition*. Berkeley, CA.
Herzog, R. 1989. 'Fest, Terror und Tod in Petrons *Satyrica*'. In Haug, W. and R. Warning, eds. 1989: 120–50.
Heusch, H. 1951. 'Der Grabspruch des Sardanapal und die Entgegnung des Krates von Theben'. *RhM* 94: 250–6.
Heyne, C. G. 1826. *P. Vergilii Maronis opera*. London.
Highet, G. 1954. *Juvenal the satirist*. Oxford.
Hilgers, W. 1969. *Lateinische Gefäßnamen. Bezeichnungen, Funktion und Form römischer Gefäße nach den antiken Schriftquellen*. Düsseldorf.
Hill, G. B. and L. F. Powell, eds. 1934. *Boswell's Life of Johnson; together with Boswell's Journal of a tour to the Hebrides and Johnson's Diary of a journey into North Wales*. 6 vols. Vol. 2. Oxford.
Himmelmann-Wildschütz, N. 1973. 'Ein antikes Vorbild für Guercinos "Et in Arcadia ego"?' *Pantheon* 31: 229–36.
Himmelmann, N. 1980. *Über Hirten-Genre in der antiken Kunst*. Opladen.
Hinds, S. 1998. *Allusion and intertext. Dynamics of appropriation in Roman poetry*. Cambridge.
Hobden, F. 2013. *The symposion in ancient Greek society and thought*. Cambridge.
Hock, H. H. 1991. *Principles of historical linguistics*. 2nd ed. Berlin.
Högg, H. 1971. *Interpolationen bei Juvenal*. Diss. Freiburg.
Hollander, J. 1981. *The figure of echo. A mode of allusion in Milton and after*. Berkeley, CA.
Holliday, P. J., ed. 1993. *Narrative and event in ancient art*. Cambridge.
Hollis, A. S. 1972. 'Two notes on Callimachus'. *CR* 22: 5.
Holzberg, N. 1991. 'Die Fabel von Stadtmaus und Landmaus bei Phaedrus und Horaz'. *WJA* 17: 229–39.
Holzberg, N. 1998. 'Review of G.B. Conte, The hidden author'. *CJ* 94: 96–9.
Holzberg, N. 2009. *Horaz. Dichter und Werk*. Munich.
Hooley, D. M. 1997. *The knotted thong. Structures of mimesis in Persius*. Ann Arbor, MI.
Hopkins, D. 1993. 'Cowley's Horatian mice'. In Martindale, C. and D. Hopkins, eds. 1993: 103–26.
Hopkinson, N. 2020. *A Hellenistic anthology*. 2nd ed. Cambridge.

Bibliography

Horsfall, N. 1989a. '"The uses of literacy" and the *Cena Trimalchionis*: I'. *G&R* 36: 74–89. [= (2020) 230–44]
Horsfall, N. 1989b. '"The uses of literacy" and the *Cena Trimalchionis*: II'. *G&R* 36: 194–209. [= (2020) 244–57]
Horsfall, N. 2003. *Virgil. Aeneid 11. A commentary*. Leiden and Boston, MA.
Horsfall, N. 2020. *Fifty years at the Sibyl's heels. Selected papers on Virgil and Rome*. Edited by A. Crofts. Oxford.
Horster, M. and C. Reitz, eds. 2010. *Condensing texts – condensed texts*. Stuttgart.
Höschele, R. 2010. *Die blütenlesende Muse. Poetik und Textualität antiker Epigrammsammlungen*. Tübingen.
Höschele, R. 2014. '"Er fing an zu singen, und sang lauter Mägdchen". Johann Wolfgang Ludwig Gleim, the German Anacreon'. In Baumbach, M. and N. Dümmler, eds. 2014: 199–226.
Höschele, R. 2019. 'Greek epigram in Rome in the first century CE'. In Henriksén, C., ed. 2019: 475–90.
Hose, M. 2008. '"Der Leser schneide dem Lied Länge ab". Vom Umgang mit Poesie im Hellenismus'. *Hermes* 136: 293–307.
Houghton, L. B. T. 2009. 'Two letters to Horace. Petrarch and Andrew Lang'. In Houghton, L. B. T. and M. Wyke, eds. 2009: 161–81.
Houghton, L. B. T. and M. Wyke, eds. 2009. *Perceptions of Horace. A Roman poet and his readers*. Cambridge.
Housman, A. E. 1890. 'Horatiana III'. *Journal of Philology* 18: 1–35. [= (1972) i.136–61]
Housman, A. E. 1923. 'Horace, Epode XIII 3'. *CR* 37: 104. [= (1972) iii.1087]
Housman, A. E. 1931. *Iuuenalis Saturae*. 2nd ed. Cambridge.
Housman, A. E. 1972. *The classical papers of A. E. Housman*. Edited by J. Diggle and F. R. D. Goodyear. 3 vols. Cambridge.
Hubbard, T. K. 1994. 'Elemental psychology and the date of Semonides of Amorgos'. *AJPh* 115: 175–97.
Hubbard, T. K. 1996. '"New Simonides" or old Semonides? Second thoughts on POxy 3965, fr. 26'. In *The New Simonides*, edited by D. Boedeker and D. Sider, *Arethusa* 29.2: 255–62. [= Boedeker and Sider (2001) 226–31]
Hunter, R. L. 1996a. 'Callimachus swings (frr. 178 and 43 Pf.)'. *Ramus* 25: 17–26. [= (2008) i.278–89 = Fantuzzi and Hunter (2004) 76–83]
Hunter, R. L. 1996b. *Theocritus and the archaeology of Greek poetry*. Cambridge.
Hunter, R. L. 2008. *On coming after. Studies in post-classical Greek literature and its reception*. 2 vols. Berlin and New York.
Hunter, R. L. 2010. 'Language and interpretation in Greek epigram'. In Baumbach, M., A. Petrovic, and I. Petrovic, eds. 2010: 265–88. [= (2021) 131–55]
Hunter, R. L. 2014. *Hesiodic voices. Studies in the ancient reception of Hesiod's Works and days*. Cambridge.

Bibliography

Hunter, R. L. 2018. *The measure of Homer. The ancient reception of the Iliad and the Odyssey.* Cambridge.

Hunter, R. L. 2021. *The layers of the text. Collected papers on classical literature 2008–2021.* Edited by Antonios Rengakos and Evangelos Karakasis. Berlin.

Hunter, R. L. and S. P. Oakley, eds. 2015. *Latin literature and its transmission. Papers in honour of Michael Reeve.* Cambridge.

Hunter, R. L., A. Rengakos, and E. Sistakou, eds. 2014. *Hellenistic studies at a crossroads. Exploring texts, contexts and metatexts.* Berlin and Boston, MA.

Hunter, R. L. and A. Uhlig, eds. 2017. *Imagining reperformance in ancient culture. Studies in the traditions of drama and lyric.* Cambridge.

Hutchinson, G. O. 2008. *Talking books. Readings in Hellenistic and Roman books of poetry.* Oxford.

Hutchinson, G. O. 2013. *Greek to Latin. Frameworks and contexts for intertextuality.* Oxford.

Hutchinson, G. O. 2016. 'Hierarchy and symposiastic poetry'. In Cazzato, V., D. Obbink, and E. E. Prodi, eds. 2016: 247–70.

Hutchinson, G. O. 2018. 'What is a setting?' In Budelmann, F. and T. Phillips, eds. 2018: 115–32.

Huxley, H. H. 1970. '"Marked literary inferiority" in the poems of the "Satyricon"'. *CJ* 66: 69–70.

Hyman, W. B. 2019. *Impossible desire and the limits of knowledge in Renaissance poetry.* Oxford.

Immisch, O. 1932. *Horazens Epistel über die Dichtkunst.* Leipzig.

Indelli, G. and V. Tsouna-McKirahan. 1995. *[Philodemus]. [On choices and avoidances].* Naples.

Jackson, V. and Y. Prins, eds. 2014. *The lyric theory reader. A critical anthology.* Baltimore, MD.

Jacob, C. 2000. 'Athenaeus the librarian'. In Braund, P. and J. Wilkins, eds. 2000: 85–110.

Jacob, C. 2004. 'La citation comme performance dans les *Deipnosophists* d'Athénée'. In Darbo-Peschanski, C., ed. 2004: 147–74.

Jacobs, F. 1794–1814. *Anthologia Graeca siue Poetarum Graecorum lusus ex recensione Brunckii. Indices et commentarium adiecit Fridericus Iacobs. Animadversiones in epigrammata Anthologiae Graecae.* 13 vols. Leipzig.

Jacoby, C. 1875. 'Ktesias und Diodor. Eine Quellenuntersuchung von Diodor *B*. II, c. 1–34'. *RhM* 30: 555–615.

Jaeger, W. 1933–47. *Paideia. Die Formung des griechischen Menschens.* 3 vols. Berlin. [tr. = (1939–45)]

Jaeger, W. 1939–45. *Paideia. The ideals of Greek culture.* Translated by G. Highet. 3 vols. Oxford.

Jansen, L., ed. 2014. *The Roman paratext. Frame, texts, readers.* Cambridge.

Jauß, H. R. 1967. *Literaturgeschichte als Provokation der Literaturwissenschaft.* Konstanz.

Bibliography

Jensen, R. M. 2008. 'Dining with the dead. From the *mensa* to the altar in Christian late antiquity'. In Brink, L. and D. A. Green, eds. 2008: 107–43.

Johnson, T. S. 2002. 'Horace, *Carmina* 1.36.13. Should Damalis outdrink Bassus?' *Philologus* 146: 187–9.

Johnson, T. S. 2004. *A symposion of praise. Horace returns to lyric in Odes IV.* Madison, WI.

Johnson, W. A. and H. N. Parker, eds. 2009. *Ancient literacies. The culture of reading in Greece and Rome.* Oxford.

Johnson, W. R. 1982. *The idea of lyric. Lyric modes in ancient and modern poetry.* Berkeley, CA.

Kajanto, I. 1969. '*Balnea uina uenus*'. In Bibauw, J., ed. 1969: ii. 357–67.

Kannellou, M., I. Petrovic, and C. Carey, eds. 2019. *Greek epigram from the Hellenistic to the early Byzantine era.* Oxford.

Kantzios, I. 2018. 'Peleus' ὄλβος in the symposion. Alc. 42 V'. *Phoenix* 72: 1–18.

Kassel, R. and C. Austin, eds. 1983–2001. *Poetae comici Graeci.* 9 vols. Berlin and New York.

Keane, C. 2015. *Juvenal and the satiric emotions.* Oxford.

Kenney, E. J. 2014. *Lucretius. De rerum natura Book III.* 2nd ed. Cambridge.

Kenney, E. J. and W. V. Clausen, eds. 1982. *The Cambridge history of classical literature. Vol. II. Latin literature.* Cambridge.

Kießling, A. 1867. 'Horatianische Kleinigkeiten'. In *Gratulationsschrift der philosophischen Facultaet in Basel zu dem fünfzigjährigen Doctorjubilaeum ihres Seniors des Herrn Professor Fr. Dor. Gerlach*, 1–16. Basel.

Kießling, A. and R. Heinze. 1961a. *Q. Horatius Flaccus. Briefe.* 7th ed. Berlin.

Kießling, A. and R. Heinze. 1961b. *Q. Horatius Flaccus. Satiren.* 8th ed. Berlin.

Kießling, A. and R. Heinze. 1966. *Q. Horatius Flaccus. Oden und Epoden.* 12th ed. Dublin and Zurich.

Kilbansky, R. and H. J. Paton, eds. 1963. *Philosophy and history. Essays presented to Ernst Cassirer.* New York.

Kilpatrick, R. S. 1970. 'An interpretation of Horace, *Epodes* 13'. *CQ* 20: 135–41.

King, R. A. H., ed. 2015. *The good life and conceptions of life in early China and Graeco-Roman antiquity.* Berlin, Munich, and Boston, MA.

Kirstein, R. 2002. 'Companion pieces in the Hellenistic epigram'. In Harder, M. A., R. F. Regtuit, and G. C. Wakker, eds. 2002: 113–35.

Kißel, W. 1978. 'Petrons Kritik der Rhetorik (*Sat.* 1–5)'. *RhM* 12: 311–28.

Kißel, W. 1990. *Aules Persius Flaccus. Satiren.* Heidelberg.

Kleinlogel, A. 2019. *Scholia Graeca in Thucydidem. Scholia vetustiora et Lexicon Thucydideum Patmense.* Berlin and Boston, MA.

Klingner, F. 1938. '*Herculis ritu* 3,14'. In *Werke und Tage. Festschrift für Rudolf Alexander Schröder zum Geburtstage*, 74–82. Berlin. [= (1961) 395–405]

Klinger, F. 1940. 'Zur *Ars poetica*'. *Hermes* 75: 326–9. [= (1964) 405–9]

Klingner, F. 1959. *Q. Horatius Flaccus. Opera.* 3rd ed. Leipzig.

Klingner, F. 1961. *Römische Geisteswelt.* Munich.

261

Bibliography

Klingner, F. 1964. *Studien zur griechischen und römischen Literatur.* Edited by K. Bartels. Zurich.
Klingner, F. 1967. *Virgil. Bucolica Georgica Aeneis.* Zurich.
Knoche, U. 1950. *D Iunius Iuvenalis. Saturae.* Munich.
Knorr, O. 2004. *Verborgene Kunst. Argumentationsstruktur und Buchaufbau in den Satiren des Horaz.* Hildesheim, Zurich, and New York.
Knox, P. E. 1992. 'Love and horses in Virgil's *Georgics*'. *Eranos* 90: 43–53.
Knox, P. E. 2013. 'Language, style and meter in Horace'. In Günther, H.-C., ed. 2013: 527–46.
König, F. W. 1972. *Die Persika des Ktesias von Knidos.* Graz.
König, J. 2012. *Saints and symposiasts. The literature of food and the symposium in Greco-Roman and early Christian culture.* Cambridge.
König, J. and T. Whitmarsh, eds. 2007a. *Ordering knowledge in the Roman Empire.* Cambridge.
König, J. and T. Whitmarsh. 2007b. 'Ordering knowledge'. In König, J. and T. Whitmarsh, eds. 2007a: 3–39.
König, R. 1994. *C. Plinius Secundus d. Ä. Naturkunde. Buch XXXVII.* Munich.
Konstan, D. 2011. 'Excerpting as reading practice'. In Reydams-Schils, G., ed. 2011: 9–22.
Krasser, H. and E. A. Schmidt, eds. 1996. *Zeitgenosse Horaz. Der Dichter und seine Leser seit zwei Jahrtausenden.* Tübingen.
Krauß, H. 1957. *Die Vergil-Zitate in Senecas Briefen an Lucilius.* Diss. Hamburg.
Krömer, D., ed. 1995. *Wie die Blätter am Baum, so wechseln die Wörter. 100 Jahre Thesaurus Linguae Latinae.* Stuttgart and Leipzig.
Krznaric, R. 2017. *Carpe Diem regained. The vanishing art of seizing the day.* London.
Kühn, K. G. 1821–33. *Claudii Galeni opera omnia.* 20 vols. Leipzig.
Kurke, L. 1996. 'Pindar and the prostitutes, or reading ancient "pornography"'. *Arion* 4: 49–75.
Kurke, L. 2000. 'The strangeness of "song culture". Archaic Greek poetry'. In Taplin, O., ed. 2000: 58–87.
Kuttner, A. 2005. 'Cabinet fit for a queen'. In Gutzwiller, K., ed. 2005: 141–63.
La Penna, A. 1995. 'Il vino di Orazio'. In Murray, O. and M. Tecuşan, eds. 1995: 266–82.
Ladewig, T. 1870. *De Vergilio, verborum novatore.* Neustrelitz.
Lämmle, R. 2013. *Poetik des Satyrspiels.* Heidelberg.
Lampe, K. 2015. *The birth of hedonism. The cyrenaic philosophers and pleasure as a way of life.* Princeton, NJ and Oxford.
Landels, J. G. 2009. *Music in ancient Greece and Rome.* London and New York.
Landolfi, L. 1995. 'Metro e forma. Lettura di Hor. *c.* I, 11'. *AC* 64: 217–35.
Lanfranchi, G. B. 2003. 'Il "monumento di Sardanapalo" e la sua iscrizione'. In *Studi trentini di scienze storiche* 82: 79–86.
Lanfranchi, G. B. 2011. 'Gli ΑΣΣΥΡΙΑΚΆ di Ctesia e la documentazione assira'. In Wiesehöfer, J., R. Rollinger, and G. B. Lanfranchi, eds. 2011: 175–223.

Bibliography

Lanfranchi, G. B., M. Roaf, and R. Rollinger, eds. 2003. *Continuity of empires (?). Assyria, Media, Persia*. Padua.

Lange, W., J. P. Schwindt, and K. Westerwelle, eds. 2004. *Temporalität und Form. Konfigurationen ästhetischen und historischen Bewußtseins*. Heidelberg.

Lattimore, R. 1942. *Themes in Greek and Latin epitaphs*. Urbana, IL.

Leach, E. W. 1993. 'Horace's Sabine topography in lyric and hexameter verse'. *AJPh* 114: 271–302.

Lee, C. and N. Morley, eds. 2015. *A handbook to the reception of Thucydides*. Malden, MA, Oxford, and Chichester.

Lefèvre, E. 1993a. *Horaz. Dichter im augusteischen Rom*. Munich.

Lefèvre, E. 1993b. 'Waren horazische Gedichte zum "öffentlichen" Vortrag bestimmt?' In Vogt-Spira, G., ed. 1993: 143–57.

Leigh, M. 2017. 'Nero the performer'. In Littlewood, C., K. Freudenburg, and S. Bartsch, eds. 2017: 21–33.

Lejay, P. 1966. *Œuvres d'Horace. Satires*. Hildesheim. Original edition, 1911.

Lelièvre, F. J. 1958. 'Parody in Juvenal and T. S. Eliot'. *CPh* 53: 22–6.

Lemaire, N. E. 1824. *Poetae Latini minores (ex recensione Wernsdorfiana)*. Paris.

Lenfant, D. 2001. 'De Sardanapale à Élagabal. Les avatars d'une figure du pouvoir'. In Molin, M., ed. 2001: 45–55.

Lenfant, D. 2004. *Ctésias de Cnide. La Perse. L'Inde. Autres fragments*. Paris.

Leo, F. 1897. *Die plautinischen Cantica und die hellenistische Lyrik*. Berlin.

Leroy, M. 1948. 'Encore la "callida iunctura"'. *Latomus* 7: 193–5.

LeVen, P. A. 2013. 'Reading the octopus. Authorship, intertexts and a Hellenistic anecdote (Machon, *fr.* 9 Gow)'. *AJPh* 126: 23–35.

LeVen, P. A. 2014. *The many-headed muse. Tradition and innovation in late classical Greek lyric poetry*. Cambridge.

LeVen, P. A. 2018. 'Echo and the invention of the lyric listener'. In Budelmann, F. and T. Phillips, eds. 2018: 213–33.

LeVen, P. A. 2021. *Music and metamorphosis in Graeco-Roman thought*. Cambridge.

Levene, D. S. and D. P. Nelis, eds. 2002. *Clio and the poets. Augustan poetry and the traditions of ancient historiography*. Leiden, Boston, MA, and Cologne.

Liberman, G. 1999. *Alcée. Fragments*. 2 vols. Paris.

Liberman, G. 2016. 'Some thoughts on the symposiastic catena, Aisakos, and skolia'. In Cazzato, V., D. Obbink, and E. E. Prodi, eds. 2016: 42–62.

Liceti, F. 1653. *Hieroglyphica sive antiqua schemata gemmarum anularium*. Padua.

Liddel, P. P. and P. Low, eds. 2013. *Inscriptions and their uses in Greek and Latin literature*. Oxford.

Lieberg, G. 1965. 'Die Bedeutung des Festes bei Horaz'. In Flashar, H. and K. Gaiser, eds. 1965: 403–27.

Liebeschuetz, W. 1965. 'Beast and man in the Third Book of Virgil's *Georgics*'. *G&R* 12: 64–77.

Lier, B. 1904. 'Topica carminum sepulcralium Latinorum. Pars III'. *Philologus* 63: 54–65.

Bibliography

Lissarrague, F. 1987. *Un flot d'images. Une esthétique du banquet grec*. Paris. [tr. = (1990)]
Lissarrague, F. 1990. *The aesthetics of the Greek banquet. Images of wine and ritual*. Translated by A. Szegedy-Maszak. Princeton, NJ.
Littlewood, C., K. Freudenburg, and S. Bartsch, eds. 2017. *The Cambridge companion to the age of Nero*. Cambridge.
Lloyd-Jones, H. 1967. 'Review of B. Snell, Gesammelte Schriften'. *CR* 17: 214–17.
Lowrie, M. 1992. 'A sympotic Achilles. Horace *Epode* 13'. *AJPh* 113: 413–33.
Lowrie, M. 1997. *Horace's narrative odes*. Oxford.
Lowrie, M. 2002. 'Beyond performance envy. Horace and the modern in the *Epistle to Augustus*'. In Paschalis, M., ed. 2002: 141–71. [= (2009a) 235–50]
Lowrie, M. 2005. 'Inside out. In defense of form'. *TAPhA* 135: 35–48.
Lowrie, M. 2006. 'Review of T. N. Habinek, The world of Roman song. From ritualized speech to social order'. *BMCR* 2006.04.34.
Lowrie, M. 2009a. *Writing, performance, and authority in Augustan Rome*. Oxford.
Lowrie, M., ed. 2009b. *Horace. Odes and Epodes. Oxford readings in classical studies*. Oxford.
Lowrie, M. 2010. 'Performance'. In Barchiesi, A. and W. Scheidel, eds. 2010: 281–94.
Lynch, T. A. C. 2020. 'Rhythmics'. In Lynch, T. A. C. and E. Rocconi, eds. 2020: 275–95.
Lynch, T. A. C. and E. Rocconi, eds. 2020. *A companion to ancient Greek and Roman music*. Hoboken, NJ.
Lyne, R. O. A. M. 2005. 'Structure and allusion in Horace's Book of *Epodes*'. *JRS* 95: 1–19.
Lyons, S. 2007. *Horace's Odes and the mystery of do-re-mi*. Liverpool.
Lyons, S. 2010. *Music in the Odes of Horace*. Oxford.
Maas, E. 1895. *Orpheus. Untersuchungen zur griechischen, römischen, altchristlichen Jenseitsdichtung und Religion*. Munich.
Maaskant-Kleibrink, M. 1978. *Catalogue of the engraved gems in the royal cabinet in The Hague*. 2 vols. The Hague.
MacGinnis, J. D. A. 1988. 'Ctesias and the fall of Nineveh'. *ICS* 13: 37–42.
Maehler, H. 1989. *Pindarus. Fragmenta*. Leipzig.
Maehler, H. 2003. *Bacchylides*. 11th ed. Munich and Leipzig.
Magnelli, E. 1997. 'Review of G. Massimilla, Callimaco, *Aitia*. Libri primo e secundo'. *RFIC* 125: 445–59.
Maltby, R. 1991. *A lexicon of Latin etymologies*. Leeds.
Mandruzzato, E. 1985. *Orazio. Odi e Epodi*. Milan.
Mankin, D. 1995. *Horace. Epodes*. Cambridge.
Mann, W.-R. 2006. 'Learning how to die. Seneca's use of *Aeneid* 4.653 at *Epistulae morales* 12.9'. In Volk, K. and G. D. Williams, eds. 2006: 103–22.

Bibliography

Männlein-Robert, I. 2007. *Stimme, Schrift und Bild. Zum Verhältnis der Künste in der hellenistischen Dichtung*. Heidelberg.
Marquardt, J. and A. Mau. 1964. *Das Privatleben der Römer*. Darmstadt. Original edition, 1886.
Marmodoro, A. and J. Hill, eds. 2013. *The author's voice in classical and late antiquity*. Oxford.
Martha, C. 1867. *La poëme de Lucrèce*. Paris.
Martindale, C. and D. Hopkins, eds. 1993. *Horace made new*. Cambridge.
Marx, F. 1904. *C. Lucilii carminum reliquiae*. Leipzig.
Marx, F. 1906. 'De Sicili cantilena'. *RhM* 61: 145–8.
Marx, F. 1925. 'M. Agrippa und die zeitgenössische römische Dichtkunst'. *RhM* 74: 174–94.
Marzillo, P. 2010. *Der Kommentar des Proklos zu Hesiods 'Werken und Tagen'*. Tübingen.
Massimilla, G. 1996. *Aitia. Libri primo e secundo*. Pisa.
Mastrorosa, I. G. 2010. 'Collectables, antiques and sumptuary trends in ancient Roma. A look around the dining halls of the late Republic and early Empire'. In Gahtan, M. W. and D. Pegazzano, eds. 2010: 102–8.
Mathiesen, T. J. 1999. *Apollo's lyre. Greek music and music theory in antiquity and the Middle Ages*. Lincoln, NE and London.
Maurach, G. 1995. *Lateinische Dichtersprache*. Darmstadt.
Mayer, R. G. 1982. 'Neronian classicism'. *AJPh* 103: 305–18.
Mayer, R. G. 1994. *Horace. Epistles Book I*. Cambridge.
Mayer, R. G. 1999. 'Grecism'. In Mayer, R. G. and J. N. Adams, eds. 1999: 157–82.
Mayer, R. G. 2009. '*Vivere secundum Horatium*. Otto Vaenius' *Emblemata Horatiana*'. In Houghton, L. B. T. and M. Wyke, eds. 2009: 200–18.
Mayer, R. G. 2012. *Horace. Odes I*. Cambridge.
Mayer, R. G. and J. N. Adams, eds. 1999. *Aspects of the language of Latin poetry*. Oxford.
Mazzoli, G. 1970. *Seneca e la poesia*. Milan.
Mazzoli, G. 1991. 'Il giorno "lacerato" e il tempo "sfruttato"'. In *Studi di filologica classica in onore di G. Monaco*, 1025–1037. Palermo.
McCarthy, K. 2019. *I, the poet. First-person form in Horace, Catullus, and Propertius*. Ithaca, NY.
McGill, S. 2005. *Virgil recomposed. The mythological and secular centos in antiquity*. Oxford.
McKeown, J. C. 1987–. *Ovid. Amores. Text, prolegomena and commentary in four volumes*. 4 vols. Leeds.
McKinlay, A. P. 1946. 'The wine element in Horace'. *CJ* 42: 161–7.
McKinlay, A. P. 1947. 'The wine element in Horace (Part II)'. *CJ* 42: 229–35.
Meier, L. 2017. 'Sprechende Steine, Gesang und "professionelles" Wissen. Kulturhistorische Überlegungen zur Grabsäule des Seikilos (I. Tralleis 219)'. *Tyche* 32: 101–18.

Bibliography

Meineke, A. 1854. *Q. Horatius Flaccus*. Berlin.
Melo, W. D. C. de. 2019. *Varro. De lingua Latina*. 2 vols. Oxford.
Merkelbach, R. 1967. 'Kallimachos, *Aitia fr.* 178, 11–12'. *ZPE* 1: 96.
Merlan, P. 1949. 'Epicureanism and Horace'. *JHI* 10: 445–51.
Meyer, D. 1993. 'Die Einbeziehung des Lesers in den Epigrammen des Kallimachos'. In Harder, M. A., R. F. Regtuit, and G. C. Wakker, eds. 1993: 161–75.
Meyer, D. 2005. *Inszeniertes Lesevergnügen. Das inschriftliche Epigramm und seine Rezeption bei Kallimachos*. Stuttgart.
Meyer, D. 2007. 'The act of reading and the act of writing in Hellenistic epigram'. In Bing, P. and J. S. Bruss, eds. 2007a: 187–210.
Meyer, E. 1892–9. *Forschungen zur Alten Geschichte*. 2 vols. Halle a.d.S.
Micheli, M. E. 2016. '*Dactyliothecae Romanae*. Tra publica magnificentia e privata luxuria'. *RAL* 27: 73–113.
Miller, P. A. 1994. *Lyric texts and lyric consciousness. The birth of a genre from archaic Greece to Augustan Rome*. London.
Mindt, N. 2007. *Die meta-sympotischen Oden und Epoden des Horaz*. Göttingen.
Mindt, N. 2013. 'Griechische Autoren in den Epigrammen Martials'. *Millennium* 10: 501–16.
Mindt, N. 2017. 'Horace, Seneca, and Martial. "Sententious style" across genres'. In Stöckinger, M., K. Winter, and A. T. Zanker, eds. 2017a: 315–44.
Moles, J. 2007. 'Philosophy and ethics'. In Harrison, S. J., ed. 2007a: 165–80.
Molin, M., ed. 2001. *Images et représentations du pouvoir et de l'ordre social dans l'antiquité*. Paris.
Momigliano, A. 1950. 'Ancient history and the antiquarian'. *JWI* 13: 285–315.
Momigliano, A. 1982. 'The origins of universal history'. *ASNP* 12: 533–60. [= (1987) 31–57]
Momigliano, A. 1987. *On Pagans, Jews, and Christians*. Middletown, CT.
Monerie, J. 2015. 'De Šamaš-Šum-Ukin à Sardanapale. Histoire d'un mythe de la décadence'. *Topoi(Lyon)* 20: 167–85.
Morgan, H. 2017. 'Music, sexuality and stagecraft in the pseudo-Vergilian *Copa*'. *Greek & Roman Musical Studies* 5: 82–103.
Morgan, L. 2005. 'A yoke connecting baskets. *Odes* 3.14, Hercules, and Italian unity'. *CQ* 55: 190–203.
Morgan, L. 2010. *Musa pedestris. Metre and meaning in Roman verse*. Oxford.
Morpurgo, A. 1927. 'Οἵη περ φύλλων ... (*Iliade*, vi)'. *A&R* 8: 1–7.
Morrison, A. D. 2007. *The narrator in archaic Greek and Hellenistic poetry*. Cambridge.
Morson, G. S. 2011. *The words of others. From quotations to culture*. New Haven, CT and London.
Moss, A. 1996. *Printed commonplace-books and the structuring of Renaissance thought*. Oxford.
Mosshammer, A. A. 1979. *The Chronicle of Eusebius and Greek chronographic tradition*. Lewisburg, PA.

Bibliography

Most, G. W. 2010. 'Horace'. In Grafton, A., G. W. Most, and S. Settis, eds. 2010: 454–60.
Most, G. W. 2014. 'Τὸν Ἀνακρέοντα μίμου. Imitation and enactment in the Anacreontics'. In Baumbach, M. and N. Dümmler, eds. 2014: 145–59.
Moul, V., ed. 2017. *A guide to neo-Latin literature*. Cambridge.
Muecke, F. 1993. *Horace. Satires II*. Warminster.
Müller, K. 1995. *Petronii Arbitri Satyricon reliquiae*. 4th ed. Stuttgart.
Mundt, F. 2018. *Römische Klassik und griechische Lyrik. Transformationen der Archaik in augusteischer Zeit*. Munich.
Murray, O. 1983. 'The Greek symposion in history'. In Gabba, E., ed. 1983: 257–72. [= (2018) 11–23]
Murray, O. 1985. 'Symposium and genre in the poetry of Horace'. *JRS* 75: 39–50. [= (2018) 313–30 = Rudd, N., ed. 1993: 89–105]
Murray, O. 1988. 'Death and the symposion'. *AION(archeol)* 10: 239–57. [= (2018) 215–36]
Murray, O., ed. 1990. *Sympotica. A symposium on the symposion*. Oxford.
Murray, O. 2016. 'The symposium between east and west'. In Cazzato, V., D. Obbink, and E. E. Prodi, eds. 2016: 17–27. [= (2018) 77–88]
Murray, O. 2018. *The symposion. Drinking Greek style. Essays on Greek pleasure, 1983–2017*. Edited by V. Cazzato. Oxford.
Murray, O. and M. Tecuşan, eds. 1995. *In vino veritas*. London.
Mynors, R. A. B. 1969. *P. Vergili Maronis opera*. Oxford.
Mynors, R. A. B. 1990. *Virgil. Georgics*. Oxford.
Naeke, A. F. 1817. *Choerili Samii quae supersunt*. Leipzig.
Nagy, G. 1994–5. 'Genre and occasion'. *Mètis* 9–10:11–25.
Nardi, P., ed. 1966. *Arte e cultura nella civiltà contemporanea*. Florence.
Nesselrath, H.-G. 1990. *Die attische Mittlere Komödie*. Berlin and New York.
Newton, I. 1728. *The chronology of ancient kingdoms amended*. London.
Niese, B. 1880. *De Sardanapalli epitaphio disputatio*. Marburg.
Nietzsche, F. W. 1889. *Götzen-Dämmerung oder, Wie man mit dem Hammer philosophirt*. Leipzig. [tr. = (1911)]
Nietzsche, F. W. 1911. *Twilight of the idols*. Translated by A. M. Ludovici. New York.
Nisbet, R. G. M. 1962. 'Review of K. Müller, Petronii Arbitri *Satyricon*, and W.V. Clausen, A. Persi Flacci et D. Iuni Iuvenalis *Saturae*'. *JRS* 52: 227–38. [= (1995) 6–28]
Nisbet, R. G. M. 1966. 'Review of D. Bo, Lexicon Horatianum' *CR* 16: 325–7.
Nisbet, R. G. M. 1983. 'Some problems of text and interpretation in Horace *Odes* 3.14 (*Herculis ritu*)'. *Papers of the Liverpool Latin Seminar* 4: 105–9.
Nisbet, R. G. M. 1987. 'The oak and the axe. Symbolism in Seneca, *Hercules Oetaeus* 1618ff'. In Whitby, M., P. R. Hardie, and M. Whitby, eds. 1987: 243–51. [= (1995) 202–12]
Nisbet, R. G. M. 1995. *Collected papers on Latin literature*. Edited by S. J. Harrison. Oxford.

Bibliography

Nisbet, R. G. M. and M. Hubbard. 1970. *A commentary on Horace. Odes Book I.* Oxford.

Nisbet, R. G. M. and M. Hubbard. 1978. *A commentary on Horace. Odes Book II.* Oxford.

Nisbet, R. G. M. and N. Rudd. 2004. *A commentary on Horace. Odes Book III.* Oxford.

Nollé, J. 1985. 'Grabepigramme und Reliefdarstellungen aus Kleinasien'. *ZPE* 60: 117–36.

Norden, E. 1905. 'Die Composition und Litteraturgattung der horazischen *Epistula ad Pisones*'. *Hermes* 40: 481–528.

Norden, E. 1956. *Agnostos theos. Untersuchungen zur Formengschichte religiöser Rede.* Darmstadt. Original edition, 1913.

Nünlist, R. 1998. *Poetologische Bildersprache in der frühgriechischen Dichtung.* Stuttgart and Leipzig.

Oates, W. J. 1932. *The influence of Simonides of Ceos upon Horace.* Diss. Princeton University.

Obbink, D., ed. 1995. *Philodemus and poetry. Poetic theory and practice in Lucretius, Philodemus, and Horace.* Oxford.

Obbink, D. 2014. 'Two new poems by Sappho'. *ZPE* 189: 32–49.

Oberhelman, S. and D. Armstrong. 1995. 'Satire as poetry and the impossibility of metathesis in Horace's *Satires*'. In Obbink, D., ed. 1995: 233–54.

O'Gorman, E. 2002. 'Archaism and historicism in Horace's *Odes*'. In Levene, D. S. and D. P. Nelis, eds. 2002: 81–101.

O'Hara, J. J. 2017. *True names. Vergil and the Alexandrian tradition of etymological wordplay.* 2nd ed. Ann Arbor, MI.

Oliensis, E. 1998. *Horace and the rhetoric of authority.* Cambridge.

Olson, S. D. and A. Sens. 2000. *Archestratos of Gela. Greek culture and cuisine in the fourth century BCE.* Oxford.

Oppermann, H., ed. 1972. *Wege zu Horaz.* Darmstadt.

Orelli, J. K. von and J. G. Baiter. 1850. *Q. Horatius Flaccus.* 3rd ed. 2 vols. Zurich.

Otto, A. 1962. *Die Sprichwörter und sprichwörtlichen Redensarten der Römer.* Hildesheim. Original edition, 1890.

Page, D. L. 1978. *The Epigrams of Rufinus.* Cambridge.

Page, D. L. 1981. *Further Greek epigrams.* Cambridge.

Pailler, J.-M. 1981. 'Martial et l'espace urbain'. *Pallas* 28: 79–87.

Palmer, F. R. 1981. *Semantics.* 2nd ed. New York and Cambridge.

Pamir, H. and N. Sezgin. 2016. 'The sundial and convivium scene on the mosaic from the rescue excavation in a late antique house of Antioch'. *Adalya* 19: 251–80.

Panayotakis, C. 1995. *Theatrum mundi. Theatrical elements in the Satyrica of Petronius.* Leiden.

Panayotakis, C. 2009. 'Petronius and the Roman literary tradition'. In Prag, J. and I. D. Repath, eds. 2009: 48–64.

Bibliography

Panofsky, E. 1963. 'Et in Arcadia ego'. In Kilbansky, R. and H. J. Paton, eds. 1963: 225–54.
Paolucci, P. 2015a. 'Ovidio in Pentadio. Musicalità del *De adventu veris*'. *Paideia* 70: 121–36.
Paolucci, P. 2015b. 'Pentadio poeta ovidiano'. *AL. Rivista di studi di Antholiga Latina* 6: 57–103.
Paolucci, P. 2016. *Pentadius Ovidian poet. Music, myth and love*. Hildesheim.
Papadopoulou, I. N. 2005. 'Sardanapallus' gesture'. In Cairns, D., ed. 2005: 107–22.
Parker, H. N. 2009. 'Books and reading Latin poetry'. In Johnson, W. A. and H. N. Parker, eds. 2009: 186–229.
Parry, A. 1972. 'The idea of art in Virgil's *Georgics*'. *Arethusa* 5: 35–52.
Parsons, P. 2001. 'These fragments we have shored against our ruin'. In Boedeker, D. and D. Sider, eds. 2001: 55–64.
Paschalis, M. 1995. 'Names and death in Horace's *Odes*'. *CW* 88: 181–90.
Paschalis, M., ed. 2002. *Horace and Greek lyric poetry*. Rethymnon.
Pasquali, G. 1964. *Orazio lirico*. *Studi*. Florence. Original edition, 1920.
Paton, W. R. 1916–18. *The Greek Anthology*. 5 vols. London and New York.
Payne, M. 2006. 'On being vatic. Pindar, pragmatism, and historicism'. *AJPh* 127: 159–84.
Pearce, S. M. 1995. *On collecting. An investigation into collecting in the European tradition*. London.
Peek, W. 1979. 'Die Inschriften am Grabbau des Patron an der Via Latina'. *ZPE* 35: 255–63.
Pelliccia, H. N. 2002. 'The interpretation of *Iliad* 6.145–9 and the sympotic contribution to rhetoric'. *ColbQ* 38: 197–230.
Pelttari, A. 2016. 'Sidonius Apollinaris and Horace, *Ars poetica* 14–23'. *Philologus* 160: 322–36.
Peponi, A.-M. 2002. 'Fantasizing lyric. Horace, *Epistles* 1.19'. In Paschalis, M., ed. 2002: 19–45.
Perri, A. 2011. '*Il Giambo di Nino* di Fenice di Colofone e la tradizione dell'autoepitafio fittizio'. *ARF* 13: 59–68.
Petrovic, A. 2005. '"Kunstvolle Stimme der Steine sprich!"'. *A&A* 51: 30–42.
Petrovic, A. 2007. 'Inscribed epigram in pre-Hellenistic literary sources'. In Bing, P. and J. S. Bruss, eds. 2007a: 49–68.
Petrovic, A. 2019. 'The materiality of text. An introduction'. In Petrovic, A., I. Petrovic, and E. Thomas, eds. 2019: 1–25.
Petrovic, A., I. Petrovic, and E. Thomas, eds. 2019. *The materiality of text. Placement, perception, and presence of inscribed texts in classical antiquity*. Leiden and Boston, MA.
Pezzini, G. 2016. 'Comic lexicon. Searching for "submerged" Latin from Plautus to Erasmus'. In Adams, J. N. and N. Vincent, eds. 2016: 14–46.
Pezzini, G. 2018. 'Caesar the linguist. The debate about the Latin language'. In Grillo, L. and C. B. Krebs, eds. 2018: 173–92.

Bibliography

Pichois, C. 1975–6. *Baudelaire. Œuvres complètes*. 2 vols. Paris.
Pfeiffer, R. 1949–53. *Callimachus*. 2 vols. Oxford.
Phillips, T. 2014. 'A new Sapphic intertext in Horace'. *APF* 60: 283–9.
Phillips, T. 2016. *Pindar's library. Performance poetry and material texts*. Oxford.
Phillips, T. and A. D'Angour, eds. 2018. *Music, text, and culture in ancient Greece*. Oxford.
Pierson, W. 1860. 'Bacchus bei Horaz'. *RhM* 15: 39–61.
Plaza, M., ed. 2009. *Persius and Juvenal. Oxford readings in classical studies*. Oxford.
Pöhlmann, E. 1960. *Griechische Musikfragmente. Ein Weg zur altgriechischen Musik*. Nuremberg.
Pöhlmann, E. 1965. 'Marius Victorinus zum Odengesang bei Horaz'. *Philologus* 109: 134–40.
Pöhlmann, E. 1970. *Denkmäler altgriechischer Musik. Sammlung, Übertragung und Erläuterung aller Fragmente und Fälschungen*. Nuremberg.
Pöhlmann, E. 1988. 'Sulla preistoria della tradizione di testi musica e per il teatro'. In Gentili, B. and R. Pretagostini, eds. 1988: 132–44.
Pöhlmann, E. and M. L. West. 2001. *Documents of ancient Greek music*. Oxford.
Ponzio, A. 2001. 'Tradizione di un frammento alcaico (*frg.* 347 V.)'. In Cannatà Fera, M. and G. B. D'Alessio, eds. 2001: 63–9.
Porter, D. H. 1975. 'The recurrent motifs of Horace, *Carmina* IV'. *HSPh* 79: 189–228.
Porter, J. I. 2011. 'Sublime monuments and sublime ruins in ancient aesthetics'. In *Image, word and the antiquity of ruins*, edited by A. Kahane, *European Review of History* 18: 829–50.
Pöschl, V. 1970. *Horazische Lyrik*. Heidelberg.
Pöschl, V. 1992. 'Horazens Lebenskunst'. In Froning, H., T. Hölscher, and H. Mielsch, eds. 1992: 375–81.
Pöschl, V. 1994. 'Die Horazode "Aequam memento" (*C.* 2,3)'. *RhM* 137: 118–27.
Postgate, J. P. 1919. *Phaedri Fabulae Aesopiae*. Oxford.
Prag, J. and I. D. Repath, eds. 2009. *Petronius. A handbook*. Malden, MA, Oxford, and Chichester.
Prauscello, L. 2006. *Singing Alexandria. Music between practice and textual transmission*. Leiden.
Preger, T. 1891. *Inscriptiones Graecae metricae. Ex scriptoribus praeter Anthologiam collectae*. Leipzig.
Prentice, W. K. 1923. 'Callisthenes, the original historian of Alexander'. *TAPhA* 54: 74–85.
Pretagostini, R. 1997. 'La ripresa teocritea della poesia erotica arcaica e tardoarcaica (*Idd.* 29 e 30)'. *MD* 38: 9–24.
Price, S. 2012. 'Memory and ancient Greece'. In Dignas, B. and R. R. R. Smith, eds. 2012: 15–36.

Bibliography

Prinz, K. 1911. *Martial und die griechische Epigrammatik*. Vienna and Leipzig.
Prioux, É. 2007. *Regards alexandrins. Histoire et théorie des arts dans l'épigramme hellénistique*. Leuven, Paris, and Dudley.
Prioux, É. 2008. *Petits musées en vers. Épigramme et discours sur les collections antiques*. Paris.
Prioux, É. 2014. 'The jewels and the dolls. Late Hellenistic ecphrastic epigrams as metapoetic texts'. In Hunter, R. L., A. Rengakos, and E. Sistakou, eds. 2014: 185–212.
Prioux, É. 2015. 'Poetic depictions of ancient dactyliothecae'. In Gahtan, M. W. and D. Pegazzano, eds. 2015: 54–71.
Putnam, M. C. J. 1969. 'Horace *c.* 1.20'. *CJ* 64: 153–7.
Putnam, M. C. J. 1979. *Virgil's poem of the earth. Studies in the Georgics*. Princeton, NJ.
Putnam, M. C. J. 1986. *Artifices of eternity. Horace's Fourth Book of Odes*. Ithaca, NY and London.
Putnam, M. C. J. 1996a. 'Horace *C.* 3.14 and the designing of Augustus'. In Krasser, H. and E. A. Schmidt, eds. 1996: 442–64.
Putnam, M. C. J. 1996b. 'Horace's arboreal anniversary (*C.* 3.8)'. *Ramus* 25: 27–38.
Race, W. H. 1988. *Classical genres and English poetry*. London, New York, and Sydney.
Race, W. H. 1993. 'Carpe Diem'. In *The new Princeton encyclopedia of poetry and poetics*, edited by A. Preminger and T. V. F. Brogan, 171–2. Princeton, NJ.
Rackham, H., W. H. S. Jones, and D. E. Eichholz. 1938–63. *Pliny. Natural History*. 10 vols. Cambridge, MA, and London.
Raible, W. 1995. 'Arten des Kommentierens, Arten der Sinnbildung, Arten des Verstehens. Spielarten der generischen Intertextualität'. In Assmann, J. and B. Gladigo, eds. 1995: 51–73.
Ramage, E. S. 1973. *Urbanitas. Ancient sophistication and refinement*. Norman, OK.
Rawles, R. 2018. *Simonides the poet. Intertextuality and reception*. Cambridge.
Reade, J. E. 1995. 'Symposion in ancient Mesopotamia. Archaeological evidence'. In Murray, O. and M. Tecuşan, eds. 1995: 35–56.
Reeve, M. D. 1970. 'Seven notes'. *CR* 20: 135–6.
Reeve, M. D. 1983. 'Petronius'. In Reynolds, L. D., ed. 1983: 295–300.
Reeve, M. D. 1985. 'Review of D. R. Shackleton Bailey, *Anthologia Latina* 1.1'. *Phoenix* 39: 174–80.
Reid, J. S. 1925. *M. Tulli Ciceronis De finibus bonorum et malorum libri I, II*. Cambridge.
Reitzenstein, R. 1893. *Epigramm und Skolion. Ein Beitrag zur Geschichte der alexandrinischen Dichtung*. Gießen.
Reitzenstein, R. 1924. 'Eine neue Auffassung der horazischen Ode'. *Neue Jahrbücher für das klassische Altertum* 53: 232–41. [= (1963) 73–82]
Reitzenstein, R. 1963. *Aufsätze zu Horaz*. Darmstadt.

Bibliography

Reydams-Schils, G., ed. 2011. *Thinking through excerpts. Studies on Stobaeus*. Turnhout.
Reynolds, L. D., ed. 1983. *Texts and transmission. A survey of the Latin classics*. Oxford.
Ribbeck, O. 1865. *Der echte und der unechte Juvenal*. Berlin.
Ribbeck, O. 1869. *Des Q. Horatius Flaccus Episteln und Buch von der Dichtkunst*. Berlin.
Richter, A. 1970. 'La vertu du vin dans les *Odes* d'Horace'. *Bulletin de la faculté des lettres de Mulhouse* 3: 3–10.
Richter, W. 1957. *Vergil. Georgica*. Munich.
Riechel, D. C., ed. 1978. *Wege der Worte. Festschrift für Wolfgang Fleischhauer*. Cologne.
Riemschneider, M. 1955. '"Sei gegrüßt"'. *Altertum* 1: 131–6.
Riese, A. (1894–1906). *Anthologia Latina. Carmina in codicibus scripta*. 2nd ed. 2 vols. Leipzig.
Rigato, D. and M. Mongardi. 2016. '*Tituli picti* con datazione consolare su anfore vinarie italiche. Indagini preliminari'. In Buora, M. and S. Magnani, eds. 2016: 101–29.
Rimell, V. 2002. *Petronius and the anatomy of fiction*. Cambridge.
Rimell, V. 2007. 'Petronius' lessons in learning – the hard way'. In König, J. and T. Whitmarsh, eds. 2007a: 108–32.
Rimell, V. 2008. *Martial's Rome. Empire and the ideology of epigram*. Cambridge.
Rimell, V. 2020. 'Name means fame. Egos, authorship and uncertainty. [Review of K. McCarthy, *I, the poet. First-person form in Horace, Catullus, and Propertius*; T. Geue, *Author unknown. The power of anonymity in ancient Rome*]'. *Times Literary Supplement* 6107: 29.
Riposati, B. 1939. *M. Terenti Varronis De vita populi Romani*. Milan.
Robert, L. 1933. 'Inscriptions grecques inédites au Musée du Louvre'. *RA* 2: 121–47.
Robert, L. 1936. *Collection Froehner. Inscriptions grecques*. Paris.
Robert, L. 1937. *Études anatoliennes. Recherches sur les inscriptions grecques de l'Asie Mineure*. Paris.
Robert, L. 1943. 'Notes et discussions'. *RPh* 17: 170–201.
Robert, L. 1965. *Hellenica. Recueil d'épigraphie de numismatique et d'antiquités grecques*. Vol. 13. Paris.
Rodríguez Almeida, E. 2014. *Marziale e Roma. Un poeta e la sua città*. Rome.
Rohland, R. A. 2019. 'Highway to hell. *AP* 11.23 = Antipater of Thessalonica 38 G-P'. *Mnemosyne* 72: 459–70.
Roller, M. B. 2006. *Dining posture in ancient Rome. Bodies, values, and status*. Princeton, NJ.
Rollinger, R. 2017. 'Assyria in classical sources'. In Frahm, E., ed. 2017: 570–82.
Rood, T. 2015. 'The reception of Thucydides' Archaeology'. In Lee, C. and N. Morley, eds. 2015: 474–92.

Bibliography

Roos, A. G. 1967. *Flavii Arriani quae exstant omnia. I. Alexandri Anabasis.* G. Wirth ed. of 2nd ed. Leipzig.
Rosati, G. 1983. 'Trimalchione in scena'. *Maia*: 213–27. [tr. = (1999)]
Rosati, G. 1999. 'Trimalchio on stage'. In Harrison, S. J., ed. 1999: 85–104.
Rose, V. 1886. *Aristotelis qui ferebantur librorum fragmenta.* Leipzig.
Rosenmeyer, P. A. 1992. *The poetics of imitation. Anacreon and the Anacreontic tradition.* Cambridge.
Rosenmeyer, P. A. 2018. *The language of ruins. Greek and Latin inscriptions on the Memnon colossus.* New York and Oxford.
Rösler, W. 1980. *Dichter und Gruppe. Eine Untersuchung zu den Bedingungen und zur historischen Funktion früher griechischer Lyrik am Beispiel Alkaios.* Munich.
Rösler, W. 1983. 'Über Deixis und einige Aspekte mündlichen und schriftlichen Stils in antiker Lyrik'. *WJA* 9: 7–28.
Ross, W. D. 1955. *Aristotelis fragmenta selecta.* Oxford.
Rossi, L. E. 1983. 'Il simposio greco arcaico e classico come spettacolo a se stesso'. In *Spettacoli conviviali dall'antichità classica alle corti italiane del '400. Atti del VII convegno di studio, Viterbo, 27–30 maggio, 1982*, 41–50. Viterbo. [= (2020) ii.333–50]
Rossi, L. E. 1998. 'Orazio, un lirico greco senza musica'. *SemRom* 1: 163–81. [= (2020) i.383–402; tr. = (2009)]
Rossi, L. E. 2009. 'Horace, a Greek lyrist without music'. In M. Lowrie, ed. 2009b: 356–77.
Rossi, L. E. 2020. *Κηληθμῷ δ' ἔσχοντο. Scritti editi e inediti.* Edited by G. Colesanti and R. Nicolai. 3 vols. Berlin and Boston, MA.
Rostagni, A. 1930. *Arte poetica di Orazio.* Turin.
Rostovtzeff, M. I. 1957. *The social and economic history of the Roman Empire.* P. M. Frazer ed. of 2nd ed. Oxford.
Rothmaler, A. 1862. *De Horatio verborum inventore.* Berlin.
Rubensohn, M. 1888. *Crinagorae Mytilenaei Epigrammata.* Berlin.
Ruch, M. 1963. 'Horace et les fondements de la "iunctura" dans l'ordre de la création poétique (*AP*, 46–72)'. *REL* 41: 246–8.
Ruckdeschel, F. 1911. *Archaismen und Vulgarismen in der Sprache des Horaz.* Erlangen.
Rudd, N. 1960. 'Patterns in Horatian lyric'. *AJPh* 81: 373–92.
Rudd, N. 1966. *The Satires of Horace.* Cambridge.
Rudd, N. 1989. *Horace. Epistles Book II and Epistle to the Pisones (Ars Poetica).* Cambridge.
Rudd, N., ed. 1993. *Horace 2000. A celebration, essays for the bimillennium.* London.
Ruperti, G. A. 1818. *D. Iunii Iuvenalis Aquinatis Satirae XVI.* 2nd ed. Leipzig.
Rüpke, J. 1995a. 'Fasti. Quellen oder Produkte römischer Geschichtsschreibung?' *Klio* 77: 184–202.

Bibliography

Rüpke, J. 1995b. *Kalendar und Öffentlichkeit. Die Geschichte der Repräsentation und religiösen Qualifikation der Zeit in Rom*. Berlin and New York. [tr. = (2011)]

Rüpke, J. 1997. 'Geschichtsschreibung in Listenform. Beamtenlisten unter römischen Kalendern'. *Philologus* 141: 65–85.

Rüpke, J. 2011. *The Roman calendar from Numa to Constantine*. Translated by D. M. B. Richardson. Oxford.

Rüpke, J. 2017. 'Doubling religion in the Augustan age'. In Ben-Dov, J. and L. Doering, eds. 2017: 50–68.

Russell, A. 2019. 'The Augustan senate and the reconfiguration of time on the *Fasti Capitolini*'. In Gildenhard, I., U. Gotter, W. Havener, and L. Hodgson, eds. 2019: 157–86.

Russell, D. A. 1973. '*Ars poetica*'. In Costa, C. D. N., ed. 1973: 113–34.

Said, E. W. 1978. *Orientalism*. New York.

Saint-Denis, E. de. 1972. *Pline L'Ancien. Histoire Naturelle. Livre XXXVII*. Paris.

Santirocco, M. S. 1986. *Unity and design in Horace's Odes*. Chapel Hill, NC and London.

Sawicki, L., and D. Shalev, eds. 2002. *Donum grammaticum. Studies in Latin and Celtic linguistics in honour of Hannah Rosén*. Leuven.

Schäfer, E. 1970. 'Erasmus und Horaz'. *A&A* 16: 54–67.

Schetter, W. 1986. 'Zum anonymen *Libellus* epanaleptischer Monodisticha des Salmasianischen Corpus'. *Hermes* 114: 231–39.

Schmeling, G. 2011. *A commentary on the Satyrica of Petronius*. With the collaboration of Aldo Setaioli. Oxford.

Schmidt, E. A. 1980. 'Alter Wein zum Fest bei Horaz'. *A&A* 26: 18–32. [= (2002) 248–65]

Schmidt, E. A. 1994–5. '"Vornehm par excellence". Über Noblesse und Takt in Horazens Philippi-Gedichten (*Epode* 13 – *Ode* 2, 7 – *Ode* 3, 14)'. *WS* 107/108: 377–96. [= (2002) 266–85]

Schmidt, E. A. 1997. *Sabinum. Horaz und sein Landgut im Licenzatal*. Heidelberg.

Schmidt, E. A. 2002. *Zeit und Form. Dichtungen des Horaz*. Heidelberg.

Schmitt Pantel, P. 1992. *La cité au banquet. Histoire des repas publics dans les cités grecques*. Rome.

Schmitz, C. 2000. *Das Satirische in Juvenals Satiren*. Berlin and New York.

Schnapp, A. 1993. *La conquête du passé. Aux origines de l'archéologie*. Paris. [tr. = (1996)]

Schnapp, A. 1996. *The discovery of the past. The origins of archaeology*. Translated by I. Kinnes and G. Vardndell. London.

Schnurbusch, D. 2011. *Convivium. Form und Bedeutung aristokratischer Geselligkeit in der römischen Antike*. Stuttgart.

Schwienhorst-Schönberger, L. 1996. *'Nicht im Menschen gründet das Glück' (Koh 2,24). Kohelet im Spannungsfeld jüdischer Weisheit und hellenistischer Philosophie*. Freiburg.

Bibliography

Schwindt, J. P. 2004a. 'Blinde Mimesis. Über Ordo und Kontingenz in der literaturgeschichtlichen Traditionsbildung (Horaz und Petron)'. *Dictynna* 1.

Schwindt, J. P. 2004b. '*Dislocatio temporis*. Struktur und Ereignis in Horaz' Lyrik'. In Lange, W., J. P. Schwindt, and K. Westerwelle, eds. 2004: 77–93.

Schwindt, J. P., ed. 2005a. *La représentation du temps dans la poésie augustéenne. Zur Poetik der Zeit in augusteischer Dichtung.* Heidelberg.

Schwindt, J. P. 2005b. 'Zeiten und Räume in augusteischer Dichtung'. In Schwindt, J. P., ed. 2005a: 1–18.

Schwindt, J. P. 2016. 'The magic of counting. On the cantatoric status of poetry (Catullus 5 and 7; Horace *Odes* 1.11)'. In Hardie, P. R., ed. 2016: 117–33.

Scodel, R. 2010. 'Iambos and parody'. In Clauss, J. J. and M. Cuypers, eds. 2010: 251–66.

Scriverius, P. 1619. *M. Val. Martialis nova editio.* Leiden.

Seaford, R., J. Wilkins, and M. Wright, eds. 2017. *Selfhood and the soul. Essays on ancient thought and literature in honour of Christopher Gill.* Oxford.

Sedley, D. 1976. 'Epicurus and his professional rivals'. In Bollack, J. and A. Laks, eds. 1976: 119–59.

Sedley, D. 1998. *Lucretius and the transformation of Greek wisdom.* Cambridge.

Sedley, D. 2017. 'Epicurean versus Cyrenaic happiness'. In Seaford, R., J. Wilkins, and M. Wright, eds. 2017: 89–106.

Seel, O. 1972. *Verschlüsselte Gegenwart. Drei Interpretationen antiker Texte.* Stuttgart.

Seel, O. and E. Pöhlmann. 1959. 'Quantität und Wordakzent im horazischen Sapphiker'. *Philologus* 103: 237–80.

Sens, A. 2007. 'One thing leads back to another. Allusion and the invention of tradition in Hellenistic epigrams'. In Bing, P. and J. S. Bruss, eds. 2007a: 373–90.

Sens, A. 2011. *Asclepiades of Samos. Epigrams and fragments.* Oxford.

Sens, A. 2015. 'Hedylus (4 and 5 Gow-Page) and Callimachean poetics'. *Mnemosyne* 68: 40–52.

Sens, A. 2016. 'Party or perish. Death, wine, and closure in Hellenistic sympotic epigram'. In Cazzato, V., D. Obbink, and E. E. Prodi, eds. 2016: 230–46.

Sergueenkova, V. and F. Rojas. 2017. 'Asianics in relief. Making sense of Bronze and Iron Age monuments in classical Anatolia'. *CJ* 112: 140–78.

Setaioli, A. 1965. 'Esegesi virgiliana in Seneca'. *SIFC* 37: 133–56.

Setaioli, A. 2011. *Arbitri nugae. Petronius' short poems in the Satyrica.* Frankfurt.

Shackleton Bailey, D. R. 1982. *Anthologia Latina. Vol. 1, carmina in codicibus scripta. Fasc. I, libri Salmasiani aliorumque carmina.* Stuttgart.

Shackleton Bailey, D. R. 1990. *M. Valerii Martialis Epigrammata.* Stuttgart.

Shackleton Bailey, D. R. 2001. *Horatius. Opera.* 4th ed. Stuttgart.

Sider, D. 1996. 'As is the generation of leaves in Homer, Simonides, Horace, and Stobaios'. In *The New Simonides*, edited by D. Boedeker and D. Sider, *Arethusa* 29.2: 263–82. [= Boedeker and Sider (2001) 272–88]

Bibliography

Sider, D. 1997. *The Epigrams of Philodemos*. Oxford.
Sider, D., ed. 2017. *Hellenistic poetry. A selection*. Ann Arbor, MI.
Sider, D. 2020. *Simonides. Epigrams and elegies*. Oxford and New York.
Skutsch, O. 1985. *The Annals of Q. Ennius*. Oxford.
Slater, N. W. 1990. *Reading Petronius*. Baltimore, MD, and London.
Slater, N. W., ed. 2017. *Voice and voices in antiquity*. Leiden and Boston, MA.
Slater, W. J., ed. 1992. *Dining in a classical context*. Ann Arbor, MI.
Small, S. G. P. 1951. 'Marcus Argentarius. A poet of the *Greek Anthology*'. *YClS* 12: 65–145.
Smereka, J. 1935. 'De Horatianae vocabulorum copiae certa qadam lege'. In *Commentationes Horatianae*, 65–91. Kraków.
Smith, K. F. 1971. *The Elegies of Albius Tibullus*. Darmstadt. Original edition, 1913.
Smith, M. 2004. 'Elusive stones. Reading Posidippus' *Lithika* through technical writing on stones'. In Acosta-Hughes, B., E. Kosmetatou, and M. Baumbach, eds. 2004: 105–17.
Snell, B. 1946. *Die Entstehung des Geistes. Studien zur Entstehung des europäischen Denkens bei den Griechen*. Hamburg. [tr. = (1953)]
Snell, B. 1953. *The discovery of the mind. The Greek origins of European thought*. Translated by T. G. Rosenmeyer. Oxford.
Solomon, J. 1986. 'The Seikilos inscription. A theoretical analysis'. *AJPh* 107: 455–79.
Sontag, S. 1966. *Against interpretation and other essays*. New York.
Sourvinou-Inwood, C. 1995. *'Reading' Greek death. To the end of the classical period*. Oxford.
Spelman, H. L. 2018. *Pindar and the poetics of permanence*. Oxford.
Spentzou, E. and D. P. Fowler, eds. 2002. *Cultivating the muse. Struggles for power and inspiration in classical literature*. Oxford.
Squire, M. 2009. *Image and text in Graeco-Roman antiquity*. Cambridge.
Squire, M. 2014. 'Reading a view. Poem and picture in the *Greek Anthology*'. *Ramus* 39: 73–103.
Stein-Hölkeskamp, E. 2005. *Das römische Gastmahl*. Munich.
Stöckinger, M., K. Winter, and A. T. Zanker, eds. 2017a. *Horace and Seneca. Interactions, intertexts, interpretations*. Berlin and Boston, MA.
Stöckinger, M., K. Winter, and A. T. Zanker. 2017b. 'Introduction'. In Stöckinger, M., K. Winter, and A. T. Zanker, eds. 2017a: 1–23.
Stronk, J. P. 2010. *Ctesias' Persian history*. Vol. 1. Düsseldorf.
Stucchi, S. 2002. 'Esempi di sapienza oraziana nel *Satyricon*. Tra svilimento e rovesciamento'. In Castagna, L. and G. Vogt-Spira, eds. 2002: 213–22.
Sullivan, M. B. 2014. 'On Horace's pyramids (*C*. 3.30.1–2)'. *The Cambridge Classical Journal* 60: 100–108.
Suriano, M. J. 2017. 'Kingship and *carpe diem*, between Gilgamesh and Qoheleth'. *VT* 67: 285–306.

Bibliography

Svenbro, J. 1988. *Phrasikleia. Anthropologie de la lecture en Grèce ancienne.* Paris. [tr. = (1993)]

Svenbro, J. 1993. *Phrasikleia. An anthropology of reading in ancient Greece.* Translated by J. Lloyd. Ithaca, N,Y and London.

Syndikus, H. P. 1972–3. *Die Lyrik des Horaz. Eine Interpretation der Oden.* 2 vols. Darmstadt.

Tammaro, V. 2014. 'Un riesame di Alex. *fr.* 25 K.-A'. In Tulli, M., M. Magnani, and A. Nicolosi, eds. 2014: 55–66.

Taplin, O., ed. 2000. *Literature in the Greek and Roman worlds. A new perspective.* Oxford.

Tarán, S. L. 1979. *The art of variation in the Hellenistic epigram.* Leiden.

Tarrant, R. J. 1983. 'Horace'. In Reynolds, L. D., ed. 1983: 182–6.

Tarrant, R. J. 2012. *Virgil. Aeneid Book XII.* Cambridge.

Tarrant, R. J. 2015a. 'Virgil and Vergilius in Horace *Odes* 4.12'. In Günther, H.-C., ed. 2015: 429–52.

Tarrant, R. J. 2015b. 'A new critical edition of Horace'. In Hunter, R. L. and S. P. Oakley, eds. 2015: 291–321.

Tarrant, R. J. 2016. *Texts, editors, and readers. Methods and problems in Latin textual criticism.* Cambridge.

Taylor, B. 2020. *Lucretius and the language of nature.* Oxford.

Tchernia, A. 1986. *Le vin de l'Italie romaine.* Paris and Rome.

Tchernia, A. 1995. 'Le vin et l'honneur'. In Murray, O. and M. Tecuşan, eds. 1995: 297–303.

Tchernia, A. and J.-P. Brun. 1999. *Le vin romain antique.* Grenoble.

Thiel, H. van 1996. *Homeri Ilias.* Hildesheim.

Thomas, R. F. 1986. 'Virgil's *Georgics* and the art of reference'. *HSPh* 90: 171–98.

Thomas, R. F. 1987. 'Prose into poetry. Tradition and meaning in Virgil's *Georgics*'. *HSPh* 91: 229–60. [= Volk (2008) 142–72]

Thomas, R. F. 1988. *Virgil. Georgics.* 2 vols. Cambridge.

Thomas, R. F. 1998. 'Melodious tears. Sepulchral epigram and generic mobility'. In Harder, M. A., R. F. Regtuit, and C. C. Wakker, eds. 1998: 205–23.

Thomas, R. F. 2010. 'Grist to the mill. The literary uses of the quotidian in Horace *Satires* 1.5'. In Dickey, E. and A. Chahoud, eds. 2010: 255–65.

Thomas, R. F. 2011. *Horace. Odes Book IV and Carmen Saeculare.* Cambridge.

Thurmond, D. L. 2017. *From vines to wines in classical Rome. A handbook of viticulture and oenology in Rome and the Roman west.* Leiden and Boston, MA.

Tigay, J. 1993. 'On evaluating claims of literary borrowing'. In Cohen, M. E., D. C. Snell, and D. B. Weisberg, eds. 1993: 250–5.

Tischer, U. 2017. '*Nostra faciamus.* Quoting in Horace and Seneca'. In Stöckinger, M., K. Winter, and A. T. Zanker, eds. 2017a: 289–314.

Tolman, J. A. 1910. *A study of the sepulchral inscriptions in Buecheler's Carmina epigraphica Latina.* Chicago, IL.

Bibliography

Topper, K. 2012. *The imagery of the Athenian symposium*. New York and Cambridge.
Traina, A. 1973. 'Semantica del *carpe diem*'. *RFIC* 101: 5–21. [= (1975–98) i.227–51]
Traina, A. 1975–98. *Poeti latini (e neolatini). Note e saggi filologici*. 5 vols. Bologna.
Traina, A. 1985. 'Introduzione a Orazio lirico. La poesia della saggezza'. In Mandruzzato, E. 1985: 5–45. [= (1975–98) v.133–68]
Traina, A. 1991. 'Orazio e Aristippo. Le *Epistole* e l'arte di *convivere*'. *RFIC* 119: 285–305. [= (1975–98) iv.161–86; tr. = (2009)]
Traina, A. 1993. 'La linea e il punto (ancora sul *carpe diem*)'. *Paideia* 48: 100–103. [= (1975–98) iv.191–5]
Traina, A. 2009. 'Horace and Aristippus. The *Epistles* and the art of *couiuere*'. In Freudenburg, K., ed. 2009: 287–307.
Trédé-Boulmer, M. 2015. *Kairos. L'à-propos et l'occasion. Le mot et la notion, d'Homère à la fin du IVe siècle avant J.-C.* 2nd ed. Paris.
Trimble, G. 2018. 'Echoes and reflections in Catullus' long poems'. In Frangoulidis, S., S. J. Harrison, and T. D. Papanghelis, eds. 2018: 35–54.
Trumpf, J. 1973. 'Über das Trinken in der Poesie des Alkaios'. *ZPE* 12: 139–60.
Tsagalis, C. C. 2008. *Inscribing sorrow. Fourth-century Attic funerary epigrams*. Berlin.
Tueller, M. A. 2008. *Look who's talking. Innovations in voice and identity in Hellenistic epigram*. Leuven, Paris, and Dudley.
Tueller, M. A. 2010. 'The passer-by in archaic and classical epigram'. In Baumbach, M., A. Petrovic, and I. Petrovic, eds. 2010: 42–60.
Tsouna, V. 2009. 'Epicurean therapeutic strategies'. In Warren, J., ed. 2009: 249–65.
Tulli, M., M. Magnani, and A. Nicolosi, eds. 2014. Φιλία. *Dieci contributi per Gabriele Burzacchini*. Bologna.
Uhlfelder, M. L. 1963. 'The Romans on linguistic change'. *CJ* 59: 23–30.
Ullman, B. L. 1930. 'Petronius in the mediaeval florilegia'. *CPh* 25: 11–21.
Van Oyen, A. 2020. *The socio-economics of Roman storage. Agriculture, trade, and family*. Cambridge.
Venuti, R. and A. Boriani. 1736. *Collectanea antiquitatum Romanarum*. Rome.
Vérilhac, A.-M. 1978–82. Παῖδες ἄωροι. *Poésie funéraire*. 2 vols. Athens.
Veyne, P. 1967. '*Sapias, vina liques*'. *RPh* 41: 105–8.
Vogt-Spira, G., ed. 1993. *Beiträge zur mündlichen Kultur der Römer*. Tübingen.
Vogt-Spira, G. 2002. '*Ars pervertendi*. I *Satyrica* di Petronio e i limiti del rovesciamento'. In Castagna, L. and G. Vogt-Spira, eds. 2002: 193–212.
Vogt-Spira, G. 2017. 'Time in Horace and Seneca'. In Stöckinger, M., K. Winter, and A. T. Zanker, eds. 2017a: 185–210.
Voigt, E.-V. 1971. *Sappho et Alcaeus*. Amsterdam.
Volk, K. 2002. *The poetics of Latin didactic. Lucretius, Vergil, Ovid, Manilius*. Oxford.

Bibliography

Volk, K., ed. 2008. *Vergil's Georgics. Oxford Readings in classical studies*. Oxford.
Volk, K. and G. D. Williams, eds. 2006. *Seeing Seneca whole. Perspectives on philosophy, poetry, and politics*. Leiden and Boston, MA.
Vössing, K. 2004. *Mensa regia. Das Bankett beim hellenistischen König und beim römischen Kaiser*. Munich.
Vössing, K., ed. 2008. *Das römische Bankett im Spiegel der Altertumswissenschaften*. Stuttgart.
Vout, C. 2009. 'The *Satyricon* and Neronian culture'. In Prag, J. and I. D. Repath, eds. 2009: 101–13.
Vout, C. 2018. *Classical art. A life history from antiquity to the present*. Princeton, NJ.
Vredeveld, H. 1987. 'Two philological puzzles in Erasmus' *Poem on old age*'. *BiblH&R* 49: 597–604.
Vredeveld, H. 1993. *Collected works of Erasmus. Poems*. Vols. 85–6. Toronto, ON.
Wachter, R. 2004. 'Drinking inscriptions on Attic Little-Master Cups. A catalogue (AVI 3)'. *Kadmos* 42: 141–89.
Wakefield, G. 1789–95. *Silva critica, sive in auctores sacros profanosque commentarius philologus*. 5 vols. Cambridge.
Wallace-Hadrill, A. 1987. 'Time for Augustus. Ovid, Augustus and the *Fasti*'. In Whitby, M., P. R. Hardie, and M. Whitby, eds. 1987: 221–30.
Walsh, P. G. 1970. *The Roman novel*. Cambridge.
Waltz, A. 1881. *Des variations de la langue et de la métrique d'Horace dans ses différents ouvrages*. Paris.
Wankel, H. 1983. '"Alle Menschen müssen sterben". Variationen eines Topos der griechischen Literatur'. *Hermes* 111: 129–54.
Warmington, E. H. 1935–40. *Remains of old Latin*. 4 vols. Cambridge, MA and London.
Warmuth, G. 1992. *Autobiographische Tierbilder bei Horaz*. Hildesheim.
Warren, J., ed. 2009. *The Cambridge companion to Epicureanism*. Cambridge.
Waszink, J. H. 1964. 'De poëtische expressie in Horatius' lyrische gedichten'. *Forum der Letteren* 5: 1–22. [German tr. = (1972)]
Waszink, J. H. 1972. 'Der dichterische Ausdruck in den *Oden* des Horaz'. In Oppermann, H., ed. 1972: 271–301.
Waters, M. W. 2017. *Ctesias' Persica and its Near Eastern context*. Madison, WI.
Watson, L. C. 2003. *A commentary on Horace's Epodes*. Oxford.
Watson, L. C. and P. A. Watson. 2003. *Martial. Select epigrams*. Cambridge.
Watson, P. A. 1998. 'Ignorant Euctus. Wit and literary allusion in Martial 8.6'. *Mnemosyne* 51: 30–40.
Węcowski, M. 2014. *The rise of the Greek aristocratic banquet*. Oxford.
Weeber, W.-K. 1993. *Die Weinkultur der Römer*. Zurich.
Wehrli, F. 1967–9. *Die Schule des Aristoteles. Texte und Kommentar*. 2nd ed. 10 vols. Basel.
West, D. 1967. *Reading Horace*. Edinburgh.

Bibliography

West, D. 1973. 'Horace's poetic technique in the *Odes*'. In Costa, C. D. N., ed. 1973: 29–58.
West, D. 1974. 'Of mice and men'. In Woodman, A. J. and D. West, eds. 1974: 67–80.
West, D. 1995. *Horace Odes I. Carpe diem*. Oxford.
West, M. L. 1969. 'Near Eastern material in Hellenistic and Roman literature'. *HSPh* 73: 113–34.
West, M. L. 1978. *Hesiod. Works & days*. Oxford.
West, M. L. 1989–92. *Iambi et Elegi Graeci*. 2nd ed. 2 vols. Oxford.
West, M. L. 1990. 'The *Anacreontea*'. In Murray, O., ed. 1990: 272–6. [= (2011–3) ii.385–90]
West, M. L. 1992. *Ancient Greek music*. Oxford.
West, M. L. 1993. *Carmina Anacreontea*. 2nd ed. Stuttgart.
West, M. L. 1997. *The east face of Helicon. West Asiatic elements in Greek poetry and myth*. Oxford.
West, M. L. 2011–13. *Hellenica. Selected papers on Greek literature and thought*. 3 vols. Oxford
West, S. 1985. 'Herodotus' epigraphical interests'. *CQ* 35: 278–305.
Whitby, M., P. R. Hardie, and M. Whitby, eds. 1987. *Homo viator. Classical essays for John Bramble*. Bristol.
Whitehead, J. 1993. 'The *Cena Trimalchionis* and biographical narration in Roman middle class art'. In Holliday, P. J., ed. 1993: 299–325.
Whitmarsh, T. and S. Thomson, eds. 2013. *The romance between Greece and the East*. Cambridge.
Wieland, C. M. 1752. *Anti-Ovid, oder die Kunst zu lieben*. Amsterdam.
Wieland, C. M. 1776. *Sammlung poetischer Schriften*. Vol. 2. Karlsruhe.
Wieland, C. M. 1798. *Sämtliche Werke*. Supplemente Vol. 2. Leipzig.
Wieland, C. M. 1813. *Sämtliche Werke. Horazens Satyren*. Vol. 59. Vienna.
Wieland, C. M. 1816. *Horazens Briefe*. 3rd ed. Leipzig.
Wiesehöfer, J., R. Rollinger, and G. B. Lanfranchi, eds. 2011. *Ktesias' Welt. Ctesias' world*. Wiesbaden.
Wifstrand, A. 1926. *Studien zur griechischen Anthologie*. Lund.
Wilamowitz-Moellendorff, U. von. 1900. *Die Textgeschichte der griechischen Lyriker*. Berlin.
Wilamowitz-Moellendorff, U. von. 1913. *Sappho und Simonides. Untersuchungen über die griechischen Lyriker*. Berlin.
Wilamowitz-Moellendorff, U. von. 1924. *Hellenistische Dichtung in der Zeit des Kallimachos*. 2 vols. Berlin.
Wilkinson, L. P. 1959. 'The language of Virgil and Horace'. *CQ* 9: 181–92.
Wilkinson, L. P. 1974. 'A. E. Housman, scholar and poet'. *Housman Society Journal* 1: 32–46.
Will, E. L. 1982. 'Ambiguity in Horace *Odes* 1. 4'. *CPh* 77: 240–5.
Wille, G. 1977. *Einführung in das römische Musikleben*. Darmstadt.
Williams, C. A. 2004. *Martial. Epigrams Book Two*. Oxford.

Bibliography

Williams, G. D. 2003. *Seneca. De otio. De brevitate vitae*. Cambridge.
Willis, J. 1989. 'Juvenalis male auctus'. *Mnemosyne* 42: 441–68.
Willis, J. 1997. *D. Iunii Iuvenalis Saturae sedecim*. Stuttgart and Leipzig.
Wills, J. 1996. *Repetition in Latin poetry. Figures of allusion*. Oxford
Wiseman, T. P. 2015. *The Roman audience. Classical literature as social history*. Oxford.
Wöhrle, G. 1990. '"Eine sehr hübsche Mahn-Mumie..." Zur Rezeption eines herodoteischen Motivs'. *Hermes* 118: 292–301.
Wolkenhauer, A. 2011. *Sonne und Mond, Kalender und Uhr. Studien zur Darstellung und poetischen Reflexion der Zeitordnung in der römischen Literatur*. Berlin and New York.
Woodall, N. J. 1971. 'Trimalchio's limping pentameters'. *CJ* 66: 256–7.
Woodman, A. J. 1970. 'Horace, *Odes*, II, 3'. *AJPh* 91: 165–80.
Woodman, A. J. 1972. 'Horace's *Odes* "Diffugere niues" and "Soluitur acris hiems"'. *Latomus* 31: 752–78.
Woodman, A. J. and J. Powell, eds. 1992. *Author and audience in Latin literature*. Cambridge.
Woodman, A. J. and D. West, eds. 1974. *Quality and pleasure in Latin poetry*. Cambridge.
Wörrle, M. 1996–7. 'Die Inschriften am Grab des Apollonios am Asartaş von Yazir in Ostlykien'. *Lykia* 3: 24–37.
Wörrle, M. 1998. 'Leben und Sterben wie ein Fürst. Überlegungen zu den Inschriften eines neuen Dynastengrabes in Lykien'. *Chiron* 28: 77–86.
Yeh, W.-J. 2007. *Structures métriques des poésies de Pétrone. Pour quel art poétique?* Leuven, Paris, and Dudley.
Yona, S. 2018. *Epicurean ethics in Horace. The psychology of satire*. Oxford.
Ypsilanti, M. 2018. *The epigrams of Crinagoras of Mytilene. Introduction, text, commentary*. Oxford.
Ypsilanti, M. 2019. 'Critical notes on Greek epigrams'. *CPh* 114: 626–37.
Yunis, H. ed. 2002. *Written texts and the rise of literate culture in ancient Greece*. Cambridge.
Zahn, R. 1923. Κτῶ χρῶ. *Glasierter Tonbecher im Berliner Antiquarium*. Berlin.
Zangemeister, K. F. W. 1862. *De Horatii vocibus singularibus dissertatio*. Berlin.
Zanker, G. 2003. 'New light on the literary category of "ekphrastic epigram" in antiquity. The New Posidippus'. *ZPE* 149: 59–62.
Zanker, G. 2004. *Modes of viewing in Hellenistic poetry and art*. Madison, WI.
Zeitlin, F. 2013. 'Figure. Ekphrasis'. *G&R* 60: 17–31.
Ziolkowski, T. 2005. 'Uses and abuses of Horace. His reception since 1935 in Germany and Anglo-America'. *IJCT* 12: 183–215.
Zwierlein-Diehl, E. 2007. *Antike Gemmen und ihr Nachleben*. Berlin and New York.

GENERAL INDEX

Achilles, 10, 11, 80 n.40, 153, 156, 238
Actium, Battle of, 104
address, 23, 31, 34, 129–30, 194
   and Horace, 93 n.62
   and wayfarer in epigram, 17–19, 50
admonition (to enjoyment): see exhortation (to enjoyment)
Aeneas, 130, 196
aetiology
   and calendar, 84
Agricola, Rodolphus, 195 n.38
Alcaeus, 15, 116, 212–14, 232, 233
   and banquet, 13–14, 144–5, 155, 187–93, 212–14
   and performance, 26
   and transience, 19 n.72
Alexander the Great, 42–5, 54, 58 n.62, 158
Alexis, 68–71
allusion
   and echo, 232, 233 n.19, 236–8
   and epigram, 59–67, 73, 153–6
   and etymology, 156, 192, 231
   and excerpt, 183–226
   and *exemplum*, 211
   and *hapax legomenon*, 13 n.44, 130, 137, 153, 154
   and interpolation, 219–21
   and intertexual marker, 201 n.59
   and *locus communis*, 210, 216
   and lyric appropriation of Homeric material, 112–13
   and *oppositio in imitando*, 130
   and quotationality, 185
   and Vergil, 192
   as pluckable textual object, 219
   as quotation, 13, 113
   integrative, 210
   reflective, 210
   through editing, 154
Amyntas, pseudo-Bematist, 53–5

Anacreon, 14, 165, 183
Anacreontea, 14, 16, 172, 185
Anchiale, 42–5, 49, 54, 73
anthology, 186–7, 207–8, 209, 212–14, 221 n.133
Antiphilus, epigrammatist, 161 n.65
Antonia Minor, 161
Apollo, 112
   Palatine temple of, 165
Apollonides, epigrammatist, 150–5
archaeology (of literary predecessors)
   and *carpe diem*, 39
   and Sardanapallus, 52
   in Hellenistic literature, 15
archaism, 34, 119–25, 135
   and wine, 103–7
Archestratus of Gela, 23–4
   and Epicurus, 67
Archilochus, 12, 147–8
archive, 105
Argentarius, Marcus, epigrammatist, 155–6
argumentum a fortiori, 13, 61
Aristippus of Cyrene, 21–2, 56 n.56
Aristobulus of Cassandria, 42–5, 51
Aristophanes of Byzantium, 69
Aristotle, 41, 54 n.54, 55–6, 118
Arrian, 42–5, 51–2
Asclepiades of Samos, 16, 17, 56, 155–6, 166
   as lyric poet, 15
Ashurbanipal, 44 n.17
Athenaeus, 11, 41, 59–61, 68–9, 143, 153, 189, 212–14
Athens, 70
Auden, W.H., 112 n.14
Augustus, 73, 104, 161
   and banquet, 102
   and calendar, 84 n.23, 88, 90
   and Horace, 101–2

282

General Index

and poetic memory, 93–4
Ausonius, Decimus Magnus, 217 n.116, 218–19
Austin, J.L., 26

Bacchus, 84, 85, 97
banquet, 104, 141, 149–50, 159, 217
  and Alcaeus, 13, 144–5, 188–92, 212–14
  and Augustus, 102
  and command, 52 n.50, 79 n.10, 149–50, 212
  and cutting meat, 208–9
  and epigram, 27, 143–60, 167–72, 176–82
  and excerpting poetry, 205–14
  and fable, 198–205
  and Greek culture, 62
  and Homer, 112–13, 153, 156–7
  and Horace, 36, 76–107, 135–8
  and learning, 144, 153–6, 212–14
  and luxury, 168
  and music, 5–7
  and performance, 25–7, 129
  and popular Epicureansism, 20–1
  and popular song, 15 n.56
  and presence, 94–7, 144–5
  and Roman emperor, 142
  and Rome, 10 n.31
  and Sardanapallus, 46, 52–3
  and setting, 95–6
  and textuality, 149–55
  and the erotic, 10
  and Theognis, 12, 25–7
  and tomb, 176–82
  and warfare, 12
  as place for pleasure, 8–10
  as space for lyric, 18
  in classical period, 14 n.51
Barthes, Roland, 140, 144, 176
Batrachomyomachia, 202 n.66
bath (as pleasure), 10
Baudelaire, Charles, 225
Berossus, historian, 44 n.17
Bibulus, Marcus Calpurnius, 98–9
Boscoreale cups, 145–9
Brutus, Marcus Iunius, 104
Byron, Lord, 44 n.15, 77 n.4

Caesar, Gaius Julius, 86 n.31, 98–9, 161
  and *De Analogia*, 118 n.24

calendar, 136
  and aetiology, 84
  and annalistic historiography, 91
  and anniversary, 84–5
  and Augustus, 84 n.23, 88, 90
  and chronology, 57–9
  and consular date, 79, 86–102
  and cyclicality, 86
  and *Fasti Capitolini*, 90
  and political events, 97–9
  and presence, 94–7
  and reperformance, 84–5
  and Roman holiday, 84, 86, 95, 97
  and wine, 236
  and wine label, 89
  and wine storage, 90–1
callida iunctura, 119–25, 131–3, 202
Callimachus, 65, 69, 136–8, 154, 165
Callisthenes of Olynthus, 42
Carmina Burana, 224
carpe diem
  and cliché, 224–6
  and Epicurus, 20–1
  and luxury, 142
  and music, 1–6
  and sex, 172–6, 218–19
  expression of, 36–7, 131–3, 199, 209
  in "Eastern" culture, 39
  in first centuries BC and AD, 141–2
  survey of, 8–25
Cassius, Gaius Cassius Longinus, 80 n.14, 104
Catullus, Gaius Valerius, 127 n.56, 230, 236–8
  and *carpe diem*, 19
Cena Cypriani, 207 n.82
Chagall, Marc, 87 n.37
Charisius, grammarian, 103
Charles IV, Holy Roman Emperor, 187, 221
Choerilus of Iasus, 53–9, 66, 70, 73
Chrysippus of Soli, 65–7, 68, 69, 70
Cicero, Marcus Tullius, 55–6, 67, 69, 71, 80, 118, 171
Cleopatra, Cleopatra VII Philopator, 104
Clitarchus, historian, 42
coinage, of words, 103, 117, 124–5, 130
collecting (in ancient world), 143, 156–9, 160, 165–7

283

General Index

comedy, 68, 70, 212
   and *carpe diem*, 24
commonplace-book, 222
convivium: *see* banquet
Crates of Thebes, 63–5, 66, 68, 70
Crinagoras of Mytilene, 161–7
Ctesias of Cnidus, 46–7, 58
Culler, Jonathan, 31, 34, 125, 225, 234 n.23
Cynic philosophy: *see* Crates of Thebes, Diogenes the Cynic, Monimus of Syracuse
Cyrenaic philosophy: *see* Aristippus of Cyrene, Hegesias of Cyrene

Dante Alighieri, 114 n.17
deconstruction, 30–1
deixis, 144–5
   and epigram, 50
   and Horace, 95–6
   and lyric, 95–6
Delacroix, Eugène, 44 n.15
Dellius, Quintus, 94–6, 105
didactic poetry, 23–4, 183, 194
dining hall, 176–82
Diodorus Siculus, 44
Diogenes the Cynic, 64
Dionysius of Halicarnassus, 58 n.62
Domitian, 142
drinking party: *see* banquet
dum licet, 9 n.28, 193, 206
Dunbar, William, 238 n.29

echo, 227–38
ekphrasis, 142, 161–72, 180–2
elegy, 6, 7
   and *carpe diem*, 11–13, 24
   and epigram, 18
   in late antiquity, 20, 227–38
epic, 112–13
   and *carpe diem*, 10–11, 24
Epicurus, 41, 73, 147
   and Archestratus of Gela, 23 n.95, 67 n.98, 70
   and belly, 69–71
   and *carpe diem*, 20–1, 65–7, 69–71
   and comedy, 69–71
   and divination, 171
   and Horace, 21, 77 n.5
   and linguistic theory, 119
   and Sardanapallus, 65–7, 69–71
   misrepresentation of, 65–7, 69–71
epigram, 16–19, 38–75, 99, 140–82
   and allusion, 73
   and companion pieces, 63
   and deixis, 50
   and elegy, 18
   and *Ergänzungsspiel*, 49
   and gems, 160–76
   and performance, 27
   and reader-response theory, 48–9
   and riddles, 48–9
   and Rome, 177–80
   and tomb, 16–18, 176–82
   and variation, 59–67
   and wayfarer, 163
   definition of, 16
   Latin, 19–20
Erasmus of Rotterdam, 10 n.29, 223–4
   Adagia, 224
Eusebius of Caesarea, 58
exhortation (to enjoyment), 2 n.4, 3, 5, 8, 55, 71, 162
   and banquet, 99–100
   and choice of words, 129–30
   and death, 104, 159
   and inscription, 50, 59 n.69, 61
   and *kairos*, 81–2
   and performance, 71
   and presence, 53, 70, 129–30
   and present tense, 70
   and Sardanapallus epitaph, 52–3, 59 n.67
   plucking and seizing, 14, 81–2, 85–6, 99–100, 131–3, 193
   through object, 159
   types of, 8–10

Fermor, Patrick Leigh, 76–7
Fish, Stanley, 45, 53
flâneur, 178–9
Florilegium Gallicum, 209
Foucault, Michel, 39
Frost, Robert, 112 n.14

Galen of Pergamum, 91
Gellius, Aulus, 118, 123
gem, 160–76
   see also luxury
genre

General Index

and Horace's lyric, 19
lyric and satire, 198–205
relation of epic and lyric, 13, 112–13
relation of epigram and elegy, 18
Gracchus, Gaius Sempronius Gracchus, 97
Grecism, 119–25, 128–30, 131, 136–8
Guercino, 162
Gumbrecht, Hans Ulrich, 31–4, 125, 140, 234 n.23, 235–6
see also presence

Hannibal, 102
Hedylus of Samos, 154
Hegesias of Cyrene, 22
Hegesippus, chronicler, 70
here and now, 7, 25, 96
see also occasion, setting
Herrick, Robert, 11, 223
Hesiod, 187–93
hic et nunc: *see* here and now
Homer, 8, 10, 11 n.23, 41, 137, 153–5, 156–7
and banquet, 112–13, 153
and *carpe diem*, 11
and lyric, 13, 112–13
and Simonides, 113–16
and transience of nature, 11, 111–13, 221
in Petronius, 208–9
scholia of, 155–6
Horace, Quintus Horatius Flaccus, 11, 13, 15, 16, 19, 39, 76–139, 183, 184, 185, 198, 205, 206, 215, 222, 224, 232, 236
and Augustus, 101–2
and civil wars, 101, 104
and Epicurus, 21, 76, 77
and performance, 28–31
and poetic memory, 91–4, 102
and presence, 28–31, 78–82, 94–7, 124–5, 129–30, 139
and reperformance, 30, 84–5
and textuality, 28–9, 86, 93, 105–6, 116–17
in Renaissance, 221
Housman, A.E., 32–4, 121, 200 n.55

iam, 9 n.28, 230
iambus, 6, 7
Ida, Mount, 76–7

imperative (to enjoyment): *see* exhortation (to enjoyment)
interpolation, 215 n.102, 216
and allusion, 219–21
interpretative communities: *see* Fish, Stanley
Ion of Chios, 14, 52
Isidorus of Seville, 103 n.98, 203 n.70, 231 n.13

Johnson, Samuel, 195
Julian, epigrammatist, 16 n.59
Jullian, Philippe, 87
Juno Lucina, 84
Juvenal, 102, 131, 214–26

kairos, 81–2
katabasis, 130
Kreipe, Karl Heinrich, 76

leaves, fallen: *see* nature, transience of – and leaves
Leonidas of Tarentum, 17
linguistic theory
and atoms, 119
and presence, 116–17
in antiquity, 117–19
of Epicurus, 119
of Horace, 108–39
Lucilius, Gaius, 204
Lucretius, Titus Lucretius Carus, 119, 196, 206
and *carpe diem*, 20–1
Luke, the Evangelist, 66 n.86
Lupercalia, 85
luxury, 7 n.18, 8, 18, 145–9, 157–76
see also gem
Lycia, 61–3
lyric, 3, 6 n.17, 7, 11, 111
and banquet, 105
and choice of words, 116–17
and cliché, 224–6
and deixis, 95–6
and echo, 233
and epic, 12–13, 112–13
and Homer, 112–13
and Horace, 28–31
and hyperbole, 224–6
and poetic memory, 91–4, 105–6

285

General Index

lyric (cont.)
  and popular song, 15–16
  and presence, 25–35, 124–5
  and repetition, 116–17
  and satire, 198–205
  and setting, 25, 95–6
  and transience of nature, 112–13
  and wine, 105–6
  and word coinage, 124–5
  Hellenistic book editions of, 29
  in Rome, 116
  in the classical period, 14
  in the Hellenistic period, 15
  Latin, 19
  melic, 7, 11, 13–14
  origin of, 13, 39
  song culture of, 25–9
  theory of, 31

Macedonius, epigrammatist, 154
Machon, 57
Macrobius Ambrosius Theodosius, 143, 237 n.27
Maecenas, Gaius Cilnius, 80 n.40, 84, 85, 88, 90, 98 n.78, 124, 233
Marcellus, Marcus Claudius, 161, 165
Mark Antony, Marcus Antonius, 71–5, 98 n.79, 102 n.91, 104
Mars, 84
Martial, Marcus Valerius Martialis, 20, 88, 106, 156–7, 165, 177–80
Meineke's Law, 15 n.55, 29
Mimnermus, 11–12, 112, 115
Monimus of Syracuse, 64, 147
Montand, Yves, 112 n.14
motto
  and Anacreontea, 16
  and Horace, 19, 200 n.53
Musaeus of Athens, 112
music, 20, 35
  and banquet, 25–6, 138, 147–9, 208
  and echo, 227–38
  and Horace, 29
  see also notation (musical)

Nachleben (of *carpe diem*): *see* reception (of *carpe diem*)
Narcissus, 229, 233

nature (transience of), 13, 19, 32–4, 100, 123 n.41, 136, 231
  and choice of words, 109–17, 122
  and cyclical time, 110, 116, 125–31
  and flower of youth, 115, 132 n.74
  and fruits, 131–3
  and Homer, 12, 111–13
  and leaves, 11, 76, 109–17, 127–8, 130 n.68, 186, 221
  and lyric, 112–13
  and rose, 219 n.126
  and Simonides, 113–16
  and wine, 78, 105–6
neologism, 119–25, 135
Nero, 157–60, 207 n.81, 208 n.84
Newton, Isaac, 40
Nietzsche, Friedrich, 108
Nineveh, 54, 57–9, 60, 66
Niobe, 11 n.23
notation (musical), 1, 4–6, 29

occasio: *see kairos*
occasion, 30 n.126, 31, 32, 86, 97, 226
  see also here and now, setting
octopus, 57
Odeon, 69 n.93
Odysseus, 10, 12, 153
Opimius, Lucius, 97, 98
  see also wine – and Opimian
orientalism, 47
Ovid, Publius Ovidius Naso, 10, 84, 85, 229
Ozymandias, 44

Paetus, Lucius Autronius, 89
Palladas, epigrammatist, 11 n.33, 16 n.59, 17
pastoral poetry
  and *carpe diem*, 24
Pentadius, elegiac poet, 227–38
performance, 3–7, 25–35, 73, 129, 159, 198, 235–6
  and *Anacreontea*, 16
  and choice of words, 135
  and Horace, 28–31
  and music, 20
  and Nero, 158
  and reperformance, 26–7, 30, 129–30, 189, 233, 234 n.24
  and speech act, 26–7

286

General Index

and theatre, 71, 198
in classical period, 14 n.51
Pergamum, 69
Persius, Aulus Persius Flaccus, 201, 217–18
Petrarch, Francesco Petrarca, 221–3
Petronius, 108, 142, 159, 180–2, 205–14
Philaenis of Samos, 67
Philippi, Battle of, 80 n.40, 104
Philodemus of Gadara, 20, 119, 189 n.20
Philomela, 229
Philoxenus of Cythera, 57
Picasso, Pablo, 87 n.37
Pindar, 14 n.50, 28 n.113, 47 n.26, 106
  n.109, 132 n.74, 225 n.144
Plancus, Lucius Munatius, 102, 104
Plautus, Titus Maccius, 117
Pliny the Elder, Gaius Plinius Secundus, 157–60
Plutarch, 153
Polemon II, king of Pontus, 167–72
Poliziano, Angelo, 223
Polybius, historian, 102
Pompeii, 142 n.7, 168, 180
Pompey, Gaius Pompeius Magnus, 102 n.91
  theatre of, 158
Porphyrio, Pomponius, 94, 133 n.75, 136
  n.89, 201 n.57, 202 n.63, 222 n.137
Posidippus of Pella, 160, 175 n.100
presence, 4, 7, 25–35, 73, 144–5, 150, 153, 235–6
  and banquet, 94–7
  and calendar, 94–7
  and choice of words, 108, 116–17, 129–30, 135, 139
  and comparative literature, 31
  and echo, 233–4
  and exhortation (to enjoyment), 53
  and Horace, 28–31, 76–7, 116–17, 124–5, 129–30, 139
  and lyric, 124–5
  and materiality, 141
  and present tense, 55–9, 61–2
  and repetition, 77
  and sex, 176
  and song, 234
  and sound, 230, 236–8
  and textuality, 116–17
  and wine, 78–82, 141

and wine storage, 94–7
and word coinage, 124–5
see also Gumbrecht, Hans Ulrich
prescription (to enjoyment): see exhortation (to enjoyment)

Quintilian, Marcus Fabius Quintilianus, 108, 202
Quintus of Smyrna, 112 n.14

Rabirius, Gaius, 108–12, 71–5
Raleigh, Walter, 19
reader-response theory
  and epigram, 48–9
reception (of *carpe diem*), 7 n.18, 7 n.20, 10 n.29, 17 n.63, 221–4
Renaissance, 7 n.18, 10 n.19, 17 n.63, 221–4
Richards, Keith, 112 n.14
ritual, 25–31, 84–5, 86
Rome
  cityscape of, 177–80
Ronsard, Pierre de, 17 n.63, 223
Rothschild, Baron Philippe de, 87
Rufinus, epigrammatist, 16 n.59, 219

Sappho, 14 n.50, 28
Sardanapallus
  and Dionysus statue, 74
  as legendary figure, 44–5
  as role model, 59–61, 74
  death of, 46–7
  in fifth-century sources, 45–6
Sardanapallus epitaph
  and banquet, 52–3
  and comedy, 68–71
  and Greek lyric, 52–3
  and Mark Antony, 71–5
  as *interpretatio Graeca*, 42–5
  in prose, 42–5, 47–53
  in Rome, 20, 71–5
  in verse, 41–2, 53–9
  reception of, 59–67, 68–75
satire, 7, 198–226
Scaliger, Julius Caesar, 109, 118
Seikilos, 1–8, 15, 35, 148 n.25
semiotics: *see* Barthes, Roland
Seneca, Lucius Annaeus, 21, 22–3, 195–6, 197–8, 221
  and Horace, 23

287

General Index

Sennacherib, 45, 49
Sestius, Lucius, 93
setting, 18, 25, 78, 95–6
  see also here and now, occasion
sex, 172–6, 218–19
  and banquet, 10, 99–100
  and cows, 194–8
  and Sardanapallus, 51, 56
  denial of, 8, 17, 166, 218–19
  teaching of, 10
Shelley, Percey Bysshe, 44
Simon and Garfunkel, 112 n.14
Simonides of Ceos, 13, 112, 113–16, 128–30
skeleton, 18, 21, 38 n.3, 141, 145–9, 159, 161–72
Social War, 102
Soracte, Mount, 76–7, 116
Sotion of Alexandria, 69
Spartacus, 102
Speichergedächtnis: *see* wine storage – and storage memory
Stimmung, 34 n.141
  see also Gumbrecht, Hans Ulrich
Stobaeus, Joannes, 187, 207–8
storage memory: *see* wine storage – and storage memory
Strato of Lampsacus, 16
Suetonius, Gaius Suetonius Tranquillus, 99
Swift, Jonathan, 97
symposium: *see* banquet

Take That, 2 n.4
Terence, Publius Terentius Afer, 117
textuality, 4, 7, 25–35, 165, 235–6
  and Alexandrian book editions, 16 n.59
  and echo, 233–4
  and epigram, 65, 144, 149–55
  and Horace, 86, 93, 105–6
  and inscription, 19
  and poetic memory, 105–6
  and wine labels, 93
Thaliarchus, 77
Theognis of Megara
  and *carpe diem*, 12
  and Homer, 12
  and performance, 26–7
Thucydides, 38–9
Tiberius, 98 n.79

Tibullus, Albius, 193
tomb, 149–50, 176–82
  and epigram, 16–18, 176–82
  of Apollonius (Lycian dynast), 61–3
  of Augustus, 177–80
  of Bacchidas, 59–61
  of Cornelius Vibrius Saturnius, 180
  of Sardanapallus, 42–5, 47–53, 59
  of Trimalchio, 159, 180–2
Torquatus, Lucius Manlius, 81
Totenmahl, 62, 180
tragedy
  and *carpe diem*, 24
translatio imperii, 58 n.62
triclinium: *see* dining hall
Trimalchio, 10, 142, 156, 159, 180–2, 205–14
Tullus, Lucius Volcatius, 86, 88, 89

Ungaretti, Giuseppe, 112 n.14
urbanitas, 200, 201, 208, 217, 225

Vaenius, Otto, 222 n.136
Varro, Marcus Terentius, 118, 191
Vergil, Publius Vergilius Maro, 130–1, 187–98, 221

Waits, Tom, 112 n.14
Warhol, Andy, 87 n.37
Wieland, Christoph Martin, 186, 199
wine
  and archaism, 103–7
  and calendar, 236
  and choice of words, 133–5
  and consular date, 86–8
  and Horace, 78–107, 210
  and lyric, 105–6
  and nature (transience of), 78
  and Opimian, 88 n.40, 90 n.50, 97–8, 106, 205, 209–10
  and optimal maturation time, 80–1
  and poetic memory, 102, 105–6
  and presence, 141
  and reperformance, 84–5
  and seasons, 105–6
  appelation
    Alban, 93
    Caecuban, 91
    Falernian, 94, 179, 212

288

General Index

Fundi, 89, 106
Sabine, 91
as remedy against worries, 85 n.26
being unmixed, 13 n.44, 136–8, 153–5, 156–7
vessel
  amphora, 88, 89–90, 93 n.62, 97, 99, 159
  Amystis cup, 136, 138
  cadus, 105
  cup, 143–60
  cup of Nestor, 157
  cups from Boscoreale: *see* Boscoreale cups
  diota, 78
  dolium, 87
  mixing bowl, 153, 157 n.52
  skyphus, 157 n.52
wine label, 87, 88–95, 104, 209
  and calendar, 89
  and Château Mouton Rothschild, 87
  and Maecenas, 98 n.78
  and wine storage, 94
  in epigraphic evidence, 79
  in literature, 79
wine storage
  access to, 94–5
  and apotheca, 89, 97
  and archaism, 103–7
  and calendar, 90–1
  and *condo*, 91–3
  and *diffundo*, 93
  and fume, 90
  and poetic memory, 91–4, 105
  and presence, 94–7
  and seasons, 105–6
  and spatial visualisation of time, 90–1, 94–5
  and storage memory, 105
  and war, 102
Winnie-the-Pooh, 51 n.46
word choice
  and cyclical time, 116, 117–31
  and Lucretius, 119
  and lyric, 116–17
  and performance, 135
  and presence, 108, 116–17, 135, 139
  and transience of nature, 109–17
  and wine, 133–5
worry (about future, death), 9, 88
  and Horace, 88
  and wine, 85

Young, Neil, 1

Zonas, epigrammatist, 149–50

INDEX LOCORUM

Achaeus
  Omphale TrGF 33, 152 n.39
Aeschylus
  Persians
    840, 24, 47 n.28
Aesop
  314 Hausrath and Hunger, 204
Alcaeus
  fr. 38a, 13, 52 n.49
  fr. 42, 13 n.45
  fr. 286, 232
  fr. 335, 10, 41–2, 53–9, 213
  fr. 335.4, 13 n.45
  fr. 338, 10, 65–7, 79 n.11
  fr. 346, 79 n.10, 156 n.50
  fr. 346.1, 13 n.45
  fr. 347, 24, 187–93
  fr. 352, 189, 220 n.131
  fr. 367, 232
  fr. 401a, 52
  fr. 401a and b, 144–5
[Alexis]
  fr. 25, 68–71
Amipsias
  fr. 21, 5 n.12, 138
Amphis
  fr. 8, 4 n.9, 175
  fr. 8.1, 52 n.48
Amyntas
  FGrHist 122 F 2, 53–5
Anacreon
  fr. 356, 14 n.49
  fr. 356a, 14 n.48
  fr. 395, 14 n.48
Anacreontea
  8, 16
  18.1–4, 189 n.22
  45.5, 175 n.99
  60.32–6, 189 n.22
Anaxandrides
  fr. 33, 150 n.29
Antipater of Thessalonica
  20 *GP*, 140
  38 *GP*, 16 n.59, 201
  38.1–2 *GP*, 171
Antiphanes, comic poet
  fr. 85, 152 n.37
Antiphanes, epigrammatist
  7 *GP*, 218 n.119
AP
  5.12, 10
  5.21, 219
  5.79, 201
  5.85, 17, 166
  5.85.4, 150 n.31
  5.118.2, 151 n.34
  6.161, 161
  6.244, 161
  7.217, 56
  7.271.3–4, 60 n.70
  7.326, 63–5
  7.452, 16–17
  7.472, 165 n.73
  9.50.1, 148 n.24
  9.229, 152
  9.239, 161
  9.412, 20 n.83
  9.439, 161–7
  9.545, 161
  10.47, 11 n.33
  10.100, 218 n.119
  10.105.2, 113 n.15
  11.20, 140
  11.23, 16 n.59, 201
  11.23.1–2, 171
  11.25, 150–5
  11.26.1, 151 n.34
  11.28, 155–6
  11.30, 218 n.119
  11.34.7, 189 n.20

Index Locorum

11.38, 167–72
11.43, 149–50
11.56.6, 62 n.72
11.59, 154
12.49, 154
12.50, 155–6
APl
  89.4, 171 n.90
  275, 81 n.19
Apollodorus
  FGrHist 244 F 303, 42 n.11, 46 n.22, 51 n.45
Apollonides
  27 *GP*, 150–5
Archestratus of Gela
  fr. 25 Olson and Sens, 23
  fr. 59.2–3 Olson and Sens, 81 n.17
  fr. 60 Olson and Sens, 23, 67
  test. 6 Olson and Sens, 67
Archilochus
  fr. 19, 16
  fr. 2, 147
Argentarius
  11.2 *GP*, 151 n.34
  24 *GP*, 152
  27.1 *GP*, 151 n.34
  30 *GP*, 155–6
Aristippus
  SSR IV A 96, 56 n.56
  SSR IV A 174, 22 n.88
Aristobulus
  FGrHist 139 F 9, 42–5, 46 n.22
Aristophanes
  Birds
    1021, 45 n.21
  Knights
    120, 150
    123, 150
  Wasps
    1181–5, 202 n.65
Aristotle
  Eudemian Ethics
    1.5 1216a 16, 41
  Nicomachean Ethics
    1.3 1095b 22, 41
  Poetics
    22 1458a–1459a, 118 n.24
    25 1461a 14, 153 n.42

Protrepticus
  fr. 16 Ross = 90 Rose, 54 n.54, 55–6
Arrian
  Anabasis
    2.5.2–4, 42–5
    2.5.4, 46 n.22, 50 n.42
Asclepiades
  2 *HE*, 17, 166
  2.4 *HE*, 150 n.31
  16 *HE*, 155–6
  41 *HE*, 56
Athenaeus
  1.26 c–27d, 80 n.15
  7.278e–9d, 70 n.98
  8.335d–336 f, 213
  8.335e–337a, 41, 60 n.68
  10.423d–424a, 153
  10.426b, 212
  10.426b–427d, 155
  10.430a–d, 213
  10.430c, 213
  11, 144
  11.783d–e, 138
  12.529a, 46 n.25
  12.529b–d, 46–7
  12.529e–530a, 53–5
  12.530 c–531b, 41, 60 n.68
Ausonius
  De Rosis Nascentibus, 20 n.81, 223 n.140
  Epigrams
    14.1–3, 218–19
  Epitaphia Heroum
    17.2 Green, 217 n.116

Babrius
  60, 57 n.60
  108, 204
Bacchylides
  3.78–84, 9, 14 n.50, 62 n.74
  fr. 11 Maehler, 40, 14 n.50
  fr. 12 Maehler, 14 n.50
Bion
  Epitaphius Adonis
    37–8, 232 n.18

Callimachus
  Aetia
    fr. 43.12–17 Harder, 10, 65

Index Locorum

Callimachus (cont.)
   fr. 178.11–12 Harder, 136–8
   fr. 178.12 Harder, 154
  Epigrams
   45.3–4 *HE*, 60 n.70
  Fragments,
   fr. 544 Pfeiffer, 147
Callisthenes
  FGrHist 124 F 34, 42 n.10
Cassius Dio
  38.6, 98 n.79
  67.9.1–4, 142
Catullus
  5, 19, 127 n.56
  64, 234 n.23, 236–8
  66.39, 199 n.50
Choerilus of Iasus
  SH 335, 10, 41–2, 53–9, 63–5
  SH 335.3, 13, 65
Chrysippus
  SH 338 = *SVF* iii.200 *fr.* 11, 10, 65–7
  SVF iii.178 *fr.* 709, 67 n.89
Cicero
  Ad Atticum
   2.19.2, 98 n.79
   6.8.5, 99 n.80
  Brutus
   287, 80, 105, 209 n.86
  De Divinatione
   2.12, 171
  De Finibus
   2.106, 55–6, 67, 69
  De Oratore
   3.149–58, 118 n.24
  In Pisonem
   30, 98 n.79
   67, 90 n.51
  De Inventione
   1.33, 118 n.24
  Philippica
   13.11, 102 n.91
  Tusculan Disputations
   5.101, 55–6, 72
Clearchus
  fr. 51d Wehrli, 42 n.11, 46 n.22
Clitarchus
  FGrHist 137 F 2, 42 n.10
Crates
  fr. 8 Diels = *SH* 355, 63–5

Crinagoras
  7 *GP*, 161
  10 *GP*, 161
  11 *GP*, 161
  12 *GP*, 161
  47 *GP*, 161–7
Ctesias
  fr. 1 b 23–7 Lenfant, 47 n.29
  fr. 1b 27 Lenfant, 46–7
  fr. 1q Lenfant, 46–7
De rosis
  Anthologia Latina i.84 Riese = 72 Shackleton Bailey, 20 n.81
Diodorus Siculus
  1.47, 44 n.15
  2.23–7, 44 n.15, 47 n.29
  2.27, 46–7
Diogenes Laertius
  2.93–6, 22 n.89
  10.6–8, 66 n.88
Dionysius of Halicarnassus
  Antiquitates Romanae
   1.2.2, 58 n.62
Duris
  FGrHist 76 F 42, 46 n.25
Ennius
  Annales
   fr. 304–8 Skutsch, 123 n.41
   fr. 363 Skutsch, 98 n.79
   fr. 476 Skutsch, 105 n.106
Epicurus
  Letter to Menoecus
   130–2, 67 n.90
  fr. 15 Arrighetti, 171
  fr. 212 Arrighetti, 171
Euripides
  Alcestis
   780–802, 24, 186
   782, 9 n.27, 197
  TrGF 973, 171
Florus
  Anthologia Latina i.87 Riese = 75 Shackleton Bailey, 20 n.81
Galen
  Ant.

Index Locorum

2.15 = xiv.25–6 Kühn, 90, 91
Gallus
  2 *FGE*, 171 n.90
Gellius
  11.7.2, 118
  11.12, 123
  12.9, 123
  19.9.4, 5 n.12
Hedylus
  3 *HE*, 136 n.88
  4 *HE*, 154
Hegesippus
  Philetairoi
    fr. 2.5–6, 70
Hellanicus
  FGrHist 4 F 6, 45 n.21
  FGrHist 687a F 2, 45
Herodotus
  2.78, 38 n.3
  2.150, 45 n.21
  6.84.3, 153 n.42
Hesiod
  Works and Days
    582–96, 187–93
Homer
  Iliad
    6.145–9, 11
    6.146, 13 n.44
    6.146–49, 186
    9.203, 13 n.44, 137, 153
    21.461–7, 112
    24.128–32, 11
    24.602–20, 11
  Odyssey
    2.305, 52 n.49
    8.248–9, 10 n.31
    9.1–15, 8
    10.174–7, 13 n.44
    11.568, 126 n.54
    12.21–7, 13 n.44
    12.208–12, 13 n.44
Horace
  Ars Poetica
    14, 200 n.53
    14–23, 184, 200, 214 n.100
    45–59, 119–25
    45–72, 106
    55, 131

    58–9, 117
    60–72, 109–17
    71–2, 124
    95, 203
    139, 203
    141, 203
    240–3, 120
    291–4, 134
    331–2, 94–6
    388, 93 n.62
    445–50, 134
  Epistles
    1.1.10, 93
    1.1.12, 92
    1.2.69–70, 105 n.106
    1.3.8, 93
    1.4, 21 n.86
    1.5.4, 88 n.42, 93 n.63
    1.6.17–18, 161 n.63
    1.14.34, 100 n.86
    1.19.26–34, 116
    1.19.32–4, 28
    2.1.34–5, 106 n.109
    2.1.144, 202
    2.1.250–1, 203
    2.2.112, 123 n.42
    2.2.115–25, 134–5
    2.2.122–3, 106
    2.2.163, 103 n.97, 105
    2.2.180–2, 161
    2.2.217, 123 n.41
  Epodes
    2.19–20, 132
    6, 204 n.74
    9.1, 97 n.75, 104
    9.37–8, 88 n.43
    11.5–6, 124 n.46
    13, 78–82
    13.4, 224 n.142
    13.6, 97
  Odes
    1.1, 29, 88
    1.1.35–6, 19
    1.4, 19 n.72, 93 n.62, 127, 231
    1.4.16, 135
    1.4.16–20, 185 n.84
    1.7.25–32, 13 n.44
    1.9, 76–8

Index Locorum

Horace (cont.)
  1.9.9, 14 n.50
  1.11, 36, 131–5, 199–200
  1.11.1–2, 171
  1.11.8, 14 n.50, 21 n.86
  1.12.1–3, 200 n.53
  1.20, 91, 98 n.78, 233
  1.36, 135–8
  1.36.10, 95 n.66
  1.36.13–16, 14 n.49
  1.37.5–6, 104
  2.3, 94–6
  2.3.8, 79
  2.7.13–16, 104 n.101
  2.11.9–10, 124
  2.11.13–14, 96 n.73
  2.14.22, 96
  2.14.24, 202
  2.14.25–8, 81 n.17, 94
  3.2.2–3, 97
  3.8, 82–8, 89–90
  3.8.27–8, 22 n.93
  3.14, 101–7
  3.14.13–14, 85 n.26
  3.17.13, 3 n.6
  3.21.1, 81 n.16, 88 n.41
  3.21.7, 97
  3.22, 86 n.30
  3.23.8, 131 n.70
  3.28, 98–100
  3.28.2–3, 91
  3.29.1–2, 103 n.97
  3.29.18–20, 189
  3.29.29–32, 171
  3.29.41–3, 21 n.86
  3.29.51–2, 124
  3.30, 93 n.60
  4.2.27–32, 224
  4.6.39–40, 121 n.34
  4.7, 19 n.72, 32–4, 125–31
  4.7.16, 217
  4.11, 93
  4.12, 189
  4.12.5, 230 n.8
  4.12.13, 192 n.28
  4.13.13–16, 92
  4.14.1–4, 94
  Sermones
    1.1.33, 201 n.57

  1.10.21, 201
  1.5.73–4, 199 n.50
  2.1.85, 204 n.74
  2.3.115–16, 93 n.61
  2.3.115–17, 90
  2.6.16–23, 200 n.53
  2.6.17, 203
  2.6.71, 203
  2.6.90–7, 198–203
  2.6.93, 203
  2.6.99–100, 203
  2.6.106, 205
  2.6.110–15, 203–5
  2.8.61–74, 212 n.96

Inscriptions
  CEG
    28, 50 n.44
    37, 50 n.39
    113, 6 n.16
    153, 60 n.70
    429, 152 n.38
    596, 50 n.41
  CIG
    3846 l, 62 n.72
    7298, 168–9
    7299, 4 n.4, 172–6
  CIL
    i² 2929, 209 n.86
    iii 14524, 72 n.107
    iv 2554–9, 88 n.42
    iv 9313, 88 n.41
    vi 15258, 72
    vi 15258.5–8, 229 n.4
    vi 18131, 72
    viii 22640, 89 n.46
    ix 2114, 72 n.107
    xii 4548, 159 n.60
    xv 4566, 89
  CLE
    187, 72 n.107
    244, 72
    706.10, 224 n.140
    1499.1–2, 229 n.4
    2207, 72 n.107
  Courtney (1995) 160, no. 169, 72
  Courtney (1995) 186–7, no. 199, 223 n.140

Index Locorum

GV
58, 50 n.39
1016.5, 175
1112, 4 n.9
1112.10, 62 n.72
1219, 4 n.9
1225, 50 n.44
1364.3, 167
1364.4, 201
1368, 59–61, 129
1955, 1–8
Heberdey and Wilhelm (1896) 126,
   no.211, 4 n.9, 185
IG
  xii² 35, 161 n.64
IK Kibyra I
  300–2, no.362, 62 n.72
IK Kios
  138–9, no. 78, 173 n.98
Kaibel
  546.16, 65 n.83
  1129, 168–9
Pöhlmann and West (2001) 62–85,
  no. 20–1, 4 n.11
Pöhlmann and West (2001) 88–91,
  no. 23, 1–8
Rigato and Mongardi (2016) 108, no. 1,
  209 n.86
Rigato and Mongardi (2016) 111, no. 29,
  89 n.46
Rigato and Mongardi (2016) 113, no. 51,
  88 n.41
Rigato and Mongardi (2016) 121,
  no. 115, 89 n.46
Robert (1943) 182, 4 n.91
SGO
01/12/05, 152 n.38
02/02/07, 1–8
02/09/32, 4 n.9
02/09/32.5, 173
05/01/62.3, 167 n.77
05/01/62.4, 201
09/08/04, 4 n.9
09/08/04.10, 62 n.72
10/05/04.1–2, 148 n.25
18/01/19.9–10, 173 n.98
18/01/20, 4 n.9

Ion of Chios
Elegies
fr. 26, 14
fr. 26.15–16, 52 n.48
fr. 26.16, 62
fr. 27, 14, 71
fr. 27.7, 52

Juvenal
1.7–14, 214
4.56–7, 131 n.71
5.33–5, 90 n.49
5.34, 79
5.122, 208 n.84
9.9–11, 217
9.32–7, 218 n.119
9.53, 84 n.21
9.96–7, 217 n.111
9.118–23, 214–15
9.124–9, 215–23
9.134, 218 n.119
11.137, 208 n.84

Leonidas
67 HE, 16–17
77 HE, 165 n.73
Lucian
DMort.
  2.1, 64 n.81
  20.6, 64 n.81
Luct.
  21, 39
Merc. Cond.
  18, 5 n.12
Lucilius
fr. 2 Marx = 3–4 Warmington,
  204 n.74
fr. 377–80 Marx = 389–92 Warmington,
  204 n.74
fr. 917 Marx = 878 Warmington, 210,
  132 n.74
fr. 1095–6 Marx = 1000–1 Warmington,
  204 n.74
Lucretius
1.832, 119
3.260, 119
3.912–30, 20 n.83, 67

Index Locorum

Lucretius (cont.)
  3.914, 206
  5.925–47, 196 n.42
  5.944, 196

Machon
  9 Gow, 57
Macrobius
  5.21, 144, 219
Martial
  1.105, 89 n.44, 90 n.49
  2.57, 178
  2.59, 177–9
  5.64, 179–80
  7.47.11, 223 n.140
  8.6, 156–7
  13.111, 88
  13.113, 89 n.44, 106 n.47
Meleager
  113 *HE*, 154
Mimnermus
  fr. 1.4, 11
  fr. 2, 186
  fr. 2.3, 11, 115
  fr. 2.7–8, 11
  fr. 2.9, 11
  fr. 3.1, 11
  fr. 5.2, 11
  fr. 5.5, 201
  fr. 7.1, 148 n.24
Monimus
  SSR V G 2, 64
Musaeus
  fr. 5 *DK*, 112

Ovid
  Amores
    1.4.29, 199 n.51
  Ars Amatoria
    2.113–22, 10
    3.30, 183
    3.59–80, 24 n.97
    3.79, 209, 223 n.140
  Fasti
    2.267–380, 85
    2.359, 84 n.22
    3.170, 84
    5.517–18, 93 n.63, 97 n.75

    6.201, 104
  Metamorphoses
    1.565, 124 n.46
    3.334–510, 233

Papyri
  P.Mil.Vogl. VIII, 143 n.9
  P.Oxy. 761, 221 n.132
  P.Oxy. 1362, 154 n.43
  P.Oxy. 1795, 5 n.12
  P.Oxy. 1795.25–6, 165 n.73
  P.Oxy. 3724.iv.20, 189 n.20
  P.Oxy. 3965 *fr.* 26, 207
  P.Oxy. 4547, 187 n.15
  P.Oxy. 5486, 187 n.15
Pausanias
  3.3, 47 n.31
Pentadius
  Anthologia Latina i.234 Riese = 226
    Shackleton Bailey, 229
  Anthologia Latina i.235 Riese = 227
    Shackleton Bailey, 20 n.81,
    227–38
  Anthologia Latina i.265
    Riese = 259 Shackleton Bailey,
    229
Persius
  1.25, 210 n.87
  1.109–10, 204 n.74
  5.151, 186, 209, 223 n.140
  5.151–3, 217–18
  5.153, 201
  5.167, 199 n.51
Petronius
  1–5, 210
  1.15, 210
  5.34, 79
  29, 180
  31.10, 210
  34, 205–8, 209–10
  34.7, 156, 189 n.20
  34.8, 159
  34.10, 217
  36, 208–9
  52.1, 181
  55, 211–12
  59, 208
  71–2, 180–2

Index Locorum

71.11, 159
72.2, 159
73.6, 189 n.20
78.5, 22 n.91
118.5, 108, 210
Phaedrus
Fables
  4.24, 203 n.67
Fabulae nouae
  9 Postgate, 204
Philodemus
Epigrams
  6.7 Sider, 189 n.20
  19 Sider, 218 n.119
  29 Sider, 20 n.83
  [*On Choices and Avoidances*] 17, 20 n.83
Phoenix of Colophon
  CA 231–2, *fr.* 1, 57 n.60, 66 n.87, 70 n.99
  CA 234, *fr.* 3, 70 n.99
Pindar
Olympians
  2.1–2, 200 n.53
  9.48–9, 106 n.109
Pythians
  6.48, 14 n.50, 132
Fragments
  fr. 89a Maehler, 200 n.53
  fr. 122.19 Maehler, 47 n.26
  fr. 123.1–2 Maehler, 14 n.50, 132
Plato
Hippias Maior
  285d–e, 38 n.2
[Plato]
  4 *FGE*, 201
Pliny
Natural History
  8.176–7, 195 n.37
  10.81–5, 229 n.7
  14.55, 88 n.40, 97, 106 n.110, 209
  14.55–6, 90 n.50
  14.65, 89 n.47
  14.94, 88 n.41, 209 n.86
  14.142, 81 n.19, 158 n.56
  36–7, 161 n.63

37.11, 165
37.19, 157–60
37.20, 159 n.60
37.66, 162 n.68
37.139, 172
37.142, 175
Plutarch
Moralia
  107b–c, 186 n.15
  148a, 38 n.3
  336c, 50 n.42, 51
  336d, 53
  357f, 38 n.3
  546a, 63
  622c, 5 n.12
  677c–678b, 153
  711d, 5 n.12
PMG Adespota
  902.1, 52 n.49
  913, 5 n.12, 138
Polemon
  2 *GP*, 167–72
Polybius
  3.88, 102 n.91
Posidippus
  2 Austin and Bastianini, 160
  3 Austin and Bastianini, 160
  16 Austin and Bastianini, 172 n.94
  142 Austin and Bastianini, 81 n.19

Quintilian
Inst.
  8.5.28, 210 n.89
  10.96, 108, 202
Quintus of Smyrna
  9.502–4, 112 n.14

Rabirius
  fr. 2 Courtney, *FLP* = 2 Blänsdorf, *FPL* = 231 Hollis, *FRP*, 11, 71–5
Rufinus
  2 Page, 10 n.32

Sappho
  fr. 55, 14 n.50
  fr. 58, 14 n.50
  'Brothers poem', 9–10, 14 n.50

Index Locorum

Seneca
  De Beneficiis
    6.31, 71
  Dialogues
    7.13, 21
    10.8.5, 23 n.94, 216 n.106
    10.9, 22 n.90, 23 n.94
    10.9.2, 195, 197–8, 222 n.136
    10.17.2., 80 n.15
  Epistulae Morales
    12.9, 22
    33.1, 186
    33.3, 185
    33.7, 186
    78.14, 133 n.77
    99.5, 22
    108.24–9, 22 n.90, 195
    114.26, 90
  Hercules Furens
    179, 216 n.106
  Natural Questions
    4B.13.3, 90
  Phaedra
    450, 198
Sidonius
  Epistles
    8.11.5, 237 n.28
    9.1.14.4, 237 n.28
Silius Italicus
    13.474–6, 38 n.3
Simonides
  Elegies
    frr. 19 + 20, 13 n.44, 113–16, 207
[Simonides]
  Epigrams
    79.2 *FGE* = 46 Sider, 113 n.15
Sophocles
  Electra
    1158–9, 217 n.116
Stobaeus
    4.34.28, 207
    4.51.13, 186 n.15
Strabo
    14.5.9, 42, 50, 54 n.53
Suetonius
  Julius Caesar
    20.2, 99

Tacitus
  Annales
    3.17–18, 98 n.79
  Theocritus, 116
    23.29–40, 165 n.73
    29, 15
  Theognis
    33, 52, 98
    567, 52 n.48
    795, 148 n.24
    1047–8, 27
    1063–8, 12
  Thucydides
    1–23, 38
  Tibullus
    2.5.56, 193
  Timotheus
    PMG 791.149, 46 n.23
  TrGF Adespota
    fr. 95.1, 197
    fr. 331, 11 n.33
  TrRF Adespota
    21, 24 n.98

Varro
  De Vita Populi Romani
    fr. 125a Riposati, 90
    fr. 125b Riposati, 90
  Lingua Latina
    5.5, 118 n.24
  Res Rustica
    2.2, 192 n.28
    2.2.10–311, 191
    2.2.18, 195 n.37
Velleius Paterculus
    2.7.5, 98 n.77
Vergil
  Aeneid
    2.310–12, 199 n.50
    6.309–10, 130 n.68
    6.460, 199 n.50
    6.629, 199 n.50
    7.740, 130
    10.861–2, 197
    11.230, 103 n.96
  Georgics
    2.176, 191

3.60–1, 196 n.41
3.63–71, 194–8, 218, 222
3.323–38, 187–93
[Vergil]
  Copa, 20
  25–38, 189

Xenarchus
  Twins
    fr. 3.1, 212
Zonas
  9 *GP*, 149–50

Lightning Source UK Ltd.
Milton Keynes UK
UKHW022132021222
413185UK00011B/152